TURNING
THE
TIDE

TURNING THE TIDE

U.S. INTERVENTION IN CENTRAL AMERICA AND THE STRUGGLE FOR PEACE

NOAM CHOMSKY

11

91-884

South End Press   **Boston, Massachusetts**

Manufactured in the USA
Production at South End Press, Boston
Cover design by Michael Prokosch
Fourth printing
Library of Congress Cataloguing in Publication Data
Chomsky, Noam.
    Turning the tide.

    Bibliograhy: p.
    Includes index.
    1. Central America—Politics and government—1979-   . 2. Violence—Central America—History—20th century. 3. Civil rights—Central America—History—20th century. 4. Central America—Foreign relations—United States. 5. United States—Foreign relations—Central America. I. Title.
F1439.5.C53 1985   327.730728   85-27940

ISBN: 0-89608-266-0 paper
ISBN: 0-89608-267-9 cloth

SOUTH END PRESS 116 St Botolph St Boston MA 021115

TABLE OF CONTENTS

Introduction   1
Chapter One: Free World Vignettes   3
  1 The Miseries of Traditional Life   5
  2 Challenge and Response: Nicaragua   9
  3 Challenge and Response: El Salvador   14
    3.1 The Carter Years   14
    3.2 Reagan Takes Command   16
  4 Challenge and Response: Guatemala   28
  5 The Reagan Administration and Human Rights   31
  6 The Contribution of the Mercenary States   33
  7 The Planning of State Terror   36
  8 The Miseries of Traditional Life: A Further Note   39
Chapter Two: The Fifth Freedom   43
  1 Rhetoric and Reality   43
  2 The Perceptions of the Planners   47
  3 Latin America: "An Incident, Not An End"   58
  4 Planning for Global Hegemony   63
  5 The Crimes of Nicaragua   72
Chapter Three: Patterns of Intervention   85
  1 Defending Our Sovereignty   85
  2 The Rule of Law and the Rule of Force   89
  3 The US and El Salvador in Historical Perspective   95
  4 Contemporary State Terrorism: The System Established   97
  5 The System Applied: Torturing El Salvador   101
    5.1 Carter's War   101
    5.2 Duarte's Role   109
    5.3 Towards "Democracy" in El Salvador   117
    5.4 The Propaganda System Moves Into High Gear   118
    5.5 The War Moves Into High Gear   122
    5.6 Reaction at Home: Successful Terror and its Rewards 124
  6 Torturing Nicaragua   127
    6.1 Before the Crisis   127
    6.2 The Proxy War   128
    6.3 The Elections and the Opposition   137
    6.4 The Free Press at Work   140
    6.5 A Glimpse into the Civilized World   143
  7 Elsewhere in the Region   146
    7.1 Torturing Hispaniola   146
    7.2 Torturing Guatemala   154
  8 Human Rights, the Raising of the
    Living Standards and Democratization   157
  9 The Awesome Nobility of Our Intentions   162

Chapter Four: The Race To Destruction   171
  1 The Threat of Global War   171
  2 The Nuclear Freeze Campaign: Successes and Failures   177
  3 The Lessons to be Drawn   178
  4 Defense Against the Great Satan:
    The Doctrine and the Evidence   189
    4.1 Defending the National Territory   189
    4.2 The Defense of Western Europe   191
    4.3 The Containment Doctrine   193
    4.4 Containing the Anti-Fascist Resistance:
      From Death Camps to Death Squads   194
    4.5 Escalation of the Pentagon System:
      The Pretexts and the Evidence   202
  5 The Roots of the Pentagon System   202
  6 The Consequences   215
  7 Cold War Realities   217
Chapter Five: The Challenge Ahead   221
  1 The "Conservative" Counterattack   221
    1.1 Confronting the Threat of Democracy at Home   221
    1.2 The Attack Against Labor   226
    1.3 The Attack Against Rights   227
    1.4 The Attack Against Independent Thought   228
    1.5 Investing to Control the State:
      The Political System of Capitalist Democracy   232
    1.6 The "Ultimate Target": The Public Mind   234
    1.7 The Domestic Successes of "Conservatism"   236
  2 The Opportunities for Constructive Action   237
    2.1 The System of Control: its Points of Weakness 237
    2.2 The "Shift to the Right": Rhetoric and Reality 240
    2.3 Turning the Tide   245
Footnotes   255
Index   292

INTRODUCTION

We live entangled in webs of endless deceit, often self-deceit, but with a little honest effort, it is possible to extricate ourselves from them. If we do, we will see a world that is rather different from the one presented to us by a remarkably effective ideological system, a world that is much uglier, often horrifying. We will also learn that our own actions, or passive acquiescence, contribute quite substantially to misery and oppression, and perhaps eventual global destruction.

But there is a brighter side. We are fortunate to live in a society that is not only rich and powerful—and hence, as any student of history would expect, dangerous and destructive—but also relatively free and open, perhaps more so than any other, though this may change if the reactionary jingoists who have misappropriated the term "conservative" succeed in their current project of diminishing civil liberties, strengthening the power of the state, and protecting it from public scrutiny. For those who are relatively wealthy and privileged, a very large sector of a society as rich as ours, there are ample opportunities to discover the truth about who we are and what we do in the world. Furthermore, by international standards the state is limited at home in its capacity to coerce. Hence those who enjoy a measure of wealth and privilege are free to act in many ways, without undue fear of state terror, to bring about crucial changes in policy and even more fundamental institutional changes. We are fortunate, perhaps uniquely so, in the range of opportunities we enjoy for free inquiry and effective action. The significance of these facts can hardly be exaggerated.

I want to consider here some aspects of the reality that is often concealed or deformed by the reigning doctrinal system, which pervades the media, journals of opinion, and much of scholarship.[1] An honest inquiry will reveal that striking and systematic features of our international behavior are suppressed, ignored or denied. It

1

will reveal further that our role in perpetuating misery and oppression, even barbaric torture and mass slaughter, is not only significant in scale, but is also a predictable and systematic consequence of longstanding geopolitical conceptions and institutional structures. There is no way to give a precise measure of the scale of our responsibility in each particular case, but whether we conclude that our share is 90%, or 40%, or 2%, it is that factor that should primarily concern us, since it is that factor that we can directly influence. It is cheap and easy to deplore the other fellow's crimes in the manner of the official peace movements of the so-called "Communist" states, or their counterparts in the West who, with comparable sincerity, denounce the crimes of official enemies while dismissing or justifying our own. An honest person will choose a different course.

These are among the questions I want to examine here, concentrating primarily on relations between the US and its southern neighbors—and victims—in the post-World War II period, although the pattern that emerges is by no means new and is not limited to this region.[2]

Chapter 1 is concerned with the grim reality of normal life for a large majority of the population in our dependencies in Central America, and with the consequences that regularly ensue, at our initiative and with our crucial support, when efforts are undertaken to bring about constructive change. In chapter 2, I will turn to the backgrounds for US policy and the geopolitical conceptions that guide planners, as exhibited in the documentary record and, more significantly, in the actual pattern of events. Chapter 3 places these matters in the broader context of US history, both in Central America and elsewhere, and discusses recent US policies in Central America in this context. In chapter 4, I will turn to national security policy, the Cold War system of global management, and the drift towards global war which is, in significant measure, a result of US government programs that have little to do with security, but are deeply rooted in the structure of power in our society and the global concerns of dominant institutions. Finally in the last chapter, I want to consider the domestic scene: the dedicated efforts that have been undertaken by dominant elites to overcome the democratic revival of the 1960s, and the opportunities that now exist to engage in constructive work to deter terrible crimes, to reverse the race towards global destruction, and to enlarge the sphere of freedom and justice.

1 Free World Vignettes

John Jay, the President of the Continental Congress and the first Chief Justice of the US Supreme Court, held that "the people who own the country ought to govern it."[1] His prescription is, in fact, close to the reality. The United States is furthermore unusual in the high degree of class consciousness among the business classes, the extremely low degree of class consciousness (particularly in the current period) on the part of workers, and the general conformity of the intelligentsia. Since World War II, the United States has held a position of dominance in world affairs with few if any historical parallels, though long before, it had become the greatest industrial power by a large margin. US elites were naturally aware of these conditions and determined to exploit the expanded opportunities they offered. They have engaged in careful planning, and have been willing to resort to subversion and violence on an impressive scale to maintain or extend their dominant position, which, according to the reigning doctrinal system, is theirs by right, given the unique virtue of the state that they or their representatives govern.

There are aspects of American history and institutions that lend support to the pretensions of ideologues, but the full story is less pleasant to contemplate, as many have recognized over the years. The founder of the utopian Oneida community, John Humphrey Noyes, described the US in 1830 as "a bloated, swaggering libertine...with one hand whipping a negro tied to a liberty-pole, and with another dashing an emaciated Indian to the ground."[2] At the turn of the century, as his compatriots turned from slaughtering Indians to wiping out resisting "niggers" in the Philippines, Mark Twain gave his version of "The Battle Hymn of the Republic":[3]

3

Mine eyes have seen the orgy of the launching of the
Sword
He is searching out the hoardings where the strangers'
wealth is stored
He hath loosed his fateful lightnings, and with woe and
death has scored.
His lust is marching on.

If some Third World revolution today were to reenact US
history, with literal human slavery as well as decimation and
brutal expulsion of the native population, the reaction would be one
of horror and disbelief. We may recall, for example, that the first
emancipation proclamation was issued by the British governor of
Virginia in 1775, and that slavery was abolished in 1821 in Central
America by nations to whom we must teach lessons in "civilization," according to Theodore Roosevelt and other interven-
tionists until the present day.[4] The conquest of the national
territory and the exercise of US power in large areas of the world
also hardly merit the accolades of the faithful.

No region of the world has been more subject to US influence
over a long period than Central America and the Caribbean. The
extent and character of US influence are illustrated, for example,
by the establishment early in the century of a National Bank of
Nicaragua in which the New York Brown Brothers Bank held
majority ownership; its board of directors "met in New York and
consisted entirely of Brown Brothers' US representatives, except
for a token Nicaraguan" while US banks received the revenues of
the national rail and steamship lines and a US-run commission
required Nicaragua to pay fraudulent "damage claims" that
exceeded total US investment in the country for alleged "damages
from civil disorder." Or to take another case, a coup attempt in
Honduras in 1923 by a local client of the United Fruit company
(which virtually owned the country) led to US military intervention and a settlement arranged by the State Department: "North
American power had become so encompassing that U.S. military
forces and United Fruit could struggle against each other to see
who was to control the Honduran government, then have the
argument settled by the U.S. Department of State." The United
Fruit client took power in 1932 "and hand-in-hand with United
Fruit ruled his country for the next seventeen years."[5] Throughout
modern history, much the same has been true.

We naturally look to the Central America-Caribbean region,
then, if we want to learn something about ourselves, just as we look
to Eastern Europe or the "internal empire" if want to learn about
the Soviet Union. The picture we see is not a pretty one. The region
is one of the world's most awful horror chambers, with widespread
starvation, semi-slave labor, torture and massacre by US clients.
Virtually every attempt to bring about some constructive change

has been met with a new dose of US violence, even when initiated by Church-based self-help groups or political figures who modelled themselves on Roosevelt's New Deal. We are, once again, living in such a period, in fact, the worst such period, which is saying a good deal.[6]

The region evokes little attention inside the United States as long as discipline reigns. The prevailing unconcern is revealed, for example, by the treatment of Woodrow Wilson's bloody counterinsurgency campaign in the Dominican Republic—or lack thereof; it received its first detailed scholarly examination after 60 years.[7] Or consider the case of William Krehm, *Time* correspondent in Central America and the Caribbean in the 1940s. His book on the region—a rare event in itself—was published in Mexico in 1948 and then elsewhere in Latin America; the original English version appeared 36 years later.[8] The book jacket states that *Time* refused to publish much of what he submitted for fear of offending large corporations, and that his book was regarded as too controversial by American publishers. Lack of interest, the consequence of lack of credible threats to US control at the time, might well suffice to explain its unavailability. The two books just cited appeared in 1984, a time of challenge to US dominance, hence much concern over the fate of the region. Our lack of interest when the lower orders make no unseemly noises should be a matter of no great pride.

The brutal and corrupt Somoza dictatorship had long been a reliable US ally and a base for the projection of US power: to terminate Guatemalan democracy in 1954, to attack Cuba in 1961, to avert the threat of democracy in the Dominican Republic in 1965 and in El Salvador in 1972.[9] The fall of the dictatorship in 1979, along with a renewed threat to the military regime in Guatemala and the growth of popular organizations in El Salvador, led to increasing US intervention and brought the region to the front pages. Let us consider the picture that comes into focus with this renewed attention.

1 The Miseries of Traditional Life

Among the many dedicated and honorable Americans who went to see for themselves, one of the most impressive is Charles Clements, a graduate of the US Air Force Academy and former pilot in Vietnam, who was sent to a psychiatric hospital when he refused to fly further missions. A committed pacifist, he went to El Salvador in March 1982 and spent a year as the only trained physician in the rebel-controlled Guazapa region 25 miles from San Salvador, a free-fire zone in which any person or object is a legitimate target. There he witnessed the terror of the US-run war against rural El Salvador at first hand, living with the *campesinos*, "many of [whom] have been tortured and mutilated by tormenters who have been trained in the sophisticated tactics of violence—often by our own military advisers," in the words of Murat Williams, US Ambassador to El Salvador from 1961 to 1964, when the system of efficient state terror was established by the Kennedy Administration.

Clements observed the attacks on villages by planes and helicopter gunships and artillery, the strafing by US-supplied jets aimed specifically against defenseless peasants, the ruins of villages gutted by government forces, the destruction of crops and livestock to ensure starvation, always imminent. As is the regular pattern, the worst atrocities were carried out by US-trained elite battalions (Atlacatl, Ramón Belloso) and by air and artillery units employing tactics designed by the US in Vietnam and taught by US advisers. He treated the bodies mutilated by torture and the victims of attacks with napalm and gasoline bombs and white phosphorus rockets used as anti-personnel weapons against civilians. He heard the stories of people whose families had been hacked to death by National Guardsmen or who had crawled from under a pile of bodies of trapped civilians cut to pieces with machetes and mutilated by US-trained troops, or who had themselves been subjected to horrifying torture receiving no medical aid, since physicians were unwilling to "endanger their lives by treating someone who had been tortured by the security forces." Using a US-made scanner, he could hear the voices of American advisers directing troops on their mass murder missions.

He also witnessed the courage of the *campesinos*, their "sense of community and hope," their schools and rudimentary health services and community programs in the base Christian communities—a revelation to people who had lived for a century as virtual slaves, ever since the oligarchy had taken over most of the land by a combination of legal chicanery and violence to enjoy the profits of the coffee boom—and their "determination to build their new society even while the Salvadoran government sought to destroy them."[10]

But what seems to have impressed him the most were the words of a lay minister of one of the base Christian communities:

> You gringos are always worried about violence done with machine guns and machetes. But there is another kind of violence that you must be aware of, too. I used to work on the hacienda. My job was to take care of the *dueno*'s dogs. I gave them meat and bowls of milk, food that I couldn't give my own family. When the dogs were sick, I took them to the veterinarian in Suchitoto or San Salvador. When my children were sick, the *dueno* gave me his sympathy, but no medicine as they died.
>
> To watch your children die of sickness and hunger while you can do nothing is a violence to the spirit. We

have suffered that silently for too many years. Why aren't you gringos concerned about that kind of violence?

The old man was wrong. We gringos are not worried about violence done with machine guns and machetes. Rather, we devote our incomparable wealth and power to ensuring that such violence proceeds unhindered, and we laud its successes, joined by the suppliers of French tanks, Israeli guns and planes and napalm, German, Swiss and Belgian weapons, and other civilized people whose outrage knows no bounds when the lower orders threaten to break their bonds, but who are otherwise content to look the other way. But his comment is nevertheless to the point. The violence of everyday life in the domains of our influence and control is not deemed a fit topic of attention or concern except at moments when order is threatened.

A vignette of normal life is given by US journalist Tom Buckley, who visited a coffee plantation in El Salvador in 1981.[11] Most of the workers and their families lived in a long one-story building, with a room about 10 feet square for each family of 2 adults and many children, and privies 50 feet down the hill. Some of the new showcase *ranchitos* were a bit larger:

> As residences for agricultural labor go in El Salvador, they were not bad, but the furnishings were mean and sparse, and the atmosphere was one of hopelessness and squalor.
>
> An old woman sat in front of one of the *ranchitos*. Her left ankle and leg were bandaged with rags halfway to the knee. She said she thought her ankle might be broken. Hernandez [the manager, who ran the plantation for absentee landlords in Florida] asked her if she had been to see the paramedic. She hadn't, she said. She was unable to hobble to the clinic, and he, it seemed, did not make house calls. A younger woman sat in a hammock in front of another *ranchito*. At her side was a cradle improvised out of a basket. An infant lay in it, motionless. Its belly was bloated, and its limbs and face were so thin that the skin was translucent. Hernandez asked what was wrong. "It is his stomach," the woman said. "The food does him no good." She said that she had taken the infant to a physician but that he had told her nothing could be done. Her voice was vague and monotonous, as though speaking taxed her energy unbearably.
>
> "I don't think she took him at all," Hernandez said when we had returned to the station wagon. "It may sound terrible to say, but having children die is so common that it is accepted. It's no big thing to these people."

Hernandez's point is reiterated by Jeane Kirkpatrick, chief sadist-in-residence of the Reagan Administration, on the basis of her vast experience with peasant life in the Third World:[12]

Traditional autocrats [the ones we do and should support, Kirkpatrick explains] leave in place existing allocations of wealth, power, status, and other resources which in most traditional societies favor an affluent few and maintain masses in poverty. But they worship traditional gods and observe traditional taboos. They do not disturb the habitual rhythms of work and leisure, habitual places of residence, habitual patterns of family and personal relations. Because the miseries of traditional life are familiar, they are bearable to ordinary people who, growing up in the society, learn to cope, as children born to untouchables in India acquire the skills and attitudes necessary for survival in the miserable roles they are destined to fill.

Kirkpatrick adds further that "Such societies create no refugees": only 20% of the population of the Caribbean who have come to the United States, many illegally, to escape grinding poverty and oppression (40% from Puerto Rico where access is easier), including 40,000 from Haiti since 1979, many of them "boat people" whom the Carter Administration attempted to force back to the misery from which they fled "with full regard to the Administration policy of human rights," so its spokesman assured us—not to speak of a huge flow of refugees from the terror-and-torture states established since the 1960s with US backing, including some 20% of the population of Uruguay, well over 100,000 victims of Somoza's terror by 1978, 140,000 boat people fleeing the Philippines to Sabah in the mid-1970s, and on, and on; and the even greater numbers of internal refugees fleeing state terror or herded into "secure areas" by the state terrorists.[13] This vast flood of refugees furthermore increased dramatically as a direct consequence of the policies to which Kirkpatrick was to make a notable contribution soon after having delivered herself of these pronouncements, which much impressed Reagan's staff. In El Salvador, "approximately one quarter of all Salvadorans have fled [or have been forcibly expelled] from their homes," including many who flee in terror to the United States, where US authorities seek to return them to privation, torture and assassination. In 1984, only 93 Salvadorans and no Guatemalans, of the 1 million who had fled these countries, were legally admitted to the US as refugees; only 1% of Guatemalans and 3% of Salvadorans were granted asylum as compared with 52% of Bulgarians and 51% of Russians, countries where the miseries of ordinary life, or the very threat to existence, do not begin to compare with what is endured in these long-term beneficiaries of US solicitude.[14]

The picture described by the lay minister in El Salvador or by Tom Buckley can be duplicated in large parts of the world. The "habitual patterns" are captured by a character in Ignazio Silone's rendition of peasant life in southern Italy in his classic *Fontamara*, describing the hierarchy of "traditional life":

> At the head of everything is God, the Lord of Heaven.
> Everyone knows that.
> Then comes Prince Torlonia, lord of the earth.
> Then come Prince Torlonia's guards.
> Then come Prince Torlonia's guards' dogs.
> Then, nothing at all.
> Then, nothing at all.
> Then, nothing at all.
> Then come the peasants. And that's all.

Adapting the picture to our domains, it is only necessary to insert the United States, a shade removed from the Lord of Heaven and doing His holy work, as our leaders have often told us.

2 Challenge and Response: Nicaragua

What Buckley saw is the kind of society that we have helped to create and sustain through a century of intervention, and that we are now attempting to secure or restore. Sometimes, these habitual patterns are threatened, as today in Nicaragua, where the priorities of the Sandinista government "meant that Nicaragua's poor majority would have access to, and be the primary beneficiaries of, public programs" in accordance with the "logic of the majority," a concept which "implies redistribution of access to wealth and public services" to the benefit of the poor majority, and support for "mass organizations" that "involve very large numbers of people in the decisions that affect their lives."[15] At such moments, normal life undergoes some changes: two kinds of change, in fact. Let us look further into each of these.

One kind of change is illustrated in a report by Jethro Pettit, Desk officer for Latin America of Oxfam America:[16]

> "Before the revolution we didn't participate in anything. We only learned to make tortillas and cook beans and do what our husbands told us. In only five years we have seen a lot of changes—and we're still working on it!"
>
> Esmilda Flores belongs to an agricultural cooperative in the mountains north of Esteli, Nicaragua. Together with seven other women and 15 men, she works land that was formerly a coffee plantation owned by an absentee landlord.
>
> After the revolution in 1979, the families who had

worked the land became its owners. They have expanded production to include corn, beans, potatoes, cabbages, and dairy cows.

"Before, we had to rent a small plot to grow any food," Flores said. "And we had to pay one-half of our crop to the landlord! Now we work just as hard as before—both in the fields and at home—but there's a difference, because we're working for ourselves."

Women in Nicaragua, as in most of rural Latin America, carry an enormous workload [as throughout the Third World]. Not only are they a mainstay of the agricultural labor force (40 percent of Nicaragua's farm laborers are women), but they are responsible for child care, food preparation, and most domestic chores.

Women's roles did not suddenly change with the revolution. But there has been a pronounced shift in cultural attitudes as a result of their strong participation in Nicaragua's social reconstruction. Women have taken the lead in adult literacy programs, both as students and teachers. They have assumed key roles in rural health promotion and in vaccination campaigns...

Pettit goes on to describe the new rural organizations that aim to improve living and working conditions for farm laborers, offer training, technical advice, credit, seeds and tools, and so on. Clements reports similar developments in the rebel-held area of El Salvador where he worked, as have many others, though rarely in the US press.[17]

But these are not the only consequences that ensue when the pack animals who endure traditional life fail to appreciate properly that its miseries are quite bearable in Washington. Here is an example of a different kind of change, reported by a mother of two from Estelí, near Esmilda Flores's cooperative:[18]

Five of them raped me at about five in the evening... they had gang-raped me every day. When my vagina couldn't take it anymore, they raped me through my rectum. I calculate that in 5 days they raped me 60 times.

The "freedom fighters" dispatched from Washington also beat her husband and gouged out the eyes of another civilian before killing him, as she watched.

Another witness describes a *contra* attack on his cooperative in April 1984:

They had already destroyed all that was the cooperative; a coffee drying machine, the two dormitories for the coffee cutters, the electricity generators, 7 cows, the plant, the food warehouse. There was one boy about 15 years old, who was retarded and suffered from epilepsy.

We had left him in a bomb shelter. When we returned...,
we saw...that they had cut his throat, then they cut open
his stomach and left his intestines hanging out on the
ground like a string. They did the same to Juan Corrales
who had already died from a bullet in the fighting. They
opened him up and took out his intestines and cut off his
testicles.

In Miami—along with Washington, the base for the war
against Nicaragua and one of the major world centers of international terrorism—Adolfo Calero, political-military director of the
central component of the US proxy army (the FDN), stated that
"There is no line at all, not even a fine line, between a civilian farm
owned by the government and a Sandinista military outpost"—so
that arbitrary killing of civilians is entirely legitimate. Calero is
regarded as a meritorious figure and leading democrat by our
domestic partisans of mass slaughter, mutilation, torture and
degradation.[19]

A mother describes how her husband, a lay pastor, and her five
children were kidnapped; when she found them the next day,
"They were left all cut up. Their ears were pulled off, their throats
were cut, their noses and other parts were cut off." An American
parish priest reports that in this region of three towns and
scattered mountain communities, *contra* attacks have caused
"hundreds of deaths and thousands of displaced people," including
many taken to Honduras. A Miskito teacher kidnapped by the
contras describes the tortures to which he and eight others were
subjected in Honduras, where US authorities can pretend no
ignorance about their agents:

> In the evening, they tied me up in the water from 7 PM
> until 1 AM. The next day, at 7 AM they began to make me
> collect garbage in the creek in my underwear, with the
> cold. The creek was really icey. I was in the creek for four
> hours... Then they threw me on the ant hill. Tied up, they
> put me chest-down on the ant hill. The ants bit my body. I
> squirmed to try to get them off my body, but there were
> too many... They would beat me from head to heels. They
> would give me an injection to calm me a little. Then they
> would beat me again.

A French priest who trains nurses in the north testified before
the World Court about a handicapped person murdered "for the fun
of it," of women raped, of a body found with the eyes gouged out and
a girl of 15 who had been forced into prostitution at a *contra* camp
in Honduras. He accused the *contras* of creating an atmosphere of
terror through kidnappings, rapes, murder and torture.[20]

These matters are considered of scant interest by US journalists in Nicaragua or Honduras, who do not seek out or publish such

testimony, though it is permissible to concede that some unpleasant things may have happened in the past while reporting that the *contras* now "vow to end rights abuses...after reports that the insurgents in Nicaragua have been executing Government soldiers, officials and village militiamen"—not exactly the content of the testimony that has largely been suppressed in the field. The same news item informs us that the *contra* official placed in charge of human rights with much fanfare "said that he had found only six 'small cases' of violations" so far and "suggested that some apparent violations had been the work of Government soldiers dressed as guerrillas." *Contra* political spokesman Arturo Cruz said that "it was 'a delicate thing' to persuade rebel fighters to respect the lives of prisoners and pro-Sandinista civilians without demoralizing the fighters,"[21] offering an interesting insight into the "democratic resistance" that he seeks to legitimate and that is lauded by respected figures in the United States (see note 19).

The foreign press has been less circumspect. There we can read of "the contras' litany of destruction": the destruction of health and community centers, cooperatives, kindergartens and schools with such methods as these, described by one of the survivors:[22]

> Rosa had her breasts cut off. Then they cut into her chest and took out her heart. The men had their arms broken, their testicles cut off, and their eyes poked out. They were killed by slitting their throats, and pulling the tongue out through the slit.

And we can learn of a 14-year-old girl who was gang-raped and then decapitated, her head placed on a stake at the entrance to her village as a warning to government supporters; of nurses who were raped, then murdered; a man killed by hanging after his eyes were gouged out and his fingernails pulled out; a man who was stabbed to death after having been beaten, his eyes gouged out and a cross carved in his back after he fled from a hospital attacked by the *contras*; another tortured then skinned; another cut to pieces with bayonets by *contras* who then beheaded her 11-month-old baby before his wife's eyes; others who were raped to a background of religious music; children shot in the back or repeatedly shot "as though she had been used for target practice," according to a North American priest; along with much similar testimony provided by American priests, nuns, and others working in the border areas where the terrorist forces rampage, attacking from the Honduran bases established by their US advisers, instructors and paymasters.[23]

The chairmen of Americas Watch and Helsinki Watch, after a personal visit to study the "great divergence between President Reagan's rhetoric and the conclusions of the [Americas Watch] report" on *contra* atrocities, concluded that "there can be no doubt, on the basis of what we heard and saw, that a planned strategy of terrorism is being carried out by the contras along the Honduras border" and that "the U.S. cannot avoid responsibility for these atrocities."[24] Nor can the US apologists for the "democratic resistance" or those who front for it.

This is a brief sample of the methods we are compelled to undertake when the orderly regime of traditional life is challenged in our dependencies. They constitute what the press describes as "a military and economic annoyance to the Sandinista regime," and since it does not appear likely to achieve the aim of overthrowing this regime, this "annoyance" is often considered unwise.[25] Our chosen instruments for such annoyance are blandly described as the "democratic opposition" in the news columns of the nation's press, for example, in a lengthy account of US government preparations for invasion of Nicaragua in the *New York Times*.[26] In keeping with the principle of objectivity, no intimation is given that there might be something questionable about the contemplated crime of aggression, for which people were hanged at Nuremberg and Tokyo, nor could the *Times* editors express or even consider this point. But reference to the butchers as "the democratic opposition" in news columns is in keeping with the requirements of objectivity.

A more accurate description is that "The civilization and justice of bourgeois order comes out in its lurid light whenever the slaves and drudges of that order rise against their masters. Then this civilization and justice stand forth as undisguised savagery and lawless revenge."[27]

Our friends are quite aware of what they do. Arturo Cruz, who has been dubbed "the leading Nicaragua democrat" by the US media, concedes that his *contra* associates have committed "damnable atrocities" against civilians. Before joining them, he warned that their victory might lead "to a possible mass execution of the flower of our youth" while describing some of them as "civic cadavers" and noting that "most of those persons in positions of military authority within the FDN are ex-members of the National Guard, who unconditionally supported Somoza until the end, against the will of the Nicaraguan people"—not "most," but virtually all, from the top military commander on down; Edgar Chamorro, chosen by the CIA to serve as spokesman for its proxy army, writes that "by mid-1984, 46 out of 48 of the *contra commandantes* were former National Guardsmen." Cruz is unhappy about the fact that the *contras* "are almost totally controlled by right-wingers, many of them followers of" Somoza, Dennis Volman reports. The new unified command (UNO) set up by the CIA is "dominated by Adolfo Calero, according to all sources interviewed"; "Mr. Calero is an ultra-conservative Nicaraguan businessman closely allied to those FDN field commanders who were top officers in Somoza's army." Volman reports further that

Cruz is also "very concerned about alleged human rights abuses by contra forces in Nicaragua"; as Cruz knows, the "damnable atrocities" are not merely "alleged" and will continue in the course of a war waged by a mercenary army lacking any program other than restoration of the traditional order. While fronting for the terrorists attacking Nicaragua from Honduran bases, Cruz proclaims in the *New York Times* that the Sandinistas "will also, in time, provoke conflicts with their neighbors in order to justify ever more repressive measures at home"; in his view, Constable reports, "the central issue is the 'mistrust' they have aroused among Central American leaders."[28]

We return to Cruz's "democratic credentials" and his claim that he was excluded from the 1984 election—while secretly on the CIA payroll.

Edgar Chamorro writes that since 1982, the war "has left more than 12,000 Nicaraguans dead, 50,000 wounded and 300,000 homeless." The figure of 12,000 dead was also given by Nicaraguan President Daniel Ortega, including civilians and fighters on both sides. In an affidavit to the World Court given little notice in the press, Chamorro said that *contras* "would arrive at an undefended village, assemble all the residents in the town square and then proceed to kill—in full view of the others—all persons working for the Nicaraguan government, including police, local militia members, party members, health workers, teachers and farmers" on government cooperatives, actions which made it "easy to persuade those left alive to join" the *contra* forces. In the same affidavit, he testified that the FDN had been advised by the CIA to "murder, kidnap, rob and torture," and stated that he had been given funds by the CIA to bribe some 15 Honduran journalists to write pro-*contra* articles calling for the overthrow of the Sandinista government.[29]

3 Challenge and Response: El Salvador

3.1 The Carter Years

Atrocities in Nicaragua are, however, a small-time affair by US standards. Our concepts of civilization and justice are revealed more graphically in El Salvador, where the growth of unions, Church-based self-help organizations, peasant associations and other such threats to order in the 1970s called forth the familiar response. In the muted words of the State Department: "Faced with increasing demands for social change in the 1970s, traditional ruling groups continued their dominance by employing electoral fraud and repression."[30] As traditional ruling groups in the US took over the task, terror rapidly escalated.

For the year 1980, the Human Rights office of the Archdiocese of San Salvador tabulated 8062 murders of "Persons of the popular and progressive sectors killed for political reasons, not in military confrontations, but as a result of military operations by the Army, Security Forces, and paramilitary organizations coordinated by the High Command of the Armed Forces." These are cases where the data could be "fully checked," not including victims of bombardments or the more than 600 *campesinos* murdered in the Rio Sumpul massacre by a joint Honduran-Salvadoran military operation, and unknown numbers of others, primarily in the countryside where "verification was impossible."[31]

To rephrase these facts in Carter Administration Newspeak:[32]

> The Church has condemned the violence of left, right, and the security forces... Killings and terrorist acts are the work of both leftist "Democratic Front" forces who often claims [sic] responsibility for them, and of rightist elements with whom some members of the security organizations are associated... The government has been unable to end such abuses.

Through 1980 and beyond, the US press generally kept to the Party Line, though it was subsequently conceded that "Under the Carter Administration, United States officials said security forces were responsible for 90 percent of the atrocities," not "'uncontrollable' right-wing bands"[33]—so that the assertions in the Human Rights Report and other public statements were deliberate lies, reiterated as conscious deception by the media.

The *Washington Post* maintained that "There is no real argument that most of the estimated 10,000 political fatalities in 1980 were victims of government forces or irregulars associated with them"—only the detailed accounting by the Church Human Rights office and what the press was being told by US officials, but chose to conceal. Jeane Kirkpatrick stated: "And I think it's a terrible injustice to the Government and the military when you suggest that they were somehow responsible for terrorism and assassination." No commissar could be more loyal in defending state terror. The first major massacre, at Rio Sumpul, was suppressed for over a year, though it was reported at once in the Church and international press. A congressional report to which we return directly received the same treatment as did much other evidence that was readily available but not considered appropriate for the general population.[34] This is quite typical; it is always more rewarding to gaze with horror at the crimes of official enemies.

The claim that "the government has been unable to end such abuses" by right-wing death squads continues to be widely echoed in the press; thus we read in the *New York Times*, without comment, that "The death squads have been linked by United States officials to...the extreme right-wing Republican Nationalist Alliance, which has sought to block social changes proposed by President José Napoleón Duarte's moderate Christian Democratic Party." The report from San Salvador continues: "Archbishop Romero's killing is widely believed here to have been planned by right-wing death squads..."[35]

This *Times* report illustrates the typical device of insinuating official propaganda in the news columns by selective choice of sources and vague unattributed references. In fact, what is "widely believed" in San Salvador and is well supported by credible evidence, as we shall see, is that the government was directly implicated in the Archbishop's killing and sought to prevent any inquiry into it. And US officials, as we noted earlier, concede privately that the atrocities are carried out by the security forces of the government that Duarte seeks to legitimate. The Senate Select Committee on Intelligence reports that "Death Squad activities...have originated in the Salvadoran security services, including the National Police, National Guard and Treasury Police," and that "numerous Salvadoran officials in the military and security forces as well as other official organizations have been involved in encouraging or conducting death squad activities or other violent human rights abuses," including "officials in the civilian government, representatives of the private sector organizations, and various individuals associated with the traditional oligarchy of that country." Salvadoran interim President Álvaro Magaña (the US candidate) stated earlier that "All of the death squads are related to the army or paramilitary."[36]

The pretense transmitted by the *Times* is impossible to sustain in the light of available evidence and never was even remotely tenable. The vice-chairman of Americas Watch and Helsinki Watch writes:[37]

> death squads were never apprehended or prosecuted; they operated with impunity during curfew hours; they passed police checkpoints without challenge; the security forces sometimes blocked streets to permit death squads to operate without interruption; uniformed forces sometimes conducted joint operations with nonuniformed death squads; bodies were dumped in heavily patrolled areas; death squads had access to good intelligence; the volume of death squad killing was adjusted in response to pressure on governmental forces; and so on.

Evidence from defectors and other sources simply confirms the obvious, recognized indirectly by US authorities who seek to deny it. An Embassy spokesman in San Salvador comments: "If you pursue the squads it is going to cut so far back into the fabric of Salvadorean society you may face the destabilisation of the society." In other words, we must not interfere with the practices of the elite groups who constitute that part of the society that matters, or we might disturb its stability. The same problem was noted by Arturo Cruz with regard to the *contras* (see p. 12).

It is not easy to employ killers for your work and then expect them to act like gentlemen—particularly, when their professional skills are instrumental for the task at hand. Furthermore, it is impossible to deny the crucial "Washington connection" in forming, training and maintaining this system of highly organized state terror.[38]

Occasionally the press does concede that security forces are responsible for atrocities. In a report on repression in Nicaragua, Stephen Kinzer notes that "Nicaragua has not reached the level of abuse attained a few years ago in Guatemala and El Salvador, when squads of security men in civilian clothes arrested, tortured or killed hundreds of dissidents." An accurate report would state that Nicaragua does not begin to approach the level of abuse today—not "a few years ago"—in Guatemala or El Salvador. And it was not *hundreds* "arrested, tortured or killed," but rather "tens of thousands of murders committed since 1979 by military-manned death squads," as the London *Economist* accurately observes, with many more tortured and arrested, in El Salvador alone, many thousands or possibly tens of thousands more in Guatemala.[39] In reference to our friends, the occasional recognition of the source of the violence must be given with a reduction by a factor of 100 and the US role omitted, and placed in the past; things are always improving in our domains.

The practice is standard. Barbara Crosette writes in the *Times* that after a military coup "which is believed" (namely, by approved unnamed sources) to have involved the Communist Party, Indonesian General Suharto "and others loyal to him" killed "thousands of Communist suspects." In fact, the number of people killed, mostly landless peasants, was in the neighborhood of 1/2 million by conservative estimate; again, diminution by a factor of 100, with the US support omitted.[40] In contrast, in early 1977, when the Khmer Rouge had killed perhaps tens of thousands of people (after having been turned into "totalitarian fanatics" by "American ruthlessness," as Philip Windsor comments, referring to the horrendous bombings of the early 1970s that killed unrecorded tens or hundreds of thousands), the press was satisfied with no less than 2 million murdered, ignoring the far lower estimates by US intelligence, later supported by Western scholarship. Jean Lacouture, who invented the 2 million figure, observed a few weeks later that the actual numbers might be in the thousands, not millions, but held that this did not matter, a statement that won great admiration here. His earlier 2 million figure, fabricated as he conceded, remained the official one in the media here and abroad.[41]

In short, atrocities committed by US clients are to be reduced by a factor of 100 with the crucial US role eliminated (if they are mentioned at all), while the rather comparable atrocities of official enemies are to be multiplied by a similar factor, with an enormous chorus of righteous indignation and with the background US role generally ignored.

Returning to El Salvador in the Carter years, the obvious place to learn about what was happening in the interior was the Honduran border, where 25,000 peasants fled the rampaging army that was destroying and burning down their villages in 1980, many more since. But this is not Cambodia under Pol Pot, where a trip to the Thai-Cambodian border could unearth stories that had ideological serviceability, so well-behaved journalists have given the refugee camps a wide berth. These camps were, however, visited by a congressional delegation in January 1981. The delegation concluded that "The Salvadoran method of 'drying up the ocean' involves, according to those who have fled from its violence, a combination of murder, torture, rape, the burning of crops in order to create starvation conditions, and a program of general terrorism and harassment." Refugees described mutilation, decapitation, "children around the age of 8 being raped, and then they would take their bayonets and make mincemeat of them"; "the army would cut people up and put soap and coffee in their stomachs as a mocking. They would slit the stomach of a pregnant woman and take the child out, as if they were taking eggs out of an iguana. That is what I saw."[42] This report was suppressed by the media, along with the facts generally; see note 34. But in the foreign press one could read refugee accounts of bombing, napalm attacks, destruction of villages, massacres, rape, torture by military forces, stories of "an existence of almost incomprehensible brutality."[43]

3.2 Reagan Takes Command

As Reagan took over in 1981, the massacres increased both in sadism and scale, with 12,501 cases documented by the Church Legal Aid Service for 1981 along with unknown numbers of others, again, attributed primarily to the various military and police forces. Meanwhile torture reached "extraordinary dimensions," human rights groups who investigated the matter observed; "Of the many thousands of bodies which have appeared after detentions and abductions of security personnel, a very high proportion show signs of torture including dismemberment, beating, acid burns, flaying, scalping, castration, strangulation, sexual violation, and evisceration." Churches and Human Rights offices were attacked; the judge investigating the murder of Archbishop Romero was driven from the country by death threats and assassination attempts after the government had ensured that no investigation could proceed; relatives of another judge were murdered, their heads severed and laid at his home, to prevent inquiry into state terror; patients were machine-gunned in hospitals; peasants, teachers, health workers, union leaders, students and others were brutally tortured and murdered with increasing ferocity. Meanwhile, President Duarte and US officials attempted to cover up the atrocities and denied the complicity of the military forces and police, whom they knew to be responsible.[44]

A medical mission of the US National Academy of Sciences and other professional and human rights groups investigated reports of barbarous treatment of health workers in January 1983. They report that "Wherever we turned we found the chilling effects of the ever-widening devastation to health and health care that has been caused by the breakdown of education, the slashing of budgets for national health programs, and the repression of human beings by the systematic use of terror in ways that are hideous and frightful." They report killing and kidnapping of patients and doctors in hospitals, "sometimes even during surgery"; "since merely notifying the Church and independent human-rights groups of a relative's disappearance can jeopardize the whole family, statistics on disappearances are minimal." They were shown "dirty, haggard political prisoners" in "foul, pitch-black steel-barred cells furnished with only a concrete bench and a hole in the floor for a latrine," but were forbidden to speak with them. They report that in July 1982, the Red Cross threatened to leave El Salvador because of human rights abuses by the armed forces, particularly, "their practice of not taking prisoners." The Salvadoran Ministry of Health had suffered a 50% reduction in its budget during each of the past two years (while capital flight from El Salvador was almost 2/3 as high as US aid, so that in effect US aid is a personal subsidy to Salvadoran high society). They describe horrifying conditions in hospitals as well as the breakdown of the educational system as facilities were destroyed, many teachers and university faculty were killed or imprisoned or "disappeared," or fled abroad from the terror. Another medical mission at the same time reported similar conclusions, adding grim statistics and observations about people living in "subhuman conditions" in a country where "social organization is considered subversive by the government of El Salvador." They express their surprise "to find so little evidence of international concern for their plight."[45]

A September 1985 report of a delegation of US health professionals—physicians, nurses, public health professors and others—"painted a grim picture of a war-ravaged country where countryside bombing drives children to autism, where hospitals are so ill-equipped that wounds are sutured with fishing line and where doctors are captured and tortured for treating persons suspected of antigovernment activity." The delegation "expresses special concern about violations of medical neutrality—the capture and harassment of health professionals working in the countryside," particularly near combat areas. "Medical professionals who work in rural clinics and refugee camps appear to be the target of a concerted and conscious repression by government security forces," the report asserts. It estimates more than 3000 civilians killed by government military actions in 1984, while 66 were killed by the guerrillas.[46]

As noted earlier, the US government is resolute in returning refugees from this chamber of horrors to the hands of their torturers, in striking comparison to the treatment of refugees whose suffering—real, but not remotely comparable—can be used to score ideological points. The logic is Jeane Kirkpatrick's; the refugees from El Salvador and Guatemala are not refugees, because these relatively benign societies, advancing towards democracy, "create no refugees."

These non-refugees have, however, described what they will face if forced back to their shattered homelands, to the tiny audiences they can reach, mainly church groups. One typical case is that of a 20-year-old Salvadoran woman whose appeal for asylum is being handled by the ACLU Asylum Project. In 1984, a death squad came to extort money from her uncle, who was the chairman of a peasant co-operative. She watched as the soldiers peeled her uncle's skin off with machetes before they murdered him along with her female cousin. She and two other cousins were then beaten and raped, and she was warned by the government death squad that her entire family would be killed if she recounted the story. On her first day in the US, she was picked up by the Immigration Service. She was denied political asylum and ordered deported because, in the judge's words: "you can pick up the newspaper everyday and read about this same thing happening in any urban area of the U.S."

Just as this was reported in *In These Times*, George Will devoted his nationally syndicated column to the case of a 12-year-old boy whose Russian parents wished to take him with them when they returned to the USSR, though he chose to remain here. Will scornfully denounced the "ludicrous governmental brooding about whether, were he returned, he would face persecution"; such hesitations—which were quickly overcome—are "ludicrous" in so obvious a case of protection of a person from persecution. Will also berated the ACLU for concerning itself with this case, in which the ACLU's position, upheld by the courts, was that the parents should have been granted their legal right to a custody hearing, which the government denied them. This "brooding" over legal rights is also "ludicrous," a sign of the ACLU's "swerve to the left." The fears of the Salvadoran woman elicited no such concern, nor, in fact, may they be expressed to a large audience.[47]

The Salvadoran military were trained and advised by Americans, while the security forces were instructed in torture methods by imported Argentine neo-Nazis. Elite battalions fresh from their US-training have regularly been responsible for the worst atrocities. John Loftus, who investigated Nazi war criminals for the US Justice Department, writes that "In the year 2025, when the Central American death squad documents are released in the National Archives to take their place alongside the records of Nazi genocide, I am going to take my grandchildren for a visit," so that they will learn that "those who do not know the mistakes of history [namely, ignoring hideous atrocities while they are in progress] are condemned to repeat them." Loftus also states that he knows from his investigations of Nazi war criminals brought to the US after the war that there are connections between them "and US operations in Central America"—a matter to which we return.[48]

Comparisons to some of the most extraordinary murderers of the modern age do occasionally appear in the press, in this context. Thus, at the height of Reagan's terror war in Central America, the respected liberal commentator William Shannon described the terrorism in Latin America as showing "a contempt for human life worthy of Joseph Stalin and his murderous policemen," referring, of course, to the guerrillas, not to the state terrorists organized and supported by the United States.[49] Again, no commissar could be more loyal in defending state terror.

We might recall the debates of the past few years over whether it would have been appropriate to use military force to intervene to stop the terrible massacres under the Pol Pot regime. It is not easy to take any of them very seriously. In the case of El Salvador, East Timor (where the atrocities were comparable to Pol Pot, thanks to crucial US assistance) and other places, no military intervention would have been (or would now be) required to terminate terrible massacres; it would only have been necessary to call off the hounds. The implications seem obvious.

With the crushing of the urban organizations, the increasing technical proficiency of the military, and the direct participation of US military forces in reconnaissance and coordination, the war shifted to the countryside, with no diminution of atrocities but less visibility. The Central America correspondent of the conservative London *Spectator* writes that death squad killings are "down to a handful every week," "but if the bright mood in the capital suggests that El Salvador is returning to the fold of civilized nations, it is a consummate deception: it is just that the war has moved from assassinations in the cities to indiscriminate bombing in the countryside," which is "happening every day" while Duarte's "strict rules about aerial bombardment" are simply "scoffed at" by the military command. The practice of "draining the sea" by "heavy and repeated bombing" and murderous groundsweeps "is not new but it has got worse since the elected government of President Duarte took power." Mary Jo McConahay, one of the few US reporters to have spent some time in zones under attack, reports that the peasant population in those zones was reduced by a third to a half during 1984 by air attacks, operations by US-trained elite battalions, and burning of fields to cause starvation and flight of the population, though she found no signs of combat. A religious worker says that "this is a war of attrition, and food—or an attempt at starvation—has become a weapon too"; an old US specialty, dating back to the Indian wars and employed effectively in Vietnam. The army commander blocked food deliveries by the Red Cross and the Catholic relief agency Caritas. Farmers cannot go to fields because of bombing. Peasants report that the planes, now directed by high technology US reconnaissance, "go after anything that moves."[50]

Visiting a refugee camp in Honduras, Elizabeth Hanly reports the testimony of a Salvadoran peasant woman who describes a 1983 massacre, when the National Guard came to her village in US-supplied helicopters, killing her three children among others, chopping the children to pieces and throwing them to the village pigs: "The soldiers laughed all the while," she said. Like her, other women "still had tears to cry as they told stories of sons, brothers and husbands gathered into a circle and set on fire after their legs had been broken; or of trees heavy with women hanging from their wrists, all with breasts cut off and facial skin peeled back, all slowly bleeding to death." They described how "they had worked, generations of them, all day, every day on someone else's land," their children starving or parasite-ridden. Peaceful visits to the landowners to beg for food had brought the National Guard: "We asked for food; they gave us bullets." More "annoyance" in *Christian Science Monitor* terminology, courtesy of the American taxpayer, who must be protected from awareness of these facts.[51]

The record of horrors has been compiled in regular publications of Americas Watch—only very partially of course, since the scale is so enormous—and generally ignored by the press, which is not interested in US atrocities. Reviewing the press record, Alexander Cockburn aptly comments: "All you need is a complicit or cowed press and a mendacious State Department and the American people need scarcely know that repeats of My Lai and Operation Speedy Express are taking place not far south of Miami and are sponsored by their government."[52]

As in Argentina under the generals, a Committee of Mothers of Disappeared Prisoners, formed at the initiative of assassinated Archbishop Romero, keeps a weekly vigil outside the Cathedral in San Salvador, carrying pictures of missing relatives. Two of the mothers were given the annual human rights awards of the Robert

Kennedy Foundation, but were denied visas on grounds that they had taken part in unspecified acts of violence. Roberto d'Aubuisson, one of the worst killers, was granted a visa a month later; the distinction reflects accurately the moral climate in Washington. A delegation of US labor leaders reports that the Deputy Chief of Mission of the US Embassy in San Salvador told them that one of the women "deserves" to be killed by security forces because her sons are fighting with the guerrillas.[53]

The two award recipients were, however, admitted to England, where the population apparently does not require protection from unpleasant truths. There, they described how their family members were murdered, tortured or "disappeared." One of the women had been raped, tortured and sprayed with bullets when she inquired about the whereabouts of her brothers and daughter; her right breast was cut off and she has artificial tubes for internal organs. These, apparently, were the acts of violence in which the mothers took part, making them ineligible for entry to the Land of the Free.

The Kennedy award was accepted in their name by a Salvadoran woman who came here from her exile in Mexico. She had witnessed the beating of her husband and rape of her two youngest children and "is undergoing her third operation to repair injuries incurred when Salvadoran agents attacked her [in 1981] with bayonets," Amnesty International reports. She too was raped and tortured. Her 14-year old son had been tortured by the National Guard several years earlier and two of her brothers "disappeared," one since found murdered.[54]

The refusal to grant the visas was noted here, but their testimony went largely unreported, to my knowledge.[55]

When President Duarte's daughter was kidnapped a year later, the *Times* reported: "By abducting her the guerrillas broke what [prominent families] regarded as an unspoken but traditional rule of chivalry," which had spared "the wives and daughters of the middle and upper classes."[56] The latter statement is false; women of these classes are tortured and murdered with impunity by the US client regime. But in the light of the regular sadistic treatment of women by these terrorist forces, the reference to the "traditional rule of chivalry," now broken, can only inspire amazement about the nature of our friends, and wonder about the moral and intellectual values of a country where these words can appear.

Meanwhile peasants continue to be beaten to death and mutilated, women and children are being killed in indiscriminate army attacks, and police torture remains a routine practice. In November 1983, in a leaked cable that the Reagan Administration attempted to conceal, the International Committee of the Red Cross cabled that it

> has seen a continuing deterioration in the treatment of detainees since April. Perhaps as many as ninety percent

of detainees are being tortured during interrogation. Torture is being employed in some of the formerly more humane centers, such as those run by the National Police.

As torture increased, Reagan offered his ritual Presidential Certification (July 1983) describing the progress of the government in ending torture and other human rights abuses, accepted by a supine Congress and public opinion fairly generally. Two years later the Salvadoran Commission of Human Rights stated that "Torture in El Salvador has become customary as a method of work, considered natural and necessary by those who practice it."[57]

An Americas Watch report, based on interviews in January 1985, records the testimony of refugees who fled well after President Duarte's theoretical "strict rules about aerial bombardment" were announced in September 1984 in response to protests by human rights groups. They fled, they say, because "people can't stand so much bombing." "The task of these people is to destroy," one said. The soldiers "set the mountains on fire" to drive people out of the hills, where they destroy villages and fields. "They kill anyone they find," the refugees report. Not even chickens or pigs escape as the scorched earth policies devastate crops and livestock and habitations, along with trapped civilians. Colonel Sigifredo Ochoa, who has many massacres to his credit and is much admired here for his prowess, told a reporter in January 1985 that he had established 12 free-fire zones in Chalatenango, where "Air strikes and artillery bombardments now are being carried out indiscriminately." "Without a civilian base of support, the guerrillas are nothing but outlaws," he explained.

Ochoa refused to permit the International Red Cross to provide humanitarian services and banned medical services throughout the province, also blocking entry of food provided by the Catholic relief agency Caritas. "His troops usually do not engage in combat with rebels," Chris Norton reports, "but Roman Catholic Church sources say he dislodged some 1,400 civilian rebel supporters, who fled to Honduran refugee camps between September and November [1984]." These "civilians say he turned mortar fire on them." Ochoa says there are no civilians in these areas, adding that

> We are anticommunist, democratic, or at least aspire to that, and we believe in the market system... We represent the Judeo-Christian Western civilization. We defend a system... We need a leader—someone to lead us. It's this way in Latin America. We want a strong man. Someone to lead us—to guide us.

He runs his area "like his private country," according to an observer with a human rights group "who echoes views fairly widely held here," while receiving much praise from his US advisers for his successes.

In the Guazapa area, where Dr. Clements had worked, regular air attacks against civilian targets continued after Duarte's rules of engagement were announced. The scattered remnants of the population attempt to hide from ground sweeps following the shelling and bombardment by helicopters and jet bombers, watching their children die of starvation and thirst. In Cabanas, two months after Duarte's pronouncement, one man reported that "about fifteen people got killed, children, pregnant women, adults, etc.," by A-37 planes and helicopters. Earlier, soldiers had swept through, raping, cutting the throats of victims, killing children with knives. "If they find somebody, they kill, they even kill the poor dogs and other animals," another refugee testified, reporting night bombing (an effective terror technique, now possible thanks to US air force technology and aerial support) and ambushing of people fleeing in October 1984. The soldiers also destroyed crops and houses, "even pans one uses to cook in...in order to leave one without anything." Fleeing women and children were killed by bullets and grenades, or sliced to pieces and decapitated with machetes. The attacks became particularly vicious after the "peace negotiations" between Duarte and the guerrillas—Duarte's noble and courageous "peace initiative," as the press described it, referring to Duarte's acceptance of longstanding guerrilla proposals, which he then refused to pursue further.[58]

Americas Watch reports that the testimonies they reproduce "were not selected because the events they describe were more or less horrifying than those described in other testimony," presented in extensive detail in the monthly reports of the Church Human Rights office Tutela Legal but ignored by the media. "Rather, they are representative of what is endured constantly by Salvadoran civilians in conflict zones and guerrilla controlled zones."

The Americas Watch report correctly warns that refugee testimony must be critically evaluated. In fact, on the rare occasions when US journalists investigate massacre reports, they are cautious and scrupulous in presenting and evaluating testimony—for example, in the September investigation by James LeMoyne of the July 1984 massacre at Los Llanitos,[59] carried out by the US-trained elite Atlacatl battalion, who killed 68 people according to the on-the-spot investigation of Tutela Legal a few days after the massacre, most of them women, old people and children; the bodies were then burned with gasoline brought in by helicopter.

LeMoyne writes that "the villagers' account has not been confirmed, and it may be colored by their sympathies for the guerrillas." What would count as "confirmation" he does not say, and it is, of course, the norm for reports of atrocities to come from the victims, who are not likely to be sympathetic to the murderers of their families and friends. But to raise doubts on this score is permissible only in the case of atrocities conducted by US client states, atrocities that are generally ignored or described with much skepticism and with the US role pointedly omitted, as in this case.

The need for care is regularly emphasized by analysts concerned with facts, and regularly disregarded, often with reckless abandon, when there are ideological points to be scored. In the case of El Salvador, the record compiled by human rights groups and journalists—many of them foreign or reporting out of the mainstream—is so extensive, detailed and consistent that, exercising all the care that is deemed appropriate in the case of our own state or its clients, no rational person can doubt that we are implicated in terrible crimes.

No one who surveys the record can reasonably doubt the conclusion of Aryeh Neier of Americas Watch and Helsinki Watch:[60]

> ...gross abuses of human rights are not incidental to the way the armed forces of El Salvador conduct their war against the guerrillas. In our view, the principal reason that those abuses continue at such a high rate at a point when—one would guess—the armed forces should have run out of politically suspect persons to murder is that the murders instill terror. Terror is the means whereby the armed forces maintain their authority.

As for the still more massive atrocities of the ground and air war in the countryside, there is little reason for the armed forces or President Duarte, who presides over the worst massacre in the history of his country, to be overly concerned. The paymasters will be pleased, whatever the cost, if the results are satisfactory, and most of the US population knows little more than the citizens of Moscow do about Afghanistan. "It is by the goodness of God," Mark Twain once observed, "that in our country we have those three unspeakably precious things: freedom of speech, freedom of conscience, and the prudence never to practice either of them."[61]

Terrorist violence is rarely purposeless. When its goals have been attained, it may well subside. Thus urban assassinations declined in El Salvador after the successful use of terror to subdue the urban population, a fact exploited here to justify further support for the torturers and assassins, who are seen to be mending their ways. Similarly, we can expect with some confidence that sooner or later the terror in the countryside will abate, once the resisting population is decimated or has fled, or has been forcibly removed to areas where they can be controlled. Under Col. Ochoa's rule, there will be many fewer atrocities, as a point of logic: atrocities require victims. And those that occur will be ever more difficult to document.

If Charles Clements were to return to Guazapa, he would not report horrors and atrocities of the kind he witnessed a few years ago, because "the continuing bombardment around Guazapa has driven almost all of the few hundred civilians remaining to flee to camps or hiding elsewhere, refugees and relief workers say"—that is, those who have not been murdered or removed by the army. Relief workers near Guazapa say "they observed planes bombing the mountainside at least once a week since January [1985]" though they rarely saw "air fire while troops are fighting on the ground," the only circumstance in which it is permitted according to the highly-touted Duarte rules of engagement. Since the civilians have been killed or removed, the press can inform us that things are looking up: "American and Salvadoran human rights groups in El Salvador have not reported any incidents this year [1985] in which air force fire caused large numbers of civilian casualties."[62]

This last conclusion is plainly true, again as a point of logic, with regard to the main human rights monitor in the hemisphere, Americas Watch, since its most recent report was based on testimony taken in January 1985. It is highly misleading at best with regard to other human rights groups. Two weeks before the conclusion just quoted appeared, the Council on Hemispheric Affairs (COHA, Washington) reported that according to its sources in El Salvador,·the most accurate figure is that "close to 3,000 civilians have died in rural areas in the first half of 1985 as a result of the air war." As for the major human rights group in El Salvador, the Church-based Tutela Legal, COHA reports that "unremitting public and private pressure on Tutela Legal by the Salvadoran government and the US embassy [which has been documented by Americas Watch] has caused it to adopt a lower profile and much stricter evidential standards which are difficult to meet under such restricted and dangerous circumstances, and the figures that it reports are but a fraction of the total death count, as Tutela personnel will freely admit."[63] Since the press regularly avoids the topic and virtually never reports the findings of Church or other human rights groups in El Salvador, further check is difficult. But sooner or later, such conclusions about declining body counts are bound to be correct, just as Soviet atrocities abated in Hungary after 1956, sure proof of the benign intent of the forces that had intervened to "defend Hungary" from "fascists instigated by the US."

It is notable that in El Salvador as in Nicaragua, the level of atrocities, which rival the most gruesome of recent years, increased dramatically as US involvement grew. Few seem capable of drawing the obvious conclusions, though they would be plain enough in the case of an official enemy.

Events in Nicaragua and El Salvador since 1980, as reviewed in sections 2 and 3, illustrate the second of the major consequences that characteristically ensue in US domains when efforts are made to mitigate the "miseries of traditional life." We return in chapter three to the remarkable reaction on the part of the media and educated classes fairly generally to what has been taking place in these countries.

4 Challenge and Response: Guatemala

The conditions of traditional life came under threat in Guatemala at about the same time as they did in El Salvador, and for the same reasons. Large segments of the peasant population, Indians primarily, began to lend support to guerrillas after the government moved to crush their nonviolent efforts to overcome the conditions of semi-slavery and misery to which the US has made notable and persisting contributions. The dynamics were the familiar ones. Local self-help organizations, many established by the Church, had developed during the 1970s and "functioned effectively with wide participation by the rural population," achieving "impressive results"—and calling forth the usual response: murder of priests and community leaders, and generalized massacre and repression.[64]

The response has been examined in gory detail by human rights groups. In October 1982, Amnesty International reported that in widespread massacres, the government had "destroyed entire villages, tortured and mutilated local people and carried out mass executions." To cite one example, in one village troops "forced all the inhabitants into the courthouse, raped the women and beheaded the men, and then battered the children to death against rocks in a nearby river."[65]

A Survival International delegation took depositions from refugees in Mexico, who report massacres in which "pregnant women and children have been killed, women have been raped, and people have been tortured and burned alive," with the destruction of whole towns and villages, burning of crops and destruction of livestock.[66] The stories are the familiar ones from the domains of US influence and control. Thus, a mother of 2 children fled her village as it was burned down with many killed by the army:

> In July 1982, soldiers flew into the area by helicopter. First they went to——, a nearby town, and killed five people, burned the town, and threw people, including women and children, into the flames... Children's throats were cut, and women were hit by machetes. [A man] watched as the soldiers killed fifteen people, including women, with machetes. They set fire to the houses, and sometimes opened the doors of huts and threw hand grenades inside. In all, fifty people in his village were killed. Soldiers also killed forty-nine people in the nearby

town of ——, which they burned as well... From a kilometer away, he saw women from the village who were hung by their feet without clothes and left.

Others describe how villagers were hacked to death by machetes, beaten to death, raped and tortured by soldiers, their towns burned to the ground. The perpetrators of such widespread massacres were easily recognized as Guatemalan army forces by their uniforms and their Israeli Galil rifles, standard issue for state terrorists in Latin America.

Survivors of the massacre at Finca San Francisco in July 1982 describe how 300 people were killed, the women raped and shot or burned to ashes in houses put to the torch, the old people hacked to pieces with machetes, the children disemboweled:[67]

> Finally they brought out the last child. He was a little one, maybe two or three years old. They stabbed him and cut out his stomach. The little child was screaming, but because he wasn't dead yet, the soldier grabbed a thick, hard stick and bashed his head. They held his feet together and smashed him against a tree trunk. I saw how they flung him hard and hurt his head. It split open, and they threw him inside the house.

The 1982 strategy of the Ríos Montt regime, defended by President Reagan and his Human Rights specialist Elliott Abrams, as we shall see, was described at the time by a respected journal:[68]

> The army strategy is to clear the population out of the guerrilla support areas. Troops and militias move into the villages, shoot, burn or behead the inhabitants they catch; the survivors are machine-gunned from helicopters as they flee.

Two years later, a British Parliamentary investigation concluded that "if anything, [the situation] has worsened since 1983" in a continuing slaughter that the conservative Bishops' Conference describes as "genocide." "The grim statistics summarizing Guatemala's political reality—100,000 killed since 1960, 100 political assassinations a month in 1984, 10 disappearances a week, 100,000 orphans, half a million displaced—barely reach the North American, let alone the European newspapers." Government claims that the guerrillas are responsible and that the "disappeared" have gone to Cuba or the USSR are "a brazen lie"; "The evidence points inexorably to the state security apparatus as being responsible for these crimes." Presenting testimony of gruesome torture and murder, the report cites estimates that in the most recent series of state massacres, some 25,000 had been slaughtered, mostly Indians, in three departments where a census was taken; the Roman Catholic Church administrator in the town of Quiché "estimates that in recent years about 20,000 Indians have been killed in Quiché province alone," the *Wall St. Journal* reports, quoting another churchman who says: "The roads began to stink, there were so many dead bodies." Estimates are uncertain, because the atrocities in the rural areas generally go unreported, as in El Salvador. The remnants of the terrorized population are removed to "model villages," the British report continues, where the system, "implanted by means of terror," is "designed also to sow terror." Conditions there, including the forced "civilian patrols" into which virtually the entire male population is press-ganged, "can be compared to slavery." Apart from the slaughter, eviction of peasants to make way for agro-export crops is bound to increase the already dramatic levels of severe malnutrition. The planned elections seem "more designed for the consumption of US Congress and world opinion than for the Guatemalan people."[69]

The "model villages" are inspired by the strategic hamlet program applied by the United States in the early stages of its direct attack against South Vietnam, when an attempt was made to drive several million people into areas where they could be "protected" from the guerrillas who, the aggressors conceded, they were willingly supporting. The basic concept was expressed in a USAID report of 1963:[70]

> The ultimate target is the human mind. It may be 'changed,' it may be rendered impotent for expression or it may be extinguished, but it still remains the critical target.

This was during the "hearts and minds" period of the US war against the rural population in South Vietnam, later to be modified in favor of mass murder, as more efficient, given the resources of the US military forces. The Guatemalan army with its Israeli advisers is regarded as better suited to the task than the US client forces in South Vietnam, hence capable of applying these ideas more effectively. As the London *Economist* noted in 1983, "with the help of Israeli advisers, [Guatemala] has succeeded where a similar campaign in neighbouring El Salvador, pushed by American advisers, has failed," though "the price of success has been very high," including "sadistic butchery" and one million homeless Indians. The journal suggests that El Salvador "could copy" the techniques used in Guatemala with profit. A few months earlier, the same journal had thoughtfully observed that "What liberal Americans can reasonably expect is that a condition of military help to Guatemala should be an easing of the political persecution of the centre—which played into the hands of the extreme left in the first place." The others evidently deserve their fate.[71]

The same "strategic hamlets" model is to be applied in El Salvador as well. Col. Ochoa announced the formation of "auto-defense units" that will involve the whole community, including women, in the defense of the community," noting that "plans similar to his have worked in neighboring Guatemala." "No one will be paid for their services," he said, though when the "communities are organized, they will receive government services and jobs." Funding is to come from USAID and the Inter-American Bank. Like his Guatemalan counterparts, Ochoa cites the Israeli Kibbutzim as an example; elsewhere, he has credited his training in Israel for his achievements. The whole account is straight out of Orwell, but as in Guatemala, the results will not be amusing for the enslaved population.[72]

5 The Reagan Administration and Human Rights

Throughout, the Administration has produced a steady stream of apologetics for the murderers and torturers, while conceding that in the past there had been abuses that have now been overcome. Ríos Montt, who took over the slaughter in March 1982, was "totally committed to democracy," "a man of great personal integrity" who "wants to improve the quality of life for all Guatemalans" and had received a "bum rap"; so President Reagan commented in December 1982 at a time when human rights groups and the international press estimated that some 3-8,000 had been killed with 200,000 driven from their homes by the government of this saintly figure, who, speaking on Guatemalan TV, had "declared a state of siege so that we could kill legally." A few months earlier, after four months of mounting atrocities under Ríos Montt, Stephen Bosworth of the State Department had informed Congress that "the record of the past four months, while not perfect, demonstrates that the new government has a commitment to positive change and new opportunity in Guatemala": "I cannot emphasize strongly enough the favorable contrast between the current human rights situation in Guatemala and the situation last December" under the Lucas Garcia regime. He added falsely that "Under the previous government, we did not provide military assistance because of the human rights record," but now, given the dramatic improvements, we may proceed. Melvin Levitsky of the State Department human rights office told Congress that under the Lucas Garcia regime, the US could not "easily sustain a relationship" because it engaged "in violence against its own people."

During the Lucas Garcia regime, the Administration had sung a different tune, lauding this mass murderer for "positive" developments as Guatemalan security forces have been "taking care to protect innocent bystanders" during their counterinsurgency operations—they were actually engaged in wholesale murder and torture of civilians—and lauding also the army's "program of civic action" in "backward areas."

When General Mejía Víctores took over from Ríos Montt in another coup, it turned out that Ríos Montt hadn't been quite such a saint after all. The State Department human rights report conceded that under his rule, "there were many allegations of abuses against Guatemala's Indian population, some of which were confirmed"— a forthright denunciation, Reagan-Abrams style, of *past* abuses of the sort briefly reviewed earlier. Now, however, the situation has improved, the Administration alleged. Assistant Secretary of State for Human Rights Elliott Abrams added that the violence and refugees should be blamed "on the guerrillas who are fighting the government"; violence and refugees are "the price of stability." As for the refugees in Mexico, their testimony can be discounted, Abrams held, because some may be "guerrilla sympathizers"; in any event, they "are not a representative proportion of the population." "Reporting on events in Guatemala without stepping foot into the country is not recommended," Abrams explained— naturally enough, since it is only in the refugee camps that testimony can be taken freely, without fear of the state terrorists. In congressional testimony in May 1984, Abrams stated that General Mejía Víctores had "continued a large number of the [human rights] improvements that Ríos Montt had begun," thus expressing his admiration for the most savage of the thugs who have ruled Guatemala with US support. State Department Human Rights reports and government officials claimed constant improvements, even "dramatic decline" in violence as government atrocities soared, or blamed the guerrillas, when evidence of atrocities could not be denied. "In September 1983 as the rate of assassinations doubled and abductions quadrupled (to a hundred per month)," Americas Watch observes, a State Department official said that "we see a trend toward improvement in human rights." In March 1985, Edward Fox of the State Department stated that "democracy is on track in Guatemala... The overall human rights situation in Guatemala has also improved, and the trends are encouraging," while human rights groups, and now even the press, reported the upsurge in murders and repression in preparation for forthcoming elections.

Commenting on this abysmal record, Christopher Hitchens observes: "I'm not suggesting 'moral equivalence' here. The U.S. government has fallen *below* the standards employed by the cheapest Stalinist hack."[73]

After the disappearance and murder of several USAID employees, Abrams conceded that some problems had arisen: "It has not gone from white to black... But the situation has clearly deteriorated."[74] The reports sampled above are from the period when the situation was still perfect. In the case of El Salvador, Abrams stated categorically that well-documented massacres, such as the one at Los Llanitos, had never taken place. Referring to this and another massacre by the Atlacatl Battalion at the Gualsinga river, where the toll may have reached several hundred, Abrams stated that "neither of them happened...there were no massacres in El Salvador in 1984." Abrams also claimed that the US Embassy, which "is in a better position than a newspaper which has a one-man bureau to investigate what is going on in El Salvador," always investigated such reports, and that his "memory is" that they did so in these cases, finding the reports groundless. The US Embassy denied investigating either massacre.[75] We return in chapter three to the interesting reactions of President Duarte, in these and other cases.

It is small wonder that human rights groups have referred to the Reagan Administration as "an apologist for some of the worst horrors of our time."[76] Human Rights Secretary Abrams has become particularly notorious for his denials of human rights violations or apologetics for them, in Central America and Turkey particularly, and for his attacks, in the familiar style of his Stalinist models, on human rights advocates. In recognition of his achievements in protecting human rights, Abrams was placed in charge of Latin American affairs in the State Department.[77]

Reagan's devotion to human rights was clear before his accession to the Presidency, which permitted him to put it into practice. In 1978, when the mass murders of the Argentine generals had become an international scandal, he condemned the Carter Administration for raising a fuss about such trivialities: "In the process of rounding up hundreds of suspected terrorists, the Argentine authorities have no doubt locked up a few innocent people," he wrote: "This problem they should correct without delay. The incarceration of a few innocents, however, is no reason they should open the jails and let the terrorists run free." True to his commitments, he and Jeane Kirkpatrick quickly let the murderers know that such concerns were a thing of the past, after the 1980 elections.[78]

6 The Contribution of the Mercenary States

Since the advent of the Reagan Administration, the US has provided direct military assistance to Guatemala, first in roundabout ways, then more directly, helping to facilitate the torture, murder and general brutality. The US government has not, however, been able to participate in the genocidal activities of its Guatemalan friends as fully as it would have liked, because of congressional human rights restrictions. Nevertheless, contrary to what is commonly alleged, the delivery of arms to the murderers never ceased, and as Pentagon figures show, it was barely below the norm during the Carter years.[79]

Still, there were impediments, so prime responsibility for providing the means and the advice and instruction was shifted to various clients, particularly Argentine neo-Nazis (though this ally was lost after the unfortunate return to democracy in Argentina) and Israel, which has lent its services enthusiastically to the cause, a fact commonly suppressed here.[80] The occasional articles and editorials on Guatemalan horrors in the press commonly refer to the travail of the years since 1954, without recalling the overthrow of Guatemalan democracy in 1954 and the regular US intervention since to maintain the system instituted by the CIA coup, a sordid display of moral cowardice.[81]

The US is, of course, implicated in the activities of its clients. The Argentine neo-Nazis regularly served as proxies for the US in Latin America, a fact noted without shame (see, e.g., p. 122, below), and more generally, the US was instrumental in the rise and sustenance of the neo-fascist National Security states of South America, as was the USSR in the case of Argentina.[82] But there are also other links, extending from Nazi Germany to Central America via the US, to which we return in chapter four.

In the case of Israel, US responsibility is obvious, given the massive aid Israel receives from the United States, conditioned in part on the services that it is expected to provide in return. The fact is recognized in Israel. Journalist Yoav Karni notes that "The Israelis may be seen as American proxies in Honduras and Guatemala." In discussing the memorandum of understanding with the US regarding strategic cooperation, the well-informed correspondent Gidon Samet writes that its most important features have to do not with the Middle East, but with Central America and Africa. Israeli services to the US in the Third World, he adds, were the prime topic of discussion when Israel's representative David Kimche visited Washington in early summer 1983. "The US needs Israel in Africa and Latin America, among other reasons, because of the government's difficulties in obtaining congressional authorization for its ambitious aid programs and naturally, for military actions." Israel aided the US through its contacts with Zaire in Chad and the US has "long been interested in using Israel as a pipeline for military and other aid" to Central America. US aid to Israel, diverted to Central America, can thus serve indirectly to bypass congressional restrictions. These are among the "secrets" relating to US-Israeli contacts with regard to Central America. Furthermore, the Administration requires support from congressional liberals for Grenada and other adventures, and the Israeli connection can help materially here, given Israel's influence in Congress.[83] The Washington correspondent of the *Jerusalem Post* elaborates, referring to criticism of Israel "for selling weapons to various Latin American regimes—many of which are not exactly democratic or enlightened":[84]

> Israeli officials have countered by pointing out that most of the sales have had the blessings of the Reagan administration, which often has been frustrated by Congress in its arms sales to these countries. Israel, therefore, could legitimately argue that it was doing America's dirty work—and making a nice profit in the process.

The profits are not insignificant. The Israeli press reports that "Latin America has become the leading market for Israeli arms exports," estimated at $1.2 billion for 1982, and that the market should grow in the light of the effectiveness of Israeli arms in the Lebanon war. The US is secretly helping Israel to establish military relations with various states, according to US sources, and is encouraging Israel to use American aid to assist US clients, so that they can "in effect obtain Israeli arms with US funding." Former Knesset Member Michael Kleiner states that the sale of arms to Honduras and to El Salvador, arms which indirectly find their way to the war against Nicaragua, "are made in accordance with the explicit request of the United States."[85]

Not surprisingly, Israeli arms sales to Latin America rapidly increased when the congressional human rights restrictions took effect. Shortly after Israel agreed to provide military aid to Guatemala, the Guatemalan army's Staff College review "published a prominent feature article by a Guatemalan officer in praise of Adolf Hilter, National Socialism, and the 'Final Solution'," in which the author, a Guatemalan military officer, quoted extensively from *Mein Kampf* and traced Hitler's anti-Semitism to his "discovery" that Communism was part of a "Jewish conspiracy" so that Germany's fight against the Jews was "in self defense" as part of its struggle against Russia, which was "dominated by the strength of a Marxist-Jewish nucleus." Despite his admiration for Hitler, he added that Nazism is not "a political panacea," and urged that Guatemala find its own variant of National Socialism, similar to the fascist Spanish Falange, "which is eminently nationalist and Catholic." Neither such sentiments nor the genocidal uses to which the military aid was put cut short the flow of Israeli weapons and advisers; Israeli military assistance was estimated at $90 million by 1982, when the Rios Montt regime took power, offering thanks for the Israeli training which made this possible.[86]

Israel's close relations with the Argentine neo-Nazis and others like them in Latin America were also unaffected by their virulent anti-Semitism. To cite one of numerous examples of regular cozy relations, when Israel faced an international arms embargo after the 1967 war, it approached Bolivia with a plan, which was implemented, to divert to Israel Belgian and Swiss arms ostensibly destined for Bolivia, to be transported by a company managed by Klaus Barbie, the Nazi war criminal who was spirited to Latin America by US intelligence when it was no longer possible to benefit from his services in postwar Europe. A report in the Israeli press alleges that Barbie also had frequent dealings with Israel concerning supplies of Israeli arms to Latin American countries and "various underground organizations."[87]

Any possible moral qualms concerning arms sales to Guatemalan Himmlers and other murderers and torturers may be put aside by the familiar principles expressed by the director of Israeli State military industry (*Ta'as*), Michael Shur:[88]

> The welfare of our people and the state supersedes all other considerations. If the state has decided in favor of export, my conscience is clear.

Some do feel a degree of discomfort. The revered moralist Elie Wiesel, whose thoughts are featured in the media whenever it is deemed appropriate to denounce someone else's crimes, received a letter from a Nobel Prize laureate containing documentation on Israel's contributions to atrocities in Guatemala with a suggestion that he might use his prestige and close Israeli contacts to help mitigate genocidal acts while they are in progress. The matter came up in an interview in the Israeli press. Wiesel "sighed," and said that he had not responded: "I usually answer at once, but what can I answer to him"? To make a public statement would violate his principle, frequently expressed, never to say anything in public critical of Israel. But he did sigh.[89]

7 The Planning of State Terror

The striking correlation between US assistance and barbarism in Central America has its roots in deliberate planning, both in global terms and in specific application to this region. We will take up these matters later on, merely noting here that the essentials are understood in Washington, however easy it may be to disguise the reality with familiar pieties. A USAID report of 1967, reviewing the US program to train the National Guard and National Police, commented that by virtue of this assistance,[90]

> ...authorities have been successful in handling any politically motivated demonstrations in recent years... With the potential danger that exists in a densely populated country where the rich are very rich and poor extremely poor El Salvador is fortunate that the Guard and Police are well trained and disciplined...

Here it is necessary to decode, once again, from Newspeak to English: it is not El Salvador that is fortunate, plainly, but rather those who own and rule the country, those whom we dare not disturb by trying to inhibit their pleasure in torture and mass murder (see p. 17).

After its successful destruction of Guatemalan democracy in 1954, the US undertook to ensure that no such problems would ever arise again. The US began to train army officers and security forces, including elements of the police specializing in political repression and the Mobile Military Police, later implicated in many massacres. The goal was to increase efficiency in the operations that are bound to be necessary as the miseries of traditional life and continued repression evoke resistance, and to ensure that domestic order will be maintained even if some pretense of formal democracy is occasionally permitted for the benefit of the US home front. After the CIA coup, LaFeber notes, US advisers took a "rag-tag force" and converted it into an efficient modern army with "institutional pride and allegiance" and an understanding of its political as well as its military mission, a fit force to rule the country, as the US determined again in 1963, when Kennedy supported a military coup. Similarly in Honduras, the army, "not yet a self-conscious, professional institution," could do little to block social and political development in earlier years, but is currently more capable of doing so, now that "US training raised the military's self-awareness, and North American equipment made it the decisive political force." As Americas Watch observes, "what the United States is doing for the army of El Salvador today, it did for the army of Guatemala twenty years ago," and there is every reason to expect the long-term consequences to be the same. The major steps in providing the Latin American military and internal security forces with an understanding of their political mission and with the proficiency to realize it were taken under the Kennedy Administration, in part through the Alliance for Progress; we return to that topic in chapters three and four.[91]

The model for these programs was Nicaragua, where in the late 1920s, the US undertook to create an efficient domestic military force to replace the US Marines who occupied the country for two decades. The result was that "Nicaragua was clearly a nation occupied by its own army,...one of the most totally corrupt military establishments in the world," maintained with enthusiastic US support from the days of FDR to the fall of Somoza.[92] Guatemala's turn came in the fifties, and after early steps under the Alliance for Progress, El Salvador is undergoing the same process today, with Honduras not far behind. Costa Rica has been spared the fate of the other Central American countries, largely because it has no professional army to occupy the country in the interests of the generals, the oligarchs, and their foreign overseer, but the Reagan administration is working hard to overcome this defect while laboring to restore the traditional system in Nicaragua. Lester Langley observes that "Costa Ricans, who have suffered no American military penetration and only isolated cases of Washington's political chastisement, are the only truly pro-American people in Central America" (elite groups aside).[93] With a little help from their friends in Washington, this should soon change as Costa Rica goes the way of the rest of Central America.

The current pro-American mood in Costa Rica derives not only from the lack of US intervention and the sensible rejection, until recently, of substantial US-trained domestic armed forces, but also from the fact that the Costa Rican economy is in a shambles, with one of the highest per capita debts in the world and ¾ of its exports used to cover debts to foreign (primarily US) banks, so that the economy remains viable only because it is "rolling in aid from Uncle Sam," receiving the highest per capita aid of any country apart from Israel (a case to itself). "This year's aid of $198 million equals the total of U.S. support for Costa Rica in the 18 years before the Nicaraguan revolution," the *Wall St. Journal* comments, quoting a leading Costa Rican figure who says that "Our best industry is the Sandinistas," as the US works to shore up its anti-Nicaraguan alliance. "We're recycling money from the U.S. government and paying it out to U.S. banks," the president of the central bank of Costa Rica observes; in other words, the US taxpayer is paying US banks via the aid program, permitting Costa Rica to "combine bankruptcy with relative prosperity"—as long as it toes the line.[94]

A secret State Department report of May 1984 urges military aid to Costa Rica "to prevent any backsliding into neutralism" and to "push it more explicitly and publicly into the anti-Sandinista camp." The report notes that "for public relations, it is important to neutralize the 'ARDE' factor"—referring to the US-supported *contra* attacks from Costa Rica—or this will weaken the "rationale for a vigorous U.S. response" to Nicaraguan military actions; "our provision of assistance and accompanying public and background statements can help to focus the spotlight on Costa Rica as the victim of Nicaraguan aggression." The *Washington Post* quoted a Costa Rican close to President Monge as saying that he had tried to handle border incidents by diplomatic means, but was being "pushed to create a scandal" by the the US. The State Department report warned of the danger that "An effective rationale for urgent U.S. military supplies could be dissipated somewhat if there are no further attacks and press stories focus on mediation and lessened tensions... Attacks against a small democracy with no standing army put Nicaragua in a bad light." Costa Rica had, in the past, "sought to defuse tensions, avoid confrontation, and fall back on the moral protection of its unarmed neutrality," the report continues, a course that "still retains its strong attraction for many

Costa Ricans." This course must be changed, with the US exploiting incidents arising from *contra* attacks to make it appear that Costa Rica is the victim of unprovoked Nicaraguan aggression, whatever the consequences for Costa Rica.[95]

8 The Miseries of Traditional Life: A Further Note

This review, which barely samples what the US has helped to institute and maintain in Central America, is seriously misleading in one crucial respect: it overlooks the silent suffering of normal life, the "violence to the spirit" and to the flesh described by the lay minister quoted earlier (p. 6). In Honduras, for example, one in eight infants dies before age two and of those who survive to age five, ¾ are undernourished. The problem is not that food production is insufficient; in 1980, Oxfam reports, "the harvest of bananas was three times greater than the harvest of corn, rice, sorghum and beans combined" while Honduras has become a net importer of all of these staple foods. Coffee, beef, cotton, fruit and palm oil are major export crops, enriching US agribusiness and the tiny elite of Hondurans who are "junior partners with US-based agribusiness companies." Beef production more than doubled since 1960 while per capita consumption of beef declined and exports increased over 500% for hamburgers, hot dogs and pet foods in the US. Forests are being destroyed for cattle ranching, with the assistance of USAID grants funding the expansion of beef production for export. In one typical region, 68% of loans from US government and private sources went to cattle ranchers, 22% to cotton growers, 5% to corn farmers. Peasants are compelled to clear land which they farm for two or three years, after which they are forced to move on to repeat the process while the land loses its fertility and becomes "a weeded, dusty wasteland" from over-grazing. While Central America was expanding beef production rapidly under the Alliance for Progress, beef consumption dropped 41% in Costa Rica, 38% in El Salvador, and 13% in Guatemala and Nicaragua from 1960 to the mid-seventies.[96]

When the land is finally denuded and devastated, we may tolerate the victory of some future guerrilla movement, then denouncing its failure to carry out real economic development, another proof of the evils of Communism.

The process extends back many years in Central America, to the Spanish conquest in fact, when grazing by cattle introduced by the conquerors, unrestricted under Spanish law, was a factor in the elimination of close to 20 million people in about 50 years, a notable chapter in the history of genocide.[97] The major factors that caused Honduras to "lose the ability to feed its own people," the Oxfam report continues, include "the economic power of US corporations, the interests of a small Honduran elite, and the policies of US and international banks and aid agencies," which have driven these developments throughout Central America. Just in the past few years, US corporations, which have virtually owned Honduras since 1900, bribed Honduran officials to avoid paying taxes and hired Honduran army officers to bring troops to arrest members of a peasant cooperative who sought to evade their market control, while US government policies are designed to guarantee their increasing profits. All of this is quite apart from the regular subversion and military intervention over the years if the society held in thrall to the foreign investor threatens to change in the wrong direction, towards concern for the needs of its own population.

In part these developments simply reflect the dynamics of the market, given the distribution of economic power. "With the fastest growing and most profitable markets for agricultural commodities located in the advanced capitalist countries, the most dynamic sector of capital accumulation is in export production," so it is here that modernization has taken place; those who have only their labor to sell can expect to fall by the wayside, or to be removed by force if they are in the way of greater profits. The state, controlled by the US-backed oligarchy, will naturally observe the same priorities. Thus in Guatemala, 87% of all government credit in the decade following the military coup of 1963 went to finance export production, while rice, corn, and beans received 3%.[98] Had democratic elections been permitted in 1963, the story would very likely have been different, but the Kennedy-backed military coup prevented any such outcome. A similar pattern of government credit holds in Brazil and elsewhere.

Throughout the Central American dominions of the US, the same has been true, particularly under the Alliance for Progress, when US aid to agriculture rapidly increased; not, however, to alleviate hunger but primarily to "improve the productivity of Central America's agricultural exporters and at the same time to advance the sales of American companies that manufacture pesticides and fertilizer... AID accepts as fundamental doctrine the notion that its funds should not be directed toward reducing food prices for domestic consumers," Langley observes, or for improving domestic food consumption. Quite the contrary: as AID disbursements show, its concern is the export market dominated by US agribusiness, expansion of the market for American grain exporters as domestic production of food for the population declines, and improving opportunities for the foreign investor. An executive of a US fertilizer firm observed that "there would be scarcely any [US] investment if it were not for the infrastructure, the education, the training, and the support provided by our aid programs...very few investors would be in any of the underdeveloped countries were it not for our effort at economic assistance"—and, as noted, the investment is not for the benefit of the population, in fact is harmful to them, despite the statistics concerning production increase. The Food for Peace program (PL 480), which the US Department of Agriculture described in 1982 as "one of the United States' most successful market development tools," has opened up new markets for US grain producers, allowing them to export more than $20 billion worth of grain under the program. Furthermore, as President Carter's Secretary of Agriculture John Block explained, "Food is a weapon" that we use "to tie countries to us. That way they'll be reluctant to upset us." [99]

The picture is the same throughout Latin America, where "the terrifying reality is that most of the population is hungry, malnourished and sick" while "the actual purchasing power of the worker has been declining since the early 1960s" despite impressive growth rates and "economic miracles" under the National Security states that the US has helped to impose and sustain. Latin America is a net exporter of foods, including grains, meats, sugar, bananas, coffee, cacao, and soybeans as well as non-food crops such as cotton, "because the large landowners, foreign as well as domestic, earn handsome profits from such exports, more than they might earn selling food in the domestic market," as does US agribusiness with its indirect state subsidies. At the same time, only about 10% of the arable land is in use. "Latin America is fully capable not only of feeding its own population well but of contributing significantly to world food supplies...we are challenged to understand why Incan technology, efficiency and productivity surpassed Western technology, efficiency, and productivity."[100] Particularly in the past quarter-century, the US has made a material contribution to these consequences with its political, military and economic policies ranging from subversion to "aid."

The phenomenon is, in fact, worldwide. The US is the world's largest food importer, primarily from the Third World, including countries where malnutrition is rampant. The US is also the world's largest food exporter, but the food rarely goes to the starving. Two-thirds of US agricultural exports go to developed countries, primarily Europe and Japan. "In 1982, the Netherlands alone received more of our agricultural products (over 3 billion dollars worth) than the entire continent of Africa," and agricultural exports to Canada were twice as high as to the 17 countries of the world with a food supply of less than 2,000 calories per person, with a population of almost 1 billion people. Furthermore, 55% of US grain exports are for animals, much of it for beef exports to the US, and most of the food for Third World governments is not aid (only 3% was aid in 1982) but rather is sold with low-interest financing (and hence is in effect a taxpayer subsidy to US agribusiness), then for the most part resold at prices that the poor cannot afford.[101]

Forty thousand children die every day from malnutrition and disease resulting from starvation. We help kill them, with policies designed to have this predictable consequence.

Let us now turn away from the children dying of malnutrition while crops are exported to the US, from the bodies hacked to pieces by machetes and the villages burned to the ground in free-fire zones, and consider the background for all of this at home.

2 The Fifth Freedom

1 Rhetoric and Reality

In April 1944, *Time* reporter William Krehm described a failed coup attempt he had just witnessed in El Salvador:[1]

> The people here drank their sedition directly from the slogans of the United Nations. It was possible for the *Diario Latino* to conduct an anti Martinez campaign for a whole year merely by featuring phrases of Roosevelt and Churchill on the Four Freedoms. Perhaps naively, they believed them. They were convinced that by its utterances the United States would not look unkindly on their efforts to unfurl the Atlantic Charter on this bit of Pacific coast. Their leaders botched matters, and the first thing they knew, the embassy doors were slammed in their faces when they sought asylum from their hangmen.

The *Time* reports elicited a response from the State Department which, in Krehm's words, explained that

> asylum might be extended to those threatened by mob violence, but never to anybody pursued by the constituted authorities. In less stuffy language, a dictator fleeing the retribution of his people would find embassy doors ajar, but for democrats hunted by the dictator's goons they would be bolted. It was an elucidation that could not fail to impress the Salvadoran public.

The coup attempt, by military officers with middle class backing, aimed to depose General Maximiliano Hernández Martínez, who had ruled El Salvador since 1931. One of a group of Central American dictators supported by the United States, Martínez had won notoriety by presiding over the 1932 *Matanza* ("massacre"), a slaughter of some 10-30,000 peasants while US and Canadian naval vessels stood offshore and US Marines were alerted in Nicaragua. "It was found unnecessary for the United States forces and British forces to land," US Chief of Naval Operations Admiral William V. Pratt testified before Congress, "as the Salvadoran Government had the situation in hand." Martínez was granted informal recognition at once on grounds of his success in "having put down the recent disorders" (State Department), with full recognition following in 1934 in defiance of an agreement with the Central American states that military dictators were not to be recognized without free elections; the latter condition was presumably satisfied the next year when Martínez was elected, unopposed, after having eliminated or suppressed any political opposition. Martínez maintained his rule until 1944 with bloody repression and corruption while openly siding with European and Japanese fascism through the 1930s—and, in limited ways, introducing some social reforms in the style of his fascist models. Thus a government housing program constructed 3000 houses from 1932 to 1942 while the population of San Salvador alone increased by 80,000, and 0.25% of the population received land (including squatters, required to pay for the land on which they lived or be expelled) in a land reform program. There was little support for the 1944 coup attempt by labor, the peasantry or the urban poor, who had been traumatized by the *Matanza*.[2]

All of this was during the peak years of the Good Neighbor policy, which was to replace the earlier rampant US military interventionism. Its exalted rhetoric concealed something rather different. The lessons taught once again by these events have been learned and relearned throughout Central America, and not only there, for many years. US rhetoric is often noble and inspiring, while operative policy in the real world follows its own quite different course, readily discernible in the actual history and rooted in institutional structures that change very slowly, if at all, and often outlined frankly in internal documents. We understand such facts with regard to official enemies. The rhetoric of Soviet propaganda is also elevated and developments in Eastern Europe vary under the influence of local particularities and historical contingencies. But it would be absurd to ignore their systematic pattern and its roots in the institutions and planning of the regional superpower; in fact, we learn a good deal about the USSR by observing the domains of its authority and control. Much the same is true of the United States. The history of Central America and the Caribbean in the shadow of an emerging superpower is particularly enlightening in this regard, as noted earlier.

The rhetorical flourishes of political leaders, which resound through the ideological institutions, play their assigned role in concealing the evolving reality from the domestic population of the hegemonic power, who would be unlikely to tolerate the truth with equanimity. The rhetoric, however fanciful, may be sincerely believed by the purveyors of propaganda; in public as in personal life, it is easy to come to believe what it is convenient to believe. As John Adams once said, "Power always thinks it has a great soul and vast views beyond the comprehension of the weak; and that it is doing God's service when it is violating all his laws.[3]

The Four Freedoms and the Atlantic Charter illustrate very well the true significance and domestic utility of noble ideals. President Roosevelt announced in January 1941 that the Allies were fighting for freedom of speech, freedom of worship, freedom from want, and freedom from fear. The terms of the Atlantic Charter, signed by Roosevelt and Churchill the following August, were no less elevated. These lofty sentiments helped to maintain domestic cohesion during the difficult war years, and were taken seriously by oppressed and suffering people elsewhere, who were soon to be disabused of their illusions.

It was not the first time, nor the last. Truman Doctrine rhetoric in 1947 about supporting "free peoples who are resisting attempted subjugation by armed minorities or by outside pressures" concealed plans for counterinsurgency in Greece, soon implemented, which led to unspeakable carnage and terror. Meanwhile perennial presidential adviser Clark Clifford happily observed that the Doctrine served as "the opening gun in a campaign to bring people up to [the] realization that the war isn't over by any means," setting off a new era of domestic militarism and intervention abroad in the context of Cold War confrontation.[4] The true meaning of Jimmy Carter's soulful devotion to human rights would be learned by hundreds of thousands of victims of torture, starvation, or outright slaughter in El Salvador, Timor, Laos, and elsewhere. John F. Kennedy's Alliance for Progress, launched with great fanfare out of fear that the Cuban model might inspire others to pursue the same course, was again a rhetorical triumph. Its real world impact for 1960-1965 was summarized by the editor of *Inter-American Economic Affairs*:[5]

> During that period the distribution of income became even more unsatisfactory as the gap between the rich and poor widened appreciably. During most of the period a very heavy proportion of the disbursements went to military regimes which had overthrown constitutional governments, and at the end of the period, with almost half of the population under military rule, a significant portion of the aid was going *not* to assist "free men and free governments" [in Alliance rhetoric] but rather to hold in power regimes to which the people had lost their freedom.

These consequences were the direct and predictable results of fateful decisions of the Kennedy Administration, to which we return. Meanwhile "Alliance funds in massive amounts went to US-owned firms and to the Central American oligarchs that controlled banks and mercantile businesses, as well as the best tillable land." US investment rose rapidly, and while the first decade did record statistical growth of their economies, its effect was to shift subsistence production to export crops for the benefit of foreign corporations and local oligarchs, while every country of Central America increasingly lost the capacity to feed itself and starvation and misery grew; again, the result of specific decisions with predictable consequences. The substantial growth of military forces trained for internal repression was a natural concomitant of the Alliance for Progress, which "helped make such a force necessary" as the expansion of the export economy "took lands from campesinos and set the class war in motion."[6]

Few statesman were more given to uplifting pronouncements about the rights of the weak and oppressed than Woodrow Wilson, "the greatest interventionist of all,"[7] who celebrated his doctrine of self-determination by invading Mexico, Haiti, and the Dominican Republic. One supplicant approached Wilson's Paris residence during the Versailles conference in 1919, hoping to present a petition entreating the victorious allies to support his country's "permanent representation in the French Parliament by elected natives in order to keep it informed of native aspirations." But in vain. "The appeal went undelivered. United States Marines, guarding President Wilson in his quarters, chased the would-be petitioner away, 'like a pest'"—an important phase in the education of the man later known as Ho Chi Minh.[8]

The noble rhetoric remains unsullied in Western discourse (including much scholarship). But many poor and suffering people have a much clearer understanding of the reality it has always masked.

In the privileged countries of the West, there have also been a few who refrained from joining the celebrations of the True Believers. The revolutionary pacifist A. J. Muste once quoted this remark, thinking no doubt of World War II:[9]

> The problem after a war is with the victor. He thinks he has just proved that war and violence pay. Who will now teach him a lesson?

The sentiment was to the point, as postwar events revealed.

2 The Perceptions of the Planners

In the chambers of power, a clearer vision is also sometimes expressed. In mid-1941, while schoolchildren were memorizing the Four Freedoms and—soon after—the Atlantic Charter, the War and Peace Studies Project of the Council on Foreign Relations, which included top government planners and members of the foreign policy elite with close links to government and corporations, explained privately that "formulation of a statement of war aims for propaganda purposes is very different from formulation of one defining the true national interest," recommending further that[10]

> If war aims are stated, which seem to be concerned solely with Anglo-American imperialism, they will offer little to people in the rest of the world, and will be vulnerable to Nazi counter-promises. Such aims would also strengthen the most reactionary elements in the United States and the British Empire. The interests of other peoples should be stressed, not only those of Europe, but also of Asia, Africa and Latin America. This would have a better propaganda effect.

In accordance with this conception, Roosevelt spoke of Four Freedoms, but not of the Fifth and most important: the freedom to rob and to exploit. Infringement of the four official freedoms in enemy territory always evokes much agonized concern. Not, however, in our own ample domains. Here, as the historical record demonstrates with great clarity, it is only when the fifth and fundamental freedom is threatened that a sudden and short-lived concern for other forms of freedom manifests itself, to be sustained for as long as it is needed to justify the righteous use of force and violence to restore the Fifth Freedom, the one that really counts.

A careful look at history and the internal record of planning reveals a guiding geopolitical conception: preservation of the Fifth Freedom, by whatever means are feasible. Much of what US governments do in the world can be readily understood in terms of this principle, while if it remains obscured, acts and events will appear incomprehensible, a maze of confusion, random error and accident. Many other factors also operate—fortunately, or there would be no hope of modifying state policies and actions short of social revolution. But this principle is an invariant core, deeply rooted in the basic institutions of American society.

Public discussion of the facts would plainly not have "a good propaganda effect," so the ideological institutions—the schools, the media and much of scholarship—keep to a familiar refrain, extolling our profound concern for human rights, the raising of the living standards, and democratization. In private, the more intelligent planners reveal that they labor under few illusions and urge that we not be "hampered by idealistic slogans" of this sort. The central point was lucidly explained in an internal document written in 1948 by George Kennan, head of the State Department planning staff in the early post-World War II period:[11]

> ...we have about 50% of the world's wealth, but only 6.3% of its population... In this situation, we cannot fail to be the object of envy and resentment. Our real task in the coming period is to devise a pattern of relationships which will permit us to maintain this position of disparity without positive detriment to our national security. To do so, we will have to dispense with all sentimentality and day-dreaming; and our attention will have to be concentrated everywhere on our immediate national objectives. We need not deceive ourselves that we can afford today the luxury of altruism and world-benefaction... We should cease to talk about vague and—for the Far East—unreal objectives such as human rights, the raising of the living standards, and democratization. The day is not far off when we are going to have to deal in straight power concepts. The less we are then hampered by idealistic slogans, the better.

This prescription is noteworthy not only for its clarity and forthrightness, but also because of its source, one of the most thoughtful and humane of US planners, who left his position not long after because he was considered not sufficiently tough-minded for this harsh world.[12]

Note that this is a Top Secret document. The "idealistic slogans" must constantly be trumpeted in public in order to pacify the domestic population, as in the 1984 report of the bipartisan Kissinger Commission, which opens by explaining that "The international purposes of the United States in the late twentieth century are cooperation, not hegemony or domination; partnership, not confrontation; a decent life for all, not exploitation."[13] The historical and contemporary record reveal just how seriously these fine words are to be taken.

There is, to be sure, an exception to Kennan's advice, explained by the Joint Strategic Survey Committee in a Top Secret discussion of US assistance to other countries a few months earlier. This report stipulates that "assistance should be concentrated on those countries of primary strategic importance to the United States in case of ideological warfare, excepting in those rare instances which present an opportunity for the United States to gain worldwide approbation by an act strikingly humanitarian."[14] In such a case, we may briefly live up to our inspiring ideals. Etzold and Gaddis observe that the ranking of interests in this document "to a large extent established priorities for the programs of economic and military assistance implemented in the name of 'containment' during the next three years."

Kennan's prescriptions refer to the Far East, but the US is a global power, and this general geopolitical conception, amply illustrated over many years, is applicable elsewhere as well, as Kennan among others made clear.

Before considering its more general application, we might observe that some questions can be raised about Kennan's formulation of the goals of national policy. One has to do with his concept of the disparity between "us" and "them." Ignored here are certain disparities among "us." In fact, planners recognized early on that more egalitarian social arrangements at home might reduce the need to protect the Fifth Freedom abroad. One participant in the War and Peace Studies Project observed that the domains of US control must be sufficient to provide it with "the 'elbow room'...needed in order to survive without major readjustments"; it was understood that changes in the domestic distribution of power, wealth, ownership and control might reduce the significance of the Fifth Freedom for the American economy.[15] Furthermore, the harsh measures required to maintain the (somewhat abstract) disparity between "us" and "them" carry severe costs, both material and moral. Perhaps in the present narrow context the latter should be put aside as irrelevant sentimentality. But it is far from clear that "we" benefit materially from the national commitment to "maintain this position of disparity" by force, a commitment that entails global confrontation with the constant threat of nuclear war, an economy driven by military production, loss of jobs to regions where US-supported thugs ensure low wages and miserable living standards, almost 60,000 soldiers killed in an attempt to enforce "our" will in Indochina, and so on.

The idea that "we" confront "them" is a staple of the ideological system, one that has as much merit as the tenets of other religious cults. With this cautionary note, I will nevertheless continue to use these misleading formulations, thus adopting— with some misgivings —one of the conventional devices employed to prevent understanding of the world in which we live.

A second question is whether Kennan is correct in suggesting that "human rights, the raising of the living standards, and democratization" should be dismissed as irrelevant to American foreign policy (except when points can be scored in "ideological warfare"). A review of the historical record suggests a different picture: that US policy has not been neutral in these regards, but has sought to destroy human rights, to lower living standards, and to prevent democratization, often with considerable passion and violence. The reasons are not difficult to discern: commitment to these values is often at odds with the Fifth Freedom. Preservation of the Fifth Freedom quite regularly requires measures that tend to harm human rights and living standards, and with meaningful steps towards democracy, governments will tend to be more responsive to domestic needs, thus threatening our control of the human and material resources that must be at our command if we are to "maintain the disparity." We therefore quite regularly oppose human rights and raising of the living standards in practice, and we oppose meaningful democracy in much of the world to ensure that the Fifth Freedom will not be threatened. We return in chapter 3, section 8, to a closer look at these specific issues. In chapter 1, we took note of the means to which we habitually resort when the Fifth Freedom is challenged. Chapter 3 will be devoted to a more detailed examination of the facts of the matter, which can hardly be comforting to a person of any honesty and integrity.

Kennan extended the same thinking to the Western Hemisphere in a briefing for Latin American ambassadors in 1950. He observed that a major concern of American foreign policy must be "The protection of our raw materials"—in fact, more broadly, the material and human resources that are "ours" by right. To protect our resources, we must combat a dangerous heresy which, as US intelligence noted, had been spreading through Latin America for many years: "The wide acceptance of the idea that the government has direct responsibility for the welfare of the people,"[16] what is called "Communism," whatever the political commitments of its advocates, in US political theology.

From whom must we protect our "our raw materials"? For the public, throughout our history we have been defending ourselves from one or another Evil Empire; currently, from the USSR. In the real world, the enemy is the indigenous population which may attempt to use domestic resources for their own purposes, thus joining what the President called "the monolithic and ruthless conspiracy" to thwart our ends; President Kennedy, in this case.[17] Those who undertake this course may not be Soviet allies to begin with; in Latin America, they have commonly been Church-based self-help groups, advocates of capitalist democracy such as Juan José Arévalo in Guatemala, popular organizations of the sort defended by the martyred Archbishop Romero in El Salvador, and so on. But they are likely to become Soviet clients, for the simple reason that they will have nowhere else to turn for protection against the violence that we regularly unleash against them. This is a net gain for American policy, since it justifies the attacks we must carry out to destroy the conspiracy to steal our resources. When the Fifth Freedom is threatened in its domains, the US regularly resorts to subversion, terror or direct aggression to restore it, declaring the target of these actions a Russian client and acting to make this required truth a reality.

The Indochina wars are enlightening in this regard. By the late 1940s, the US had committed itself to support the French effort to reconquer their former colony, having rejected repeated overtures from the Viet Minh, the anti-French resistance whom the State Department recognized in secret to be the representatives of Vietnamese nationalism; a favorable response might have permitted the Communist-led national movement to maintain its independence, thus undermining the official rationale for the US-French attack. US intelligence was then assigned the task of demonstrating the required truth: that Vietnamese nationalists were simply agents of the "Commie-dominated bloc of slave states," in Dean Acheson's elegant phrase.

Intelligence sought desperately to find links between Ho Chi Minh and his masters in the Kremlin or "Peiping"; either would do. It failed. State Department intelligence found evidence of "Kremlin-directed conspiracy...in virtually all countries except Vietnam," which appeared to be "an anomaly," and found "surprisingly little direct cooperation between local Chinese Communists and the Viet Minh." The problem, then, was to show how these facts demonstrated the required conclusion: that Ho was an agent of the Commie conspiracy.

The problem was readily solved. Perhaps "a special dispensation for the Vietnam government has been arranged in Moscow," presumably because Ho was such a loyal slave of his masters that they did not even have to provide direct guidance. Later, a National Intelligence Estimate noted that "We are unable to determine whether Peiping or Moscow has ultimate responsibility for Viet Minh policy"; it is axiomatic that it must be one or the other. One of the most astonishing revelations in the *Pentagon Papers* is that in a record of over two decades, the analysts were able to discover only one staff paper "which treats communist reactions primarily in terms of the separate national interests of Hanoi, Moscow, and Peiping, rather than primarily in terms of an overall communist strategy for which Hanoi is acting as an agent." Even US intelligence, which is paid to get the facts straight, not to rave about the Commie-dominated bloc of slave states, was unable to perceive the possibility that the Vietnamese Communists might be guided even in part by their own interests and concerns rather than merely acting as agents of their foreign masters.

The higher truths of the state religion, which blinded intelligence to the most elementary facts, also pervade the mainstream scholarly literature, where we find as a point of doctrine that Vietnamese Communists were "enflamed" by Stalin after World War II (Walt Rostow) and that US intervention was "aimed at

forestalling a southward expansion of Chinese communism"
(John King Fairbank; an analytic error, this distinguished his-
torian and critic of the war believes). In the real world, the
Vietnamese Communists did not need Stalin to "enflame" them;
French tyranny and then US subversion and aggression sufficed.
And it was clear enough, early on, that far from being an agency of
Chinese expansionism, Vietnamese nationalism (whether Communist or not) would be an obstacle to it. The role of Stalin and Mao
in the US doctrinal system was to legitimate the US assault,
motivated on quite different grounds, as internal documents make
clear.[18]

When the attempt to subdue South Vietnam failed, the US
widened the war to all of Indochina in a manner that predictably
led to eventual North Vietnamese dominance after desperately
blocking efforts on all sides to neutralize South Vietnam, Laos and
Cambodia. After failing in its larger aims, the US devoted itself to
maximizing suffering and repression in the societies that it had
destroyed, and helping to drive them more firmly into the hands of
the USSR by systematically closing off all other options, insofar as
possible.[19]

Much the same was true as the US sought to overcome the
heresy of capitalist democracy in Guatemala, which threatened the
interests of US corporations. Guatemala was declared an agency of
the global Communist conspiracy and serious threats were
mounted against it, including even the dispatch of nuclear armed
SAC bombers to Nicaragua, "meant, it would appear, as a signal of
American commitment."[20] When in desperation the Guatemalan
government sought military aid from the Soviet bloc, much to the
delight of the US government, this fact was used as part of the
official justification for restoring a military dictatorship. Shortly
before the CIA coup, Guatemalan Foreign Minister Toriello commented accurately that US policy amounts to

> cataloguing as 'Communism' every manifestation of
> nationalism or economic independence, any desire for
> social progress, any intellectual curiosity, and any in-
> terest in progressive or liberal reforms... any Latin
> American government that exerts itself to bring about a
> truly national program which affects the interests of the
> powerful foreign companies, in whose hands the wealth
> and the basic resources in large part repose in Latin
> America, will be pointed out as Communist; it will be
> accused of being a threat to continental security and
> making a breach in continental solidarity, and so will be
> threatened with foreign intervention.

Toriello's words were applauded by his Latin American col-
leagues, who then proceeded to line up against him in support of

John Foster Dulles's resolution opposing the threat of "international communism" in Guatemala (issued in Caracas, the capital of one of the most notorious dictatorships in the continent), in the hope of receiving US aid.[21]

We might note that the dual Latin American reaction to Toriello's words has been duplicated more than once. UN correspondent Louis Wiznitzer, commenting on how "United States standing in Latin America has reached an all-time low" because of US actions against Nicaragua, observes that "one sign of Latin American feelings toward the US was the cool reception Vice-President George Bush and Secretary of State George Shultz received" when they appeared at the inauguration of the new Brazilian president. They "are not personally unpopular in Latin America," he notes, "Yet at this reception they were booed, while Nicaragua's President Daniel Ortega was applauded," a fact generally unreported here. Two months earlier, ABC reported that on a visit to Uruguay, Ortega was "greeted by wildly enthusiastic crowds, cheering his name as if he was about to be named president of Uruguay," a fact again generally ignored in the media.[22] But few Latin Americans will risk offending the hemisphere's Big Brother when the chips are down.

Returning to Guatemala, the relevant point is that whatever the facts, Guatemala had to be an agency of the Commie conspiracy so as to justify the U.S. overthrow of its democratic government, motivated on quite different grounds.

This characteristic device of US foreign policy is now being employed in the familiar manner in Nicaragua, where the Reagan Administration is attempting to drive the Sandinista regime securely into the hands of the Evil Empire just as it is acting to undermine the private sector through embargo, so as to create the "totalitarian" state that is required to justify US violence, to the distress of business groups and the conservative Nicaraguan Church hierarchy that we purport to favor.[23]

Harvard Business School professor James Austin describes the embargo as "a flagrant violation of international agreements," and also "an affront to the basic values of our society" and a "foreign policy blunder" that is "counterproductive" because it drives Nicaragua towards dependence on the Soviet Union. The first point is correct; the second reflects a serious misunderstanding both of the basic values of our society as they are expressed in historical practice, and of the goals of the policy. Austin observes that the boycott violates the GATT agreements on trade as well as treaties between Nicaragua and the US; it expresses the position "that other countries should adhere to the agreements, laws and treaties, but the United States need not." True, but quite consistent with our historical practice. He quotes an "outraged and bewildered marketing manager [who] exclaimed: 'This is the most absurd thing the United States has done, because it is mostly hurting the private sector'," and he observes that it has even been criticized by the US-financed rightist press *La Prensa*. Austin comments accurately that the effect will be similar to the Cuban boycott, which increased Cuban dependency on the USSR, concluding that "the president has failed to learn from history." But US planners understand all of this well enough, and are following a rational course (in their terms) with ample historical precedent, fully expecting the consequences that Austin deplores, and recognizing that these consequences will be readily exploited to justify the attack against Nicaragua in defense of the Fifth Freedom. There is nothing "absurd" about this, though it does "stand with the moral repulsiveness of providing aid to the *contras*," as Austin states. He particularly deplores the fact that the embargo will undermine the US-made potable water system and Nicaraguan hospitals, which rely on US equipment; all "inhumane" and "morally reprehensible," but fully in accord with our operative values, throughout our history.[24]

To ensure that Nicaragua will become part of "the Commie-dominated bloc of slave states," the US has been waging a proxy war of mounting intensity against Nicaragua while blocking any source of arms from other than the preferred source: the USSR and its clients. This serves a dual purpose: (1) to maintain a level of destruction and terror sufficient to reduce the danger of constructive developments in Nicaragua, and (2) to justify these efforts on the grounds of self-defense against the Evil Empire. In March 1983, Under Secretary of Defense Fred Iklé testified before Congress that the USSR had provided $440 million in aid to Nicaragua since the revolution while "express[ing] irritation" that nearly four times that much, some $1.6 billion, had come from non-Soviet sources, mostly what he called "misguided" European governments. The US has predictably devoted itself to terminating this pluralism and ensuring sole dependency on the Evil Empire. "In 1982, the French sold Nicaragua about $17 million worth of arms before US anger made them steer clear of sending any more military items into the area," the press reports; the statement is only partly true, since France, which will gladly sell arms to the devil himself unless prevented by higher authority, may continue to provide state terrorists in El Salvador and Guatemala with the required means of destruction, with our full acquiescence. But only the Soviet bloc is permitted to provide Nicaragua with arms for self-defense against our attack.[25]

When arms do not flow at the approved level from our favored source, US propaganda invents the required facts, as in the case of Guatemala in 1954, or the guerrillas in El Salvador during the Reagan years.

Much the same was true in the case of Maoist China and Castro's Cuba, among other examples; in the former case, the US not only helped create a Sino-Soviet bloc that was not inevitable, given longstanding conflicts between the Chinese Communists and the USSR that extend back to the Chinese Civil War, but even insisted with some passion that the Sino-Soviet bloc remained solid when it was evident to any rational observer that it was riven by deep conflicts. The important point is that such behavior is systematic and quite rational, given the guiding geopolitical conceptions, which are essentially invariant, since they are rooted in the unchanging institutional structure of ownership and domination in our own society.

It is commonly remarked that indigenous factors have played a role in driving the various enemies of the Fifth Freedom into the hands of the Russians. That is true, but not pertinent here. The point is that for quite understandable reasons, US policy has regularly labored to reinforce precisely these tendencies and to block alternatives. Nevertheless, tactical considerations may on occasion dictate a different course, as when Nixon and Kissinger finally recognized that the Sino-Soviet bloc was unresurrectible and decided, rationally, to exploit the conflict and to accept Chinese overtures, hoping ultimately to draw China into the US-dominated sphere and convert it to what we call a more "open" society—one open to US economic penetration and political control.

In an important study of the Guatemalan intervention, Richard Immerman argues that top US planners and corporate representatives closely linked to government (or running it) really believed that Guatemala's moderate reforms constituted *prima facie* evidence for "the penetration of Central America by a frankly Russian-dominated Communist group" (Adolf Berle, on behalf of the Council on Foreign Relations, to the State Department), thus justifying US intervention in defense of freedom.[26] He may well be right, but the point is of little significance except for the (rather boring) study of the psychology of leaders and ideologues. It is a rare individual who consciously believes that what he or she does is genuinely evil; as noted earlier, it is easy enough to come to believe whatever is convenient. There is no reason to doubt the sincerity of Japanese fascists who explained that they were creating an "earthly paradise" as they swept across China 50 years ago, not for crass economic motives—Japan was, after all, spending more than it could hope to gain in protecting the "true nationalists" under its wing from bandits such as Chiang Kai-shek—but to bring the benefits of civilization to benighted and oppressed people who had been victimized by Western imperialism.[27] Similarly, Hitler doubtless sincerely wanted peace—on his terms—and the integrity and vitality of the German nation, as he proclaimed, and Soviet leaders yearn for stability and economic development in Eastern Europe and Afghanistan. We should have no difficulty in understanding their self-image and picture of the world, if we can look honestly at ourselves. Not only state planners, but the educated classes generally, are given to sincere belief in the most astonishing (and self-serving) fantasies, a fact of little relevance to the study of policy formation. In the case of official enemies or precursors in imperial aggression we readily understand that true interests are disguised in propaganda, perhaps even disguised to those who propound it. Only in studying the record of our own state is such elementary rationality proscribed.

There is, however, a related point that is of some significance for the study of state policy. A system of rationalizations and propaganda, once constructed and internalized, may come to be a factor influencing policy decisions as ideology overwhelms interests. The same may be true of other irrational factors—e.g., heroic posturing, and the like. A close analysis of policy will generally unearth a structure of rational calculation based on perceived interests at its core, but in the complex world of decision-making and political planning, many other elements may also intervene, sometimes significantly, including the system of self-serving beliefs that is regularly constructed to disguise—to others, and to oneself—what is really happening in the world.

Failure to understand the roots of US foreign policy, and a curious unwillingness to perceive its highly systematic nature over many years, makes it appear that this policy is confused and is failing, when it is succeeding brilliantly. Thus conservative British correspondent Timothy Garton Ash finds a "striking inconsistency" in the way the US "has pursued its principles in Central America," Nicaragua being a "prime example."[28] The inconsistency is that the US is devoted to pluralism, respect for human rights, and other good things, and to persuading the Sandinistas to cut their ties with the USSR. But the "*contra* aggression" sponsored by the US has precisely the opposite effects: increasing internal repression, undermining "advocates of a 'third way' like [President] Daniel Ortega," "supplying arguments to the Leninists," increasing the militarization of the country, and strengthening its ties to the USSR. The situation, he states, "is comparable to that of Cuba twenty years ago."

The "inconsistency" arises only if we assume that official US pronouncements aimed at the general public are necessary truths. If we subject them to the test of history, as in the case of states that do not merit such loyalty and adulation, we will discover, not surprisingly, that they are without merit and that the "inconsistency" disappears. Refusing to accept the elementary canons of rationality, we will fail to comprehend that the consequences Ash perceives are precisely the intent of US policy: to ensure that constructive developments in Nicaragua will not "infect" the region (see below, p. 67f.), and to strengthen its ties with the USSR to justify our assault against those who violate the Fifth Freedom. The behavior of the US government over many years will appear to yield further "inconsistencies"—curiously systematic ones, as anyone whose eyes are open will quickly discover. Ash finds the "inconsistency" puzzling because he credits childish inanities about the US "dedication to the liberal creed" and "dedication to a value system...virtually alone among nations" (citing Michael Howard, Regius Professor of Modern History at Oxford). Putting these delusions aside, a rational pattern emerges, and a highly familiar one.

One might note, incidentally, the remarkable "colonization" of sophisticated British intellectuals, who regard themselves as independent and critical but in fact react to US power and propaganda in a manner reminiscent of some of the more absurd Anglophile Indian intellectuals under the Empire.

It is particularly important for people who hope to influence government policy to be clear about these matters. There is no point wasting time in patiently explaining to our leaders that the policies they pursue are inconsistent with the goals they profess; they know this well enough without our help. Nor is there any reason to suppose that a different group of leaders would react in any essentially different way to the same institutional imperatives. It is not failure to understand a simple point so clear to us that regularly leads the political leadership to commit the same "error" over and over again.

Returning to Kennan's prescriptions, what means must we use against our enemies who fall prey to the heresy that threatens our resources? Kennan explains, in the same briefing to the Ambassadors:

> The final answer might be an unpleasant one, but...we should not hesitate before police repression by the local government. This is not shameful since the Communists are essentially traitors... It is better to have a strong regime in power than a liberal government if it is indulgent and relaxed and penetrated by Communists.

Again, as policy becomes practice, the term "Communists" takes on its technical sense in American political discourse, referring to people who do not appreciate the sanctity of the Fifth Freedom.

It is small wonder, then, that John F. Kennedy should have held that "governments of the civil-military type of El Salvador are the most effective in containing Communist penetration in Latin America." This was after a military coup overthrew a liberal civilian government, with US approval, while the Kennedy Administration was organizing the basic structure of the military and paramilitary "death squads" that have massacred tens of thousands of civilians since, within the framework of the Alliance for Progress—in fact, the most lasting effect of that program apart from its contributions to dependent development in the US interest.[29]

The concept of "Communism" was further elaborated by a prestigious study group of the National Planning Association and the Woodrow Wilson Foundation, headed by William Yandell Elliot of Harvard, in 1955. The study observed, quite accurately, that the primary threat of what they call "Communism" is the economic transformation of the Communist powers "in ways which reduce their willingness and ability to complement the industrial economies of the West."[30] This insightful comment provides a good operational definition of the term "Communism" as it is used in American political discourse. If a government or popular movement is so evil as to undertake a course of action of this sort, it at once becomes an enemy. It has joined the "monolithic and ruthless conspiracy" to steal what is ours, namely, their resources, and by definition, it has been taken over by the Russians—and we will act to ensure that it is, so that we may legitimately proceed to terminate this scandal by subversion or intervention, all with the noblest intent and in defense of the highest values. "In other words," as the Argentinian-Mexican writer Gregorio Selser explains with a somewhat clearer vision, "the North American puritans meekly sacrifice themselves to care for the flock, gobbling any willful lamb that proved intractable to their protection."[31]

3 Latin America: "An Incident, Not An End"

Selser is, of course, not the first Latin American to discover that "the United States [seems] destined to plague and torment the continent in the name of freedom" (Simón Bolívar, 1829).[32] Nor was Kennan the first to enunciate the doctrine that the US has special rights in Latin America. Thomas Jefferson declared that "America has a hemisphere to itself," and John Quincy Adams, while formulating the thinking that led to the Monroe Doctrine, stated to the cabinet that the world must be "familiarized with the idea of considering our proper dominion to be the continent of North America." It is, he said, "as much a law of nature that this should become our pretension as that the Mississippi should flow to the sea," while in his diary he recorded his statement to British minister Canning: "Keep what is yours, but leave the rest of this continent to us."[33] Connell-Smith comments that while it is not entirely clear what Jefferson, a well-known expansionist, meant by the term "America," "the appropriation by United States citizens of the adjective 'American', not surprisingly resented by Latin Americans, has encouraged a proprietary attitude towards the hemisphere already present in 1823."

This propietary interest was expressed in the Monroe Doctrine, announced by the President in 1823. This doctrine has no more standing in international affairs than the Brezhnev Doctrine a century and a half later, expressing the right of the USSR to protect the "socialist" world from influences regarded as subversive. In the major scholarly study of the Monroe Doctrine and its subsequent history, Dexter Perkins comments that "The Doctrine is a policy of the United States, not a fixed principle of international law," a conclusion that is surely correct. Latin Americans "have seen [the Monroe Doctrine] as an expression of United States hegemony employed to justify that country's own intervention," not as protection against Europe, and since the days of Simón Bolívar have sought "to summon Europe to their aid against the Colossus of the North," with good reason.[34]

The operative meaning of the Doctrine was lucidly explained by Woodrow Wilson's Secretary of State Robert Lansing, in what Wilson described as an "unanswerable" argument but one that it would be "impolitic" to state openly:

> In its advocacy of the Monroe Doctrine the United States considers its own interests. The integrity of other American nations is an incident, not an end. While this may seem based on selfishness alone, the author of the Doctrine had no higher or more generous motive in its declaration.

A few years earlier President William Howard Taft had sagely explained that "the day is not far distant" when "the whole hemisphere will be ours in fact as, by virtue of our superiority of race, it already is ours morally." The attitude towards Latin Americans remains as expressed by Wilson's Secretary of the Interior to Lansing: "They are naughty children who are exercising all the privileges and rights of grown ups," requiring "a stiff hand, an authoritative hand."[35]

The essence of the Doctrine, and the "protection" it conveyed for Latin America, was expressed succinctly by Secretary of State Richard Olney in 1895, when Great Britain was still the Evil Empire:

> Today the United States is practically sovereign on this continent, and its fiat is law upon the subjects to which it confines its interposition. Why? It is not because of the pure friendship or good will felt for it. It is not simply by reason of its high character as a civilized state, nor

because reason, justice, and equity are the invariable characteristics of the dealings of the United States. It is because, in addition to all other grounds, its infinite resources combined with its isolated position render it master of the situation, and practically invulnerable as against any òr all other powers.

Much of the subsequent history of the region is elegantly summarized in these lines, as it is in a confidential memorandum of 1927 by Under-Secretary of State Robert Olds, expressing US policy goals in Nicaragua as the US once again sent the Marines:

The Central American area down to and including the Isthmus of Panama constitutes a legitimate sphere of influence for the United States, if we are to have due regard for our own safety and protection.... Our ministers accredited to the five little republics stretching from the Mexican border to Panama...have been advisors whose advice has been accepted virtually as law...we do control the destinies of Central America and we do so for the simple reason that the national interest absolutely dictates such a course.... We must decide whether we shall tolerate the interference of any other power [i.e., Mexico] in Central American affairs or insist upon our own dominant position. If this Mexican maneuver succeeds it will take many years to recover the ground we shall have lost... Until now Central America has always understood that governments which we recognize and support stay in power, while those which we do not recognize and support fall. Nicaragua has become a test case. It is difficult to see how we can afford to be defeated.

We were not defeated, and rarely are; for the people of Nicaragua, the verdict of history was different.[36]

Summarizing his three-volume work, Dexter Perkins writes that "In the development of the Monroe Doctrine, one of the most extraordinary and interesting objects of study must be the evolution of a doctrine which was intended for the protection of Latin-American states by the United States into one that justified and even sanctified American interference in and control of the affairs of the independent republics of this continent."[37] The assessment of the early intention may be questioned, and one might be slightly taken aback by Perkins's lack of comment over what this "interference" has meant to Latin America, evident enough when he wrote in 1937. But the basic thrust of his summary is much to the point.

Over the years, there have been various "corollaries" to the Monroe Doctrine, most notably, the "Roosevelt Corollary" announced by President Theodore Roosevelt in 1904, after he had succeeded in stealing the Panama Canal route from Colombia and with an eye on the Dominican Republic:

> Chronic wrongdoing, or an impotence which results in a general loosening of the ties of civilized society, may in America, as elsewhere, ultimately require intervention by some civilized nation, and in the Western Hemisphere the adherence of the United States to the Monroe Doctrine may force the United States, however reluctantly, in flagrant cases of such wrongdoing or impotence, to the exercise of an international police power.

This pronouncement was described by the Argentine newspaper *La Prensa* as "the most serious and menacing declaration against South American integrity which has come out of Washington." For Roosevelt, Connell-Smith comments, "the dominant position of the United States in the western hemisphere was exactly like that of 'the English speaking race' in South Africa. Both were in the interests of civilization."[38] Colombia not being a civilized nation, the chicanery involved in the Panama Canal robbery was entirely legitimate. The Colombians who objected to Roosevelt's maneuvers were, after all, nothing but "damned dagoes," as he explained, who had to be taught proper behavior. In the words of one American historian, Roosevelt "made it clear how he would deal with refractory Latin Americans; he would 'show those Dagos that they will have to behave decently'."[39]

Woodrow Wilson took matters a step further: "...as a Progressive he thought a good system was one that was orderly and slightly reformed—by which he came to mean replacing European concessions with North American," and so produced what LaFeber calls "the Wilson corollary."[40] Wilson issued a "Declaration" extending the Monroe Doctrine to "European financiers and contractors" of whose acts he disapproved, that is, to European financial as well as political and military intervention. The Latin American order would rest on cooperation with "those who act in the interest of peace and honor, who protect private rights," meaning in effect the rights of US business. A case in point was control over oil, just becoming an important resource. Britain was the major threat. Wilson's State Department warned Costa Rica that "Department considers it most important that only approved Americans should possess oil concessions in the neighborhood of Panama Canal. Amory concession [British, supported by Costa Rica] does not appear to meet these requirements." Guatemala was warned that "It is most important that only American oil interests receive concessions," and US pressure ensured that this result was achieved in the Western Hemisphere, despite some meaningless gestures designed to support the right of US access to Middle East oil; the US declared an "open door," after all concessions were safely in US hands, under the Wilson corollary.[41]

The concept of the "open door," as understood in practice, is well illustrated by US petroleum policy over the years. It is explained clearly in a State Department memorandum of 1944 entitled "Petroleum Policy of the United States." There must be equal access for American companies everywhere, but no access for others in the Western Hemisphere (the major oil producing region then and for over two decades to come), where the US was safely in control. This policy, it was explained, "would involve the preservation of the absolute position presently obtaining, and therefore vigilant protection of existing concessions in United States hands coupled with insistence upon the Open Door principle of equal opportunity for United States companies in new areas."[42] The "Open Door policy," so construed, is a corollary to the principle of the Fifth Freedom.

Interventionism was theoretically renounced by Presidents Hoover and Roosevelt in favor of the Good Neighbor policy, though the renunciation was conditional on good behavior; the Roosevelt Administration relied on the threat of force to install the dictatorship of Fulgencio Batista in Cuba when it was feared that US commercial interests might be threated by the civilian government of Dr. Ramón Grau San Martín.[43] But this was an exception. By that time, European competition—the major concern—had been effectively contained, and the US reigned unchallenged, capable of attaining its objectives by political and economic power. Furthermore, domestic military forces trained and supplied by the US could impose order and stability—that is, could guarantee the Fifth Freedom—without the Marines. Dictatorships, however brutal and corrupt, were acceptable to the Hoover and Roosevelt Administrations as long as they satisfied this condition.

By the time the Good Neighbor policy was officially announced, Nicaragua was effectively controlled by the most important of these domestic guardians of order, Somoza's National Guard, while the Trujillo dictatorship ruled in the Dominican Republic through the medium of the National Guard, also established as a result of US intervention. Martínez had taken over in El Salvador after the *Matanza*, soon to be recognized by the US, and most of the rest of the region was also in safe hands by 1940 as the US replaced France and Britain. Meanwhile Roosevelt created the Export-Import Bank to subsidize US exports and in general acted to increase the dependency of the Central American nations on the US for food, as they shifted to export crops to the US, with grim long-term effects. The Good Neighbor policy relied on regimes which occasionally went through the forms of elections for propaganda purposes, meanwhile maintaining a status quo in which the Fifth Freedom was preserved and "2 percent or less of the population in four of the five Central American nations controlled the land and hence the lives of the other 98 percent." Dictatorships were thus "not a paradox but a necessity for the system, including the Good Neighbor policy," which "carried on interventionism in Central America and tightened the system far beyond anything Theodore Roosevelt and Woodrow Wilson probably imagined."[44] The Good Neighbor policy was summed up by journalist William Krehm, who observed its effects on the spot: "First there had been intervention to impose a puppet and then—in the name of non-intervention—propaganda, funds, and connivance to keep him in the saddle."[45]

Quite generally, state policy served to guarantee business interests. In the rare conflicts between them, the state generally prevailed, a consequence to be expected, as LaFeber aptly observes, "if a *system* was to be maintained." This pattern is quite a regular one. The state is concerned to maintain a system based on the Fifth Freedom, and the parochial interests of particular corporations, even major ones such as the oil companies, sometimes conflict with this end, in which case the state, representing the long-term global interests of US capitalism, generally prevails. At times, the very same individuals will reach different decisions in their institutional roles as corporate executives or state managers, not surprisingly, given the different framework of planning guided by essentially the same interests. Such cases may foster a conception of independence of the state from dominant business interests, largely an illusion, though not entirely so as a close examination indicates.[46]

4 Planning For Global Hegemony

As World War II came to an end, US ideas concerning Latin America were clarified by Secretary of War Henry Stimson (May 1945), in a discussion of how we must eliminate and dismantle all regional systems dominated by any other power, particularly the British, while maintaining and extending our own. With regard to Latin America, he explained privately: "I think that it's not asking too much to have our little region over here [namely, Latin America] which never has bothered anybody."[47]

It should be noted that US officials had a ready explanation for the distinction between control by the US and by other powers. As Abe Fortas explained with regard to US trusteeship plans in the Pacific, which Churchill regarded as a cover for annexation: "When we take over the Marianas and fortify them we are doing so not only on the basis of our own right to do so but as part of our obligation to the security of the world... These reservations were being made in the interest of world security rather than of our own security...what was good for us was good for the world."[48] On such assumptions, naturally regarded highly by US officials and ideologists, quite a range of actions become legitimate.

In keeping with Stimson's conception, the Joint Chiefs of Staff, through 1945 and early 1946, insisted that non-American forces must be kept out of the Western Hemisphere, which "is a distinct military entity, the integrity of which is a fundamental postulate of our security in the event of another world war."[49] In January 1947, Secretary of War Patterson added that the resources of Latin America were essential to the US because "it is imperative that our war potential be enhanced...during any national emergency." Patterson gave an expansive interpretation of the Monroe Doctrine, consistent with the Wilson corollary: the Doctrine meant "that we not only refuse to tolerate foreign colonization, control, or the extension of a foreign political system to our hemisphere, but we take alarm from the appearance on the continent of foreign ideologies, commercial exploitation, cartel arrangements, or other symptoms of increased non-hemispheric influence." The US must have "a stable, secure, and friendly flank to the South, not confused by enemy penetration, political, economic or military." The prime concern was not the USSR but rather Europe, including sales of arms by the British to Chile and Ecuador, by Sweden to Argentina, and by France to Argentina and Brazil.

From January 1945, military and civilian officials of the War and Navy departments argued for an extensive system of US bases, curtailment of all foreign military aid and military sales, training of Latin American military officers and supply of arms to Latin America by the US under a comprehensive military assistance program. While laying these plans for "our little region over here which never has bothered anybody," the US was in no mood to allow others similar rights elsewhere, certainly not the USSR. Secretary of State Byrnes in fact objected to these plans for Latin America because it might prejudice US initiatives elsewhere that he regarded as more important, in particular, in Greece and Turkey, which "are our outposts"—on the borders of the USSR, which had far more serious security concerns than the US. The "outposts" were also intended to buttress US ambitions in the crucial Middle East region with its incomparable energy reserves, then passing into American hands.

Commenting on an array of material of this sort laying out US plans, much of it classified and recently released, Leffler notes that these moves were made while US officials were "paying lip service to the United Nations and worrying about the impact of regional agreements in the Western Hemisphere on Soviet actions and American influence in Europe." The problem was the one that

concerned Stimson: how to extend our own regional systems while
dismantling all others, particularly those of Britain and the USSR.
The same problems were arising in Europe, where the USSR
observed the unilateral US and British takeover in Italy, Belgium
and elsewhere with equanimity, later using this as a model for its
brutal takeover of Eastern Europe, to much outrage in the West—
justified, but not lacking in hypocrisy.[50] In chapter 4, we return to
the more general concept of postwar "national security" in which
the plans just sketched for Latin America were a small element.

The geopolitical conception that underlies Kennan's nutshell
presentation of US foreign policy had been elaborated during the
war by the War and Peace Studies project of the Council on Foreign
Relations, whose thoughts on the suppression of war aims and on
"elbow room" were cited earlier. These high-level sessions took
place from 1939-1945, producing extensive plans for the postwar
period. Their concern was to elaborate the requirements of the
United States "in a world in which it proposes to hold unquestioned
power." It was clear by the early 1940s that the US would emerge
from the war in a position of unparalleled dominance, initiating a
period in which it would be the "hegemonic power in a system of
world order," in the words of an elite group 30 years later.[51] The
group developed the concept of the "Grand Area," understood to be
a region subordinated to the needs of the US economy. As one
participant put it, the Grand Area was a region "strategically
necessary for world control." A geopolitical analysis concluded
that the Grand Area must include the Western Hemisphere, the Far
East, and the former British empire, then being dismantled and
opened to US penetration and control—an exercise referred to as
"anti-imperialism" in much of the literature.

As the war proceeded, it became clear that Western Europe
would join the Grand Area as well as the oil-producing regions of
the Middle East, where US control expanded at the expense of its
major rivals, France and Britain, a process continued in the
postwar period. Specific plans were outlined for particular regions,
and institutional structures were proposed for the Grand Area,
which was regarded as a nucleus or model that could be extended,
optimally to a global system.[52] It is in this context that Kennan's
proposals should be understood.

The memoranda of the National Security Council and other
government documents in subsequent years often closely follow
the recommendations of the wartime planners, not surprisingly,
since the same interests were represented, often the same people.
They also accord with Kennan's principles. For example, NSC 48/1
in December 1949 states that "While scrupulously avoiding
assumption of responsibility for raising Asiatic living standards, it
is to the U.S. interest to promote the ability of these countries to
maintain...the economic conditions prerequisite to political stabil-

ity." Thus in accordance with Kennan's precepts, we should not be "hampered by idealistic slogans" about "the raising of the living standards," though economic aid may be in order when we have something to gain by it.

It is not, of course, proposed that we should assist—or even permit — the nationalist movement of Vietnam to achieve economic health and political stability; on the contrary, a State Department Policy Statement of September 1948 had explained that it is "an unpleasant fact" that "Communist Ho Chi Minh is the strongest and perhaps the ablest figure in Indochina and that any suggested solution which excludes him is an expedient of uncertain outcome," a serious problem, since plainly we must seek to exclude him in pursuit of the Fifth Freedom.[53] Political stability under his leadership was not what was contemplated. Rather, "stability" is a code word for obedience. Those familiar with the peculiar terminology of US ideological discourse will understand that it is no contradiction when James Chace, editor of *Foreign Affairs*, cites "our efforts to destabilize a freely elected Marxist government in Chile" as an illustration of the efforts of Nixon-Kissinger *Realpolitik* "to seek stability."[54] Destabilization in the interest of stability makes perfect sense in the age of Orwell. The problem, when noted, is placed under the rubric of "irony" in mainstream commentary, including much scholarship.[55]

NSC 48/1 proceeds to develop the conventional explanation found in secret documents of the period for US participation in the French war against Indochina, then the US takeover of that war. The reasoning, which extends directly to Latin America, merits attention. Despite references by Eisenhower and others to Vietnam's resources, Indochina was not of major concern in itself. Rather, its importance derived from the context of the domino theory. This theory has two versions. One, invoked when there is a need to frighten the public, warns that if we don't stop them there, they'll land in California and take all we have. As expressed by President Lyndon Johnson at the height of US aggression in Vietnam:

> There are 3 billion people in the world and we have only 200 million of them. We are outnumbered 15 to one. If might did make right they would sweep over the United States and take what we have. We have what they want.

"If we are going to have visits from any aggressors or any enemies," Johnson said in a speech in Alaska, "I would rather have that aggression take place out 10,000 miles from here than take place here in Anchorage," referring to the aggression of the Vietnamese against US forces in Vietnam. Therefore, as he had warned 20 years earlier, we must maintain our military strength, particularly air power: "without superior air power America is a bound and throttled giant; impotent and easy prey to any yellow dwarf with a pocket knife."[56]

The sense that we will be "a pitiful, helpless giant" unless we act forthrightly in defense against the overwhelming power of our Third World adversaries, in the terms used later by President Nixon in announcing the invasion of Cambodia, is a common refrain in US political discourse, reminiscent of a rich and spoiled child who whines that he does not have *everything*—though to render the image more accurate, we should place a squadron of storm troopers at the child's command.

This version of the domino theory is undoubtedly believed at some level of consciousness, and expresses in a vulgar way the concerns over maintaining the "disparity" outlined in more sophisticated terms by Kennan at the time when Lyndon Johnson was voicing his fears about the "yellow dwarves." This crude domino theory is, however, regularly dismissed with scorn if things go sour and policy must be revised. But there is also a rational version of the domino theory, the operative version, which is rarely questioned and has considerable plausibility; adopting the terminology of the planners, we might call it the "rotten apple theory." The rotten apple theory was outlined by Dean Acheson when he concocted a remarkable series of fabrications concerning alleged Soviet pressure on Greece, Turkey and Iran in February 1947 in a successful effort to convince reluctant congressional leaders to support the Truman Doctrine, an incident that he cites with much pride in his memoirs; "Like apples in a barrel infected by one rotten one, the corruption of Greece would infect Iran and all to the east" and would "carry infection" to Asia Minor, Egypt and Africa, as well as Italy and France, which were "threatened" by Communist participation in democratic politics.[57] This adroit and cynical invocation of a fabricated "Russian threat" to prepare the way for measures to prevent "infection" from spreading has been imitated with great efficacy since.

The prime concern throughout is that if there is one rotten apple in the barrel, then "the rot will spread," namely, the "rot" of successful social and economic development of a form that would constrain the Fifth Freedom. This might have a demonstration effect. To cite another case, Kissinger's aides recall that he was far more concerned over Allende in Chile than over Castro because "Allende was a living example of democratic social reform in Latin America," and Allende's success within the democratic process might cause Latin America to become "unraveled" with effects as far as Europe, where Eurocommunism, operating within parliamentary democracy, "scared him" no less. Allende's success would send the wrong message to Italian voters, Kissinger feared. The "contagious example" of Chile would "infect" not only Latin America but also southern Europe, Kissinger stated, using the conventional imagery.[58] Soon, we might find that the Grand Area is beginning to erode.

These concerns are persistent. The CIA warned in 1964 that "Cuba's experiment with almost total state socialism is being watched closely by other nations in the hemisphere and any appearance of success there would have an extensive impact on the statist trend elsewhere in the area," to the detriment of the Fifth Freedom.[59] Hence the appearance of success must be aborted by a major terrorist war including repeated attempts to assassinate Castro, bombing of petrochemical and other installations, sinking of fishing boats, shelling of hotels, crop and livestock poisoning, destruction of civilian airlines in flight, etc.

We might observe that none of this counts as "terrorism," by definition, since the US or its associates are the perpetrators. In fact, it is a staple of Western propaganda that the Communist bloc is immune to terrorist acts, sure proof that they are responsible for this scourge of the modern age. Walter Laqueur, for example, writes that Claire Sterling, who pioneered this concept to much acclaim, has provided "ample evidence" that terrorism occurs "almost exclusively in democratic or relatively democratic countries"; as examples of such "multinational terrorism" he cites Polisario in the western Sahara (its defense of its territory counts as terrorism, since it is fighting a takeover by Morocco, a US ally), and also terrorism in "some Central American countries," referring, as the context makes clear, to the guerrilla forces, not the state terrorism of El Salvador and Guatemala, which are apparently "relatively democratic countries," like Morocco, and being US clients, by definition cannot be engaged in terrorism. Similarly, the London *Economist* notes sagely in reviewing Sterling's *Terror Network* that "no terrorist has ever attempted anything against the Soviet-controlled regimes." Many others also chimed in, and the point is now a cliché of learned discourses on the topic.[60] In the real world, Cuba has been the major target of international terrorism, narrowly construed to exclude the US proxy war against Nicaragua.

Returning to the rotten apple theory, the State Department warned in 1959 that "a fundamental source of danger we face in the Far East derives from Communist China's rate of economic growth," while the Joint Chiefs added that "the dramatic economic improvements realized by Communist China over the past ten years impress the nations of the region greatly and offer a serious challenge to the Free World." Similar fears were expressed concerning North Vietnam and North Korea. The conclusion drawn was that the US must do what it can to retard the economic progress of the Communist Asian states.[61]

The larger concern was Japan—the "superdomino" as John Dower called it. Japan, it was recognized, would become again the "workshop of Asia," but requires access to raw materials and markets. We must therefore guarantee Japan such access, so that the entire region can be incorporated within the Grand Area instead of developing as part of a "new order" with Japan as its industrial center, from which the US might be excluded; concern over this prospect was a factor in the complex interactions that led to the Japanese-American war. But, it was feared, social and economic development in Indochina in terms that might be meaningful to the Asian poor might cause the rot to spread through Southeast and South Asia, leading Japan to associate itself with a bloc of nations independent of the Grand Area, or even worse, to accommodate to the Soviet bloc. A 1949 report of the State Department Policy Planning Staff urged that Washington should "develop the economic interdependence between [Southeast Asia] as a supplier of raw materials, and Japan, Western Europe and India as suppliers of finished goods...," so that "the region could begin to fulfill its major function as a source of raw materials and a market for Japan and Western Europe."[62] In this context, Vietnam gained a significance as a rotten apple that it did not have for American planners on its own.

Such thinking is not original to American planners; similar concerns had been evoked, for example, by the American revolution. A few days before the Monroe Doctrine was announced, the Czar of Russia warned:

> Too many examples demonstrate that the contagion of revolutionary principles is arrested by neither distance nor physical obstacles. It crosses the seas, and often appears with all the symptoms of destruction which characterize it, in places where not even any direct contact, any relation of proximity might give ground for apprehension. France knows with what facility and promptitude a revolution can be carried from America to Europe.

Metternich feared that the Monroe Doctrine would "lend new strength to the apostles of sedition, and reanimate the courage of every conspirator. If this flood of evil doctrines and pernicious examples should extend over the whole of America, what would become of our religious and political institutions, of the moral force of our governments, and of that conservative system which has saved Europe from complete dissolution?" One of the Czar's diplomats warned that "we must work to prevent or defer this terrible revolution, and above all to save and fortify the portion [of the Christian world] which may escape the contagion and the invasion of vicious principles," namely, "the pernicious doctrines of republicanism and popular self-rule."[63]

The contemporary heirs of Metternich and the Czar are animated by similar fears, and have even adopted similar rhetoric—in Kissinger's case, perhaps with full awareness—as the United States took over the role of the Czar in the 19th century as the defender of "civilization" against the yellow dwarves and others whose pretensions threaten the "disparity."

Note incidentally that the US achieved its major objectives in Indochina: it is a mistake to describe the Vietnam war simply as a US "defeat," as is commonly done, a fact that became evident as the war reached its peak of violence in the late 1960s. The devastation of Indochina by US violence guarantees that it will not be a model for anyone for a long time to come, if ever. It will be lucky to survive. The harsh and cruel measures undertaken by the US in the past decade are intended to ensure that this partial victory is maintained.[64] Meanwhile, behind the "shield" provided by the destruction of South Vietnam, then much of Indochina, the US worked to buttress the second line of defense by supporting a military coup in Indonesia in 1965 that wiped out hundreds of thousands of landless peasants (a development much applauded by Western liberals as vindication of the war against Vietnam), backing the imposition of a Latin American-style terror-and-torture state in the Philippines in 1972, etc.

A further useful consequence of the attack against South Vietnam, Laos and Cambodia was to ensure North Vietnamese dominance. It was clear enough by 1970, if not before, that "by employing the vast resources of violence and terror at its command" the US might be able to destroy the NLF in South Vietnam and independent forces in Laos and Cambodia, thus "creat[ing] a situation in which, indeed, North Vietnam will necessarily dominate Indochina, for no other viable society will remain."[65] This predictable consequence of US savagery is regularly invoked in retrospective justification for it, another ideological victory that would have impressed Orwell. Note that this achievement is a special case of the device discussed earlier: when conquest fails, efforts are made to encourage assimilation to the Soviet bloc, to justify further hostile acts and to limit the danger that independence and success will "infect" others.

Still another notable achievement of US violence was to ensure control by the harshest elements, those capable of surviving an attack of extraordinary barbarism and destructiveness; people whose homes and families are destroyed by a cruel invader have a way of becoming angry, even brutal, a fact that Westerners profess not to comprehend, having effectively suppressed the memory of their own behavior under far less onerous circumstances.[66] Then their terrible acts can be invoked to justify the attack that helped to create this outcome. With a docile intelligentsia and well-behaved ideological institutions, Western Agitprop can achieve quite notable results.

The US is intent on winning its war against Nicaragua in the same way. Nicaragua must first be driven to dependence on the USSR, to justify the attack that must be launched against it to punish it for its violation of the Fifth Freedom. If this attack does not succeed in restoring the country to the happy state of Haiti or the Dominican Republic, or of the Somoza years, then at least it must ensure that no successful social and economic development can take place there; the rotten apple must not be allowed to infect the barrel. It is very hard for a great power with the strength of the US to be defeated in a conflict with such adversaries, and it rarely is, though a failure to achieve maximal objectives is naturally regarded as a great defeat by those of limitless ambition and aims, further proof that we are a pitiful, helpless giant at the mercy of yellow dwarves.

The same essentially invariant nexus of principles and assumptions, often internalized to the point of lack of conscious awareness, explains another curious feature of US international behavior: the hysteria evoked by threats to "stability" in countries of no economic or strategic interest to the US, such as Laos or Grenada. In the case of Grenada, US hostility was immediate after the Bishop government took power in 1979. It was seriously maintained that this speck in the Caribbean posed a security threat to the United States. Distinguished military figures and commentators issued solemn pronouncements on the threat posed by Grenada to shipping lanes in the event of a Soviet attack on Western Europe; in fact, in this event, if a Russian toothpick were found on Grenada the island would be blown away, on the unlikely assumption that such a war would last long enough for anyone to care. Laos, half way round the world, is perhaps a still more remarkable case. Laos actually had a relatively free election in 1958, despite massive US efforts to subvert it. The election was won by a coalition dominated by the Pathet Lao, the Communist-led anti-French guerrillas. The government was immediately overthrown by US subversion in favor of "pro-western neutralists," soon replaced by right-wing military elements so reactionary and corrupt that even the pro-American groups found themselves lined up with the Pathet Lao, and supported by the USSR and China. By 1961, a US-organized army of highland tribesmen (utterly decimated, finally, as a result of their mobilization for US subversion and aggression) was fighting under the leadership of former French collaborators under CIA control. Through the sixties, Pathet Lao-controlled areas were subjected to the fiercest bombing in history (soon to be exceeded in Cambodia), in an effort "to destroy the physical and social infrastructure" (in the words of a Senate subcommittee). The government conceded that this bombardment was not related to the war in South Vietnam or

Cambodia. This was what is called in American Agitprop a "secret bombing"—a technical term referring to US aggression that is well-known but concealed by the media, and later blamed on evil men in the government who have departed from the American Way—as also in the case of Cambodia, a fact that is suppressed until today. The purpose of this attack against a country of scattered villages, against people who may not have even known that Laos existed, was to abort a mild revolutionary-nationalist movement that was attempting to bring about some reforms and popular mobilization in northern Laos.[67]

Why should such great powers as Grenada and Laos evoke this hysteria? The security arguments are too ludicrous to consider, and it is surely not the case that their resources were too valuable to lose, under the doctrine of the Fifth Freedom. Rather, the concern was the domino effect. Under the rotten apple theory, it follows that the tinier and weaker the country, the less endowed it is with resources, the more dangerous it is. If even a marginal and impoverished country can begin to utilize its own limited human and material resources and can undertake programs of development geared to the needs of the domestic population, then others may ask: why not us? The contagion may spread, infecting others, and before long the Fifth Freedom may be threatened in places that matter.

5 The Crimes of Nicaragua

On the same grounds, we can explain the reaction of US elites to the Sandinista revolution. The mood in Washington is conveyed by Representative William Alexander, who describes "the lust members [of Congress] feel to strike out against Communism."[68] It is, in fact, notable that even congressional and media critics of the war against Nicaragua feel obliged, with only the rarest of exceptions, to make clear that they have nothing good to say about the Sandinistas; their position, rather, is that US interests do not require such an attack, or that its means are inappropriate. "Only the bravest will say a word for the Sandinistas or question the president's premise that he has a perfect right to practice unlimited 'behavior modification' in a small, peasant nation," Mary McGrory writes.[69]

What is the reason for this "lust," this mood reminiscent of Khomeinist frenzy (but more extreme, since Iranians had sound historical reasons for hatred of their "Great Satan")? The official claims can hardly be taken seriously; even if all minimally credible charges are accepted, the Sandinista record compares favorably with that of US clients in the region today, and in the past, and elsewhere, to put it rather mildly.[70] The conclusions that follow from comparisons within the region are too obvious for discussion among sane people, so let us consider the state that is by far the major recipient of US aid, asking how it would fare under the charges brought against the Sandinistas. If the charges cannot withstand this test, then the level of hypocrisy is profound indeed.

US propaganda regularly denounces the failure of the Sandinistas to meet their alleged "obligations" to the Organization of American States (OAS). The President claimed in July 1983 that they had "literally made a contract to establish a true democracy" with the OAS before taking power in July 1979. This claim is without foundation; Roy Gutman observes that this charge, constantly reiterated by apologists for US atrocities, was concocted as part of a "successful U.S. disinformation campaign... According to the OAS, in a July 16, 1979, telex to then General Secretary Alejandro Orfila the Sandinistas said they planned to convoke 'the first free elections in this century' but made no reference to timing and said nothing about creating a 'true democracy'."[71] But although the charge has no merit with regard to the Sandinistas, it does apply to Israel; with considerably more force, in fact. Israel does have obligations, of a far more more serious nature than those falsely attributed to the Sandinistas, which it has always rejected. Israel was admitted to the UN on the express condition that it would observe UN resolutions on return or compensation of refugees.[72] As would be expected in the age of Orwell, this charge against Nicaragua is featured prominently in Israeli propaganda journals, such as the *New Republic*, which naturally remain silent on Israel's obligations.

Another major charge against Nicaragua is censorship of *La Prensa*. A State Department official commented that the Sandinistas "know the censorship is the worst thing they can do, from the American point of view." Naturally if the US were being attacked by a state of unimaginable power, we would not impose censorship on a journal that offered them support and that received a $100,000 grant from the aggressor;[73] that is, in fact, correct, since the editors and anyone remotely connected to them would be in concentration camps; recall the fate of Japanese during World War II.

Censorship in Israel, however, is so severe that an Arab woman lecturing at the Hebrew University was denied permission even to publish an Arab language social and political journal. The Arab press in East Jerusalem was seized by the authorities when it reported settler attacks against Arabs after a prisoner exchange. An Arab bimonthly was shut down permanently in 1983, and the censor closed an Arab newspaper in Jerusalem for three days when it published an obituary of two young Arabs who died in a mysterious car explosion in 1985. 350 books are officially banned in the occupied territories, along with others known to him personally, Knesset member Matti Peled (an Arabist and retired general) reports, including Hebrew translations of Theodore Herzl's diaries,

Isaac Deutscher's *Non-Jewish Jew*, books on Israeli military and political history, a translation of "To live with Arabs" by Elie Eliachar, the dovish president of the Council of the Sephardic Community in Israel, a book on the religious West Bank settlers (Gush Emunim) by the well-known Israeli journalist Danny Rubinstein, among others. Art exhibitions are censored; a Palestinian artist was given a six-month jail sentence on the charge that the colors of the Palestinian flag appeared in the corner of a painting. Arab plays have repeatedly been banned on political grounds, and a Hebrew play by an Israeli jailed for refusing military service was banned in September 1985 "on purely political grounds," Dan Fisher reports. The Hebrew press is also subject to censorship—as well as extensive self-censorship. Journalists are not permitted by the censor to publish abroad material that has appeared in the Hebrew press. All outgoing mail and packages are subject to censorship, and may be opened freely by the 58 people assigned to this task. Surveillance of telephone conversations is so extensive that the censor has intervened directly in telephone conversation, Knesset member Michael Bar-Zohar reports.[74]

But we hear no cries that the US must arm and direct terrorist forces to attack Israel. Nor does the US Congress offer "humanitarian aid" (another Orwellism) to guerrilla forces resisting South African repression or opposing the illegal South African occupation of Namibia, or defending themselves against Israeli occupation in southern Lebanon; rather they are all "terrorists," whose actions we deplore. The President, always quick to defend South Africa, even justified the murderous South African attack on Botswana on grounds that it may have been "retaliation" against the African National Congress (there is "no question," he said, about its "violence" and "murdering," but about South Africa we must withhold judgment).[75]

As for the "humanitarian aid" offered by Congress to the *contras*, the *Times* cites without comment the statement of rebel leader Adolfo Calero that it will be used for the purchase of "at least two helicopters."[76] No doubt Elliott Abrams will personally ensure that the helicopters are used solely for medical aid.

Another major charge against the Sandinistas has to do with their treatment of the Miskitos, surely the best-known American Indian group in the hemisphere and the only one whose travail merits agonized expressions of concern. That they were treated very badly by the Sandinistas is beyond question; they are also among the better treated Indians in the hemisphere. If an Indian group to their north were to put forth the demands for autonomy now being considered in Nicaragua, they would simply be slaughtered, if ridicule did not suffice. Miskito leader Armstrong Wiggins holds that the arrangement the Miskitos are demanding "has never been granted by any other country in the world to indigenous peoples, and goes beyond [their] status under the previous government" (which largely ignored the Atlantic coast); hitherto, he states, "the Sandinista policy towards indigenous people is just like the Mexican policy, just like the United States policy, just like Chilean policy."[77]

Sandinista abuses against the Miskitos were "more massive than any other human rights violations that I'm aware of in Central America," so Jeane Kirkpatrick testified before the Senate Foreign Relations committee in March 1982—at a time when thousands of Indians were being slaughtered in Guatemala, and some 13,000 civilians had been murdered in El Salvador by US clients in the preceding year alone, not to speak of torture, mutilation, starvation, semi-slave labor and other standard Free World amenities. The President chimed in with the news that the Sandinistas are conducting a "campaign of virtual genocide against the Miskito Indians" (June 6, 1985). In fact, some 10% of the Miskito population had been removed from war zones under a "policy [that] was clearly prompted by military considerations" and compares quite favorably with US treatment of Japanese-Americans during World War II, an Americas Watch report comments, and 21 to 24 Miskitos had been killed three years earlier by government forces along with 69 unresolved cases of "disappearance"; major atrocities, no doubt, but undetectable in the context of the behavior of the US and its clients in the region.[78]

Reviewing the human rights situation in Nicaragua, the Americas Watch report finds that Nicaraguan government atrocities, which it believes it was able to review in full, are far slighter than those of the US-organized terrorist army, and have sharply declined since 1982 in contrast to those of the *contras*, which can only be sampled given their scale and the lack of sources. Even in the case of the Miskitos, not the prime target of the US-sponsored terrorists, Americas Watch finds that "the most serious abuses of Miskitos' rights have been committed by the *contra* groups," and "the *contras'* treatment of Miskitos and other Indians has become increasingly more violent" while that of the government has notably improved. Miskito leader Brooklyn Rivera comments that the FDN "has been very hostile and aggressive toward us. They consider us an enemy because we maintain our independent positions and will not become soldiers in someone else's army." He alleges further "that the Reagan Administration was blocking Miskito unity because it wanted a group it could control" under Adolfo Calero of the FDN, who the US sees "as the future leader of Nicaragua," and states that the US-controlled Honduran military kept him and other prominent Miskitos from entering Honduras to attend a Miskito conference, as part of this strategy.[79]

Again, it is pointless to compare the abuse of the Miskitos with the wholesale slaughter conducted by US clients in Central

America in the same years. So we might recall some moments of early US history, for example, the Sullivan Expedition against the Iroquois in 1779, pursuant to General Washington's orders that the towns and territories of the Iroquois were "not to be merely overrun but destroyed." The orders were "fulfilled to the hilt," Fairfax Downey records in his upbeat account of "an outstanding feat in military annals," leading to "total destruction and devastation" of "cultivated fields and well-built towns," of "the North American Indian's finest civilization north of Mexico" with richly cultivated fields and orchards, stone houses and log cabins beyond the level of most of the colonial farmers. Nothing was left but "smoking ruins and desolation"; "all this industry and plenty was doomed to be scorched earth." One column destroyed forty towns and 160,000 bushels of corn along with orchards and other crops, while a smaller one destroyed hundreds of houses and 500 acres of corn. "The towns and field of the hostile Iroquois had been ruthlessly ravished," though one officer "sadly" observed that "The nests have been destroyed, but the birds are still on the wing." They survived in "miserable destitution" after "the wastage of their lands."[80]

Or we might consider one of the early exploits of our most favored client state, the massacre on Oct. 28, 1948 at Doueimah, an undefended town north of Hebron in an area where there had been no fighting. The massacre was conducted by a unit with tanks, leaving 580 civilians killed according to the accounting by its Mukhtar—100 to 350, according to Israeli sources, 1000 according to testimonies preserved in US State Department records—including 75 old men praying in a mosque and 35 families, of whom only three people escaped, in a cave outside of the destroyed town where they took refuge. The conquest of the town—but not the massacre—was noted at once in Israel's major journal, Ha'aretz, in a report on the conquest of "historical sites" from the days of Bar Kochba and the Romans, "renewing again the connection between the people of Israel and the Land of Israel." Israeli military historians say that the affair is known, though not recorded. The first report appears to be in a letter in the Labor Party journal Davar (Sept. 4, 1979) by a kibbutz member who deplores the "ghetto mentality" of those who refrain from expelling Arabs. He cites eyewitness testimony by a participant who alleges that women and children were killed by crushing their skulls with sticks and that people were blown up in houses, among other atrocities, "not during the heat of battle" but "as a system of expulsion and elimination." The story was finally unearthed by a correspondent for Hadashot in 1984 and presented as newly discovered. Historian Yoram Nimrod writes that the background for this slaughter, and the general attitude of the time that "the Arabs and their possessions are fair game," can be traced to the attitudes of the leadership, who wanted the Galilee to be "free [literally, "clean"] of Arabs" and asserted that "for the Arabs of the Land of Israel there remains only one function: to flee" (David Ben-Gurion),[81] that the country must be "homogeneous" and hence with as few Arabs as possible (Moshe Dayan), and who insisted that the Arab civilians who had fled or had been expelled "cannot and need not return" (Chaim Weizmann), or even be settled nearby, even if this means rejecting peace overtures (Ben-Gurion).[82]

Nothing comparable to these early post-independence atrocities against the indigenous population in the US and Israel can be charged to the Sandinistas.

Chaim Weizmann's principle was, incidentally, also followed in subsequent years, notably after the 1967 war when hundreds of thousands of Arabs fled or were expelled. A report by Eyal Ehrlich observes that "much was written, and with pride, about 'Operation Refugee,' which permitted 17,000 to return," but not about the fact, which he discovered in interviews with soldiers and officers, that the army was under orders, which it fulfilled, to kill returning refugees: "Civilians, women and children were killed. No one reported, no one counted the bodies, no one investigated and punished" these actions taken in pursuance of "policies established by such men as" Yitzhak Rabin (now Minister of Defense), Chaim Herzog (now President), and Uzi Narkis (Commander of the Jordanian front, later Head of the Department of Immigration and Absorption of the Jewish Agency, a bitter irony). Soldiers were ordered to shoot even if they heard "the crying of an infant."[83]

Other charges too have been levelled against the Sandinistas in the propaganda war. President Reagan, with a representative of the Anti-Defamation League of B'nai Brith (ADL) at his side, accused the Sandinistas of anti-Semitism on July 20, 1983— somehow overlooking a cable four days earlier from the US Embassy in Managua stating that it could find "no verifiable ground" to accuse the Sandinistas of anti-Semitism and that "the evidence fails to demonstrate that the Sandinistas have followed a policy of anti-Semitism or have persecuted Jews solely because of their religion."[84] The charges have been reiterated since, but are denied by human rights activists who are highly critical of the Sandinistas in Managua, by a delegation headed by a Rabbi who had been a leader in the struggle against the anti-Semitism and terror of the Argentine neo-Nazis, and by a Panamanian Rabbi (a former Minister of the government who had been honored by the Latin American Jewish Congress) after a visit to Nicaragua. The Jewish Student Press Service reports that the ADL had "approached Presidental advisers with the idea of a deal" in an effort to "gain clout with the Reagan White House," accepted by the Administration who saw a way "to get the Jewish community to join the bandwagon" in the campaign to enlist public support for its Central American policies; the report cites officials in leading Jewish organizations, who denied the charges of anti-Semitism.[85]

Meanwhile, the White House, the media and the ADL, while generally suppressing the cable from the Ambassador that reached Reagan four days before the July 20 accusation, also have yet to report the homilies of their favorite, Nicaraguan Archbishop Obando y Bravo, who declaims that "the leaders of Israel... mistreated [the prophets], beat them, killed them. Finally as supreme proof of his love, God sent his Divine Son; but they...also killed him, crucifying him." "The Jews killed the prophets and finally the son of God... Such idolatry calls forth the sky's vengeance."[86]

The Council on Hemispheric Affairs observes that "The White House keeps up a steady stream of calumny directed at Managua, charging the ruling Sandinistas with everything vile: drug-running, genocide, subverting their neighbors, and now international terrorism," charges that have not "been burdened with evidence" but are reported with only rare attempts at evaluation. The technique is the one pioneered during World War I, when the first major government propaganda agency, the Committee on Public Information, discovered "that one of the best means of controlling news was flooding news channels with 'facts,' or what amounted to official information."[87]

Few are willing to undertake the tedious task of refuting the regular flood of lies; they have little access to the public in any event, and they can always be dismissed by the charge that they are apologists for the enemy and its actual crimes. This standard device is sometimes used consciously as a technique to preserve the crucial Right to Lie in the Service of the State; or, for the more deeply indoctrinated, it may simply be impossible to conceive of criticism of the Holy State as anything but support for its official enemies, principled criticism of the divine institution being unimaginable. In either case, the discussion shifts to the evil deeds of the official enemy and the critic can be dismissed as an apologist for these crimes, as having a "double standard," etc.: the Holy State and the Right to Lie in its service are secure. The device was, and still is, used with tiresome regularity with reference to the Indochina wars: a critic of the US attack against South Vietnam must be a "supporter of Hanoi," so one can respond to the criticism by producing true or false charges against Hanoi, and if the critic refutes false charges, that just proves that he or she is an apologist for Hanoi as originally claimed and there is no need to consider the original criticism of the state one serves. The same device is now constantly used in the case of Central America.[88]

One would think that the transparent silliness of the procedure would embarrass its practitioners, but evidently this is not the case.

These are among the reactions which anyone who undertakes the task of principled criticism of state actions or domestic institutions should expect, if the critic is not simply ignored, a relatively simple matter in a deeply indoctrinated society in which private power can ensure fairly effective control over the means of expression.

We return to some of the further charges against the Sandinistas. The crucial point is that they have a cumulative effect, whatever their veracity. It is well-understood by Reagan's advisers, the ADL and others practiced in the skills of defamation, lies and brainwashing that repeated charges that receive wide publicity create a lasting image, even if they are disproven point by point in critical analysis that may subsequently be noted on the back pages. The chief foreign correspondent of the *London Guardian*, reviewing Ray Bonner's important book cited above, comments that Bonner (who notes that he originally accepted government deception as a journalist in El Salvador) "is rarely as angry about the journalists as about the officials who manipulated them":[89]

> He is well enough aware that the issue in El Salvador is not reality as such, but how that reality is perceived: the United States is not just conducting a political, economic and military war, but a propaganda war as well. But he seems less exercised than he might be about the degree to which journalists accept the US Government line. A lie reported as fact on the front page of the *New York Times* affects public opinion. The same lie exposed years later by anonymous officials reminiscing, or thanks to a Freedom of Information suit, is mainly of interest to historians. For every exposé which Mr Bonner and the handful of other industrious reporters make there are countless tendentious stories which are never challenged. Beside the cascade of one-sided and inaccurate reports, based on untrue data or false premises, the honest and probing accounts are no better than a trickle. Meanwhile, the policy juggernaut rolls on.

Furthermore, even if the media were to treat state propaganda with a critical eye in the manner employed for official enemies, the government would still have won the major battle: namely, setting the framework for debate. We spend little time analyzing or refuting Soviet charges about the terrorism of the Afghan resistance or Hitler's charges against Poland in 1939, but it is more difficult, it seems, to recognize the true nature of debate over Washington's charges against the Sandinistas at a time when it is launching its terrorist war against them.[90]

A fundamental reason for the great successes achieved in "brainwashing under freedom" is that the essential premises of the state terrorists are widely shared, even among their most ardent critics within the mainstream; as Jonathan Steele puts it more harshly, the problem is that "journalists share the same narrow, ignorant assumptions as the policy-makers." To take one example, consider the *Boston Globe*, perhaps the most consistent critic of Reagan's thuggery in Nicaragua, as they correctly describe it. Randolph Ryan of the *Globe* staff, the most outspoken of these critics, writes that critics have so far failed because they have not succeeded in putting forth their belief that "America's strength grows from the force of its moral example." Adopting the terminology of Kissinger and others (see p. 67), he writes that in 1980-81 "there was an impression that the revolutionary left was on a roll in Central America. The administration correctly saw that infectious spirit as a 'virus' that had to be stopped." But now Nicaragua is "no longer a subversive 'virus'" and has become just an opportunity to win a cheap victory.[91]

Illustrated here are some of the essential contributions of the critics to reinforcing state terror. First, we have the reference to "the force of [America's] moral example," as if history demonstrates any such truth. Second, the absurd Administration claim that the attack on Nicaragua was motivated by its alleged role in arming the guerrillas in El Salvador is accepted; and more important, it is explicitly assumed that if Nicaragua were indeed providing arms to people being massacred by US clients, then this crime would merit retribution—just as writers in *Pravda* no doubt thunder about the crimes of Pakistan and the US in aiding the feudal "bandits" who are "terrorizing" Afghanistan. But most important is the shared belief that the "infectious virus" must be stopped, by force if necessary. The "virus," of course, was never the flow of arms to El Salvador, but rather the threat of successful independent development, under the principles of the rotten apple theory. And if this doctrine is accepted, then the Administration has a strong case. Evidently this danger has not been averted, so there is every reason, on the premises that Ryan and Reagan share, to continue the "low intensity war" to ensure suffering, discontent, inability to develop any constructive programs, and the rise to power of the harshest elements, who will be dependent on the Soviet bloc, thus providing retrospective justification for the attack.

As was true during the war against South Vietnam, then all of Indochina, the contribution of mainstream critics to entrenching the doctrines of the state religion is a crucial one, which is why they are tolerated, indeed honored for their courage and decency.[92]

The irrelevance of government claims about the war against Nicaragua is evident from the way the motivation shifts as circumstances demand. At one point, the attack was justified by the need to prevent arms flow to El Salvador. By 1983, no significant arms flow having been detected despite massive efforts, the aim was to "bring the Sandinistas to the bargaining table" and force them to hold elections. In June 1984, the President told Congress that US aid to the *contras* must continue to pressure the Sandinistas to negotiate; unless we do, he said, "a regional settlement based on the Contadora principles will continue to elude us."[93] A few months later, elections had been held, the Sandinistas had accepted the Contadora principles causing the Administration to discover suddenly that they were a sham and a fraud, and they were continuing to request negotiations that the US refuses. So the argument shifted again: we read in the news columns that "the Reagan Administration has demanded that Nicaragua demilitarize, reduce its ties with the Soviet Union and Cuba and change its form of government to a pluralistic democracy."[94] A moment's thought suffices to show that the best way to bring Nicaragua to demilitarize and cut its ties with the Soviet bloc would be to accept the Contadora agreements blocked by US pressure and to call off the war, and that the commitment of the Reagan Administration, or its predecessors, to "pluralistic democracy" in Central America is as believable as the Soviet commitment to "socialism" or "democracy" in its domains. But this drivel, for that is what it is, is blandly reported as "news" in the nation's press. Nothing could be more plain than the absurdity of the whole game, in which the media play their assigned role, earnestly reporting each pretense and occasionally commenting on the weakness of the argument or the "inconsistency" of the highly consistent and rational policy.

The real reasons for the "lust" to destroy the Sandinista regime have nothing to do with the charges that are raised, whether valid or simply concocted. That is obvious enough. The real reasons can readily be explained on other grounds: by fear of Nicaraguan success. The Oxfam report on Sandinista social successes (chapter 1, section 2), inspires real fear; useless tanks do not. The real reasons are based on the argument that President Wilson regarded as "unanswerable": the interests of the people of Latin America are "an incident, not an end." What is paramount is a narrowly conceived American interest: "The protection of our raw materials," the Fifth Freedom. We must therefore become deeply concerned when some group becomes infected by the heresy detected by US intelligence: "the idea that the government has direct responsibility for the welfare of the people," what US political theology calls "Communism" in our Third World domains, whatever the commitments of its advocates.

In the real world, as we shall see in more detail directly, the US has consistently opposed "human rights, the raising of the living standards, and democratization," using harsh measures where necessary. These policies are natural concomitants of the geopolitical conceptions that have motivated planning and that are deeply rooted in American institutions. It is not surprising, for example, that the US should react with extraordinary hostility to democracy in Laos or should overthrow the only democratic government in the history of Guatemala, keeping in power a series of mass murderers ever since. It is familiar to students of US policy that "while paying lip-service to the encouragement of representative democracy in Latin America, the United States has a strong interest in just the reverse," apart from "procedural democracy, especially the holding of elections—which only too often have proved farcical." The reason is that democracies may tend to be responsive to popular needs, while "the United States has been concerned with fostering the most favourable conditions for her private overseas investment":[95]

> ...United States concern for representative democracy in Latin America is a facet of her anti-communist policy. There has been no serious question of her intervening in the case of the many right-wing military coups, from which, of course, this policy generally has benefited. It is only when her own concept of democracy, closely identified with private, capitalistic enterprise, is threatened by communism [or to be more accurate, by independent development, whether capitalist, socialist, or whatever] that she has felt impelled to demand collective action to defend it.

It is only when some form of democracy contributes to maintaining the Fifth Freedom that the US will tolerate it; otherwise, terror-and-torture states will have to do.

From these real world considerations, one can come to understand the "lust" to strike out against Nicaragua—or Allende, or Cuba, or the National Liberation Front of South Vietnam. It is not because of the abuses of human rights and democratic principle, often real, sometimes despicable, but rarely approaching what we tolerate with equanimity, directly support, or carry out ourselves. Rather, US policy towards Nicaragua is immediately predictable from the fact that the priorities of the new government "meant that Nicaragua's poor majority would have access to, and be the primary beneficiaries of, public programs," the fact that infant mortality fell so dramatically that Nicaragua won an award from the World Health Organization for the best health achievement in a Third World nation, health standards and literacy sharply improved, a successful agrarian reform was carried out, GDP expanded by 5% in 1983 in contrast to other countries in the region, production and consumption of corn, beans and rice rose dramatically and Nicaragua came closer to self-sufficiency than any other Central American nation and made the most impressive gains of any Latin American nation in the Quality of Life Index of the Overseas Development Council, based on literacy, infant mortality and life expectancy.[96] Burns comments that "Nicaragua should, in many ways, stand as an example for Central America, not its outcast. The grim social statistics from Honduras, a country in which the population is literally starving to death, stand in sharp contrast to the recent achievements of Nicaragua." That is just the point; the infection must be stopped before it spreads.

Similarly, the crime of the Allende government was that it quickly raised production and real wages, conducted an effective agrarian reform and such programs as milk distribution for children, "measures that increased consumer demand and permitted industry to take advantage of unutilized capacity and idle labor," and worse, did so under parliamentary democracy—though such dangerous progress could not long persist as the Nixon-Kissinger destabilization policy, designed to "make the economy scream," in Nixon's words, had its effects, along with other factors.[97]

Similarly, US policy towards Cuba is readily explained by the Quality of Life Index of the Overseas Development Council, which places Cuba well above any other Latin American country and approximately equal to the US—actually better than the US if we consider its more egalitarian character, thus with lower infant mortality rates than Chicago and far lower rates than the Navajo reservation. Tom Farer of the Rutgers Law School, member of the Inter-American Commission on Human Rights of the OAS and former State Department assistant for Inter-American Affairs, writes that:

> ...there is a consensus among scholars of a wide variety of ideological positions that, on the level of life expectancy, education, and health, Cuban achievement is considerably greater than one would expect from its level of per capita income. A recent study of 113 Third World countries in terms of these basic indicators of popular welfare ranked Cuba first, ahead even of Taiwan—which is probably the outstanding example of growth with equity within a capitalist economic framework. Data in the 1981 World Development Report of the International Bank for Reconstruction and Development also support the consensus. Cuba excelled according to all main indicators of human needs satisfaction... What has changed remarkably is not so much the gross indicators as those that reflect the changed conditions of the poor, particularly the rural poor. In 1958, for example, the one rural hospital in the entire country represented about 2 percent of the hospital facilities in Cuba; by 1982 there were 117 hospitals, or about 35 percent of all hospitals in Cuba.

Furthermore, polio and malaria have been eliminated, and the causes of death have shifted from those associated with underdevelopment (diseases of early infancy, etc.) to those of the developed world (congenital abnormalities, diabetes, etc.).[98] These are the crimes for which Cuba must pay dearly; the real ones are of little interest to policy makers, except for their propaganda effect.

As for the NLF in South Vietnam, its crime was explained ruefully by the bitterly anti-Communist journalist Denis Warner: "in hundreds of villages all over South-East Asia the only people working at the grass roots for an uplift in people's living standards are the Communists,"[99] the reason for the popular support that forced the US to resort to violence and to undermine any political settlement.

Those who set their priorities in this way are evidently deficient in their understanding of US needs and priorities. They have therefore joined the "monolithic and ruthless conspiracy," and must be driven into the hands of the Russians and subjected to aggression, terror, embargo and other means, in accord with their status as "an incident, not an end."

We turn next to a closer examination of just how it is done.

3 Patterns of Intervention

1 Defending our Sovereignty

It is natural and proper to focus attention on current atrocities, but it can also be misleading, and can hamper a proper understanding of what lies behind them. It may foster the belief that what is happening today is to be explained on the basis of the deficiencies, moral or intellectual, of a transitory political leadership and can be changed simply by "voting the rascals out." There is an element of truth to that assessment: the Reagan Administration and its cohorts are unusual in their commitment to aggrandizement of state power, state violence and terror, deception and other means to protect state actions from scrutiny by citizens, a quality noted by Congress as well as human rights groups.[1] But the element of truth is rather slight, as the historical record plainly shows, a fact of some import for people who hope to change the world, not merely to observe it.

It is important to recognize that little that is happening today is new. The United States has been tormenting Central America and the Caribbean for well over a century, generally in alleged defense against "outside threats." In the late 1920s, the Marines invaded Nicaragua in defense against the "Bolshevik threat" of Mexico. Secretary of State Frank Kellogg warned that

> The Bolshevik leaders have had very definite ideas with respect to the role which Mexico and Latin America are to play in their general program of world revolution. They have set up as one of their fundamental tasks the destruction of what they term American imperialism as a necessary prerequisite to the successful development of the international revolutionary movement in the New World... Thus Latin America and Mexico are conceived as a base for activity against the United States.

"Mexico was on trial before the world," President Coolidge declared as he sent the Marines to Nicaragua, once again.[2] Now Nicaragua is the base for the Bolshevik threat to Mexico, and ultimately the United States.

It requires no great originality, then, when Reagan, speaking on national television, warns of Soviet intentions to surround and ultimately destroy America by taking over Latin American states, as proven by a statement by Lenin, which, he said, "I have often quoted," but which happens not to exist[3]; or when his speech writers have him say that "Like a roving wolf, Castro's Cuba looks to peace-loving neighbors with hungry eyes and sharp teeth" and that the troubles in Central America are "a power play by Cuba and the Soviet Union, pure and simple"; or when the White House condemns Nicaragua for its "increased aggressive behavior" against Honduras and Costa Rica as the US proxy army attacks Nicaragua from Honduras and Costa Rica and Secretary of State George Shultz thunders that "we have to help our friends to resist the aggression that comes from these arms" that Nicaragua is acquiring to defend itself from the American onslaught, one act of a drama involving fabricated arms shipments to Nicaragua in a successful exercise in media management to deflect attention from unwanted elections there.[4] The media have yet to comment on the similarity to earlier episodes, for example, Hitler's anger at the "increased aggressive behavior" of Poland as his forces attacked in self-defense.

What of earlier years? Woodrow Wilson, the revered apostle of self-determination, invaded Mexico and sent his warriors to Haiti and the Dominican Republic, where they blocked constitutional government, reinstituted virtual slavery, tortured, murdered and destroyed, leaving a legacy of misery that remains until today. Evidently, there could be no Bolshevik threat at the time, so we claimed we were defending ourselves against the Huns.

Marine Commander Thorpe told new Marine arrivals that the war would last long enough "to give every man a chance against the Hun in Europe as against the Hun in Santo Domingo." The hand of the Huns was particularly evident in Haiti, he explained: "Whoever is running this revolution is a wise man; he certainly is getting a lot out of the niggers... It shows the handwork of the German." In actual fact, the real ruler of Haiti was Col. L. W. T. Waller of the US Marines, fresh from atrocities in the conquest of the Philippines; he was acquitted in court-martial proceedings on grounds that he had merely been following higher orders to take no prisoners and to kill every male Filipino over age 10. Waller particularly despised mulattos: "They are real nigger and no mistake...real nigs beneath the surface"; negotiations, in his eyes, meant "bowing and scraping to these coons." This murderous lout was particularly contemptuous of highly educated Haitians such as Philippe Dartiguenave, selected to be president by the Marines and then elected in a "free election" under Marine rule. Wilson's Secretary of State William Jennings Bryan, on the other hand, found the nigs amusing: after a briefing on Haiti, he remarked: "Dear me, think of it. Niggers speaking French." His successor, Robert Lansing, also stressed the fear of the Huns in justifying the invasion, while commenting that "the African race are devoid of any capacity for political organization and [have no] genius for government."[5] After the nineteen-year occupation by those who had a "capacity for political organization" that followed, Haiti was left a nightmare of misery and repression.

In 1899, we were compelled to defend ourselves against the Filipinos, who "assailed our sovereignty" as President McKinley announced angrily to Congress: "there will be no useless parley, no pause, until the [Filipino] insurrection is suppressed and American authority acknowledged and established," the pretext of rescuing the Philippines from Spanish rule having been abandoned. The cause was taken up by President Theodore Roosevelt; like Winston Churchill (see below, p. 126), he recognized few limits in war against "uncivilized tribes": "The most ultimately righteous of all wars," he wrote in his book *The Winning of the West*, "is a war with savages" which established "the foundations for the future greatness of a mighty people" as part of the process, "of incalculable importance," of suppressing the "red, black and yellow aboriginal owners" of much of the world in favor of "the dominant world races." To Roosevelt, the Filipinos were "Chinese halfbreeds," "Malay bandits," "savages, barbarians, a wild and ignorant people, Apaches, Sioux, Chinese boxers." A few years later, he was awarded the Nobel Peace prize. The young Winston Churchill told a New York audience that concentration camps and execution of prisoners and hostages were necessary because the Filipinos did "not know when they are whipped." The Filipinos were not fighting for independence, but "to control the Philippines so they could loot them," commanding General Otis told Congress, while the *New York Times* applauded his resort to force after the natives rejected "our kindness and indulgence"; the *Times* also commended Colonel Jacob Smith for using the brutal tactics of the Indian wars, which were "long overdue," and expressed outrage over a Harvard faculty petition urging Philippine independence, agreeing with a description of these "sympathizers with a public enemy" as "socialists" or "Populists." General Funston, who tortured and murdered prisoners while informing the press that "our men were wonderfully kind and considerate to the wounded and the prisoners," told a *Times* correspondent that the natives "are, as a rule, an illiterate, semi-savage people, who are waging war, not against tyranny, but against Anglo-Saxon order and decency." The military command, most of them old Indian fighters, carried out a campaign of wholesale slaughter and brutal atrocities which finally led to condemnations at home, though without shaking the conviction of American benevolence. "The war of conquest and its atrocities and courts-martial" have not fared well "in America's collective memory," Miller writes: "The subject is rarely touched upon in history texts, and when it is, this sordid episode is reduced to a bare mention of an 'insurrection against American rule'." Miller himself expresses contempt for critics who do not understand that "the American interventions both in Vietnam and in the Philippines were motivated in part by good intentions to elevate or to aid the victims"; Soviet scholars say the same about Afghanistan, with comparable justice.[6]

The scale of US achievements in pursuing its "good intentions" can only be guessed. General James Bell, who commanded operations in southern Luzon, estimated in May 1901 that one-sixth of the natives of Luzon had been killed or died from dengue fever, considered the result of war-induced famine; thus, over 600,000 dead in this island alone. A US government report indicated that ⅓ of the population of 300,000 had been killed by the army or famine and disease in one province of Luzon, where Bell had been fighting. A Republican Congressman who visited the Philippines wrote that "You never hear of any disturbances in Northern Luzon...because there isn't anybody there to rebel...our soldiers took no prisoners; they kept no records; they simply swept the country and wherever or however they could get hold of a Filipino they killed him. The women and children were spared and may now be noticed in disproportionate numbers in that part of the island." On the island of Samar, in contrast, everyone over 10 was ordered killed by Waller's commander General Smith, who was "admonished" in a court-martial proceeding and retired a year and a half early by President Roosevelt, in punishment.[7] As noted, Waller was acquitted for executing these orders.

Half a century earlier, we were compelled to take a third of Mexico in self-defense against Mexican aggression (initiated deep inside Mexico) in what General Ulysses S. Grant described as "the most unjust war ever waged by a stronger against a weaker nation" while the New York press explained that "the Mexicans are aboriginal Indians and they must share the destiny of their race." The editor of *Scientific American* lauded the expansion into Mexico as a triumph of American "mechanical genius": "We hold the keys of the Atlantic on the east and the Pacific on the far distant west. Our navies sweep the Gulf of Mexico and our armies occupy the land of the ancient Aztecs... Every American must feel a glow of enthusiasm in his heart as he thinks of his country's greatness, her might and her power." The genocidal assaults against the native population were in defense against England

and Spain. As in Central America, T. D. Allman comments, "the definition of the aggressors is that we have attacked them."[8]

The Evil Empire changes; the basic reasons and the credibility of the excuses do not.

If we are not defending ourselves from one or another Evil Empire, then we are acting in self-defense against "internal aggression," as Adlai Stevenson explained at the United Nations in 1964 with reference to South Vietnam, echoing McKinley, at the time when the US was desperately blocking attempts by our South Vietnamese enemies (who at the time included not only the Viet Cong but also the military-civilian leadership of the US client regime) to achieve neutralization and political settlement while the US planned its escalation of the war to block these nefarious schemes. Stevenson compared our defense against internal aggression in South Vietnam to the murderous counterinsurgency campaign in Greece in 1947, an operation that Reagan's Latin America adviser Roger Fontaine argued should be a model for our Central America policy. The concept of "internal aggression" was clarified further by the Joint Chiefs of Staff, who extended the scope of "aggression," which we must resist, to "overt armed attack from within the area" of a client state and even "political warfare," a special case of "aggression."[9] Thus, political activity by the natives in a country we occupy is aggression against us, justifying military action in self-defense. Defense against "internal aggression," another concept that Orwell would have admired, is a major theme of US history, from its origins until today.

2 The Rule of Law and the Rule of Force

Similarly, the US refusal to accept World Court adjudication of its conflict with Nicaragua in April 1984 was nothing new. The US proxy war against Nicaragua is patently illegal unless justified by the provision of the United Nations Charter that permits collective self-defense against armed attack, and indeed this absurd justification is the one offered those partisans who even care to construct a semblance of legality. International law is designed with enough loopholes to allow the great powers to do virtually anything they like; otherwise they would not ratify it. But the plain meaning of the law in this case is that if some state considers that it is subject to an armed attack—aggression so sudden and extreme that the necessity for action becomes "instant, overwhelming, and leaving no choice of means, and no moment for deliberation," in a conventional formulation due to Daniel Webster and relied upon in the Nuremberg judgments—then that state or its allies should make a formal complaint to the UN Security Council, requesting it to take appropriate action, and may defend the victim until it does; under other circumstances, the threat or use of force is illegal. The obligations under the Rio Treaty and the OAS Charter are much the same.

Of the states of Central America, only Nicaragua could claim to be subject to armed attack (namely, by the US-backed *contras*). The US is unwilling to bring to the Security Council or OAS the charge that it is engaged in self-defense against a Nicaraguan armed attack on El Salvador and to call upon the Council to act, a fact noted by conservative legal scholars such as Professor Alfred Rubin of the Fletcher School, who comments that "El Salvador should be complaining about being attacked" to the UN and OAS, "yet, he said, neither El Salvador nor the United States has moved in the OAS or the U.N. to formally charge Nicaragua with aggression"; the US has not even notified the Security Council of warlike measures such as the mining of Nicaraguan waters, which it claimed fell under "self-defense" when the facts were exposed, in explicit violation of the Supreme Law of the Land, which requires that measures taken in the exercise of the right of self-defense shall be "immediately reported to the Security Council" (UN Charter, Article 51).[10] Nor is the US willing to permit the World Court to hear its claims in the case brought against it, since in this forum too the US charge of armed attack would simply elicit ridicule.

The Rule of Law, however, does not apply to the US and its clients, or the USSR, or other violent powers that observe only the Rule of Force.[11]

The US refusal to accept the jurisdiction of the International Court of Justice in the matter of the Nicaraguan charges, unanimously rejected by the Court apart from the US representative, aroused much criticism. The American Society of International Law denounced it "overwhelmingly" in the first such action in its 78-year history. Their position is understandable. When the US government accepted the compulsory jurisdiction of the Court in 1946, the Senate observed that the force of that commitment "is that of a treaty" and entailed "a renunciation of any intention to withdraw our obligation in the face of a threatened legal action." A six-month notice was required "to terminate this declaration," a commitment plainly violated when the Reagan Administration, three days before Nicaragua's complaint was filed, attempted to modify the 1946 declaration so as to exclude "disputes with any Central American states or arising out of or relating to events in Central America."[12]

The Reagan Administration was also sharply criticized by Senator Daniel Patrick Moynihan of New York for "forsaking our centuries-old commitment to the idea of law in the conduct of nations" and for its "mysterious collective amnesia" in "losing the memory that there once was such a commitment," losing "all memory of a vital and fundamental tradition." Our UN Delegation headed by Jeane Kirkpatrick "does not know the history of our country," he proclaimed, echoed by Anthony Lewis, who decried Reagan's "failure to understand what the rule of law has meant to this country."[13]

Once again, history teaches a different lesson: in fact, it is Ronald Reagan and Jeane Kirkpatrick who understand "what the rule of law has meant to this country." The World Court incident serves as a clear illustration. It is a reenactment of events of the Taft and Wilson Administrations 70 years earlier. In 1907, at US initiative, a Central American Court of Justice was established to adjudicate conflicts among the American states. A few years later, the Court was destroyed by US refusal to recognize its decisions with regard to US intervention in Nicaragua. The incident that finally destroyed the Court, which had already condemned US intervention in Nicaragua in 1912 to no avail, involved the Bryan-Chamorro treaty of 1916, which granted the US perpetual rights to construct a canal through Nicaragua (the purpose being to forestall any competitor to the Panama Canal) and to lease a naval base on the Gulf of Fonseca. The Court upheld the plea of Costa Rica and El Salvador that this treaty infringed upon their rights, but the decision was ignored by the US and Marine-occupied Nicaragua, effectively destroying the Court. The treaty itself was fraudulent, as recognized by former Secretary of State Elihu Root, who noted that "It is apparent...that the present government...is really maintained in office by the presence of the U.S. Marines in Nicaragua" and has no legitimacy, surely no right "to make a treaty so serious for Nicaragua, granting us perpetual rights in that country."[14]

In short, the shameful World Court incident breaks no new ground in the history of US lawlessness. The only novelty in the present case is that the US does not have the power to destroy the World Court.

US lawlessness and coercive measures concerning Nicaragua have been condemned in other international forums. The GATT Council unanimously charged the US with violating obligations under international trade agreements by cutting Nicaragua's sugar quota and UNCTAD condemned "coercive economic measures applied for political reasons," over the objections of delegates from the US and its allies, referring to the US measures against Nicaragua, among other examples.[15]

Other aspects of the US attack on Nicaragua also evoke memories that should be more familiar than they are. Thus, consider the charge that the government of Nicaragua has "almost continuously kept Central America in tension or turmoil," exercising "a baleful influence upon Honduras" and destroying "republican institutions" while "public opinion and the press have been throttled." These "extremely insolent" and "false" charges were

issued by Secretary of State Philander Knox in 1909, Richard
Millett observes, in the course of US military intervention and
moves to undermine the government of the "capable and honest
Liberal politician" Dr. José Madriz, who "might have become
Nicaragua's best president to date" had the US not pursued its
"fixed determination to see a totally new administration in power,
refusing to recognize the Madriz government."[16] Knox went on,
with comparable insolence, to condemn Nicaragua for violating
the 1907 conventions that had established the Central American
Court, and announced support for the "revolution" (sponsored by
the US) which "represents the ideals and the will of a majority of
the Nicaraguan people more faithfully than does" the current
government of Nicaragua, appealing throughout to the "enlightened practice of civilized nations" and the deep concern of the US
for "free and honest government"—and incidentally, "for the
protection which must be assured American citizens and American
interests in Nicaragua." Pursuant to these aims, the Marines
landed to support the rebels—officially, "to protect U.S. lives and
property." They succeeded in "ushering in twenty-five years of
chaos," John Booth observes, a period of "destabilization and
destruction," terminating in a brutal and murderous six-year war
that "added additional burdens to the reeling nation's woes just as
the Great Depression began, thus still further taxing political
institutions and the economy," and leaving as their legacy "a
political monster—the National Guard in the hands of Anastasio
Somoza Garcia." The Guard was "an instrument potentially
capable of crushing political opposition with greater efficiency
than ever before in that nation," as it did in the years that followed
with enthusiastic support from Washington.[17]

Millet's characterization of Philander Knox's charges is appropriate today, for example, with respect to the statement by the
President that the US war against Nicaragua will continue until
the Sandinistas "keep their promise and restore [sic] a democratic
rule. And have elections."[18]

Note incidentally the clear statement by President Reagan,
reiterating earlier Administration stands, that the purpose of the
attack is to force a change in Nicaragua's internal order, not to
defend El Salvador against "armed attack." More recently, the
pretense has been dropped and the President has made it plain that
the purpose is to "remove" the existing government "in the sense of
its present structure" and make it "say 'uncle'."[19] The military is no
less frank. General Paul Gorman, on retiring from his position in
command of US forces in Central America, informed Congress that
"I don't think overthrow is feasible in the near future" though in
another year or more the *contras*, whom he praised as "freedom
fighters" whose goal is to oust the Sandinistas, might be able "to
march into Managua."[20]

The Administration has also made it plain that the use of US military force will be considered if other measures fail. Secretary of State Shultz stated that if Congress did not provide assistance to the *contras*, then the US would eventually have to make "an agonizing choice about the use of American combat troops," and Langhorne Motley, then Assistant Secretary of State for Inter-American Affairs, informed a House committee in closed session that failure to provide aid for the *contras* would place the US "in an accommodationist or military response dilemma at some later date when the threat to US interests becomes more obvious and when the only effective response would be on a larger scale or in less favorable circumstances." He referred specifically to direct US military involvement.[21] Since we evidently cannot adopt the "accommodationist" horn of the dilemma, as even the Democratic opposition generally agrees, we must prepare to use military force unless our mercenary armies can overthrow the government—or at least make the country bleed sufficiently so that it no longer poses a threat to the Fifth Freedom, always the tacit principle.

These warnings about an eventual invasion are simply another stage in what a classified Pentagon document in 1983 called a "'perception management' program...designed to keep the Nicaraguans concerned that the United States might attack." The regular large-scale US military maneuvers on the border are part of the same program, according to this document, though they also serve to establish US bases by subterfuge to ensure the militarization of Honduras under a facade of "democracy." Sonic booms over Managua have the same goal, the Administration noted. The purpose is explained by a State Department official: "Every time there's an invasion scare, they make some concessions."[22]

From the start, the Somozist leaders of the US proxy army have made it clear that "the goal of their organization has been to topple the government of Nicaragua. They scoff at past statements by the Reagan Administration that the original reason for forming the *contra* forces was to intercept weapons that Nicaragua allegedly was sending to the leftist rebels in El Salvador." Joel Brinkley of the *Times* reports that "All the F.D.N. officers interviewed said the group's goal never changed; it was to overthrow the Sandinista government." Edgar Chamorro, a top FDN leader, states that he was informed in 1982 by a CIA official, speaking in behalf of the President, that the goal was to overthrow the government; talk about arms interdiction came later. Chamorro, who was in charge of publishing the notorious CIA manual offering advice on political assassination and other useful actions, states that he was approached by the government to serve as a cover for the *contras* because he had not been a Somozist and they "said they needed people who they could sell to Congress." In private, he states, CIA officials never concealed their real objective: "to overthrow the government in Managua...They always said the President of the United States wants you to go to Managua."[23]

Admiral Stansfield Turner, Director of the CIA under the Carter Administration, comments that overthrow of the Nicaraguan government is "what we've been trying to do all along... All along, there's only been one objective—to overthrow the government of Nicaragua... It's been persiflage that they're trying to stop the flow of arms... However you look at it, we've been supporting people who are trying to overthrow the government of Nicaragua." The Administration "shifted the tune" in 1982 "because they didn't have the evidence to support the other charge," lacking evidence of any "significant flow of arms." Turner adds: "I'm not a peacenik who's opposed to interfering in the affairs of other countries. These are very legitimate activities, from my point of view, for our Government to undertake." But such actions "must be important to the national security," "achievable," and "capable of being kept secret." The Nicaraguan "covert action" fails in all three respects, he says: in particular, "it hasn't achieved what it set out to do, topple the government of Nicaragua."[24]

As Moore observes in his defense of the legality of the Reagan policy, such objectives are contrary to "the law of the United States" that is "binding on both the executive and legislative branches," not only the general provisions of international law but also such specific constraints as the Boland Amendment, in force until August 1985.[25] There can be little doubt that these are and have been the objectives throughout—though it would suffice to cause sufficient misery and destruction so as to keep the "infectious virus" from spreading through the dread demonstration effect. It is, however, important to stress that contempt for law and the regular resort to violence to protect US interests are a central theme of American history, contrary to the fantasies spun by those bemused by a "mysterious collective amnesia."

An accurate account was given by Major Smedley Butler, who commanded the Marine landing in Nicaragua in 1909 and again in 1912, and also fought in Mexico and Haiti, where he ran the fraudulent 1918 election that ratified the US occupation under Marine guns and the corvée system of slave labor, "an instrument for oppressing and torturing the Haitian people...and apparently some times for no other purpose than to provide [the Marine-imposed Haitian gendarmes] with the excuse to beat, if not shoot them down," as a missionary described it. In 1931, shortly before retiring, Old Gimlet Eye Butler summarized his career before a legionnaires convention:

> I spent 33 years...being a high-class muscle man for Big Business, for Wall Street and the bankers. In short, I was a racketeer for capitalism... I helped purify Nicaragua for the international banking house of Brown Brothers in

1909-1912. I helped make Mexico and especially Tampico safe for American oil interests in 1916. I brought light to the Dominican Republic for American sugar interests in 1916. I helped make Haiti and Cuba a decent place for the National City [Bank] boys to collect revenue in. I helped in the rape of half a dozen Central American republics for the benefit of Wall Street.

The historical record lends adequate support to Butler's rendition. Nothing essential has changed since.[26]

3 The US and El Salvador in Historical Perspective

Current US intervention in El Salvador also breaks little new ground, apart from scale. In 1932, thousands of peasants were massacred in the *Matanza*, as Hernández Martínez took power; he was duly recognized by the US while going through the forms of an election, in which he was the only candidate   (see p. 44). The population was traumatized and subdued by the *Matanza*. "The effectiveness of the *Matanza* at suppressing dissent was indicated by the passage of over a generation before rural organizing began again. As late as 1978 a reporter quoted a conservative lawyer who stated, 'Whenever the peasants make the least demand, people start talking about 1932 again'." Power remained in the hands of a tiny oligarchy of about 100 major families who enriched themselves and foreign investors while much of the population starved or emigrated. Here, as elsewhere, the US "wanted stability, benefited from the on-going system, and was therefore content to work with the military-oligarchy complex that ruled most of Central America from the 1820s to the 1980s."[27]

Historian Thomas Anderson comments that "the whole political labyrinth of El Salvador can be explained only in reference to the traumatic experience of the uprising and the *matanza*," while Jeane Kirkpatrick assures us that "To many Salvadorans the violence of this repression seems less important than the fact of restored order and the thirteen years of civil peace that ensued," an accurate rendition of the views of those Salvadorans who count.[28]

No problems arose in one of the world's most miserable countries until 1960, when a junior officer's coup established a "moderately leftist government [that] lasted for only a few weeks before other officers, responding to pressures from the oligarchy and the United States, staged a countercoup," a foretaste of what was to come 20 years later. The US Embassy urged support for the military regime, stating that the internal security forces "are behind the present government, are strongly anti-Communist, and constitute major force for stability and orderly political and economic development." Their rule was necessitated by "subversive anti-government activities" such as "underground propaganda," the Embassy explained, offering an insight into the concept of "subversion" as understood by the Kennedy liberals. Dr. Fabio Castillo, a former president of the National University, testified before Congress that the US had openly participated in the countercoup and had opposed the holding of free elections.[29] The conservative junta was quickly recognized by President Kennedy, whose preference for civil-military regimes was noted earlier (p.57), after they had "pledged to take tough actions against the students [who had protested against the outlawing of political parties, the main proof offered of a Communist plot], cut relations with Castro, and warmly welcomed foreign investment." The trends of earlier years continued: production, including food production, increased, largely for export, along with starvation and general misery. These trends were enhanced by the Alliance for Progress programs of Kennedy and Johnson. By 1969, 300,000 Salvadorans (one in eight citizens) had fled to Honduras to find food and work. Military aid rapidly increased along with US training and coordination of the military and other security forces of the region.[30]

The threat of such subversive acts as distributing propaganda, which justified support of a military dictatorship in 1961, still remains an unsolved problem. "Christian Democrats have recently acknowledged with candor the immediate threat that political accommodation with the rebels could pose," Sam Dillon of the *Miami Herald* reports. The problem, as explained by one of President Duarte's aides, is that "Six months after we sign a peace treaty, and these leftists start wandering around the country organizing legally, all the agrarian reform cooperatives would turn communist." Another problem is that the left might organize among school-age youth and in the labor movement.

Shirley Christian reports in the *Times* that the National Federation of Trade Unions is "making tough wage demands," and that "Christian Democrats say they are haunted by the memory of 1979, when the same groups were prominent in the near-anarchy that swept El Salvador," leading to the October 1979 coup, soon taken over with Carter's assistance by the right-wing military; "By mid-1980, the agitation dried up as many street activists joined the guerrillas and others disengaged out of fear for their lives, while the Government imposed the wage freeze and state of siege" amidst "accusations of human rights violations" (NB: only "accusations"). Now the fear is that these dangerous groups, who "acknowledge" their former affiliation with the political arm of the guerrillas, may attempt to reactivate the "mass organizations" that were thankfully destroyed by the "violent repression of strikes and demonstrations" along with other Carter-Reagan atrocities left unmentioned, for example, the murder or disappearance of thousands of union activists and workers, which somehow tends to have a dampening effect on labor organization.[31]

As always, the current problem is to devise something that will pass for "democracy" among commentators at home—not a difficult task, as we shall see—so that aid will flow unhampered to allow the security forces to do their work, while ensuring that "democracy" excludes democracy.

Though the suppression of Salvadoran labor under the US-imposed governments has elicited little interest, the diligent reader can find an occasional report. Thus, some notice was taken when in February 1984, nine labor leaders including all top officials of one major federation were arrested in a Catholic retreat center by armed police. The police raid was based on an alleged tip that rifles and bazookas were stored there, but the police conceded that they had found no weapons, "although they did confiscate most of the union files." Union leaders charged that they were forced to sign written confessions after a week of interrogation, sometimes beatings. None was charged with a crime; the official accusation was that they were planning to "present demands to management for higher wages and benefits and promoting strikes, which destabilize the economy." A US official stated that the Embassy had "followed the arrests closely and was satisfied that the correct procedures were followed." The union attacked had never held a meeting under its own name, "fearing arrest or death-squad attacks"; in 1980-81, some 8200 union members were murdered, wounded or disappeared, according to an estimate by one labor group. Salvadoran law requires yearly meetings of unions to elect leaders, while another law bans such meetings as illegal "except with police permission, which is seldom granted." The arrests in this case were part of a general government crackdown on unions in preparation for the much-praised March 25 elections; or as the press preferred: "The police action came despite government promises to loosen restrictions on political freedom in preparation for" the elections.[32] Such preparations then went unnoticed in the general ecstasy over the democratic renewal in El Salvador a few weeks later.

4 Contemporary State Terrorism: the System Established

Nicaragua was treated much as El Salvador under Kennedy's program of strengthening the power of military and security forces throughout Latin America. Under the Alliance for Progress, military aid to Somoza rose sevenfold while economic assistance doubled. "The energy the United States injected into the country in the form of moral support, economic aid, and military muscle discouraged opponents of the regime, enriched the brothers

Somoza, and increased their capacity to co-opt and to repress their compatriots" and to "weather a wave of internal unrest from 1959 to 1963." At the same time, the US formed a Central American Defense Council (CONDECA), unifying the armed forces of all Central American nations apart from Costa Rica and thus permitting more efficient internal repression. Nicaragua reciprocated by serving as a base for the attack against Cuba in 1961 (as it had for the CIA coup in Guatemala in 1954), sending troops to aid in the US invasion of the Dominican Republic in 1965, and intervening (with Guatemalan forces) to help defeat a reformist coup in El Salvador after the election was stolen by the military in 1972.[33]

The Alliance for Progress programs of strengthening internal security forces took a still more ominous turn in El Salvador, with the establishment of the military and paramilitary apparatus that was to be responsible for widespread slaughter in coming years. According to Allan Nairn's detailed study,[34] the US organized and trained the rural paramilitary force ORDEN, which has terrorized the countryside since, as well as the elite presidential intelligence service ANSESAL, which served as the intelligence arm of the "death squads." The founder of ORDEN and ANSESAL, General Medrano, was enlisted as a CIA agent. Described by José Napoleón Duarte as "the father of the Death Squads, the chief assassin of them all," he was awarded a silver medal by President Johnson "in recognition of exceptionally meritorious service." Medrano stated that "ORDEN and ANSESAL grew out of the State Department, the CIA, and the Green Berets during the time of Kennedy." Parallel domestic security agencies were established in Guatemala, Nicaragua, Panama, Honduras and Costa Rica and "would meet every three months under the supervision of the State Department and exchange information and methods of operation," Medrano added. This was part of a broad plan to organize a Central American intelligence effort under CIA coordination to control internal dissidence, paralleling CONDECA. Nairn reports further that according to US and Salvadoran officials, the close relations between the security forces and the US government have been sustained since, at times with some qualms, now overcome under the Reagan Administration. The US provided coordination and training (including training in terrorist and torture techniques, according to Salvadoran intelligence officers and former police agents) both in El Salvador and the US; the CIA also provided information about suspected dissidents and Salvadorans abroad, many of whom were assassinated by the "death squads" that are actually part of the military and security forces. Nairn concludes:

> U.S. complicity in the dark and brutal work of El Salvador's Death Squads is not an aberration. Rather, it represents a basic bipartisan, institutional commitment on the part of six American Administrations—a com-

mitment to guard the Salvadoran regime against the prospect that its people might organize in ways unfriendly to that regime or to the United States.

Nairn's conclusion considerably understates the case, since it isolates El Salvador from the general context of US foreign policy, which has had the same institutional commitments, with much the same effects, throughout a large part of the world, and for good reason, as we have seen. Death squads were, in fact, a natural if not inevitable outgrowth of the counterinsurgency ideology of the New Frontier, itself a concomitant of the Alliance for Progress programs of strengthening production for export at the expense of domestic consumption. It was necessary to prevent such "subversive" activities as distribution of propaganda and organizing. General William Yarborough of Kennedy's Special Forces urged that secret paramilitary groups capable of carrying out violent covert actions against the domestic opposition would be an effective mechanism to counter "subversion": "This Structure should be used to...as necessary execute paramilitary, sabotage and/or terrorist activities against known Communist proponents," he explained. A US Army handbook suggested that security forces impersonate guerrillas while carrying out terrorist actions against the population "to indicate to the people the need for protection of the village" and provide the government with a "pretext" for "population control." A Salvadoran military journal, reflecting the counterinsurgency doctrine of their US trainers, observes that

> wherever a guerrilla is found operating with success, there are still some among the people cooperating with them and providing information. What, then, must be done? You must annihilate this source of support and their sources of information.

The US applied a concept outlined for Vietnam, where the Joint Chiefs of Staff observed in a document on pacification that class conflict in villages could be effectively exploited, with the "young elite" who are "ambitious to get ahead in business, profession or politics" mobilized for "civilian counter-terrorist organization" (meaning: paramilitary terrorist organization). In Central America, the "young elites" were trained to sow terror to protect their interests, which happen to coincide with US interests. There was also a flow in the other direction, as US advisers who helped set up the terror system in Guatemala moved on to apply their skills in Vietnam. The US terror network is worldwide.

Police units were formed in Guatemala to "lend assistance, in cases of emergency, to the owners or administrators of estates, haciendas, agricultural lands, forests and rural properties...[and] observe all activity that tends to inflame passions among the peasant masses or in the rural communities and, when necessary, repress through licit means any disorder that should occur," according to a 1965 government decree; the concept of "licit means" covers quite a bit of ground under the US-backed dictatorships.

In general, the basic idea was to develop a paramilitary system working closely with the professional security forces to "lock the stable door before the danger ever arises," in the words of Truman's Secretary of War Robert Patterson in 1947. The Kennedy Administration succeeded in putting this system of state terror in place under the guise of "counterinsurgency," with gruesome consequences.[35]

The system was to be preventive, not reactive. In 1962, Kennedy's Ambassador to Guatemala, John Bell, sent to Washington a Guatemalan Internal Defense Plan which formulated "the primary objective of the US in Guatemala": "the prevention of the accession to power of Communists in Guatemala," not the needs of the suffering population. The danger of insurgency was remote, Bell held, but, the Internal Defense Plan observed, "the danger of other forms of subversion, forms which provide a base from which insurgency can develop, is real and present." Therefore the internal security apparatus must be improved, to nip any such dangers in the bud. Like the Duarte government today in El Salvador, Bell perceived the danger of allowing the left to organize politically, since such "subversion" might impede the Fifth Freedom and harm its local affiliates (see p. 96). Social reforms may be considered, but they are dangerous too. The Plan noted that better education might make people "all the more aware of the hopelessness of their status...and more susceptible to communist agitation." It is better to send helicopter gunships, which "will be of great utility in rescue operations and in other tasks in community assistance," as Ambassador Bell's successor thoughtfully explained in 1967 while the security forces with direct US military participation were in the process of slaughtering thousands of peasants.[36]

Kennedy's military and counterinsurgency adviser General Maxwell Taylor pointed out in 1965 that in Vietnam "We were too late in recognizing the extent of the subversive threat." By April 1965, when the outright US land invasion of South Vietnam took place, some 160,000 South Vietnamese had been killed, largely in US-sponsored terror operations, according to figures cited by the bitterly anti-Communist French military historian Bernard Fall, many of them "under the crushing weight of American armor, napalm, jet bombers and, finally, vomiting gases" (Fall), with some 80,000 killed by 1961 in state terror operations that had finally evoked resistance.[37] But this was not enough; we had not come to the rescue of the people we were assassinating in time or with sufficient violence. The "outstanding lesson" of this experience, Taylor explained to the police academy cadets, "is that we should never let another Vietnam-type situation arise again... We have learned the need for a strong police force and a strong police intelligence organization to assist in identifying early the symptoms of an incipient subversive situation," so that appropriate measures can be taken in time, by terror beyond that employed in South Vietnam, if necessary. Recall Kennan's strictures 15 years earlier about the necessity for "police repression by the local government" (p. 57).

The need for preemption runs through the thinking of American planners across the spectrum, and is not restricted to state terror directed against the civilian population as in the favored Kennedy model. General Nathan Twining, Chairman of the Joint Chiefs of Staff under Eisenhower, explained that tactical nuclear weapons, "if employed once or twice on the right targets, at the right time, would in my judgment, stop *current* aggression, and stop *future* subversion and limited wars before they start."[38] As examples of the "world-wide subversion" we must counter by nuclear weapons if necessary, he cited the Congo (where US intervention had helped to remove, finally assassinate, the leading nationalist figure and to install a corrupt and brutal military dictator), Cuba and Vietnam; by "aggression" he clearly meant to refer to the kind of aggression then being carried out by Vietnamese against the American invaders. One may imagine the reaction if such statements were found in a publication by the top Soviet or Libyan military commander.

5   The System Applied: Torturing El Salvador

5.1   Carter's War

Returning to El Salvador, in 1972 an election took place in which José Napoleón Duarte and Guillermo Ungo were the apparent victors, though the military candidate "won" through blatant fraud and intervention by two loyal US clients, Nicaragua and Guatemala. Interest here was slight. Duarte came to Washington but "found that no one cared much about the reign of terror and political repression in El Salvador." The press was unconcerned, and apart from Edward Kennedy and Tom Harkin, no one in Congress would even see him.[39] Another electoral fraud in 1977 also aroused little interest here. Terror, torture, starvation and semi-slave labor continued in the normal manner of US Third World dependencies. This recent history illustrates the traditional US contempt for democracy and the cynicism of the current flurry of interest in "elections" and "democracy" as a cover for state terror.

Two developments did, however, begin to cause concern by the late 1970s. The fall of Somoza in 1979 aroused fears in Washington that the brutal dictator of El Salvador might be overthrown, leading to loss of US control there as well. The second and still more threatening development was the growth of "popular organizations" in the 1970s: Bible study groups that became self-help groups under Church sponsorship, peasant organizations, unions and the like. There was a fearsome prospect that El Salvador might move towards meaningful democracy with opportunities for real popular participation in the political process. This was the "near-anarchy," memory of which still "haunts" the Christian Democrats, according to Shirley Christian, at least those she regards as meriting attention; see p. 96.

The Carter Administration reacted to these threats in El Salvador by backing a coup led by reformist military officers in October 1979, while ensuring that the most reactionary military elements retained a position of dominance. Killings rapidly increased, and by early 1980 the junta had collapsed. Left Christian Democrats, socialists and reformist officers were gone and power was firmly in the hands of the usual elements whom the US has traditionally supported in the region. "José Napoleón Duarte, however, joined the junta and, in December 1980, became its president—exercising little influence but providing the armed forces, which were slaughtering Salvadoran civilians by the tens of thousands in 1980 and 1981, with an effective public relations spokesman," the role he has continued to play since, to mounting applause in the US as the slaughter seemed to be achieving some results.[40]

By early 1980, the stage was set for outright war against the population. The Archbishop was assassinated in March; the war against the peasantry began in full force in May with major massacres, under the guise of "land reform"; the university was destroyed in June; the leadership of the political opposition was murdered in November; the independent media were terrorized and eliminated; and in general the popular organizations were crushed with large-scale killings and torture (accompanied by the silence of the US press). The threat of democracy was aborted, so that soon it became possible to contemplate "elections." Let us review these steps in Carter's war in El Salvador.

In February 1980, Archbishop Romero pleaded with President Carter not to provide the junta with military aid, which, he observed, "will surely increase injustice here and sharpen the repression that has been unleashed against the people's organizations fighting to defend their most fundamental human rights." Political power, he wrote, is "in the hands of the armed forces" who "know only how to repress the people and defend the interests of the Salvadorean oligarchy":[41]

It is beyond doubt that increasingly it is the people themselves that are becoming conscientized and organized, and thereby preparing itself to take the initiative and shoulder the responsibility for the future of El Salvador. The people's organizations are the only social force capable of resolving the crisis. It would be totally wrong and deplorable if the Salvadoran people were to be frustrated, repressed, or in any way impeded from deciding for itself the economic and political future of our country by intervention on the part of a foreign power.

But increasing the repression, destroying the people's organizations, and preventing independence were the very essence of US policy, so Carter ignored the Archbishop's plea and sent the aid, to "strengthen the army's key role in reforms"[42]—a statement that would have made Orwell cringe. The results were predictable: at this point, we enter into the system illustrated in chapter 1.

Romero's plea to Carter to refrain from destroying the popular organizations by violence was not unique. Three years later, Jaime Cardinal Sin, leader of the 42 million Catholic community of the Philippines, urged Reagan to halt military aid to the Marcos dictatorship because Filipinos were being "slaughtered and massacred" with American weapons. This plea too was ignored by the government and barely noted in the media.[43]

In March 1980, Archbishop Romero was assassinated. A judicial investigation was initiated, headed by Judge Atilio Ramírez. He accused General Medrano, the death squad organizer and US favorite, and rightwing leader Roberto d'Aubuisson of hiring the assassins, and shortly after, fled the country after death threats and an attempt on his life. In exile, Judge Ramírez reports that the Criminal Investigation Section of the National Police did not arrive until four days after the assassination and "did not provide the Court any data or evidence of an investigation into the crime." The same was true of the Office of the Attorney General. Judge Ramírez concludes that "it is undoubtedly the case that from the very beginning, they were involved in a kind of conspiracy to cover up the murder."

The security forces were not entirely inactive, however. They did raid the Legal Aid Office of the Archbishopric, removing all files bearing on the assassination, including testimony implicating the military. None of this evidence has surfaced, and neither the US government nor the press seems much interested. The Director of the Church Legal Aid Office also fled the country after death threats and warnings that his children and wife would be killed. The offices were repeatedly raided by security forces, and human rights leaders have been harassed and murdered, also with little notice in the press here, apart from reiteration of government lies that they were "guerrillas."[44]

Former Salvadoran intelligence chief Roberto Santivanez charged that a senior officer of the *contras*, Col Ricardo Lau, was paid $120,000 for arranging the Archbishop's assassination, working directly for Roberto d'Aubuisson, and also "played a key role" in organizing and training the death squads in El Salvador and Guatemala before joining the *contras*. Lau has also been linked to political killings inside Honduras by Honduran military officials. US officials confirm that Lau, a former officer of Somoza's National Guard, served as intelligence chief for the main *contra* force, the FDN; the *Times* reported in early 1985 that "until recently" he was head of FDN counterintelligence.[45]

The Honduran military leaked a report implicating *contra* elements in the death or disappearance of some 250 people since 1980, though Honduran human rights activists suspect the involvement of Honduran security forces, which have taken to the usual practices of our Central American clients as the US presence and training expanded. Among those killed were union activists, schoolteachers and others. In September 1985, a Honduran Army officer who was a leading figure in a group of military officers who oppose US policy in Honduras was found murdered under suspicious circumstances near a *contra* zone in Honduras; Nicaraguan exiles have been accused of the murder. He had "charged that the United States was turning a blind eye to abuses in the military and in some cases perhaps even encouraging them." According to a Western diplomat, a Senate aide who knew the assassinated officer said that if he made public what he knew about the Honduran army and US policy in Honduras, "it would be deeply embarrassing to the United States."[46]

The presence of former Somozist National Guard members working with the Salvadoran security forces was also reported by Captain Ricardo Fiallos, a former Salvadoran army doctor now in exile, who testified before Congress that he had treated and examined medical records of such mercenaries.[47] Since no evidence has surfaced of Nicaraguans working with the guerrillas, it appears that the only direct Nicaraguan involvement in violence in El Salvador is under US auspices.

Santivanez also provided detailed evidence concerning the role of leading figures in the Duarte government, as well as the rightist opposition, in the state terrorism and coverup, including the killing of four American churchwomen and the assassination of the Archbishop. He also described contacts with members of the *contra* army, who supplied hit men, and with Guatemalan state terrorists, including leaders of an ultraright party that was formed with CIA assistance as part of the 1954 campaign to destroy Guatemalan democracy. These and other charges—including the charge that the chief of the Treasury Police, who had been implicated in some of the worst atrocities, was on the CIA payroll and that elements of the US government supported or acquiesced in "death squad" activity—were investigated by the Senate, which claimed to find no evidence that the US was implicated in political violence. The report, however, "does not pretend to be the final word on the subject," Washington correspondent Daniel Southerland observed, since it did not even interview Salvadorans believed to have information about death squads and largely limited itself to US government sources.[48]

Carter's war against the peasantry began in full force in May, with large-scale massacres, primarily in areas scheduled for land reform.[49] The first major massacre was at the Rio Sumpul on May 14, when thousands of peasants fled to Honduras to escape an army operation. As they were crossing the river, they were attacked by helicopters, members of ORDEN and troops. According to eyewitness testimony reported by Amnesty International and the Honduran clergy, women were tortured, nursing babies were thrown into the air for target practice, children were drowned by soldiers or decapitated or slashed to death with machetes, pieces of their bodies were thrown to dogs. Honduran soldiers drove survivors back into the hands of the Salvadoran forces. At least 600 unburied corpses were prey for dogs and buzzards while others were lost in the waters of the river, which was contaminated from the dead bodies; bodies of five children were found in a fish trap by a Honduran fisherman.[50] The massacre is not mentioned in the State Department *Country Reports on Human Rights Practices* produced by the Carter Administration and was suppressed by the media for over a year, and then only barely noted, though the facts had been reported shortly after the events in the foreign press and Church-based press in the US. This was just one example of news suppression so extreme that reporting of El Salvador was selected as "Top 'Censored' Story of 1980" by an annual media research project, not because there were no reports, but because they were so biased and inadequate.[51] As noted earlier, it was later implicitly conceded that the media suppression was deliberate (see p. 15).

With the US press silent and the public unaware, the massacre of the peasantry could continue. Peasants were the major victims of the 1980 state terror.

In June, the university was shut down after an army attack that left many killed, including the rector, and facilities looted and destroyed. The dean of the Department of Science and Humanities reports (in exile):

> The army burned complete libraries; in the law school, where we once had about 100,000 volumes, we now have only 3,000. In the first days of the occupation, the officers of the army grabbed as much of the equipment, furniture, medical supplies [as] they could, and the rest they destroyed. Whatever equipment they didn't understand,

they ruined. For example, when they found the computer machinery, they tossed bombs and destroyed all of the university's records. In the agronomic science department, they discovered infrared equipment. The officers told their troops that the students used these 'torture rooms' against policemen and the army, so they destroyed them.

Medical equipment and most of the medical library were also destroyed. The humanities building was burned to the ground. Some 30 faculty members were murdered or disappeared, according to the new rector. As the university—what is left of it—reopened four years later, the librarian observed that no public official, "including President Duarte" (the civilian figurehead for the junta at the time) "ever condemned what happened or proposed some sort of retribution."[52] Another exercise of "the army's key role in reform," in the rhetoric of the Human Rights Administration.

The commitment to destroy the national culture by violence was, of course, not an innovation of the campaign carried out under the Carter-Duarte auspices. Predecessors include the Nazis, the neo-fascist National Security States that spread through much of Latin America since the Kennedy Administration, and Pol Pot, among others.

In November the political opposition was murdered, terminating the possibility of independent political activity and thereby helping to clear the ground for what the US press would describe as "democratic elections." The killings were condemned here, and the facts were partially reported, but the strong evidence that government security forces carried out the operation was omitted or downplayed.[53]

Meanwhile, the independent media were eliminated by bombings and terror, another prerequisite for "free elections" to legitimate the client regime. The editor and a journalist of one paper were found with their bodies hacked to pieces with machetes, and the second independent paper closed after three attempts to assassinate the editor, threats to his family, occupation of the offices by armed forces, and the arrest and torture of staff members. The Church radio station was repeatedly bombed, and shortly after Reagan's election, troops occupied the Archdiocese building, destroying the radio station and ransacking the newspaper offices.[54] As a result of these actions, there is no need for censorship in El Salvador; Western moralists may rest easy, concentrating their ire on censorship in Nicaragua, under attack by the US, where nothing remotely comparable has occurred.

On October 26, 1980, Archbishop Romero's successor, Bishop Rivera y Damas, condemned the armed forces' "war of extermination and genocide against a defenseless civilian population"; a few weeks later, Duarte hailed the armed forces for "valiant service alongside the people against subversion" as he was sworn in as civilian president of the junta.[55]

Carter's war was successful. The popular organizations, dissident political forces, and the independent media were eliminated, along with some 10,000 people, many killed after hideous torture. The threat of democracy in El Salvador had been stilled.

A further effect of state terror was to drive many people to join the guerrillas, estimated at 2000 in 1979, 5000 in mid-1981, and 10,000 by 1984.[56] But this too is a victory for the US, since it shifts the struggle away from the political arena, where the US and its clients are weak, to the arena of force and violence, where they reign supreme. Furthermore, as state terror undermines the opportunities for peaceful organization and meaningful political action, its victims either submit or turn to violence themselves; and as state terror mounts they are likely to lose their popular support because they cannot defend the population and because they may be driven to adopt more brutal methods, either in self-defense or as the advocates of force gain positions of dominance in an escalating struggle that is restricted by the outside power to the military dimension. These consequences can then be exploited by the propaganda system to provide retrospective justification for the initial resort to violence that is responsible for them, in the familiar manner already discussed.

The dynamics are obvious, and undoubtedly are well-understood by US planners and propagandists, who have ample experience in these matters. The US war against South Vietnam taught clear lessons in this regard. After the 1954 Geneva Accords, the Viet Minh (later called "Viet Cong" in US propaganda) attempted to pursue the political settlement it outlined, but were blocked by US terror, which led to the killing of tens of thousands of people in the following years. "The government terrorized far more than did the revolutionary movement," Jeffrey Race observes in the major book on this period, and the Communist Party refused even to authorize violence in self-defense for several years though US-organized terrorism was decimating "the southern organization." The leading US government specialist, Douglas Pike, notes that the southern organization, the National Liberation Front, "maintained that its contest with the GVN [the US-installed regime] and the United States should be fought out at the political level and that the use of massed military might was in itself illegitimate" until forced by the US "to use counterforce to survive." Captured documents also emphasize the essential role of social programs and political organization and the need to struggle against "an enemy who is weak politically and morally but strong militarily and materially." It took years of massacre, forced population removal, ecocide and general destruction before the aggressor succeeded in shifting the struggle to the arena of sheer violence. By then, the southern organization had been virtually destroyed, along with the society that it had successfully mobilized. Peaceful political settlement and neutralization in South Vietnam, regarded as quite realistic by South Vietnamese on both sides of the conflict and bitterly opposed by the US with increasing violence, was no longer a possible option, a substantial victory for the US, as discussed earlier.[57]

The Israeli-Arab conflict provides another example. Hysteria over Palestinian terrorism knows no bounds in the US media, which, over many years, have largely suppressed the record of the persistent US-Israeli rejectionism that has been the primary barrier to a political settlement, the barbaric treatment of the indigenous population of the occupied territories in what the press calls a "benign" occupation, and the years of murderous Israeli strikes against Lebanon, many without even a pretext of "retaliation."[58]

To take another case, in Guatemala in the 1980s, the guerrillas lost popular support as a result of their inability to protect the population from the huge slaughter carried out with the aid of the US and its clients. And now we see the same pattern repeating in El Salvador. Leonel Gómez, the chief adviser to the Salvadoran Institute for Agrarian Transformation who fled in January 1981 after the assassination of the Institute's head and death squad warnings, testified before Congress that "one is very cautious about rising up against the government when one has seen bodies of people sawed in half, bodies placed alive in battery acid or bodies with every bone broken," as he had during 1980. A woman fleeing from the Guazapa mountain, where soldiers destroyed everything after years of ferocious bombardment, says: "When it began, in 1980, [the guerrillas] promised us a better life. That's what we were fighting for. It hasn't turned out that way."[59] The struggle for a better life described by Charles Clements (see chapter 1, section 1) was totally defeated, as the population was murdered or removed to squalid refugee camps, a major victory for the Carter-Reagan policies.

Despite official pretenses, few knowledgeable people could have had much doubt about the character of what T. D. Allman properly called "Matanza II," in one of the few exceptions to media obedience.[60] In public, the Carter Administration was claiming that most of the violence was perpetrated by the guerrillas, some by "right-wing extremists," and only incidentally by "some elements of El Salvador's security forces," while the government was "unable to end such abuses." Meanwhile, it was telling reporters in confidence that 90% of the killings were attributable to the government security forces (see p. 15). Ambassador White, in a confidential 1980 cable on "El Salvador, One Year After the [October 1979] Coup," stated that "Plainly put, the military have the power: no government can exist without their approval," and members of the security corps and the army "continue to hunt down and kill suspected leftist subversives," a very broad category indeed. Ray Bonner writes that confidential cables and documents partially released under the Freedom of Information Act "reveal that El Salvador's political landscape was almost indistinguishable from that before the [1979] coup: The armed forces ruled, employing the same repressive methods they had in 1932, in 1948, in 1972, in 1979." In October 1980, the director of AIFLD stated in a confidential memorandum that "Government here operates with no real popular support" and "In the past several months, Duarte and company have sided with the conservative military (perhaps because this group holds the key to power now), which has hurt their image among the population...the conservative officials who look to a military solution are very much in control." Bonner adds that "No one in Washington was telling Congress or the American people this."[61]

The meaning of all of this, to put it plainly, is that the government was wholly illegitimate, a foreign implant supported by military forces that are hardly more than mercenaries of the foreign power that is responsible for the violent attack against the population of El Salvador under the facade it had created.

5.2 Duarte's Role

José Napoleón Duarte joined the junta in March 1980 as reformist elements were eliminated at the outset of *Matanza II* and became its president in December in an effort to provide the perpetrators of the "war of extermination and genocide" with some legitimacy after the murder of four American churchwomen. He too certainly understood what was happening. He later conceded that "the masses were with the guerrillas" when he joined the junta and the US-organized war against the population began. Now, mimicking his State Department mentors, Duarte describes the guerrillas as "an invading army," another manifestation of "the international red peril." Official party documents signed by Duarte show that a few weeks before he joined the junta, the leadership of the Christian Democratic party met with the army command to protest 19 cases in which Christian Democrats had been murdered, kidnapped or jailed by government troops, demanding the removal of officers responsible. The army leaders were enraged, and Duarte "agreed on the spot to retract the letter." Two weeks later, the Christian Democrat Attorney-General Mario Zamora was murdered by a death squad, and "two weeks after that, Duarte agreed to join a junta which other Christian Democrats had abandoned days before in protest over the violence, and which included officers Duarte himself had accused in party meetings of being death-squad leaders."[62] Duarte also sided with the right-wing military leaders against Col. Adolfo Majano, the reformist officer who had led the October 1979 coup and was described by the press as "the symbol of American policy in this country." Majano, who was disliked by the Carter Administration, was finally removed from the junta in December 1980 as Duarte became president, after having been marginalized for some time, and shortly after was arrested. Majano later described Duarte as "the military's ally, who covers up human rights violations."[63]

Duarte was also well aware of the measures undertaken under his auspices to overcome the popular support for the guerrillas: for example, the reconstitution and incorporation into the civil defense forces of the 80,000-member terrorist organization ORDEN, which, as he had explained in 1977, employed "the method that was used during the Nazi system to control the people directly."[64] US officials surely understood the scale and character of the massacre they were organizing, which has now been extensively documented by human rights groups, much to the distress of the US government, which has regularly attempted to undermine such groups, and of Duarte, who has denied the existence of documented massacres and now refuses to accept reports by the Church human rights office because, he says, "these people are permanently working under the direction of [those] trying to help the subversives." He also claimed that "we use the air force only to support ground troops under fire"; yet indiscriminate air strikes against civilians are documented in grim detail by human rights organizations.[65]

Moreover, it is not only the Church human rights office that is working for the "subversives," according to this darling of the American press. He also claimed that in 1979 and 1980, a "Marxist news structure" dominated US press coverage of El Salvador; this, it will be recalled, is the period when the atrocities committed by his government were virtually suppressed. Furthermore, Duarte explained, David MacMichael, the former CIA analyst who publicly denied unsupported government claims about a weapons flow from Nicaragua to the El Salvador rebels, is "clearly a Marxist" ("there are infiltrators everywhere"), as are many of the Mothers of the Disappeared. He also claimed that killings declined after he became junta president in December 1980; in fact, they increased, as all sources agree.[66]

The unions are also "infiltrated and used at the altar of war and destabilization," Duarte announced after he sent his troops to a hospital where workers were on strike, one of 25 hospitals and clinics raided by the police in an effort to dislodge strikers; the chief government spokesman said the action was warranted on the basis of rulings by the civilian and military courts that the strike was illegal and "subversive." Duarte stated that virtually all of the strikes "are by the unions managed by the Communists" who are not interested in reasonable settlements.[67] In fact, consumer buying power has decreased over 50% during the past five years while huge sums flow abroad and the oligarchy retains or enhances its privileges, and "diplomats, political observers, and union leaders say" that the strike resurgence "reflects widespread worker dissatisfaction with the government's economic policies, which have accelerated the steady decline of the standard of living." But as Duarte has learned, it is easier, and more effective with his Northern boss, to blame it on the Communists, while sending SWAT teams to carry out a "commando raid against unarmed nurses and doctors occupying a hospital but continuing to handle emergency cases," firing the entire strike leadership of the water utility union, and otherwise providing sufficient hints to people who well recall the terror against labor unleashed a few years before by the government for which Duarte provided a fig-leaf.[68]

Not surprisingly, Duarte's regime has been harshly anti-labor. The head of the 70,000 member industrial and civil service union states that some unions continue to operate underground and union membership is static because of the murders of union activists over the past 5 years, and that there will be no justice in El Salvador "so long as the army remains unreformed." "The *muchachos* in the mountains want peace," he says, "but they cannot leave their hideouts, surrender their arms and join the political process because the death squads would exterminate them." Francisco Acosta, US-Canadian representative of The National Federation of Salvadoran Workers, reports that peasants are denied the legal right to organize and that the government raises numerous barriers to the (technically legal) organization of urban workers, making it "very difficult to legalize a union." One difficulty is that "union organizers are immediately accused of being communists," which means that they are fair game for the security forces. "Since the labor movement started to become more active in the urban areas [in 1985], there have been many kidnappings, and murders of trade unionists, but there has been no international press coverage," he adds; media outrage (and extensive coverage) is restricted to suppression of civil liberties in Nicaragua, under attack by the United States. The peasant-labor coalition Popular Democratic Unity, which backed Duarte in two elections, accuses Duarte "of foot-dragging on trials of officers accused of violent repression, on meeting with the guerrilla movement's leaders, and on improving economic conditions," Shirley Christian reports. The organization is also "in an uproar over efforts by [AIFLD] to confine it to bread-and-butter issues," thus eliminating the danger that a popular organization might permit serious participation in democratic politics on the part of the poor. Some union leaders are accused of taking payoffs from AIFLD, the government-linked AFL-CIO organization that has a miserable record of anti-labor activities throughout the world.

Acosta places much of the blame for Duarte's anti-labor policies on AIFLD.[69]

AIFLD naturally paints a different picture. The chief of its Information Services lauds the "new political freedoms" enjoyed by trade unionists who "now live in a democracy where they can voice, no matter how loudly, their discontents with both national and trade-union leadership"[70]—as they are being dragged off by Duarte's security forces.

Duarte's 1985 apologetics for the massacres conducted by the government over which he presides conform to his regular practice. After the slaughter at Rio Sumpul, Duarte stated that about 300 were killed, all of them "Communist guerrillas"—including, presumably, the infants sliced to pieces with machetes. When the army killed 20 civilians in January 1983, some after torture, Duarte claimed they had been killed in a "battle"; that they had been murdered in scattered locations was confirmed by the press and a diplomat who investigated. In the case of the massacres at Los Llanitos and the Gualsinga river (see p. 26), Duarte denied the facts or blamed the guerrillas. He promised an investigation of the Los Llanitos massacre, but neither the survivors who had been interviewed by Church investigators, nor the journalists who looked into the massacre, nor Americas Watch were ever approached. Duarte did not release the report of the alleged investigation, but claimed that it produced no evidence of military abuses. He conducted no investigation of the Gualsinga River massacre, but denounced the "terrorists" for "using the masses as shields and...to provoke, exposing these people to be killed"; "This is horrible. This is inhuman. But this is not my problem. It's the problem of the subversives' terrorist actions and they have to be responsible," not the perpetrators of the massacre against defenseless civilians. The surviving victims see it differently: "Duarte's men went after our children, and now he'll go on television to say he didn't do it," a survivor of the Los Llanitos massacre commented bitterly.[71]

No less startling was Duarte's denial that there were any bodies at El Playón and his claim that stories about this charnel house were "fabricated." This was after the press had discovered what even Elliott Abrams conceded was a "hellish place," an "infamous body dump"—though Abrams accompanied the admission with transparent falsehoods about army innocence. What reporters found in El Playón was "a macabre scene from a surrealistic canvas," a huge mass of skulls with a single bullet hole in the back, skeletons mixed in with rotting garbage (for "El Playón was a dump for garbage as well as for humans"), vultures and dogs devouring the bodies of the latest victims of the death squads. The US Embassy investigated, concluding that the scene was even more gruesome than what reporters had described. Duarte promised an investigation after his initial denials, but "several months later, when reporters discovered new pockets of skeletons at El Playón, the embassy acknowledged that there had been no investigation." There could be none, Bonner observes, for it would have led directly to the headquarters of several major military units 3 miles away, including the elite US-trained Atlacatl Battalion. The road through the body dump "was heavily patrolled by army troops and security forces," Americas Watch observed.[72]

The Salvadoran military is naturally pleased with Duarte's performance. "Duarte is the man who has been able to open the coffers of the [US] Congress, and the military realizes that," a Salvadoran political analyst observes: "They won't get rid of the goose that is laying the golden eggs. He's the democratic facade so everybody doesn't have to worry...because there's a democratic president there." Similarly, "the economic right—the extremely conservative Salvadoran private sector—...are realizing that Duarte can deliver the goods." "Strangely, for a populist politician, President Duarte brags, in full-page newspaper ads, not about what he has done for his poor supporters, but about what he has done for his arch enemies—the coffee growers." Peasants continue to be evicted by the National Guard from lands they thought they had received under the land reform, a story that "is a common one in El Salvador." The London *Economist* notes renewed threats by death squads that people at the university leave the country or be assassinated, "a reminder that the right-wing terror machine is still in running order"; the death squads are still committing murders, "though on a smaller scale," while Duarte's government has not yet convicted anyone "for the tens of thousands of murders committed since 1979 by military-manned death squads." Duarte has blamed the legislative assembly, which he now controls, but "he has noticeably shifted to the right, reassuring the army and the businessmen that his aims are really the same as theirs." The director of the National Association of Private Enterprise says: "The man has been politically educated." The army too "has come to appreciate the president's skill, both as a tactician who can use peace talks to outmanoeuvre the guerrillas [not to lead to the peace for which the population yearns] and as a salesman in Washington."[73]

The official line in the US, repeated as fact in news reports as well as editorial comment, is that Duarte is a reformer thwarted by the military—that is, by the forces that he lauds for their "valiant service" in carrying out massacres and torture among the mass of the population, who "were with the guerrillas" when the exercise began under his auspices (in his words, pp. 106-7, 109). Defects in the Salvadoran judicial system "appear to outweigh Mr. Duarte's good intentions," James LeMoyne reports, so that his commission cannot proceed with investigation and prosecution of those responsible for the Las Hojas massacre in February 1983, when soldiers murdered 74 Indians in their usual style; the basic facts of the massacre are uncontested.[74] Similar defects account for the fact that perpetrators of other murders cannot be prosecuted, even when they are well-known, or that investigations cannot proceed. To date, the planners and organizers of mass murder and state terrorism, including the murder of Americans, have not been prosecuted and retain their positions in the government.

Ritual invocation of the theme of Duarte's "bravery," "moderation" and "progressive commitments" is a staple of news reporting. "President José Napoleón Duarte has spoken bravely," *Newsday* reports, "and has attempted without much success to move effectively against the homicidal terror," for which he has voiced approval, as noted; "Duarte has had little success in restoring the rule of law" and "has thus far been unable to achieve any sustained institutional reform," or in fact, to do anything but please his friends in the business classes and military, who applaud his "education." In a rare and hence important report on rural El Salvador, Clifford Krauss discusses the village of El Carrizal, which remains today about as it was 100 years ago, with no potable water, virtually no electricity, near-universal illiteracy, little land and general suffering. "Twice in this century," he writes, "in 1932 and in 1980, some people in El Carrizal have organized for a better life. And twice, the army has responded to those stirrings in the hinterland with repression, killing dozens of civilians." Organizing in the provinces "scarred by the [1932] matanza" is virtually "hopeless," since the population is terrorized; their renewed attempts in 1980 evoked new terror, reinforcing the trauma, with 27 shot when peasants attempted to organize peacefully. From 1980 to 1983, the army returned to the village once a month, keeping their eye on things and killing five more people. But now, Krauss reports, with "a moderate government gaining the upper hand in El Salvador's civil war" and with Duarte "beginning to succeed on a national level in checking such military abuses, some 300 residents met here with elected officials to discuss, once again, forming a co-op and getting such improvements as potable water, a school and a health clinic." The result? "An army truck barrelled into the village" and "the soldiers began asking questions and taking names." That "served its purpose." "The people here are permanently terrorized," a village representative of an Indian peasant union said.[75]

As always, Krauss' characterization of the goals and achievements of the Duarte regime is unsullied by evidence, untroubled by the impressive record to the contrary, to which he adds yet another item, in self-refutation. If "progressivism" and "moderation" are conferred by presiding over one of the great episodes of mass slaughter and torture in the modern period, one hesitates to imagine what "extremism" might be. The standard practice of the press is, nevertheless, understandable. Duarte must be a moderate progressive or we would not be justified in organizing the slaughter over which he presides; therefore he is a moderate progressive as a matter of doctrinal necessity, not fact, so that the actual facts may rightly be dispatched to Orwell's useful memory hole, with the sorrowful observation that "the problems of this turbulent region defy simple explanation or quick-fix solutions" (Krauss)—and of course, with no indication that the US has played any role in all of this, apart from the tacit assumption that we are trying, vainly, to improve the lot of the villagers traumatized by the armed forces we train, supply and direct to carry out their necessary tasks.

The standard version according to editorials and news columns (the locus of the most effective editorializing, where the tacit assumptions of propaganda are regularly entrenched) consists of two contradictory propositions: (1) Duarte is a sincere reformer but his "good intentions" are foiled by the fact that he has no power; (2) our policy in El Salvador is a success because "centrist democrats... now rule" in El Salvador.[76] One can have one's choice, depending on whether the task at hand is to explain away current atrocities and coverups, or to urge that we must proceed with the use of violence to further "democracy and reform."

The evasion of US responsibility is the norm for news reporting and analysis, not only in this case. It would be comical, were the consequences not so horrifying. The highly-regarded investigative reporter Tad Szulc, discussing the turbulence of the region in 1980, criticized the idea that Castro is the source of all the trouble, as "most people in the United States" believe, even though it is true that Castro "brought us the Bay of Pigs" (in the same sense in which Solidarity brought us the military regime in Poland and Dubcek brought us the tanks in Prague). This more sophisticated observer corrects the common error: "The roots of the Caribbean problems are not entirely Cuban"; the "Soviet offensive" in the region is to blame alongside of "Cuban adventurism," as shown by the fact that the USSR rejects "the notion that the Caribbean is an American *mare nostrum*" (Mussolini's phrase in reference to the Mediterranean). The past contributions of England, Spain, France, and the Netherlands are also mentioned; the current "unanswered question is the extent to which Cuba and the Soviet Union proposes [sic] to exploit the turbulent situation." The US is merely an onlooker, blamed only for its "indifference" to the brewing problems. Others, like Krauss, comment sadly on the lack of simple explanations or easy solutions, or blame indigenous cultural or political factors; not false, but with a notable omission. The desperate need to avoid the obvious is revealed, for example, in a review of a book that attributes the problems of Central America to "a religious failure"; "This is an appealing view," which the author "skillfully and bravely elaborates," the reviewer notes. Why it takes bravery to advance a view which is "appealing" precisely because it diverts attention from the depredations of the master of the region, the reviewer does not say.[77]

As for the atrocities, at any given point they are a thing of the past, so we can put them aside, though there is a fear that "if far rightists did not gain a share of power within the democratic framework, they might return to the campaign of terror and assassination that they intermittently waged between 1980 and late 1984"; the worst atrocities were committed by the army and the government's security forces, and if they were "intermittent," one can scarcely imagine what significant atrocities might be. As for the air war, we may now concede that "the air force once appeared to make little effort to avoid hitting civilians" (to translate from Newspeak: it aimed specifically at civilian targets). But while this was true of "1983 and early 1984," now matters are much improved (though the air war has stepped up, and guerrillas, now scattered in small groups, are relatively secure from air attack). Furthermore, evidence about the air war is suspect: "much testimony condemning bombing comes from peasants who identify themselves as rebel supporters," from witnesses who "are usually highly partisan," and therefore cannot be trusted. Curiously, little eye-witness testimony about the air war comes from business circles in San Salvador or Miami. A woman in a refugee camp states that "we could not stand the bombing. We had four years of suffering." But the reporter in San Salvador "could not confirm the accounts," most surprisingly.[78]

To learn about ongoing atrocities of the air war as reported by refugees in the Church-run camps, we must turn to the alternative press, where we read testimony about how "the enemy was bombing us almost every day—like crazy men," with many casualties and much destruction.[79]

Meanwhile, unencumbered with such trivialities, we may look forward to happier days as Duarte "can be expected to progress with reforms that the conservative majority previously had blocked."[80]

Duarte's role from the beginning has been to facilitate the slaughters and repression by exploiting his image as a democratic reformer, ensuring that Congress provides the support to allow them to proceed effectively. This image, carefully crafted by the US government and the media, is based on real achievements and courage in earlier years, when there was no interest here because the military dictatorship was safely in power. Since he lent his prestige to the military regime in March 1980, the true image is a far uglier one. Duarte's term has "been a lesson in public relations skills," but little else. The murderers proceed unpunished and "there are few signs of any imaginative approaches to ending the misery" of the country; Duarte refuses negotiation and cease-fire offers despite the pleas of his own supporters, such as the centrist Popular Democratic Union, which "demanded" that he accept these offers by the political organization of the guerrillas, and despite the evident desires of much of the population, though not the military, which holds power locally, or the superpower boss running the show to which Duarte lends a cloak of legitimacy.[81]

5.3. Towards "Democracy" in El Salvador

The US-organized massacres escalated as Reagan took over. A year later, the Church reported that some 30,000 civilians had been killed and 600,000 made refugees—13% of the population—while Jeane Kirkpatrick praised the "moral quality" of the government that was carrying out the slaughter and the *New Republic* declared itself "pleasantly surprised by the development of Reagan policy" in Central America, which is "basically right"; a few months earlier, when the massacres had reached their peak of intensity and horror, the editors had given "Reagan & Co. good marks for their performance (so far) in...El Salvador," where they had overcome Carter's obsessive concern for human rights, illustrated by the slightly lower number of victims tortured and massacred during the successful campaign launched under his administration to wipe out the popular organizations. [82] The numbers of killed and refugees have doubled since, very likely.

When the country was sufficiently terrorized and any hope of independent politics was eliminated, the US ran staged elections, which are about as meaningful as elections in Poland; the farce was repeated in 1984, when elections were held in an "atmosphere of terror and despair, of macabre rumour and grisly reality," in the words of the spokesman for the British Parliamentary Human Rights Group which observed them,[83] while the US government and media exulted in this heartening display of democracy in action, as *Pravda* does under comparable circumstances.

The chief foreign correspondent of the *London Guardian*, not constrained to observe the niceties, comments that as reporters who chose to speak to voters could quickly ascertain, it was not "the hunger for democracy which made people push and shove frantically to get to the front of the voting line" and caused "the mood [to] turn close to panic as the time for shutting the polling places drew near," but rather fear of "army, police or death-squad reprisals" if they did not manage to vote. At the conservative end of the mainstream British political spectrum, Timothy Garton Ash confirmed that most people voted out of fear of reprisals or because of the heavy fine for nonvoting, while some voted in the hope "that this mysterious ritual would somehow bring them the one thing which they desire before all others: peace." He too ridicules the blind enthusiasm of Americans on the scene.[84]

The meaningless elections appear to be another troubling "inconsistency," from Ash's point of view, along with the US policy towards Nicaragua (see p. 56). The reason is that "respect for the wishes of the majority in the country...is surely the moral principle behind the Salvadoran elections"—on the assumption, not subject to question, that the Holy State is guided by moral principles, which, by some odd quirk, it systematically violates, leading to "inconsistencies."[85]

5.4 The Propaganda System Moves into High Gear

"The immediate goal of the Salvadoran army and security forces—and of the United States—in 1980 was to prevent a takeover by the leftist-led guerrillas and their allied political organizations," the latter being "much more important than the former" at the time.[86] The popular organizations—"the only social force capable of resolving the crisis" in the words of the assassinated Archbishop—were effectively eliminated by means that merit comparison to Pol Pot but are regarded here as either a great success or an unfortunate error. But the usual consequence ensued: people joined the guerrillas, who became a significant force, sure proof that the Russians are coming. The Reagan Administration attempted to demonstrate this necessary truth in its February 1981 White Paper. This was ridiculed abroad, initially accepted at home. But a strong popular opposition caused the government to back down from its moves towards expanded US intervention, fearing that it would prejudice other programs such as the planned military build-up, and segments of the media then undertook an analysis of the White Paper, quickly showing that it was based on severe misrepresentation and that the actual documents revealed virtually nothing, perhaps a trickle of arms beginning in September 1980—that is, well after Carter's *Matanza II* was underway. The documents revealed the unwillingness of the USSR and particularly Nicaragua to permit arms shipments, and chronic shortage of arms on the part of the guerrillas.[87]

The State Department conceded that the US has not intercepted "a sizable number of weapons" since February 1981; in fact, the government has provided no credible evidence of significant weapons shipments or of Nicaraguan government involvement, despite extensive surveillance. Intelligence analysts dismiss government claims as "ludicrous," and the Pentagon refuses to release documents to support official claims.[88] In July 1984, a State Department "Background Paper" was circulated to try to help the government case, though without enthusiasm, because, as the press reported, it was virtually lacking in credible evidence.[89] A senior State Department official involved in the Nicaragua program dismisses the idea that the *contras* were organized to intercept arms shipments as "ludicrous,"[90] and the rationale has generally been dropped.

The State Department *Background Paper*, which had to serve as the main source of "facts" for those who attempted to provide at least some basis for the US war against Nicaragua,[91] is largely a compilation of press reports and official statements. Its credibility is illustrated by the charge, based on a report in Rev. Moon's *Washington Times*, that Nicaragua has recruited Costa Rican leftists, training them for subversion in Costa Rica. The government of Costa Rica states that it has no evidence to support the charge, and "a senior State Department official who has read the intelligence information behind the charge said it was 'extremely weak.' 'They've taken everything that came out of the vacuum cleaner,' he said. 'It's not the sort of thing we normally go with'."[92]

Apart from press reports of little significance, the *Background Paper* relies heavily on an ex-Sandinista security official, Miguel Bolanos Hunter, who alleges that arms were transported to Salvadoran guerrillas through Mexico and Guatemala, so presumably they too should be attacked by the US in accordance with the logic of the case presented by the government and its partisans. As for the *contras*, their weapons include AK-47 rifles made in Poland and Bulgaria and Soviet-made SA-7 surface-to-air missiles, which they have acquired "by the dozens" in recent months according to a senior White House official.[93] It must be, then, that the *contras* attacking Nicaragua are agents of the international "terror network" sponsored by the Soviet Union, if we accept the logic employed by the "experts on terrorism" whose dire pronouncements dominate media discussion of this plague that threatens civilization in the modern era. The truth of the matter is that the United States is one of the leading world centers of international terrorism, perhaps the leading center, but this fact and the evidence that demonstrates it are under a strict ban and can never be permitted expression to a mass audience.[94]

Claims about "captured weapons from the Soviet bloc" should always be inspected with a skeptical eye. Consider, for example, the arms cache "discovered" in Venezuela in 1963 and presented by the US government, with the press loyally trailing along, as proof of Cuban subversion. Arthur Schlesinger described this "great cache of weapons" as "unquestionably Cuban in origin and provenance, secreted for terrorists at a point along the Caribbean coast," sure proof of the "central threat" posed by Castro to the Americas. But former CIA agent Joseph Smith, in a book written in defense of the CIA after Philip Agee's exposures had appeared, writes that the cache may have been a CIA plant inspired by Kennedy's anti-Castro crusade, including the terrorist war against Cuba (which Schlesinger does not mention, and which has largely been kept under wraps until today in the mainstream). The public relations director of the United Fruit company, while outlining the success of the company's campaign to control the press at the time of the 1954 CIA coup in Guatemala, observes that "the phony weapons ploy" was "used in Guatemala in '54" as in Vietnam through the 1960s. He also describes a plan he presented to the government of Honduras "to place some Russian weapons in the hands of dead Salvadorian soldiers [during the 1969-70 Honduras-El Salvador conflict], and then to announce the 'discovery' of these weapons to the press, with pictures, at the next news conference." "Chinese weapons would be even better," he adds.[95]

Returning to the US government case against Nicaragua, apart from the worthless July 1984 document, the weakness of the government case is illustrated by the attempt of the Kissinger Commission to demonstrate Cuban-Nicaraguan instigation of violence and terrorism; the three pages devoted to this topic in the Commission report contain no evidence of any credibility or significance, and in general, the historical sections of the report are simply an embarrassment.[96] In September 1985, in a transparent attempt to shift attention away from the World Court proceedings boycotted by the United States, the State Department issued yet another document to buttress its claims; "the report contains little information not already public about alleged Nicaraguan aid to guerrillas in other countries," the press observed. Even Shirley Christian, a fervent partisan of the government cause, could find little in it of any moment.[97]

Though presenting no evidence other than undocumented assertion in support of the government's case, this latest effort is not entirely without interest. It states that since 1981, seaborne infiltration crossing the Gulf of Fonseca has been "the primary method of infiltration." The Gulf is heavily patrolled by US military forces using the highest technology at their command, and they appear unable to intercept shipments, revealing again that we are just a "pitiful, helpless giant" at the mercy of "yellow dwarves," as Richard Nixon and Lyndon Johnson whined. The historical sections are also interesting. Thus, the year 1980 in El Salvador, just reviewed, appears here in the following guise: after the "coup led by reformist officers" (who were quickly eliminated, a fact ignored), the new junta began "a series of major social and political reforms designed to address ills which seemed to justify the violence of the antigovernment guerrillas... Disturbances by groups encouraged by the Sandinista success peaked in the spring of 1980, but by summer, as the newly united guerrilla forces began to prepare for their January offensive, the reforms began to take hold, and several strike calls received only limited support." That is the whole story; the Politburo can hardly compete in this league. The account of Nicaragua describes only how "Resistance forces began to take on importance for the broader effort to counter Sandinista 'internationalism'," and from 1983, "Armed opposition within Nicaragua, generated by the policies of the Sandinistas, continued to grow." Even granting the expectations for state propaganda, it seems to me a little odd that the press can let this performance pass, merely noting that it does not prove its case. Note that this account is one that can be checked against the historical record, a fact that a rational person will use in assessing the claims made without substantiation that constitute the government's case.

Use of the term "resistance forces," with its favorable connotations (the resistance against the Nazis, etc.), to refer to the US proxy army attacking Nicaragua from its foreign bases is a neat piece of trickery by the state disinformation machine, quickly picked up by the loyal press, which sometimes even goes so far as to intimate that Nicaraguan officials refer to the terrorist forces in this way; thus we read that "President Daniel Ortega of Nicaragua said yesterday his government suspended civil liberties last week to 'guarantee' his army's defeat of US-backed resistance forces," and that "he said, however, that defeat of the resistance forces could create an even more 'dangerous situation'" by prompting US invasion.[98]

Government claims rest primarily on alleged material evidence that is classified, not a very credible tale. It may be noted that with far more meager resources, Nicaragua has no problem providing ample material evidence of US supply to the *contras* fighting within Nicaragua, evidence which for some reason they are not compelled to keep classified; and of course the support, direction and training in the foreign bases from which the attacks on Nicaragua are launched is not in question.

On Nicaragua's alleged military threat, government propaganda is entirely without credibility—indeed, barely rises to the level of absurdity—unless, of course, we adopt the assumption that it is illegitimate for a country to defend itself against attack by the US and its proxies. The fact that the topic is even discussed in a serious voice is a great tribute to the efficacy of the propaganda system. As for the claims about Nicaraguan military might, before which we must quake in terror, discussion of the military balance in Central America is nonsensical to begin with, since the US would react massively in the case of any Nicaraguan aggression— or to be more accurate, the US would welcome any act that could be interpreted as aggression with unrestrained joy, since at last the long-yearned for invasion could then be undertaken. But even if we enter this arena of state propaganda, the fevered rhetoric about Nicaraguan regional predominance is easily shown to be a carefully-contrived fraud.

Furthermore, the evidence now available indicates that Nicaragua began to acquire such military resources as it has after the *contra* attacks began. According to senior officials at the Pentagon, Nicaragua acquired its first Soviet-made tanks in mid-1981: "Until then, another Defense Department official said, they had been receiving 'small arms and light artillery, mostly'." FDN spokesman Bosco Matamoros stated "that armed rebels began attacks in 1980," which is "when Sandinista officials began complaining of attacks." They also date their "training and assistance from the Argentine military" to 1980. Rand Corporation specialist Brian Jenkins, discussing "indirect forms of warfare," observes that "Argentina acted as a proxy for the United States in Central America," referring to Argentina under the neo-Nazi generals during the period when congressional human rights restrictions were hampering direct US engagement in state terrorism. The formation of a "large citizen militia" in Nicaragua was announced in February 1981.[99] Salvadoran aid to the *contras* may have begun in 1979 (see p. 128).

The US claims to have authorized CIA aid for the *contras* in late 1981, allowing apologists for US atrocities to maintain that the Sandinista military build-up began prior to US operations, proof of Sandinista aggressive intent.[100] This is transparent deceit, as the actual record shows, quite apart from the question of how Nicaragua is to succeed in its aggression under the US shadow. Violent intervention in the region remains primarily the monopoly of the US, as in the past.

5.5 The War Moves into High Gear

Returning to El Salvador, with the popular organizations effectively demolished, the war shifted to direct attacks against the civilian population in guerrilla-controlled areas, including ground sweeps and massacres by US-trained elite units and an expanded air war. In March 1984, it was revealed publicly that US planes were rapidly increasing reconnaisance to provide intelligence for what the government and the press call "military operations." At about the same time, the rare reports on the air war observed that "bombing attacks have become much more accurate in recent weeks," quoting refugees who say: "They used to bomb and it wouldn't land near to the houses, but now they have something to detect exactly where we are" so "no one is safe in their homes, no one is safe anywhere." The reference is not to military operations but rather to what refugees call "indiscriminate" bombing raids that have turned villages into ghost towns where every structure has been hit, people cannot cook or hang laundry or they will become targets for air strikes, and the remnants who have not fled spend much of their time hiding in holes in the ground to escape the unremitting air attacks that have killed many civilians. Refugees also report the use of incendiary bombs against the civilian population, either napalm or white phosphorus according to a European doctor who inspected the wounds of victims; soldiers from the Atlacatl Battalion say that incendiary weapons are used before their operations and that "they have seen villages burned to

the ground and large tracts of land charred by incendiary bombs."
Refugees report many killed and villages and land destroyed by the
incendiary bombing, along with the recently-acquired antiperson-
nel fragmentation bombs. Use of napalm was subsequently confirmed by Dr. John Constable of Massachusetts General Hospital,
a specialist on burn victims with Vietnam war experience.
Congressman James Oberstar reports that he was informed by air
force commander Col. Rafael Bustillo that napalm bought from
Israel had been used until 1981.[101]

Military sources in the capital confirm that "improved intelligence" derived from US reconnaissance is responsible for the fact
that bombing attacks have become much more accurate. Relief
officials and Church sources report that the result, not surprisingly,
has been to increase civilian deaths from the bombardment.[102] The
correlation between US-supplied "improved intelligence" and the
increased kill-rate, including direct attacks on defenseless peasants, received little notice in the press. When noted, the reader was
offered two interpretations. The "news" columns, keeping to their
fabled objectivity, reported that "U.S. help has not enabled the Air
Force to avoid hitting civilians, according to human rights
activists." The second and rather different interpretation was the
one provided by the activists themselves: the Director of the
Church Human Rights office reports a sharp increase in civilian
fatalities, not guerrillas, but "children, women, old people," as US
reconnaissance improved bombing accuracy, and "suggested that
the Air Force was deliberately aiming at civilians who are suspected of helping the rebels." The refugee reports leave little doubt
that this is so, as it has always been so. It takes quite an act of faith
to take seriously the pretense that the US government is trying to
reduce civilian casualties, but has unaccountably "not enabled"
the Salvadoran Air Force to achieve this worthy end.[103]

The improved kill-rate extends to those trapped in military
operations by soldiers flown in by helicopter after receiving
surveillance information, as in the case of the August 30, 1984
massacre by the Atlacatl Battalion at Las Vueltas, "in which
several dozen civilians who were unable to escape military
encirclement died."[104]

Hedges observes that the Salvadoran Air Force had been
accused of using incendiary bombs a year earlier, and that the
reports were investigated by the president of the Salvadoran
Commission on Human Rights, Marianella Garcia Villas, who
collected tape-recorded testimony from victims, photographs and
soil samples. She was killed leaving the zone, by soldiers of the
Atlacatl Battalion according to people who accompanied her. Her
death was reported. The press reproduced government allegations
that she was a guerrilla, while the British human rights publication
Index on Censorship, in contrast, described her as "one of Latin

America's best-known human rights workers, highly respected internationally for her testimony" before UN and British Parliament human rights groups. A documentary film concerning her was broadcast in Europe, refused by US Public TV. It describes her early work as one of the founders of the Christian Democratic Party, her human rights work including the grisly chore of identifying bodies of victims of state terror, and her murder, which apparently did not violate "the traditional rule of chivalry" (see p. 23), to judge by the press.[105]

The Salvadoran air force also employed some novel tactics, such as bombing sites where people had gathered to receive Red Cross assistance, a practice terminated by US authorities after protest here—a clear demonstration of their complicity in the ongoing atrocities.[106] The destruction and devastation have been documented by human rights groups, but generally ignored by the media. See chapter 1, for a brief sample.

5.6 Reaction at Home: Successful Terror and Its Rewards

Let us now consider the controversy over Central America in the United States. During the 1980-81 attack against the population of El Salvador, the US client government had not even a semblance of legitimacy, and the elections staged for the benefit of the American audience after the elimination of any possible basis for democratic participation evidently changed the situation in no relevant way. Accordingly, the US has been engaged in the illegitimate use of force and serious crimes in El Salvador. This question, however, has barely been discussed here, just as there was virtually no discussion of US intervention in South Vietnam during the comparable period: 1954-1965.

Furthermore, there is virtually no debate now within the mainstream media and journals over the legitimacy of this continuing attack, which is destroying much of the country and its people. Rather, debate is strictly limited to the bounds established by the state propaganda system. Within the spectrum of respectable opinion—that which can reach any popular audience—it is permitted to discuss the legitimacy of US actions in Nicaragua; indeed, that is encouraged, since it deflects attention from the main issue. But the US war in El Salvador is excluded from discussion by the state propaganda system and is therefore off the agenda.

In fact, editorial opinion and commentary in journals quite generally lauds the wonderful progress in El Salvador, "the one region in Central America in which United States policies clearly have been successful" as the US backed "the forces of moderation," upgrading the Salvadoran Army and turning it into "a well-honed and aggressive fighting force," fully capable of the actions documented (occasionally) in the news columns and far more fully elsewhere; "So long as El Salvador continues to move forward, as it has done under Duarte, US support should remain steadfast."[107]

There is "good news from El Salvador," where "the ideal of a third force has been instilled with new life" as the army has much improved its conduct with American aid and the country is marching towards democracy and social reform under Duarte, who "is the product of an urban middle class committed to civil liberties and the economic blandishments of an open society" and is helped by "an enlightened echelon of the Salvadoran Army."[108] "He is independent-minded" and does not accept Reagan's policies, and "has begun to deliver to his battered, divided people a taste of better government, a ray of hope," though with "aficionados of violence" lurking "on both the left and the right," he may not be able to manage the "reform programs" to which he is committed.[109]

The lesson is that if terror and violence appear to be successful, and the threat to the Fifth Freedom abates, then all is well and we can return to our historical project of improving the lives of the people of Central America, those who count.

As for Nicaragua, as long as the US attack is not successful, there are "holes in the Administration's case," we learn from the *New York Times*, but these are only "practical," while the "moral argument is more compelling": "The Administration needs a strategy that is not only moral and legal but also persuasively wise," that is, successful in its aims, which are necessarily good. If the US "loses the contra option," the editors of the *Washington Post* explain, it may not be able to "ensure the progress of the democratic enterprise in Nicaragua" to which the US has always been committed—by definition, independently of any facts. Turning to the *New Republic*, we discover that the pragmatic liberal, as always, has nothing but scorn for those who are "opposed in principle, for reasons of international morality, to the exercise of military pressure against the Nicaraguan government" (though naturally we maintain this principled stand with regard to official enemies, and profess great indignation if they adopt the stance recommended here), and we must therefore continue to use military force "to push the Sandinistas, to force them to do what they promised to do when they took power in July 1979: establish a pluralist political system, a mixed economy, and a non-aligned foreign policy"—exactly our goals, as a century of involvement in Nicaraguan affairs clearly demonstrates to the faithful.[110]

The record of atrocities in Nicaragua and El Salvador is considered of little moment among sophisticated commentators. British journalist Timothy Garton Ash writes in the *New York Review of Books* that "During a month's stay in El Salvador and Nicaragua I nonetheless found—to my surprise—one or two good reasons for Western Europe's moral questioning." These reasons are rather abstract, having to do with the principle of non-interference in "the sovereignty and self-determination of weaker nations," and the "inconsistency" he perceives in elections conducted "out of respect for the wishes of the majority" in which largely illiterate peasants are forced to vote and in US policy towards Nicaragua—"inconsistencies" that arise only on condition of abandonment of rationality and naive faith in the official doctrine, as already discussed. Surely this skeptical and very knowledgeable conservative correspondent was aware before his visit of the tens of thousands of tortured and mutilated victims, the terror of the air war, the physical destruction of the political opposition and the media, and so on; but these did not provide any reason for "moral questioning" then, nor do they afterwards. Evidently the moral level in these cultivated British circles has changed little since the days when Winston Churchill, then Secretary of State at the War Office, expressed his attitude towards the use of poison gas in 1919, shortly after the furor over its use by the Germans, a major war crime: "I do not understand this squeamishness about the use of gas... I am strongly in favour of using poisoned gas against uncivilised tribes"—namely, against tribesmen in Mesopotamia and Afghanistan, and against Bolsheviks in Russia during the 1919 intervention, when the first use of chemical weapons in air warfare was considered by the British GHQ to be the primary factor in early military successes.[111]

In short, what has been done to El Salvador and Nicaragua is taken to be the prerogative of the US—or as a knowledgeable cynic might say, its historical vocation.

The debate in mainstream circles, as noted, is contained strictly within the framework established by the state propaganda system: Is Nicaragua offering assistance to guerrillas in El Salvador—that is, in the real world, to people defending themselves from American terror? The US government claims that it is, and is thus engaged in "armed attack" against El Salvador, which entitles the US to respond in "collective self-defense." Critics note that the evidence is unconvincing, and therefore question whether Nicaragua is guilty of such an armed attack. But the major issue, clearly, is the American attack against much of the population of El Salvador, and this issue is excluded from the framework of debate set by the state and accepted by the critics. Even the US peace movement is in part guilty of this moral crime: the "pledge of resistance," under which many people have been arrested for civil disobedience, refers to aggressive acts against Nicaragua, not to the far more horrifying crimes in El Salvador. Similarly, in the 1960s, the debate focused primarily on the bombing of the North, murderous and destructive but not on the scale of the war against South Vietnam. In both cases, the right of the US to attack and destroy is tacitly conceded, as long as there are no threatening international complications, a fact that reveals a good deal about the power of the state propaganda system to set the terms of discussion, and about the principles that guide critics within the mainstream, and sometimes even beyond.

What is more, it would be quite legitimate to provide military aid to people attempting to defend themselves against the depredations of a violent superpower, whether in El Salvador, South Vietnam, Afghanistan or elsewhere. If properly intimidated, a government may not do so, but that is another matter. T. D. Allman describes how an old man, after telling a harrowing tale of government atrocities and violence in a Salvadoran town, asked about a place called "Cuba" somewhere beyond the seas where, he had heard, there were people who might provide the suffering population with aid. He asked "how we might contact these Cubans, to inform them of our need, so that they might help us?"[112] Few Americans seem able to comprehend the meaning of this plea, though it would arouse great anguish if uttered by a victim of some official enemy.

In this case as in others, the formidable power and successes of our system of "brainwashing under freedom" are rarely appreciated.

6 Torturing Nicaragua

6.1 Before the Crisis

Let us turn now to the US proxy war against Nicaragua, briefly recalling some relevant history. The first major US armed attack against Nicaragua was in 1854, when the US Navy burned down the town of San Juan del Norte to avenge an alleged insult to American officials and the millionaire Cornelius Vanderbilt; the press reviewed the town's history when it was briefly conquered by *contras* in April 1984, omitting this incident.[113] A year later, the US recognized the puppet government established by the American adventurer William Walker, though conflict among US business interests (he was strongly opposed by Vanderbilt) led to withdrawal of support. The Marines landed in 1909 in support of a US-British-inspired revolution, "ushering in twenty-five years of chaos" (Booth), and from 1912 to 1933, the country was under US military occupation (apart from one year), leading to the murder of the nationalist leader Sandino and the establishment of the Somoza dictatorship after a brutal counterinsurgency campaign. Little concern was voiced here as he robbed and tortured, employing the US-trained National Guard to control the captive population, which was reduced to misery. By 1978-9, even the natural American allies, the business classes, had turned against Somoza because of his power madness and corruption and joined the FSLN rebellion. A letter from President Carter congratulating Somoza for human rights gestures was a factor precipitating the dramatic takeover of the National Palace by Edén Pastora in August 1978. Carter supported Somoza virtually to the end of his bloody rule, with Israel taking over the main burden at the end—surely with tacit US approval despite official denials—when direct US intervention was blocked by congressional human rights legislation. When all hope of maintaining Somoza was lost, the US attempted to ensure that the National Guard would remain intact and the FSLN excluded from the government, a solution that the guerrillas accurately characterized as "*somocismo* without Somoza." Some 40-50,000 people were killed and the society was reduced to ruins, devastated and bankrupt.[114]

With the failure of its attempt to maintain the basic structure of the terrorist regime, the US government, along with articulate opinion, became passionately concerned over repression and democracy in Nicaragua. In a less-indoctrinated society than ours, this sudden conversion would be dismissed with the contempt it so richly merits.

Carter proposed an "aid" package, largely credits to purchase US goods, for the country that had been left in ruins after a century of torture by the US and its clients. Much of the aid was to go to the private business sector; conditions were added barring the use of aid in facilities with Cuban personnel, who were involved in literacy and other social programs. Considerable support for the aid program came from banks, which feared default on the huge debt now that the country had been bankrupted. The new government agreed to pay the debt accumulated by Somoza, who had robbed the country blind and fled with its remaining assets.[115] This last-ditch effort to pay off US banks, to preserve the traditional Central American order, and to prevent the new government from shifting its meager resources to the needs of the disadvantaged is now described as a proof of US magnanimity and its desire for friendly relations with the new regime.

6.2 The Proxy War

Under Reagan, the US turned to a direct attack against Nicaragua. The Sandinista government, departing from historical precedents (for example, France in 1944, under US civil-military control, where tens of thousands were killed in a few months), had not carried out large-scale execution of collaborators or National Guard torturers and murderers. These elements began to reorganize on the Honduran border under the direction of Somozist officers, with assistance from Argentine neo-Nazis by 1980, and US supervision from 1981. Nicaraguan exiles and Salvadoran army officers trace Salvadoran aid to the exiled Somozists to 1979, shortly after the fall of Somoza. Salvadoran pilots bomb Nicaragua under CIA control from their sanctuaries in Honduras and El Salvador, and according to US officials in Central America, fly as many as a dozen sorties a week from El Salvador deep into Nicaragua to supply *contra* forces.[116] With CIA assistance, arms were smuggled from the US center for international terrorism in Miami, where the FDN leadership operates. CIA helicopters with American pilots provided air cover for commando raids, Ecuadoran frogmen were sent from CIA speedboats to blow up bridges, CIA transport planes dropped supplies to guerrillas deep inside Nicaragua, and a CIA "mother ship" launched seaborne commando raids to mine harbors. The *Miami Herald* reports that a secret US Army helicopter unit, a task force of the 101st Airborne Division operating out of Kentucky, is carrying out missions inside Nicaragua, with 17 fatalities in 1983 (35 casualties were reported by the entire US Army that year).[117] The early goal was "not to topple the Sandinistas by force but to push them into increased domestic repression and to spend scarce currency on military rather than social programs. That, in turn, would increase domestic opposition and quicken their downfall." Despite official denials, "most of the men running the war," including CIA director William Casey, "agreed that the goal was to topple the regime," according to senior government officials.[118]

As noted earlier, the goal from the start, apart from public relations exercises, was to overthrow the government of Nicaragua, as is now virtually conceded, or at least to sow enough terror and destruction to avert the danger that the "virus" of successful development might "infect" the region. The director of medical affairs for the New York State Department of Health, visiting in 1985, reviews the deleterious impact of US military and economic actions on health care, education, and food production, devoted to the poor for the first time in history, observing that we are "slowly strangling a poor people" who are "struggling for a better life" and "who should find it difficult to comprehend that they are alleged to be a threat to the Giant of the North."[119] Until American citizens come to understand exactly why these poor people are such a threat, and resolve to do something about state terrorism guided by respect for the Fifth Freedom, the story will continue, here and elsewhere.

The methods undoubtedly work. In a report on Central America, Oxfam America describes the terrible conditions of nutrition and health for most of the population in Guatemala, El Salvador, Honduras and Nicaragua, observing that "Among the four countries in the region where Oxfam America works [namely, these four], only in Nicaragua has a substantial effort been made to address inequities in land ownership and to extend health, educational, and agricultural services to poor peasant families. But the *contra* war has slowed the pace of social reform and compounded hunger in the northern countryside."[120] The report describes the effective agrarian reform in Nicaragua, contrasting it with the paper reform in El Salvador which "has not been carried out" and "was not intended to benefit the rural poor who had no access to land" in the first place. The US war against Nicaragua has, however, largely overcome these unique successes in Nicaragua, exactly as it was intended to do. The report describes how farmers have been forced to abandon their land because of *contra* attacks, which have severely impaired food production, as intended. Peggy Healy, a Maryknoll sister and member of Oxfam America's board of directors who has lived in Nicaragua for 10 years, comments:

> If you talk to *campesinos* in the war zones—whether they are for the Sandinistas or against the Sandinistas—and you try to pinpoint when their real problems started, inevitably you will find that those problems started when the *contras* came in. Before that, the peasants had teachers for their schools, they had low prices, and although they weren't wealthy, they had land, credit, fertilizer, they owned machetes. They had what they needed to live.

Naturally the US will do nothing to bring about desperately needed reforms in the areas under its control (apart from gestures for propaganda purposes when trouble is brewing); indeed, these would be contrary to the "national interest" for reasons already discussed. But the US can at least ensure that they will not take place elsewhere.

When Nicaragua suspended civil liberties in October 1985, the *Times* editors proclaimed in mock indignation that "There is no reason to swallow President Ortega's claim that the crackdown is the fault of the 'brutal aggression by North America and its internal allies.' A more likely explanation is an eruption of discontent over a crumbling economy and military conscription."[121] The editors presumably hope that their readers will be too stupid to draw the connection between the US aggression and the crumbling economy and military conscription. More significant is their barely concealed delight in this further success of the terrorist war they have long supported, which of course has, from the start, had as its essential aims to create an "eruption of discontent" as the society reels under imperial attack and to strengthen elements in the leadership that will demand harsher measures to mobilize resistance to it, providing the opportunity for *Times* editors and other hypocrites to pontificate about this predictable and intended consequence of the violence they advocate.

When direct CIA supervision of the US proxy army was terminated by Congress, the Reagan Administration secretly transferred control to the National Security Council. This was essential, since "the C.I.A. had managed almost every aspect of their activities" and "when left to their own devices, the rebels 'couldn't manage themselves very well,' a senior official said." "When the agency [CIA] was pulled out of this program, these guys didn't know how to buy a Band-Aid," according to the government official in charge, later identified as Marine Lt.-Col. Oliver North. The extent of CIA control has been detailed by former *contra* leader Edgar Chamorro, who describes the FDN as a "front organization" for the CIA. After the mining of harbors, for example, he was given a press release to read taking credit for the mining in the name of the FDN, who "of course" had no role in the mining carried out by CIA Latin American agents. He describes how every detail of the FDN operations, including propaganda, was stage-managed by the CIA. Chamorro also described the nature of US assistance, for example, advising the *contras* of "the precise locations of all Nicaraguan military units." Citing this testimony to the World Court, Anthony Lewis notes that new legislation introduced by Democrat Dave McMurdy permits "provision of intelligence information or advice to the contras," another congressional contribution to the war against Nicaragua.[122]

A letter by Chamorro to Congress was distributed by House Speaker O'Neill before the vote to provide renewed military aid in June 1985; in it, Chamorro described the FDN as an antidemocratic CIA front and opposed granting it "humanitarian" aid. The former spokesman for the FDN stated that it "is in the hands of the ex-National Guard who control the contra army, stifle internal dissent, and intimidate or murder those who dare to oppose them," and that it "has been subject to excessive manipulation" by the CIA. The letter had no effect.[123]

We also learn a good deal about the status of the "freedom fighters" by considering the fate of Edén Pastora, who was ditched by the Northern boss because he refused to subordinate himself sufficiently to US goals. Pastora was the only leading figure among the *contras* who could claim any popular support, apart from the business classes. His forces quickly collapsed and virtually disappeared when CIA control and assistance were terminated. "Since refusing to follow US demands," the press reports, "Pastora has been cut off from all CIA funds and from most funding by wealthy conservative individuals. The military situation of the troops he controls has deteriorated correspondingly." "The general skeptical response [to Pastora] from former comrades...and from the Central American public...was perhaps best illustrated by a remark of his older brother, Felix, who belongs to a different contra faction in Costa Rica...: 'If you people want to find my brother, go look for him in the bathroom of his house....He wants to cover up his failures with lies'." With financing from the

US government and the private corporations to whom the CIA had directed him at an end, Pastora was compelled to search for funds from Cuban exiles in Miami, the fascist murderer d'Aubuisson in El Salvador, and others like them.[124]

One might usefully compare the fate of Pastora's forces with that of the Salvadoran guerrillas, facing vastly greater military force and never enjoying a fraction of the foreign support provided to Pastora, but nevertheless surviving within El Salvador, where they originated and remain. It is difficult to avoid the conclusion that the most popular figure among the *contra* leadership was unable to mobilize significant popular support within Nicaragua.

Pastora is praised across the political spectrum in the US as the authentic "freedom fighter" and "democrat" whom we must support. If his credentials are as solid as alleged, then his fate stands as a further indictment of US policy, which is revealed as unable to tolerate a democratic alternative to the Somozist-led FDN. Whatever the truth of these claims, they have no bearing on the issue of US military aid for the attacks launched from Pastora's Costa Rican bases; it is not proposed that we support honest democrats in military attacks against far more terrible governments.

Though the issue is not strictly relevant here, it might be noted that the widespread acclaim for Pastora is difficult to assess because it has not been accompanied by an exposition of what he stands for. One exception is the "extensive statement" by Pastora published "with great pride" by the rightwing *Journal of Contemporary Studies*, which describes it as, "To our knowledge, the first time this great Central American patriot's outlook has been directly communicated, in detail, to our part of the hemisphere." Here, Pastora expresses his willingness to join with the FDN, but not as a subordinate, and expresses his support for what he calls the "democratic opposition" within Nicaragua, namely, the pro-*contra* journal *La Prensa* and COSEP, the Higher Council for Private Enterprise, representing business interests. He criticizes the Sandinistas for failing to understand the seriousness of warnings from Under-Secretary of State for Latin American Affairs Thomas Enders—"the Empire *was* speaking," he observes, but the Sandinista leadership did not appreciate the fact. He opposes the "Cubanization" of the Sandinista revolution, "dragging Nicaragua into an East-West confrontation," and describes his group as "democrats," as "genuine followers of Sandino." That is the extent of his presentation of his position. His most interesting claim is that he and his group were alone responsible for the mining of the harbors, a CIA operation according to every serious source, including US officials involved in these matters, the CIA, etc.[125] The claim does little to enhance Pastora's credibility. The editors, however, accept it as a certain truth, blaming misreporting in the US for the belief that the CIA was responsible, perhaps the same "disinformation specialists in Managua," noted for their efficient control over the US press, who are responsible for the belief in Pastora's "supposed withdrawal from the struggle."[126] All this gives us some insight into the irrationality and paranoia of so-called "conservative" thought, but leaves us little better informed about Pastora.

The CIA estimated that the FDN received about $20 million in private and foreign contributions in the preceding year, some of it from tax-exempt private US groups such as the US Council for World Freedom headed by retired General John Singlaub. This organization received approval by the Administration for its tax-exempt status, though the IRS had described its request as having "no precedent," after pledging that they would not "ever contemplate providing materiel or funds to any revolutionary, counter-revolutionary or liberation movement." Singlaub describes congressman Edward Boland (author of the Boland amendment, which barred US aid for the—strictly illegal—purpose of overthrowing the Nicaraguan government) as one of the "hard-core, leftwing" congressmen who "have always supported the communist organizations around the world." He claims to have raised "tens of millions of dollars" for arms and ammunition for the *contras*. His organization was founded with an interest-free loan from the World Anti-Communist League, which the Anti-Defamation League of B'nai Brith had once called "a gathering place for extremists and anti-Semites." According to US sources, Israel supplied the *contras* with several million dollars of aid, apparently through a South American intermediary, aid which may be repaid through the huge US subsidy to Israel, which is guaranteed a free ride through Congress.[127]

As elsewhere in the world, the US has many ways to finance and organize terror and subversion.

Participation in the war by US mercenaries has also been reported. John Gerassi interviewed captured *contra* soldiers in Nicaragua, who informed him that their chiefs were Cuban exiles. One had Puerto Rican identification papers. He estimates that there are some 5000 foreigners, mostly Cuban exiles from Miami, among the *contra* forces, and cites reports that documents found among the dead left after an attack from Costa Rica by Pastora's forces identified some as Guatemalan, Panamanian, Cuban exiles and Puerto Rican.[128]

The Israeli press reports that Israeli mercenaries are receiving salaries of $10,000 a month for service with the *contras*, and that *contra* spokesman Edgar Chamorro, before he defected, "on many occasions in the past expressed...his high regard for the contribution of Israelis to helping the *contras*."[129]

US mercenaries also serve with the Salvadoran state terrorists. A former US Marine employed as a mercenary in El Salvador dismisses the news reports, which falsely describe a war against guerrillas, whereas the reality is the "beautiful technique" of "murdering the civilians who side with them." "By terrorizing civilians, the army is crushing the rebellion without the need to directly confront the guerrillas... Kill the sympathizers and you win the war." Massacres of civilians are not scattered human rights abuses, he reports, but rather "the game plan": "The murders are not a peripheral matter to be cleaned up while the war continues, but rather, the essential strategy," and a successful one, he plausibly argues.[130] The regular Americas Watch reports yield the same conclusion, and the careful reader can discern it through the haze of press reporting.

It should be stressed, however, that reference to US and other foreign mercenaries is misleading, since even the indigenous terrorists in Central America are essentially US mercenaries, much like the native forces used to hold down the domestic population by the British, French, Russians, South African whites, and others in the past, or the forces organized by the US in South Vietnam and Laos. The elite units that carry out successful massacres in El Salvador, mass murderers such as Ríos Montt (who studied at Fort Bragg in North Carolina and served as director of studies for the Inter-American Defense College in Washington[131]), and numerous other state terrorists in Latin America and elsewhere receive their training from the United States, which also provides the means for them to carry out the lessons they have learned.

The *contra* armies can hardly be called "guerrillas," considering their origin as mercenaries organized by the US and its proxies in Honduras and their lavish support and equipment, comparable to the best-armed regular military forces in Central America.[132] They are surely the only "guerrillas" in history who complain that their air force is inadequate, or that they lost their only helicopter (the latter was Edén Pastora's problem when his helicopter crashed 30 miles inside Costa Rica, followed by claims that he had disappeared within Nicaragua; this was the event that elicited the comment from his brother, cited above, p. 131). Regular commentary by their masters, some already cited, makes it clear that the *contras* are incapable of functioning without continual direction. Their own leadership, as noted, recognizes that they are the creation of the US government, and its agents. Their actual leadership, apart from US intelligence, is overwhelmingly drawn from Somoza's National Guard, including the supreme FDN military commander and the heads of logistics, intelligence, training, operations, special forces and most of the largest combat units, and many company commanders. Several influential civilian officials were large landowners who backed the Somozas. Given their tradition and the source of their current support, it is not surprising that these forces have been engaged in ruthless terror and massacre. Early on, American Catholic missionaries reported that they were "torturing and mutilating captured peasants or Sandinista sympathizers, creating the same terror as in the past" when they were trained by the US Army.[133] The subsequent record, unearthed in part by human rights groups but largely ignored by the US journalists in Nicaragua, demonstrates the accuracy of these observations made on the scene. The US violation of international law and its responsibility for war crimes seem obvious enough.

The US government and commentators here like to speak of the "symmetry" between El Salvador and Nicaragua; in both countries, it is alleged, indigenous guerrillas with foreign support are rebelling against the government. The comparison would have some merit if the guerrillas in El Salvador lacked any domestic base, having been organized in Nicaragua by the KGB for the purpose of sowing terror in El Salvador and overthrowing its government; were launching murderous attacks against civilians in El Salvador from Nicaraguan and Cuban sanctuaries, killing, torturing and mutilating their victims; were led by thugs who had ruled El Salvador by violence for 50 years with Soviet support and had finally been driven out by an uprising of virtually the entire population; and were armed, trained and controlled by Soviet military forces in a major Nicaraguan military base while the USSR maintains large naval units offshore, carries out overflights of El Salvador to supply the guerrillas and for military operations, uses Cubans and Bulgarians to fly arms to guerrillas and to carry out major sabotage and terror operations which are attributed to the Soviet proxy army operating from its foreign bases, etc. All of this is, of course, utter nonsense. The fact that the "symmetry" can be discussed without eliciting ridicule is another tribute to the efficacy of "brainwashing under freedom."

In fact, there is a "symmetry," but not one discussed in the press. In both cases, terrorist forces are carrying out large-scale torture and massacre and in both cases these terrorist forces (the army of El Salvador, the *contras*) are organized and controlled by the lord and master of the region.

US reporters who visited *contra* camps report that they "appear to be an exclusively military force with almost no political direction other than the goal of overthrowing the Sandinistas." In this respect, they reflect the commitments of their masters, apart from rhetoric provided by domestic apologists for state terror. Their political leadership explains that "We don't need to have our own political organization," because they can "rely on [the] work" of the domestic political opposition,[134] largely business and landowner-based and hence by definition "democratic" and "moderate" in US political terminology. This domestic Nicaraguan opposition was permitted to function with few constraints, as the US press has observed, despite the fact that it was the political arm of the US proxy army attacking Nicaragua from Honduras. We might ask how a political organization would fare in the United States if it had a similar relation to an army directed and supplied by the USSR (or to be more accurate, some unimaginably awesome power) attacking the US from Mexico and Canada.

The US has sought, with some success, to block aid from other sources to Nicaragua. As noted earlier, military aid from US allies was blocked, compelling the government to rely on the USSR, as required for the purposes of justifying the aggression. The US vetoed technical assistance to agriculture in 1982 and for roads in 1983, and voted against loans for municipal development, fishing cooperatives and industry. "Angered by a 1983 IDB agreement with Nicaragua for a $30.4 million financing of its fishing industry, Secretary of State George Shultz initiated a private campaign to torpedo another such loan of more than $100 million to the private agricultural sector, the very activity that the United States has said it hoped to preserve against an alleged Marxist takeover," Mary King reports. Documents leaked from the British Foreign Office indicate that these efforts have been closely coordinated with US sabotage operations. Senior British government officials secretly condemn US actions to destabilize Nicaragua as "bully boy tactics" combined with "economic sabotage." The British representative to the Inter-American Development Bank, Kenneth O'Sullivan, reports that the US, while "financing the sabotage of the economic infrastructure of Nicaragua," is trying to make Nicaragua default on its debts by blocking new loans: "Nicaragua...is making efforts to clear arrears with the IBRD [World Bank] and the IMF...against a background of externally-financed sabotage," he informed London. In one case, the US Chair of the IADB executive board insisted that a loan for rehabilitation of fisheries (accepted after considerable US-created delay) include a clause requiring Nicaragua to provide adequate fuel for fishing boats. This "mystified" the board, but they soon came to understand this curious demand: "The following week saboteurs blew up the fuel depot in the port of Corinto, their single most effective blow to the Nicaraguan economy," O'Sullivan reported to the Foreign Office."[135]

US subversion, sabotage and aggression are carefully-plotted operations, as one would expect in the case of a terrorist state with unmatched power and only limited domestic constraints.

The commitment to overthrow the Nicaraguan government, though ritually denied, is barely concealed by Administration spokesmen, who also speak openly about the "invasion option" if all else fails. Lengthy front-page articles in the *New York Times* expound the Reagan Administration demand that Nicaragua "change its form of government to a pluralistic democracy" or face the consequences. But the facts about the historical and contemporary US attitude towards "pluralistic democracy" in Central America are virtually never discussed in this context, a Nicaraguan proposal to demilitarize the borders with the aid of the Contadora group receives a 40-word notice (a Nicaraguan proposal 3 months later for a joint patrol with Honduras to eliminate border incidents apparently was unmentioned), and the *Times* reports its neutral and objective poll which asks Americans whether they agree with Ronald Reagan, who "says the U.S. should help the people in Nicaragua who are trying to overthrow the pro-Soviet Government there"; even with this wording, they were unable to generate majority support for the operation.[136]

6.3 The Elections and the Opposition

US war aims are further clarified by the hysterical reaction to the Nicaraguan election in November 1984. In a well-crafted propaganda coup, the US government succeeded in deflecting attention from the election by regular diatribes, seriously reported as "news" in the nation's press, and by concocting a story about Russian MIGs in Nicaragua, quickly abandoned after it had served its function of eliminating the (minimal) danger of honest coverage of the election and eliciting appropriate outrage by dovish Senators—e.g., Massachusetts Democrat Paul Tsongas, who warned that the US would have to bomb Nicaragua to eliminate the MIGs because "they're also capable against the United States." The fear that Nicaragua will attack the US provides an intriguing glimpse of the mentality of US elites.[137]

A careful study of the election by the US Latin American Studies Association (LASA) was virtually ignored by the press, as were the elections themselves.[138] They reject the claim that Arturo Cruz, the official democrat according to the US government and the press, was "excluded" from the elections. Rather, his business-based group made a policy decision to exclude themselves despite protections to ensure fair access, and the LASA observers doubt that he and his group had a broad following in Nicaragua. The press reports that his "biggest rally drew no more than 1000 fans," and that his "agenda" is "more attuned to the policy debate in Washington than to the hardships of life in Nicaragua": "Nor did Cruz' calls for talks with the contras strike a popular chord in Managua. To Cruz' embarrassment, his own sister, Lilian Cruz, penned an open letter to two progovernment newspapers to remind her brother that her son, Sandinista army officer David Baez, was slain battling the contras in April."[139]

The LASA investigation concludes that the FSLN "did little more to take advantage of its incumbency than incumbent parties everywhere (including the United States) routinely do." The election "by Latin American standards was a model of probity and fairness"[140]; earlier elections were either utterly fraudulent or "meant little more than automatic ratification of candidates chosen by the incumbent party and the U.S. government," for most Nicaraguans. The report observes that "We know of no election in Latin America (or elsewhere) in which groups advocating the violent overthrow of an incumbent government have themselves been incorporated into the electoral process; particularly when these groups have been openly supported by a foreign power"; surely nothing of the sort would be tolerated for an instant in the United States. The elections were indeed "manipulated," the report notes, but by the Reagan Administration, which did everything in its power to block and discredit them, including efforts to induce Cruz and others to abstain.[141]

It was subsequently learned that Cruz was on the CIA payroll. He had "secretly received money from the Central Intelligence Agency, according to U.S. government officials... A CIA spokesman refused to comment, but intelligence sources said the money was funnelled to Mr. Cruz through organizations supported by the agency as part of an effort to encourage political opposition to the leftist Sandinista government," leading House Intelligence Committee Chairman Lee Hamilton to complain to Secretary of State Shultz that Cruz was lobbying Congress while receiving CIA funds, intelligence sources said. Confronted with the charges, Cruz "said he had received assistance in the past 'for a short period' from an 'institution' dedicated to support the 'struggle for liberty'," which he declined to name.[142] A senior official of the new United Nicaraguan Opposition organized by the US said that Cruz, along with his fellow-democrat Alfonso Robelo, "had been given money in the past by the Central Intelligence Agency to carry out what the official called 'political work'."[143]

As for Cruz's "democratic credentials," Christopher Hitchens comments that "He would not take part in an election that he felt to be insufficiently democratic, but he will take part in a war of sabotage and attrition that has no democratic pretenses at all"[144]—serving in Duarte style to legitimate the "damnable atrocities" of his associates, as he fully recognizes. Whatever the facts may be about the commitment to democracy on the part of Cruz, Robelo, and other leaders of the Nicaraguan business community, it seems clear enough that they are labelled "democrats" by US commentators not on the basis of any information about such commitment, but because their concept of democracy rejects the "'logic of the majority,' which meant that Nicaragua's poor majority would have access to, and be the primary beneficiaries of, public programs" (LASA report). This stance suffices to confer "democratic credentials."

The general counsel of the New York City Commission on Human Rights described the election as "free, fair and hotly contested," citing the access of all seven parties to free TV and radio time and campaign expenses, and reporting also a discussion with the political affairs officer at the US embassy, who described the election as "flawed" because we must use "a different measuring stick" for countries like Nicaragua that "pose a threat to United States security and interests in the area." The spokesman for the British Parliamentary Human Rights Group, whose comment on the elections in El Salvador was quoted earlier (p. 117), British Liberal Party leader David Steele, and the special envoy of the Socialist International, a former Norwegian defense minister, all compared the election favorably to the one in El Salvador.[145]

The Managua correspondent of the *London Guardian*, Tony Jenkins, observed that the political opposition in Nicaragua "has never really committed itself to trying to win power by democratic means." One of the leaders of the Democratic Coordinating Committee (CDN; the group described here as the "democratic opposition," which refused to participate in the elections) explains this posture:[146]

> It is true that we have never really tried to build up a big membership or tried to show our strength by organising regular demonstrations. Perhaps it is a mistake, but we prefer to get European and Latin American governments to put pressure on the Sandinistas.

As noted earlier (p. 135), the political leadership of the *contra* armies feel no need for political organization because they can rely on the internal domestic opposition, the CDN, which in turn feels no need for political mobilization because it can rely on outsiders (in the real world, the US). We learn something more from this about the true nature of the "democratic opposition," within Nicaragua or in Honduras or Miami, and about its US advocates.

Some of the reasons advanced for the election boycott have a degree of plausibility; we return to the question in chapter 5. But there is another and probably more fundamental reason for the refusal of the "true democrats" to attempt to organize politically or compete for political power in Nicaragua. Tony Jenkins observes that the opposition has "never accepted the basic Sandinista precept of the revolution; that society must be reorganised to the benefit of the workers and peasants." This being so, the chances of political success are slight, unless the US war succeeds in its fundamental ends: rendering conditions of life intolerable, forcing the Sandinistas to harsher measures, and reinforcing the true allies of the US among the Sandinistas, namely, the elements committed to a Leninist model of totalitarian mass mobilization and control. In such circumstances, the "democratic opposition" allied to the superpower aggressor might well have some appeal among the population at large. It makes good sense, then, for the *contra* armies and their political leadership to avoid any political goals or education, relying on the domestic opposition within Nicaragua, which in turn relies on the United States, where they can be confident of maintaining their status as "true democrats" because of their opposition to meaningful social reform.

6.4 The Free Press at Work

Throughout, the free press has ably carried out its services for the cause, as we have seen. Much insight into the contributions of the free press to establishing the Party Line is provided in a study by Edward Herman of *New York Times* reporting of the 1984 Nicaraguan and Salvadoran elections.[147] In reporting the Salvadoran election, the *Times* relied overwhelmingly on US and Salvadoran officials. The rebels were occasionally cited, but primarily with regard to their disruption plans. They were also permitted to describe the election as a "farce," but never to expand on the reasons. In dramatic contrast, the opposition in Nicaragua was cited extensively and given ample opportunity to explain their objections to the planned elections. US officials and the Nicaraguan opposition provided over 80% of the direct citations, and constituted 60% of the sources cited (meaning that there was some indirect reference to the Sandinistas). In contrast, US and Salvadoran officials provided virtually all of the direct citations in the case of the Salvadoran elections (with the exception noted above, which reinforced the government case) and 80% of total sources (peasants constituted 0.8%).

Choice of topics reflected the same *New York Times* agenda. The number of articles referring to freedom of the press, organizational freedom and limits on opposition candidates was zero in the case of the Salvadoran elections, whereas in the case of the Nicaraguan elections, 75% of the articles discussed freedom of the press, 50% discussed organizational freedom, and 62.5% discussed limits on candidates. The power of the armed forces to coerce was discussed in 37.5% of the articles on the Nicaraguan election, in 3.6% of the articles on the Salvadoran election. To fully appreciate this illustration of media servility to state power, one must bear in mind that abuses of freedom of press, organizational freedom and candidate opportunities were vastly more severe in El Salvador, and that the direct role of the armed forces in coercion was also far greater. There were also falsehoods in press reporting, but their impact is minor in comparison to the effectiveness of these more indirect methods of thought control, characteristic of the corporate media.

Notice that the news reports maintained the objectivity of which they are so proud: reporters did not state their opinions. Notice further that since we live in a free country, this devastating exposure of what the press is really up to is not suppressed and is available to the mass audience of *Covert Action Information Bulletin*. So there is plainly no problem about effective democracy here.

The devices employed to impose the state propaganda system as the basic framework for discussion are well-illustrated in the contributions of Shirley Christian of the *New York Times*, whose opinion pieces appear as "reporting" on the news pages. Thus she informs us that the Sandinistas approached the Central American countries—specifically, El Salvador—with an offer that "would address some of the concerns of each of them, asking, in turn, that the other country abandon its demand for democratization in Nicaragua." Plainly the Sandinistas never said: "Please abandon your demand for democratization in Nicaragua," or anything remotely similar. Rather, this is the paraphrase of what they said as prescribed by the state disinformation system. Presupposed as objective fact in this paraphrase is that El Salvador, Guatemala and Honduras are concerned that Nicaragua move towards democracy, and that such a concern, if it existed, would be other than comical, given the character of these states and the traditional attitude toward democracy of the superpower that backs them.[148]

Another device Christian employs is "historical engineering," to use the term devised by historian Frederic Paxson, one of the founders of a National Board for Historical Service established by US historians to serve the state during World War I: "explaining the issues of the war that we might better win it," a concept that has performed useful service since.[149] Christian observes that "in recent months diplomatic efforts have encountered many road-blocks"; in particular, "the Central American peace initiative of the so-called Contadora countries came to a standstill in June when Nicaragua demanded that the participants take up the issue of Washington's support for the anti-Sandinista forces." In the real world, the Contadora initiative foundered when the US angrily rejected the draft proposal it had previously supported after it was accepted by Nicaragua, and induced its clients in the region to do likewise, with a hysterical outburst to which we return.

Another useful device is extensive paraphrase of Administration spokesmen, as in a reference to Elliott Abrams, whose deep concern for human rights and democracy was reviewed earlier, who "said the only way to satisfy the security concerns of the United States was with a democratic government in Nicaragua." No doubt Abrams produced such words, but when the columnist reports them in her own paraphrase, this helps blur the difference between fact and opinion; and with incessant repetition, overwhelmingly one-sided, the doctrine approved by state propagandists soon becomes "fact," whatever the facts. The *Times* would not, for example, permit a reporter to write, without quotes, that a high Soviet official said that the USSR could not deal with Israel unless it established a democratic government, or that El Salvador is trying to induce Nicaragua to abandon its concern for democratization in El Salvador. Exploitation of such devices in what is called "news" is ultimately more effective in imposing the Party Line than outright state propaganda.

To take another striking case of the technique of indoctrination by selective citation, consider Christian's highly-praised book denouncing the Sandinistas, largely drawn from her Pulitzer Prize-winning news reports on Nicaragua in the *Miami Herald*. George Black observes that Christian's news stories dealt almost exclusively with Reagan Administration charges: "broken promises" to "those who wanted democracy," human rights abuses by the Sandinistas, Soviet military aid, etc. Forty of fifty-four named sources are business leaders and opposition politicians; "The remaining citations are largely *pro forma* rebuttals by government officials to the main thrust of an article." "In two years of reporting, she did not record a single sympathetic comment from the twenty-five shopkeepers, stallholders, small farmers and businessmen, baseball fans and taxi drivers she interviewed," but only a "relentless litany of complaints about Cuban influence and food lines and nostalgia for better days under Somoza." She reported charges of Sandinista "massive murder" made by a business leader (who, it has since been learned, was on the CIA payroll), but not the conclusion of Amnesty International that there was no substance to these charges. The Sandinista social programs are dismissed briefly in her book as a ruse. This unabashed state propagandist also has the gall to condemn journalists for their alleged "love affair" with the Sandinistas, who they saw "through a romantic haze"; that is, for occasionally departing from the US government propaganda line. Not surprisingly, this is the way to gain wide prestige and to merit appointment as a correspondent for the *New York Times*.[150]

The device of insinuating a Party Line by careful selection of sources is one of the standard techniques of Western Agitprop. Journalists would be departing from objectivity if they were to express their own opinions, so to serve the purposes of the free press it is necessary to proceed in a more roundabout way, for example, by extensive citation of those who express the approved doctrines and careful avoidance of alternative perspectives.

Such news reports are not without value, however. Thus Christian observes that the anti-Sandinista mood in Congress "has made it politically possible for the Administration to drop the argument that it was supporting the Nicaraguan rebels as a means of interfering with the supplying of the guerrillas fighting the Washington-backed Government in El Salvador," thus tacitly conceding that this argument was always fraudulent. Christian also quotes a classified report that Reagan sent to Congress stating that U.S. invasion "must realistically be recognized as an eventual option, given our stakes in the region, if other policy options fail." Several months earlier, the BBC had reported that a classified National Security Council document that had come into its possession indicates that the Reagan Administration is willing to use military force against Nicaragua.[151]

The Administration claim that the election was a farce, though denied by foreign and US observers including the LASA delegation, has achieved the status of unquestioned fact; more exactly, the election did not take place. Thus, nine months after the election, the Washington correspondent of *Business Week* informs us that Shirley Christian "argues convincingly that the Sandinistas never really had any intention of living up to their early promises of elections." In another review of Christian's book at the same time, Susan Kaufman Purcell, the director of the Latin-American program of the Council on Foreign Relations, informs us that when Edén Pastora broke with the Sandinistas in 1982, "it was...too late to mount an effective nonviolent opposition." Obviously, then, it was too late in 1984, independently of the facts, which are an irrelevance as usual. Purcell agrees with Christian that the US should support the *contras* but recognizes that there are some "moral dilemmas to this course of action": "Like many of us who would like to see a more democratic Nicaragua, [Christian] is not sure how far we should go."[152]

Concern for a more democratic Nicaragua is admirable, and might even be taken seriously if accompanied by similar concern for a more democratic El Salvador, which should by similar logic justify US support for the rebels, or even a more democratic United States. Lacking that, it is merely the cynical pretense of the commissar.[153]

6.5. A Glimpse into the Civilized World

The hysterical US response to the November election recapitulated the reaction two months earlier to Nicaragua's acceptance of the Contadora peace proposals, surprising US diplomats "who had been saying for months that Washington backed the Contadora effort but that Nicaragua was blocking a settlement."[154] Taken aback by Nicaragua's move, which could have led to peace in the region thus thwarting US ends, the US reacted strongly to avert any such danger. Senior US government officials demanded that a visit to Los Angeles by head of state Daniel Ortega be blocked, Philip Taubman reports, "to punish Mr. Ortega and the Sandinistas for accepting the Contadora Peace proposal," which the US was able to undermine by diplomatic and economic pressures. A National Security Council paper a few weeks later, leaked to the press, "credits U.S. foreign policy with success in blocking efforts by Venezuela, Panama, Colombia and Mexico—known as the Contadora Group—to obtain signing of a proposed regional peace treaty in Central America," while noting certain problems in ensuring that there will be no further disruption of US plans for aggression against Nicaragua.[155] "We have trumped the latest Nicaraguan/Mexican efforts to rush signature of an unsatisfactory Contadora agreement," the NSC paper exults. After Nicaragua accepted the Contadora draft treaty, the US insisted that it be revised; the amendments proposed under US pressure "tend strongly to slow and weaken the process of military de-escalation and negotiation," Tom Farer observes, by eliminating the indefinite arms freeze and firm timetables for departure of military advisers and other measures to which Nicaragua had agreed.[156] The story is a reenactment of the desperate US efforts to avoid a peaceful settlement of the Vietnam conflict in the early 1960s; the reasons are similar.

Recall that three months earlier, President Reagan had informed Congress that aid to the *contras* was essential or "a regional settlement based on the Contadora process will continue to elude us" (see p. 81). The incident can leave no doubt that once again, the US fears a political settlement and prefers that disputes remain in the arena of military conflict, in which its supremacy is unchallenged.

We might ask what term other than "hysterical fanaticism" can be used with reference to the President's declaration of May 1, 1985, announcing an embargo "in response to the emergency situation created by the Nicaraguan Government's aggressive activities in Central America":

> I, Ronald Reagan, President of the United States of America, find that the policies and actions of the Government of Nicaragua constitute an unusual and extraordinary threat to the national security and foreign policy of the United States and hereby declare a national emergency to deal with that threat.

And what term applies to the "key Congressional leaders" who, in this grim emergency situation when our very existence is under threat, "generally praised President Reagan's imposition of a trade embargo as a useful first step in pressing the Sandinista Government to change its policies"? Or to the critics who go along with the pretense that any of this is can be a topic for discussion among sane people?[157]

The reaction in the colonies is often not greatly different. The *London Times* praises the "unanimity" in Washington "about the nature of the Sandinista regime and the array of measures needed to change it." The editors write that "America's enlightenment faith in the educability, reasonableness, even the inherent liberality of most of the world is great. The Sandinistas have made their most of both qualities, cultivating the belief in Washington that they would bargain." But these wiser heads, well schooled in the task of disciplining the lower orders, remind the naive Americans that they should not rely solely on their "enlightenment faith": "the Contras are a necessary element," and "certain of the Contra groups" have "strong claims...to the status of Third World freedom fighters." The reference is presumably to Edén Pastora, who had been dismissed by the CIA as too independent and accordingly disappeared from the scene. The approving reference to Third World freedom fighters is merely comical, given the hatred and contempt of the editors for such elements, apart from those fighting the good fight against the Evil Empire. It is doubtful that any segment of the Communist Party press is more abject in its loyalty to its Soviet master. The *Times*, however, does manage a spark of insight, noting that the danger posed by Nicaragua is "the example" it may offer to others.[158]

Turning to the leading journal of our neighbor to the north, we find an indignant denunciation of Soviet military aid to Nicaragua, including even "a radar system that will allow the Nicaraguans to monitor their entire territory," under attack by the United States; an outrage of colossal proportions. The Russians have no business "running arms into Central America," the editors thunder; "the Russians have no more right to bolster a friendly regime in Central America than the Americans have to topple an unfriendly one." Employing precisely the same logic, the more servile elements of the Communist Party press might argue that the US has no business "running arms into Turkey, Israel or Denmark" (far more of a threat to the USSR than Central America is to the US); "the US has no more right to bolster a friendly regime near the borders of the USSR than the USSR has to topple an unfriendly one." In fact, if one of these countries were under attack by a well-armed mercenary force based in a Soviet satellite and armed and directed by the Soviets, the US would not even have the right to send it a radar system to monitor its territory, penetrated by Soviet planes on bombing and supply missions.[159] Since Nicaragua will not receive means of self-defense from Canada, or other US allies, the only proper course is for it to submit quietly.

There is good reason to believe that the US will not resort to the "invasion option" in Nicaragua, though a constant threat will be maintained for disruption and intimidation. A Jesuit priest working in Nicaragua, who had been active in Chile before the Pinochet coup, put the matter succinctly and accurately:[160]

In Chile, the Americans made a mistake. They cut off the revolution too abruptly. They killed the revolution but, as we can see from recent developments there, they didn't kill the dream. In Nicaragua they're trying to kill the dream.

If the dream that there might be a more just and decent society remains, there will simply be more trouble in the future. A wiser strategy is first to kill the dream by a campaign of terror, intimidation, sabotage, blocking of aid, and other means available to a superpower that is immune to retaliation, until the errant society cracks under the strain and its people recognize that in the shadow of the enforcer, there can be no hope of escaping from the miseries of traditional life. Then, order can be restored by force, with a touching display of concern for democracy and human rights, to be dispatched to oblivion once it has served the purpose of pacifying the home front and loyalists among the well-disciplined allies.

7 Elsewhere in the Region

To fully appreciate the US role in Nicaragua and El Salvador, one must consider the broader picture of US intervention in the region throughout the century. There is no space here for a comprehensive review, so a few examples must suffice.

7.1. Torturing Hispaniola

Consider the island of Hispaniola, containing Haiti and the Dominican Republic. Its population of 7-8 million "had been virtually exterminated by disease, mass murder, and oppressive labor" within a generation by Christopher Columbus, the genocidal monster whose exploits we celebrate each October.[161] The first US Marine landing was in 1800; there were eight landings in the independent Haitian republic between 1867 and 1900. The most serious intervention, however, was under Woodrow Wilson. The "nigs" were put in their place in Haiti in the manner noted earlier, but the "damned dagoes" in the Dominican Republic held out for over five years.

The occupation of Haiti lasted for nineteen years. In 1922, the president imposed in the US-run "free election" was removed in favor of "an outspoken advocate of American paternalism and intellectual devotee of Benito Mussolini's fascist experiment in Italy" when he "defied American wishes in negotiating a public loan delivering Haiti's debt to New York banks." The Duvalier dynasty was established in 1957, and remains, while the country is owned by a wealthy elite and foreign (largely US) business, and the population either flees abroad or languishes in misery in one of the poorest and most oppressed corners of the world, while the State Department heralds constant improvements and President Reagan lauds the dictatorship for its "determined opposition" to "Cuban adventurism" and its support for "private enterprise and economic reform."[162]

The first extensive study of Wilson's invasion of the Dominican Republic appeared 60 years after the war ended, in 1984;[163] here we have more important concerns. Wilson's invasion was undertaken to block constitutional government and ensure "complete satisfaction of U.S. demands for economic and military control." It initiated a brutal five-year counterinsurgency campaign and an eight-year military occupation that instituted legal-economic arrangements "which condemned the republic's population to one of the lower standards of living in Latin America," while US investors prospered, taking over most of the domestic economy, geared to sugar exports as food production declined. The military government "favored the [US] corporations" and on the major issues, "completely capitulated to foreign interests, ignoring those of the Dominican people." Its actions "advanced the fortunes of the country's existing planter and merchant elite" and "proved a tremendous boon to foreign agricultural interests," confirming "the republic's place in the world as a producer of agricultural commodities for the industrially developed North Atlantic nations." Under the US military government, "the quantity and quality of public education steadily declined" and its staff was "decimated." School enrollment did not pass the 1920 figure until 1935, when it comprised one-third of school age children in a much larger population.

There was also a "positive side," Piero Gleijeses observes, including three major roads ("largely for military purposes") and some public health development. But "these material achievements," such as they were, "were accomplished with Dominican money." The US occupying forces took over the Dominican share of customs receipts—"an economic blackmail in flagrant violation of the 1907 treaty"—and when sugar prices collapsed after World War I, the Military Government floated loans to finance its operations, which the Dominicans were compelled to assume under the 1924 evacuation treaty. In the end, about half of the meager public works program was ultimately paid, with interest, by the Dominicans themselves. Far more significant was the US takeover of the economy. The land laws promulgated by the Military Government were designed "to permit U.S. sugar concerns to get legal title to huge tracts of land. It was enforced with great zeal: Dominican peasants were driven off their lands and Dominican villages burned for the benefit of foreign—mostly American— sugar companies." When US troops finally withdrew in 1924, sugar companies owned nearly a quarter of the agricultural area of the Dominican Republic, about 2% of it owned by Dominicans, most of the rest by US companies. Americans controlled property worth about $33.7 million, the Dominicans less than $1.4 million. By 1925, exports in sugar and sugar derivatives reached 63% of total exports, profiting the foreign investor but not the local economy. The tariff structure was designed to favor US goods, eliminating protection for Dominican production so that "many local crafts and industries were ruined." "The only Dominican product favored by the American-made tariff of 1919 was sugar—an American-owned industry."[164]

During the counterinsurgency war, Calder continues, the Marines, whose "behavior was often brutish by traditional Dominican standards," machine-gunned peasants, raped, tortured, destroyed houses, imprisoned many people and sent many more to concentration camps (providing a captive labor supply for the sugar plantations), bombed and strafed "apparently as much to intimidate the populace with a show of power as to harm the guerrillas," and generally abused the "spigs" and "niggers," as they were regularly called, undertaking what the Military Governor called "the white man's burden, the duty of the big brother." Penalties, if any, were light. Testimony by the spigs and niggers was disregarded as unreliable, or dismissed as pro-German propaganda. Journalists, poets and other intellectuals were jailed and the press was censored because "any concessions on the matter of free speech would be seen as 'evidence of our weakness'," the Military Governor informed Washington. One journalist was arrested and deported for publishing a photograph of a peasant victim of Marine torture; another was fined and jailed and his editor deported for criticizing the continued occupation. Gleijeses notes that the structures of national and local government were dismantled and censorship and suppression of intellectuals was severe: "In their cells, journalists and writers had time to contemplate the merits of democracy 'Made in USA'" after their conviction by military courts presided over by US officers ignorant of the law of the country and of the Spanish language. It was a crime to make any remark, verbally or in print, that the Military Government regarded as uncomplimentary to itself or that the military courts decided tended to incite "unrest, disorder and revolt."[165]

The first major guerrilla leader, regarded by the Marines as a "negro bandit and murderer," was killed while "attempting to escape"—a standard technique for murdering prisoners—after his surrender, a foretaste of what was to happen to Sandino a few years later in Nicaragua as Somoza and his US-trained National Guard took over after another Marine operation. In 1930, dictator Trujillo took power in the Dominican Republic; his US-trained National Guard "became the tool for total control of the republic" as he established one of the most oppressive regimes in Latin America.

Throughout, he received firm US backing. President Roosevelt, who had earlier taken credit for writing the Haitian constitution under the US military occupation, is said to have remarked that Trujillo may have been an S.O.B., but "at least he's our S.O.B." DeLesseps Morrison, later President Kennedy's ambassador to the

OAS, described Trujillo in 1946 as the "man responsible for the great work of Dominican progress, the man who brought trade between the Republic and the other American nations to a peak." This was after such accomplishments as the massacre of 15-20,000 Haitians in October 1937 to prevent them from "Africanizing" the population, along with regular barbarous treatment and robbery of the Dominicans themselves.[166]

As in Haiti, the Dominican resistance was conveniently attributed to the Huns: the insurgents' "German assistants and backers have not been asleep and have been using every effort to reinforce and keep alive this lively insurrection," Marine commander Thorpe explained. Dominican President Henríquez went to the Versailles Conference in 1919 to request "inclusion of the Dominican case in the docket of oppressed nationalities whose cause President Wilson claimed to champion in his famous Fourteen Points," but without issue, since Wilson "succeeded in blocking consideration of U.S. hegemony in the Americas"; recall the treatment of Ho Chi Minh at the same time (p. 46).

The treatment of the Dominican Republic, however, was relatively benign as compared with neighboring Haiti, since its inhabitants had "a preponderance of white blood and culture" while the Haitians "are negro for the most part" and "are almost in a state of savagery and complete ignorance," therefore requiring "control" while the Dominicans need only "counsel" after US withdrawal, as explained by Ferdinand Mayer of the State Department Division of Latin American Affairs in 1921.

Calder assumes that the results of the intervention ("strengthening the system of plantation agricultural" under the control of US-owned sugar companies, condemning the population "to one of the lower standards of living in Latin America," etc.) were the "unintended" effects of "a policy neither wise nor just, a policy basically unproductive for all concerned" (though not unproductive for US investors). The general convention is to regard particular cases as deviant, the effects inadvertent, not the predictable consequences of policies that are rooted in the interests of those in a position to influence policy formation. The conclusion stands despite the fact that the same story has been reenacted over and over again with the same consequences and the same beneficiaries (by curious accident, the business interests that control state policy), and the fact that planners secretly explain exactly what they are doing—for example, Woodrow Wilson (p. 59).

The proper way to interpret these matters was elucidated by Hans Morgenthau, one of the founders of the "realist" school which eschews sentimentality and moralistic posturing in favor of hard-headed analysis. The US was founded to achieve a "transcendent purpose," Morgenthau explained: "the establishment of equality in freedom in America" and throughout the world. True, the historical record appears to show that the US, very much like every other power, pursues the interests of its own dominant elites with little regard for others. But those who express skepticism about the transcendent purpose on these trivial grounds are guilty of an error of logic: "To reason thus is to confound the abuse of reality with reality itself." It is the unachieved "national purpose," revealed by "the evidence of history as our minds reflect it" (and as our commissars interpret it), that is the reality; the actual historical record is merely the abuse of reality. The critics, who foolishly mistake the real world for reality, have fallen into "the error of atheism, which denies the validity of religion on similar grounds."[167]

These remarks were written during the Kennedy era, a period of relative ascendancy for the educated elite and correspondingly one of the low points of US intellectual culture. But the ideas, in one or another form, run through much mainstream commentary and analysis.

After torturing the Dominican Republic for 30 years, "President Trujillo and a handful of United States companies owned the Dominican Republic," but "Trujillo's share, an estimated 65-85% of the country's economy, was rather larger than that of his allies who had to content themselves with a percentage of the sugar industry."[168] He had become an annoyance, as well as an embarrassment to the rhetoric of the Kennedy Administration, which was extolling our transcendent purpose in an effort to shore up the Fifth Freedom against further disasters of the Castro variety. Trujillo was duly assassinated, after CIA efforts to eliminate him.[169]

In the country's first free elections, Juan Bosch was elected president in 1962. Though his views were basically those of the Kennedy Democrats, the Kennedy Adminstration worked to undermine him. The military structure of the Trujillo years remained, and it was evident that a military coup would be attempted unless Bosch succeeded in mobilizing substantial popular support. US officials (whose word was law) prevented Bosch from removing hostile officers who controlled the armed forces, blocked agrarian reform, and with the assistance of US labor leaders, forestalled his efforts to develop a strong, united labor movement. US military officers in the Dominican Republic meanwhile "developed rapport with their military counterparts and were critical of what seemed to some an indecisive and unreliable civilian president." Bosch's unreliability was revealed by his attempts to mobilize popular support through reform measures, his securing of a Swiss line of credit (diminishing reliance on the US), and his abrogation of a contract with Esso oil company for a refinery, all criticized by the US Embassy. "U.S. pressures hampered [Bosch's] efforts to mobilize mass political support behind his regime from his most likely sources—rural and industrial labor," and sought to "move him toward business groups." The US Embassy decided to "let him go" (Ambassador Martin's phrase) when the inevitable military coup took place in 1963. The "announced U.S. goal of promoting democracy...was subordinated to U.S. private and public vested interests," specifically, "concern for U.S. investors and traders." After some brief indications of displeasure at the "overthrow of a democratically elected government" (the State Department's official condemnation), the US quickly recognized and offered full support to the new regime.[170]

In the face of the record he reviews, Blasier nevertheless states that despite its overwhelming influence, "the United States failed in its objective of maintaining Bosch, a popularly elected president, in office in an orderly transition to a democratic system." That this was the objective is a matter of doctrine, immune to fact.

Gleijeses points out that Bosch had been the candidate of "the peasants, the urban unemployed, the working-class poor," people who "previously had never played a role in the political life of the nation." He introduced a "modern and democratic" constitution and legal system, attacked the endemic corruption, and defended civil liberties, attempting "to create a sense of civic spirit, an elementary honesty that could have sparked a true renaissance of Dominican society." He compelled the police to exercise restraint for the first time, slashed salaries of high officials, and refused the standard perquisites of office himself so that when he left for exile, he was penniless, an unprecedented phenomenon. These actions infuriated the Dominican elites and the military, and were intolerable to the Kennedy Administration. The Kennedy liberals were particularly outraged by Bosch's defense of civil liberties of leftists and by the fact that he was an ardent nationalist, unwilling to do what he was told by his US overseers, in contrast to his predecessors; earlier governments "seemed to feel that I was one of them," Ambassador Martin commented, while condemning Bosch as "ungrateful," "obstinate," and unwilling to share power. Bosch laid the basis for effective land reform, which was beginning to show promise when he was overthrown after seven months in office, and undertook efforts at education of workers and peasants for democratic participation in government and cooperatives. Even his critics recognized that economic recovery was underway, though US aid dropped sharply when he took office, to zero, in fact, apart from aid previously granted to the business-run junta. Even Ambassador Martin, "certainly no friend of Bosch, had to acknowledge: 'The indisputable fact that his brief Administration may well have been the most honest in Dominican history, if not in Latin America'." Obviously, he had to go.[171]

After he was "let go" by the Kennedy Administration, corruption returned "with a vengeance" among civilians and in the armed forces and "the country suffered a grave economic decline" and a dramatic increase in public debt: "Extreme corruption and mismanagement were responsible for the country's economic collapse after the incipient recovery brought about by the Bosch government" and "the people knew only suffering. The peasants remained silent beasts of burden."[172]

In 1965, the military-installed regime was overthrown by a constitutionalist coup aimed at restoring Bosch to power. The US sent 23,000 troops to prevent this outcome. Recently declassified records reveal that when the regime was about to be overthrown, US Ambassador Tapley Bennett was instructed by Washington to send a message changing the basis for the planned US intervention "from one of fighting communism [considered too ludicrous for plausibility] to one of protecting American lives." He gladly complied, and this became the official pretext for the US invasion, repeated in President Johnson's memoirs.[173] US troops fought the constitutionalist forces who aimed to restore the legitimate elected Bosch government, but were not permitted to interfere with the subsequent massacres by the Dominican military forces they had rescued, on the grounds that this would have violated US neutrality. The threat of democracy was averted and the traditional order restored, accompanied by an utterly fraudulent election to legitimize the restoration.

The result was the usual one: death squads, torture, repression, an increase in poverty and malnutrition for the mass of the population, slave labor conditions, vast emigration, and outstanding opportunities for US investors, whose control over the economy reached new heights. With the country demoralized and under the control of US corporations and the security forces, the US became willing to tolerate "free elections," even the election of social democrats, all possibility of social change having been terminated.[174] This permits *New York Times* correspondent Leslie Gelb to refer to "President Johnson's swift, decisive and successful takeover and redemocratization of the Dominican Republic in 1965." To Boston University President John Silber, the meaning of these events is that President Johnson "took resolute action, in concert with the Organization of American States, by sending Marines to the Dominican Republic in 1965 to protect democracy." The news columns of the press remind us that when civil war broke out in 1965, "President Johnson sent 23,000 troops to seek peace."[175] What dictator could demand more loyal service?

In 1976, the Bishop of Santiago reported that "seventy percent of the country's peasant population live on the border of starvation and misery." In 1985, a Church-based group reported further that the country had "undergone almost a decade of economic decline" with 20% of the population living in "absolute poverty" while 90% suffer malnutrition, according to Central Bank officials. The illiteracy rate is 54% and one million school age children in this country of six million do not attend school because there are no facilities. The Dominican Bishops' conference in March 1985 warned "that the foundations of Dominican society are disintegrating as a result of a crisis that has plagued the country for years," referring to the "inhuman and unjust poverty" for much of the population, the "tragic" situation of the 63% of Dominicans who are underemployed (30% unemployed) and earn less than the monthly minimum wage of $58. The Bishops' conference report states: "the situation of underdevelopment and poverty is not the result of coincidence; rather, it is the consequence of concrete economic social and political structures that overlook or fail to recognize the dignity and inherent rights of the human person." Joining with the Bishops' conference of Haiti, they urge further that something be done for the 400,000 Haitians who fled to the Dominican Republic for work under conditions of virtual slavery. Under IMF pressure, the government attempted to reduce living standards further, imposing a crackdown on opposition elements to ensure order as security forces backed up by helicopter gunships arrested thousands of citizens, also killing many.[176]

To translate this dismal story into the approved lingo of American political science: "The interventions by United States Marines in Haiti, Nicaragua, the Dominican Republic, and elsewhere in those years often bore striking resemblances to the interventions by federal marshals in the conduct of elections in the American South in the 1960s: registering voters, protecting against electoral violence, ensuring a free vote and an honest count," nothing more. So Harvard political scientist Samuel Huntington informs us in the lead article in the *Political Science Quarterly*. A human rights program was "superfluous" in those days of overwhelming US power, he continues, because "the message was there for all to see in the troop deployments, carrier task forces, foreign aid missions, and intelligence operatives." Even the Pinochet coup in Chile proves the magnificence of American virtue: if "the United States had been as active in the popular election of 1970 as it had been in that of 1964, the destruction of Chilean democracy in 1973 might have been avoided." To translate into real world terms: the US would not have had to commit itself to the overthrow of Chilean democracy and support for the subsequent slaughter and oppression if only it had intervened with sufficient vigor to prevent a democratic election in 1970. "The overall effect of American power on other societies was to further liberty, pluralism, and democracy." The Dominican Republic offers a remarkable illustration of US virtue, Huntington continues: "No Dominican could doubt but that his country was a far, far better place to live in 1922 than it was in 1916," including those tortured by the benefactors and those whose families they murdered or whose villages they burned for the benefit of US sugar companies. No less outstanding is "the extent to which the United States has over the years nurtured the development of democratic institutions in the Dominican Republic"; "to the extent that they are [established], the United States deserve a lion's share of the credit."[177]

We can learn a good deal about our own society and its intellectual culture by considering such examples as this, noting that they are respected as reputable scholarship, in contrast to "extremist" work demonstrating that the exercise of US power conforms to the historical pattern of violent hegemonic states. We might ask, for example, how we would react to an account of Soviet behavior at a similar level of veracity, and audacity, in a Communist Party journal. It is a useful exercise.

7.2 Torturing Guatemala

Returning to Central America, consider the case of Guatemala, where Juan José Arévalo was elected president in 1944, inaugurating a ten-year departure from military rule. His government, "favorably disposed initially toward the United States, was modeled in many ways after the Roosevelt New Deal." It quickly elicited US hostility because of its commitment to democratic values (Communists were not repressed), a labor code that "sought to right the balance in a society where management had long dominated" and harmed the largest employer (United Fruit), hesitation about granting concessions to US oil companies, and other similar crimes. When Arévalo's term ended in 1951, "the political rift between [the US and Guatemala] was almost complete." As he left the presidency, Arévalo, recalling his belief in the noble words of President Roosevelt, commented sadly that "Roosevelt lost the war. The real winner was Hitler."[178]

The US soon moved to prove the accuracy of these words. Arévalo's successor, Jacobo Arbenz, attempted to carry Arévalo's reforms forward, including a successful land reform that led to a rise in exports and a favorable balance of payments by 1954. The land reform not only increased productivity, but "also provided campesinos with their own food, even cash from sales, while involving them in the political system for the first time in 400 years." But this was not to be. Arbenz attempted to expropriate unused lands held by the United Fruit Company and to hand them over to landless peasants, offering compensation based on the company's fraudulent tax valuation. This and other reform measures enraged the US further. Under-Secretary of State Walter Bedell Smith, one of Eisenhower's closest advisers, reported to the President that "we have repeatedly expressed deep concern to the Guatemalan Government because it plays the Communist game," permitting Communist activists to enjoy civil rights and disturbing relations with the US "because of the merciless hounding of American companies there by tax and labor demands, strikes, and, in the case of the United Fruit Company, inadequately compensated seizures of land under a Communist-administered Agrarian Reform Law." Exploiting the pretext of a Communist takeover, with the US press loyally playing its part, the CIA engineered a coup in 1954, restoring military rule and turning the country into a literal hell-on-earth, which has been maintained by regular US intervention until today. The land reform was repealed and its beneficiaries dispossessed, peasant cooperatives were dissolved, the literacy program was halted, the economy collapsed, the labor unions were destroyed, and the killings began.[179]

It is intriguing, in this context, to consider the interpretation of international law devised by advocates of the US war against Nicaragua. Recall that the theory is that the US is exercising the right of collective self-defense against Nicaragua's armed attack upon its ally, El Salvador. Suspending momentarily the reaction that any sane person would have to this farcical claim, consider the notion of "armed attack" that must be constructed to carry through the argument. Armed attack, in this conception, "includes assistance in organizing insurgency, training of insurgents, financing of the insurgency, use of facilities for command and control, ammunition and explosives supply, intelligence and communications assistance, logistics assistance, and political and propaganda support, as well as weapons supply"[180]; thus voicing support for the Afghan rebels constitutes "armed attack" against Afghanistan, to which the USSR is "obligated" to respond by military force, by bombing offices of the US press, for example. In the light of this concept, consider the CIA-engineered coup in Guatemala, the long US terrorist war against Cuba, and innumerable other crimes. By the standards of apologists for US atrocities, many an American leader should face the bar of justice for crimes against peace, and much of the world would be permitted under international law, indeed "obligated," to attack the US in self-defense. The absurdity of this particular argument by apologists, now applied to their favored state, of course does not invalidate its conclusions, the first of which at least can be argued on rational grounds.

In 1963, Arévalo was permitted to return to take part in an election, after having been kept abroad "by an assortment of legal devices and physical threats."[181] A military coup, quickly recognized by the Kennedy Administration and perhaps encouraged by it, prevented this danger. The new regime, guided by the Kennedy counterinsurgency doctrines, rapidly expanded the instruments of state terror with enthusiastic US support.[182] Rising repression and impoverishment elicited insurgency and further US intervention. A counterinsurgency campaign in 1966-8 led to the slaughter of perhaps 10,000 peasants with the help of American Green Berets; also napalm bombing by US planes based in Panama, according to Guatemalan vice-president Rojas. In subsequent years, impoverishment of the mass of the population and indescribable terror increased, with constant US assistance and occasional notice here.

Thus, in a brief report of the murder of yet another professor at the national university, the *Times* noted in passing that more than 40,000 people have disappeared and more than 95,000 "have died in political violence here since 1954" according to "the Mexican-based Guatemalan Human Rights Commission": to translate from Newspeak, some 140,000 have been eliminated by the governments *installed and kept in power by the US since the US overthrew Guatemalan democracy in 1954* (the crucial fact, regularly omitted in news reports and editorial comment), according to a Human Rights Commission which is Mexican-based because its members could not long survive in Guatemala. In May 1982, the conservative Guatemalan Conference of Bishops stated that "never in our history have such extremes been reached, with the assassinations now falling into the category of genocide." "A new study by two American anthropologists," Douglas Foster reports, "estimates that more than 50,000 Guatemalans—most of them Mayan Indians—have been killed since 1980" (see chapter 1, section 4); one of the most powerful Guatemalan businessmen, not without reason, told him: "You Americans killed your Indians long ago, so don't lecture us." At the same time, US military aid increased, along with renewed terror, as the country strides towards democracy in official parlance.[183]

As in El Salvador, the national university has been a prime target of state terror for many years, and still is. The last two rectors were killed, in 1981 and 1983. Another fled into exile, in fear for his life. The current rector, who has received 20 death threats, narrowly escaped in 1983 when gunmen fired at his car. His possible successor was gunned down while walking to a class on campus. According to university records, 36 students and 10 teachers were killed or have disappeared in two years, 12 in early 1985. The US Ambassador, Alberto Piedra, is co-author of a 1980 book that dismisses the university as "a publicly financed echo chamber of revolutionary Communism." The rector, in contrast, "described the students of the university as members of a generation that had been wounded by state repression and political violence and that held little hope for the future," James LeMoyne reports. They do not disguise "their antipathy for the United States, which they hold responsible for supporting 30 years of repressive governments after a coup in 1954 supported by the Central Intelligence Agency."[184] LeMoyne deserves credit for departing from the norm with this reference to the US coup; he might have added that the US is not just *held* responsible, but *is* in large measure responsible for the 30 years of terror that followed.

As noted earlier, US military aid to the mass murderers never ceased during the Carter years, contrary to what is commonly alleged, and in fact remained close to the norm. Furthermore, the US military establishment maintained its close relations with the Guatemalan military, giving them a "convincing signal" that the human rights rhetoric was hardly to be taken seriously. In January

1980, top American military officials visited Guatemala, and the press noted the "particular satisfaction" the Guatemalan regime derived from the visits. Piero Gleijeses comments:

> ...it is important to understand the rationale of those State Department "liberals"... They would have advocated military assistance for the regime had they believed that it was necessary for its survival. But in their eyes [military dictator] Lucas was not yet seriously threatened—hence the United States could afford to wait (while military assistance was provided by Argentina, Israel and other countries). In this fashion, the Carter administration would avoid dirtying its hands and would preserve the facade of its human rights policy as long as possible.

In fact, military assistance also was provided by the US, and distancing from the regime was only a public posture.[185]

In short, another fine example of how "The overall effect of American power on other societies was to further liberty, pluralism, and democracy" (Huntington).

While overcoming the threat of democracy in the Dominican Republic and Guatemala, the US also succeeded, not surprisingly, in thoroughly alienating its leading advocates, who were to write bitterly about the US role, thus demonstrating to the faithful that they were really Communists at heart all along.[186]

These are only a few cases. The record is shameful and appalling. The Central America-Caribbean region has been turned into a horror chamber, with regular US intervention serving to keep matters on course.

8 Human Rights, the Raising of the Living Standards, and Democratization

We might now usefully return to Kennan's prescription in 1948 that the US should put aside "vague and...unreal objectives such as human rights, the raising of the living standards, and democratization." How well has that advice been followed? Plainly, the question is not one to be settled by ideological pronouncements, but rather by empirical research. Such research has rarely been undertaken, but some attempts have been made and their results are worth considering.

Let us begin with human rights. The relation between human rights and US foreign policy in Latin America has been studied by the leading academic specialist on the topic, Lars Schoultz. He investigated the relation between US aid and the human rights climate, finding that there is indeed a correlation: namely, US aid "has tended to flow disproportionately to Latin American governments which torture their citizens,...to the hemisphere's relatively egregious violators of fundamental human rights." Furthermore, the correlation is strong, includes military aid, and persists through the Carter period. This correlation remained strong despite the fact that support for the worst torturers and murderers was inhibited by human rights clauses that were added by Congress to US foreign assistance legislation "over the open and intense opposition of the Nixon, Ford, and Carter administrations." Furthermore, Schoultz shows, this correlation cannot be attributed to a correlation between aid and need.[187]

This study might suggest that Kennan understated the case: human rights are not irrelevant to foreign policy; rather, we send aid precisely to those governments that are committed to torture. The conclusion is supported by other research. Michael Klare and Cynthia Arnson demonstrate that "U.S. firms and agencies are providing guns, equipment, training, and technical support to the police and paramilitary forces *most directly involved in the torture, assassination, and abuse of civilian dissidents*"; "Rather than sitting in detached judgment over incidents of abuse occurring elsewhere [as official rhetoric would have it], *the United States stands at the supply end of a pipeline of repressive technology that extends to many of the world's most authoritarian regimes.*" The US is the world's leading supplier of police and prison hardware, the leader in "what can best be called the *international repression trade,*" supplying many of the worst human rights violators.[188]

But a correlation is not a theory. An explanation is required. One possibility is that US governments have a positive hatred of human rights, but this seems implausible. More likely, human rights are simply irrelevant to policy formation, in accord with Kennan's dictum, and we must search elsewhere for an explanation for the correlation between state terror and US aid.

A study by Edward Herman suggests a plausible explanation. He too investigated the relation between US aid and human rights, over a broader range and with somewhat different measures, considering changes in aid from the US and US-dominated international lending agencies as the human rights climate changed. He found the same correlation: as the human rights climate deteriorates, US aid increases. But he also carried out a second study, asking how US aid correlates with the investment climate (tax and profit repatriation laws, government controls on wages and labor organizations). The conclusion is that "US-controlled aid has been positively related to investment climate and inversely related to the maintenance of a democratic order and human rights."[189]

This study suggests a plausible explanation for the correlation between US support and human rights violations. The guiding concern of US foreign policy is the climate for US business operations, a fact well-supported in the historical and documentary record and easily explained in terms of the domestic institutional basis for foreign policy planning. But in the Third World, improvement in the investment climate is regularly achieved by destruction of popular organizations, torture of labor and peasant organizers, killing of priests engaged in social reforms, and general mass murder and repression: "it is the *function* of state terrorism to keep popular participation down, to limit services to the lower classes, and to freeze the structures that have generated" a situation of deprivation for the lower income classes.[190]

Investigation of such topics is hardly a priority for American social science; in fact, such elementary questions as the relation of corporations to formation of foreign policy have been under a virtual taboo in the literature on international relations and US foreign policy,[191] and the questions just reviewed have not exactly been on the agenda though they seem rather significant. It would, however, be no surprise to discover that the results of these few studies hold up to more extensive inquiry and that the theory they suggest proves to be valid over a large range.

What about "the raising of the living standards"? In Latin America, there has been economic growth, accompanied by widespread, often increased suffering for a very large part of the population. Consider Brazil, the most important of the Latin American countries, where the civilian government was overthrown by a US-backed coup in 1964 in what Assistant Secretary of State for Inter-American Affairs Lincoln Gordon called "the single most decisive victory of freedom in the mid-twentieth century," instituting a murderous military dictatorship that Gordon lauded as "totally democratic" and "the best government Brazil ever had." It no doubt was the best government for US investment, which rapidly increased along with profits repatriated to the US. The economy also grew in a widely heralded "economic miracle," but as President Médici commented in 1970: "The economy is doing fine, but the people aren't." The income of the majority dropped in relative terms, and for a substantial proportion, in absolute terms as well. Food consumption decreased for the poor and public health seriously deteriorated. In São Paolo, the most prosperous city of Brazil, 52% of the population was classified as suffering from malnutrition in 1970, up ten percent since the "victory of freedom," while the rate of infant mortality increased 45% between 1960 and 1973. Elsewhere, the story is still worse.[192]

In Rio de Janeiro, desperate people, including teen-agers, advertise their kidneys and corneas for sale in an attempt to survive. Others sell their blood; Red Cross officials think that Brazil has become the world's leading blood exporter, with the value perhaps reaching $.5 billion annually. The sellers are the poor, often suffering disease and malnutrition. There are no sanitary facilities or medical attention, no check on how much blood a victim has sold. Some sell blood until they die, with almost no blood left according to doctors.[193] There have been similar reports from elsewhere in Latin America, including Nicaragua, until the new regime put an end to the practice—yet another of those cases of interference with Free Enterprise that so enrage "true democrats."

Much the same is true of Guatemala, where the overthrow of the reformist democracy was hailed by Secretary of State John Foster Dulles as "a new and glorious chapter" in the "already great traditions of the American states." Four years later, in 1958, he declared on Pan American day:

> Words can scarcely express how fortunate we are in this hemisphere, how greatly blessed, to have this kind of association, which has no counterpart in all the world, and indeed in all history... Indeed, never before in history has a group of nations of comparable number enjoyed, in organized form, so high a measure of fellowship and harmony. Thus we set an example from which others can profitably learn.

In 1963, Milton Eisenhower observed that "We breathed in relief when forces favoring democracy restored Guatemala to its normal place in the American family of nations...," an interesting and rather accurate conception of the norm under US rule.[194]

The series of Guatemalan gangsters who have run their torture chamber since 1954 with constant US support have created a society with the lowest life expectancy in Central America (49 years); 35% of children (up to 60% in rural Guatemala) die before the age of 5, the minimum wage has declined to below that of the Arbenz years with a one-third decline in purchasing power of urban workers during the 1970s; caloric intake averages 83% of daily requirements and is far lower for large parts of the population; 80% of the agricultural labor force has been reduced "to a position of virtual servitude at the hands of landowners and their labour contractors" beyond that of the colonial period. It is, furthermore, "a nation of prisoners" in the words of an Americas Watch report, with a level of barbaric state terror that has few contemporary parallels.[195] This, in a country with ample resources, considerable economic growth and concentrated wealth; and encouraging steps towards democracy and economic and social progress until "big brother" stepped in to carry out "his duty" (see p. 148).

The same story can be retold throughout the continent, and elsewhere, as dependent development leads to economic growth with impoverishment for much of the population, a long-term tendency to which US policy makes regular and significant contributions.

Turning finally to democratization, the record shows clearly that the US has strenuously and often violently opposed formal parliamentary democracy when its outcome cannot be guaranteed by the domestic concentration of power and external US force, and has evinced a positive hatred for democracy, if we understand democracy to be a system that provides the population at large with ways to participate meaningfully in determining public policy and controlling state actions. In Latin America, the US has repeatedly intervened to overthrow democratic systems or prevent steps towards achieving democracy, as in the case of Chile, Brazil, the Dominican Republic in 1963 and 1965, El Salvador in 1961 and dramatically since 1979, and so on; and it has done the same elsewhere as well, as in the case of Laos and the Philippines, noted earlier. In Vietnam, US policy-makers always recognized that their problem was that the client regime they had established "lacks sufficient popular support and cohesion to enter...a political test of strength with the front [the NLF, the political front of the Vietcong]." The generals placed in power by the US recognized that "we are very weak politically and without the strong popular support of the population which the NLF have." Thus the US had to prevent any political settlement and physically destroy the political opposition and the society in which it was based, while running elections it knew to be fraudulent to appease the home front.[196]

It is no surprise at all that the US should overthrow the only democratic government in the history of Guatemala in 1954, support a military coup to avert the threat of democracy in 1963, and maintain in power a series of torturers and mass murderers, while the press in its occasional commentary deplores the violence that erupted from some unknown cause in 1954 and has mysteriously persisted since. The hostility to democracy on the part of American planners, and the reasons for it, are well-understood among serious commentators on US policy (see p. 82): the fifth Freedom is regularly threatened when governments are responsive to the needs of their own population, instead of the transcendent needs of Big Brother. Meanwhile leading American political scientists engage in childish prattle about "the overall effect of American power on other societies": namely, "to further liberty, pluralism, and democracy"; "The conflict between American power and American principles virtually disappears when it is applied to the American impact on other societies,"[197] so that we must conclude, to judge by the historical record, that "American principles" include torture, massacre, starvation, slavery, enrichment of the foreign investor, and fervent opposition to democracy when the results cannot be guaranteed.

Nor should we be surprised when President Reagan describes the vicious and corrupt President Marcos of the Philippines as a man "pledged to democracy," or when Vice-President Bush toasts the dictator for his "service to freedom and to our country," with the words: "We stand with you... We love your adherence to democratic principle and to the democratic processes."[198] In accordance with their conception of "democracy," why not?

9 The Awesome Nobility of our Intentions

Whatever we do, so our historians and commentators tell us, is guided by utterly benign intent. We are hardly alone in adopting such a stance, though it might be argued that we passed long ago beyond the norm. In 1831, de Tocqueville observed the arrival in Memphis of native Americans driven from their homes by several thousand soldiers "in the middle of winter," with snow "frozen hard on the ground." "The Indians had their families with them, and they brought in their train the wounded and the sick, with children newly born and old men upon the verge of death," a "solemn spectacle" that would never fade from his memory, "the triumphal march of civilization across the desert." He was particularly struck that the pioneers could deprive Indians of their rights and exterminate them "with singular felicity, tranquilly, legally, philanthropically, without shedding blood, and without violating a single great principle of morality in the eyes of the world." It was impossible to destroy people with "more respect for the laws of humanity," he wrote.[199]

So it has always been. As the US was massacring hundreds of thousands of natives during the conquest of the Philippines (what we call "Philippine insurrection") at the turn of the century, the press commented:

> Whether we like it or not, we must go on slaughtering the natives in English fashion, and taking what muddy glory lies in the wholesale killing til they have learned to respect our arms. The more difficult task of getting them to respect our intentions will follow.

> The struggle must continue until the misguided creatures there shall have their eyes bathed in enough blood to cause their vision to be cleared and to understand that not only is resistance useless, but that those whom they are now holding as enemies have no purpose toward them except to consecrate to liberty and to open for them a way to happiness.

Since the natives in their blindness never seem to understand the beneficence of our intentions, we must, reluctantly, continue to slaughter them.

The Republican National Convention announced in 1900—a bit prematurely—that "the American people have conducted and in victory concluded a war for liberty and human rights." Meanwhile a leading sociologist, Franklin Henry Giddings, devised the useful concept of "consent without consent": "if in later years, [the colonized] see and admit that the disputed relation was for the highest interest, it may be reasonably held that authority has been imposed with the consent of the governed," as when a parent prevents a young child from running into the street.

The beneficiaries of our endless good will failed to understand. The Filipino nationalist Sixto Lopez wrote that the Filipinos

> have already accepted the arbitrament of war, and war is the worst condition conceivable, especially when waged by an Anglo-Saxon race which despises its opponent as an alien or inferior people. Yet the Filipinos accepted it with a full knowledge of its horror and of the sacrifices in life and property which they knew they would be called upon to make.

Had they known what horror and sacrifices the invaders would bring, they might well have submitted; for example, the people of Samar, where Marine commander Waller, soon to move on to Hispaniola, carried out the orders of General "Hell Roaring Jake" Smith who wanted the area "made a howling wilderness":

> I want no prisoners. I wish you to kill and burn, the more you kill and burn the better it will please me. I want all persons killed who are capable of bearing arms in actual hostilities against the United States.

The press found the revelations at the trials of Smith and Waller "shocking," but quickly overcame their doubts. The *New York Times* explained that

> A choice of cruelties is the best that has been offered in the Philippines. It is not so certain that we at home can afford to shudder at the "water cure" [a standard form of torture used by the US forces] unless we disdain the whole job. The army has obeyed orders. It was sent to subdue Filipinos. Having the devil to fight, it has sometimes used fire.

All of this was in the best tradition of the recent Indian wars and the reaction to them.[200]

Reference to the "English fashion" of "slaughtering the natives" is, incidentally, appropriate; our Puritan forebears were particularly adept at teaching the natives that war, English-style, is a form of extermination, women and children being prime targets, using methods that had been honed in earlier trials such as the slaughter of the Irish, also "savage heathen" who merited their fate. Meanwhile, proceeding "by little and by little" in John Winthrop's words, they took the land that belonged by right to these "Saints," as the Scriptures showed. With Scriptural authority no longer in fashion, other resources sufficed. The distinguished American historian Samuel Eliot Morison wrote scornfully in 1958 of "backward peoples getting enlarged notions of nationalism and turning ferociously on Europeans who have attempted to civilize them"; four years earlier the *Times* editors had drawn the crucial lessons from the CIA coup restoring the Shah in Iran: "Underdeveloped countries with rich resources now have an object lesson in the heavy cost that must be paid by one of their number which goes berserk with fanatical nationalism." Such thoughts were echoed in 1965 by the respected British historian Hugh Trevor-Roper, when he dismissed as merely amusing the study of "the unrewarding gyrations of barbarous tribes in picturesque but irrelevant corners of the globe: tribes whose chief function in history, in my opinion, is to show to the present an image of the past from which, by history, it has escaped."[201] One of the cultural achievements of the 1960s was to open a few eyes to the meaning of such conventional talk and attitudes.

Little was to change as the years passed. When the CIA coup destroyed any hope for democracy, social justice or meaningful economic development in Guatemala in 1954, the *New York Times* editors wrote that "The expected has happened in Guatemala. Elements opposed to the slow Communist infiltration of the government have taken up arms to end it." Of course, they did not do it entirely without help from Big Brother, but the Mayans, "quiet, soft-spoken, long suffering...could not be expected to know that if their lot was hard now it would be infinitely worse if a new Moscow-linked tyranny were set up"—so we may see this as another episode of "consent without consent." A week later, they observed that "genuine agrarian reforms were needed," in contrast to the real agrarian reforms carried out by the enemy, now thankfully overcome.

The leading *New York Times* pundit, the highly-respected Arthur Krock, explained that "the world Bolshevik conspiracy to take over the country" had been foiled, solemnly parroting the idiocies and lies handed out by the US government and quoting with respect an informed diplomat who thought there was a chance that President Arbenz might be restored "after an interval devoted to shaking the conviction of this hemisphere that, for the first time, a Communist-controlled state was to be set up far from the military power of Moscow," though we might do better yet: he was "now disposed to believe in a good chance for the formation of a military junta, made reliably anti-Communist by replacements of some members of the present one, to govern Guatemala until there can be free and democratic elections again"—perhaps a millenium hence.[202]

Krock also lamented the power of the Communist propaganda apparatus that had misled the public into believing that there had been an "invasion" or that the US was somehow involved, even sponsoring "demonstrations against the United States" through "the Communist network in the Americas," while the US, so backward in these matters, had been "slow in realizing these maneuvers" or responding to them. Meanwhile, the public relations experts of the United Fruit Company were congratulating themselves on their success in peddling fanciful tales that were eagerly swallowed by the free press, including a front-page story in the

New York Times praising the Company's forward-looking policies after a successful brainwashing operation arranged for reporters in Honduras; much impressed with the fantasies spun by the United Fruit PR offices, the *Times* editors noted (June 20, 1954) that "American-controlled undertakings in Guatemala have greatly liberalized and humanized their policies." The chief PR officer for United Fruit, Thomas McCann, describes how the specialist they hired, Edward Bernays, used his contacts with the *Times* to bring the Guatemalan situation to their attention (as perceived by United Fruit) by 1951, inducing them to send publisher Arthur Hays Sulzberger to inspect at the company's invitation, witnessing a "Communist riot"—"a first-class public relations coup" by Bernays. The material successfully marketed in the press also included faked atrocity photos, and of course the whole US-fabricated story about the Bolshevik conspiracy overturned by patriotic Guatemalans. McCann later wrote that "a great deal of the news of Central America which appeared in the North American press was supplied, edited and sometimes made by United Fruit's public relations department in New York," though "It is difficult to make a convincing case for manipulation of the press when the victims proved so eager for the experience."[203] The US government and its associates in executive suites hardly need a separate state propaganda apparatus as long as they can count on the Arthur Krocks and *Times* journalists and editorial writers.

Summarizing these events on June 29, 1954, the *Times* editors concluded:

> The answer to communism in Guatemala and in other countries is not reaction but liberal reform. The road is a long one. This country [the US] may have made mistakes over the years past and in this particular episode. Now it is for us to show ourselves warm and intelligent friends of all the people of Guatemala.

And so we have been doing for 30 years, destroying agrarian reform, installing and maintaining murderous tyranny, slaughtering the natives and arming the killers and torturers, looking the other way as the long-suffering Mayans are subjected to near-genocidal assaults and slave and starve while US firms profit, all with the most noble intent, always willing to concede that "we may have made mistakes" in our innocence, as we and our subjects march forward with arms linked to an ever more brilliant future.

The same convenient innocence served well as we turned to slaughtering the natives in Indochina. In February 1965, the US extended its war against South Vietnam by initiating the regular bombardment of North Vietnam, and more significantly, as Bernard Fall observed, began "to wage unlimited aerial warfare inside [South Vietnam] at the price of literally pounding the place to bits," the decision that "changed the character of the Vietnam war" more than any other. These moves inspired the distinguished liberal commentator of the *New York Times*, James Reston, "to clarify America's present and future policy in Vietnam":

> The guiding principle of American foreign policy since 1945 has been that no state shall use military force or the threat of military force to achieve its political objectives. And the companion of this principle has been that the United States would use its influence and its power, when necessary and where it could be effective, against any state that defied this principle.

This is the principle that was "at stake in Vietnam," where "the United States is now challenging the Communist effort to seek power by the more cunning technique of military subversion" (the United States having blocked all efforts at political settlement because it knew the indigenous opposition would easily win a political contest, and after 10 years of murderous repression and three years of US Air Force bombing in the south).[204]

In November 1967, when Bernard Fall, long a strong advocate of US support for the Saigon regime, pleaded for an end to the war because "Viet-Nam as a cultural and historic entity...is threatened with extinction...[as]...the countryside literally dies under the blows of the largest military machine ever unleashed on an area of this size," Reston explained that America

> is fighting a war now on the principle that military power shall not compel South Vietnam to do what it does not want to do, that man does not belong to the state. This is the deepest conviction of Western Civilization, and rests on the old doctrine that the individual belongs not to the state but to his Creator, and therefore has "inalienable rights" as a person, which no magistrate or political force may violate.

A year later, long after the Tet offensive had caused much of the corporate elite to turn against the war as a "bad investment," one of the leading academic opponents of the war, the distinguished Asia scholar John King Fairbank, informed the American Historical Association in his presidential address that we became engaged in Vietnam "mainly through an excess of righteousness and disinterested benevolence."[205] The same touching faith in American innocence and benevolence in Indochina persists until today in any commentary that can reach a substantial audience, untroubled by the plain facts.

Returning to Latin America, William Shannon, Distinguished Professor at Boston University and noted liberal commentator, proclaims that "for a quarter century, the United States has been trying to do good, encourage political liberty, and promote social justice in the Third World," particularly in Latin America, "where we have traditionally been a friend and protector" and where we intervened "with the best of motives," though "benevolence, intelligence and hard work have proved to be not enough," as the Pinochet coup in Chile demonstrates. More recently, he has explained why the Sandinistas "hate America": "This is understandable given their limited education and their years spent in exile, in prison, or in the hills battling what they perceived as an American-backed dictatorship." These benighted creatures, so ignorant of history, use anti-Americanism to provide "the energy for their political movement, much as anti-Semitism provided the energy for Nazism."[206]

The literature of scholarship, intellectual commentary and journalism abounds with such professions of awesome benevolence, which are utterly immune to fact, illustrating a degree of fanaticism in the service of the state religion that has few historical counterparts. And the same thoughts animate the men in the field, who continue, today, to echo the message of the press at the turn of the century. Ken Anderson, a Harvard Law School student who worked in El Salvador with the Interamerican Court of Human Rights of the OAS, describes his experiences near a free-fire zone where he "watched the planes work their way across the hills" and spoke to refugees who had fled after families and friends were beaten to death by the soldiers in "a war against civilians that they will not forget."[207] He asked an American Embassy political officer about the peasant victims of the "slaughter from the air" who are "counted as combatants" by the Embassy, in particular, a nine-year-old girl whose "parents and family had been blown up in a bombing attack" and "was now headed to an orphanage filled with hundreds of children like her." The US official "shrugged off all those cases":

> A couple of years down the road, it'll all be seen as the costs of war. It's better for the military to do whatever it has to do to retake the region. Then we'll come in with food and a lot of aid—they'll eat and forget.

First we slaughter the misguided creatures until their vision is cleared, then we turn to the thankless task of getting them to respect our intentions.

To see how much our moral and intellectual life has improved since the turn of the century, we may open the pages of the *New Republic*, long the official journal of American liberalism, now perhaps with a "neo-" affixed. Three years after they had given "Reagan & Co. good marks" for their performance in El Salvador, the editors, surveying the carnage, sadly observed that there is no good solution for "America's agony" in El Salvador, and offered some sober advice to President Reagan:[208]

> The Reagan Administration, if it is honest, must argue bleakly that there are higher American priorities than

Salvadoran human rights (human rights meaning, in this context, not anything so elevated as democracy but simply the physical security of persons who may or may not be suspected of potential anti-oligarchical sympathies), and that military aid must go forth regardless of how many are murdered, lest the Marxist-Leninist guerrillas win. And indeed, the guerrillas must not win...

Leaving no doubt about their intentions, the editors explain that the aid will go to "Latin-style fascists," but no matter: "Given a choice between communism and war for the people of El Salvador, no doubt the American people will choose the latter"—and it goes without saying that it is our prerogative to choose war for them, as we suffer "the agony of responsibility." The editors explain further that "in the end the only moral choice may be military intervention," but since we are so noble, this will be intervention "not in alliance with the death squads but in opposition to them"—that is, in opposition to the death squads that we helped to establish and have since maintained, that grew inevitably out of the intelligence and paramilitary apparatus we constructed in our interest and the social conditions breeding dissidence and revolt that are in significant measure our legacy.

The injunction to persist "regardless of how many are murdered" goes a long step beyond the racist press of the turn of the century. In fact, it is not easy to find a historical counterpart; perhaps the Nazi archives might yield examples. As the right-wing moved to overturn the reformist coup in El Salvador with US backing in late 1979, Colonel Vides Casanova, then commander of the National Guard and now Minister of Defense under the Duarte government, reminded civilians in the junta that "in 1932 the country had survived the killing of 30,000 peasants. 'Today, the armed forces are prepared to kill 200,000-300,000, if that's what it takes to stop a Communist takeover'."[209] But willingness to kill two or three hundred thousand still falls short of the advice of the New Republic editors that we must proceed "regardless of how many are murdered." A closer counterpart is a statement attributed to the Khmer Rouge by François Ponchaud and widely publicized in the late 1970s as proof that its leadership matches or surpasses Hitler and Stalin: the statement that one or two million people would be enough to build the new Kampuchea, so that the rest could be eliminated. This proved to be a fabrication,[210] but at least it does come closer to the advice to proceed "regardless of how many are murdered," though it still falls short.

The sentiments themselves are remarkable enough; still more instructive, perhaps, is that they pass without comment, as apparently entirely normal.[211]

As the record clearly shows, what we are doing today in Central America, and the reaction to it, breaks little new ground, apart from scale. There should be no surprise over the undisguised pleasure so widely expressed over the relative success of five years of massacre and torture in El Salvador; a similar response will surely replace current doubts if the US succeeds in its aims in Nicaragua through its proxy armies or the "invasion option." We are only reliving history when liberal Senators warn that we must bomb if Nicaragua obtains planes to defend its national territory, thus threatening our very lives. "They attack us and then won't allow us to defend ourselves," Foreign Minister Miguel D'Escoto commented while rejecting US charges that Nicaragua plans "offensive actions" against El Salvador and Honduras. This miracle of hypocrisy is "like a torturer who pulls out the fingernails of his victim, then gets angry because the victim screams in pain,"[212] or a cowardly thug who sends a collection of goons to beat up some child in a kindergarten whom he doesn't like, then whines piteously if the child raises his hands in self-defense.

This shameful picture should remind us, if we can summon up the honesty, that our intellectual culture was virtually founded on the twin pillars of hypocrisy and moral cowardice; Ronald Reagan, George Shultz and their acolytes among the educated classes are nothing new. These elements of the intellectual culture were recognized long ago, when the Founding Fathers were preaching the doctrine of natural rights granted to each person by the Creator, and bitterly deploring their own condition of enslavement—the term constantly used—to the British tax collector. Samuel Johnson asked: "how is it that we hear the loudest yelps for liberty among the drivers of negroes?" Reflecting on the same matter, Thomas Jefferson, a slave-owner himself, remarked: "Indeed I tremble for my country when I reflect that God is just; that his justice cannot sleep forever."[213]

Why then should we feign surprise when Reagan violates the Rule of Law in attacking Nicaragua, while explaining, with reference to his South African friends who are subjected to the "surge of violence" that "resulted from the other side":[214]

> I have always believed that it is counterproductive for one country to splash itself all over the headlines, demanding that another government do something because that other government then is put in an almost impossible political position. It can't appear to be rolling over at the demands of outsiders.

Reagan loves to prate about the Bible, which "contains an answer to just about everything and every problem that confronts us," so he informed the country.[215] Perhaps he might begin his reading of the Scriptures with the definition of "hypocrite" in the Gospel according to St. Matthew, 7.5.

Why all of this elaborate pretense about our benevolence and concern for human rights, democracy, and welfare, as we go on slaughtering the natives? Why did Reagan not accept the *New*

Republic recommendation, and simply tell the American people honestly that we must proceed on our course "regardless of how many are murdered" because we have higher priorities than the survival of the people of El Salvador? Why do even the *New Republic* editors, at the outer limits, continue to intone pieties about our "moral" goals as we suffer "America's agony" in El Salvador? Why do Senator Moynihan and others proclaim absurdities about our historic commitment to the Rule of Law?

There are two basic reasons. The first is that reality is unpleasant to face, and it is therefore more convenient, both for planners and for the educated classes who are responsible for ideological control, to construct a world of fable and fantasy while they proceed with their necessary chores. The second is that elite groups are afraid of the population. They are afraid that people are not gangsters. They know that the people they address would not steal food from a starving child if they knew that no one was looking and they could get away with it, and that they would not torture and murder in pursuit of personal gain merely on the grounds that they are too powerful to suffer retaliation for their crimes. If the people they address were to learn the truth about the actions they support or passively tolerate, they would not permit them to proceed. Therefore, we must live in a world of lies and fantasies, under the Orwellian principle that Ignorance is Strength.

The real victims of "America's agony" are millions of suffering and tormented people throughout much of the Third World. Our highly refined ideological institutions protect us from seeing their plight and our role in maintaining it, except sporadically. If we had the honesty and the moral courage, we would not let a day pass without hearing the cries of the victims. We would turn on the radio in the morning and listen to the voices of the people who escaped the massacres in Quiché province and the Guazapa mountains, and the daily press would carry front-page pictures of children dying of malnutrition and disease in the countries where order reigns and crops and beef are exported to the American market, with an explanation of why this is so. We would listen to the extensive and detailed record of terror and torture in our dependencies compiled by Amnesty International, Americas Watch, Survival International, and other human rights organizations. But we successfully insulate ourselves from the grim reality. By so doing, we sink to a level of moral depravity that has few counterparts in the modern world, and we may be laying the basis for our own eventual destruction as well.

Let us turn next to this topic.

4 The Race to Destruction

1 The Threat of Global War

Senator Dave Durenberger, chairman of the Senate Select Committee on Intelligence, delivered an address to the National Press Club in March 1985 on US policy in Central America, describing it as "ill-timed" and "ill-planned," a "policy which no one understands." Durenberger was concerned that the controversy over aid to the *contras* might suggest, "incorrectly, that Congress and the Administration are not in agreement on the need to oppose the Sandinistas and all they stand for." He suggested more forceful moves to replace the current "incoherent" policy of "reacting after the fact to events which appear beyond our control." The US and its allies, he urged, should consider cutting diplomatic relations and ceasing all trade and economic cooperation with Nicaragua. "He also said the Administration should make it clear that the United States is prepared to join in an invasion of Nicaragua, 'if the other nations undertake a collective action' in response to Sandinista aggression," where "aggression" has its usual Orwellian meaning: defense against US attacks. The US should now consider a naval blockade to prevent the import of Soviet arms, he said, with the implicit consequence that the US proxy armies would then be able to conquer a defenseless Nicaragua.[1]

Secretary of the Navy John Lehman said that any attempt by the US to blockade Nicaragua to halt the flow of arms might trigger a US-Soviet naval conflict. The Navy "cannot conceive that a naval conflict which engaged Soviet forces could be localized," he added: "It is instantaneously a global war."[2] If so, then Durenberger's proposal would be a step towards a terminal nuclear war.

Democratic Presidential candidate Walter Mondale had also spoken of a possible quarantine of Nicaragua, and the proposal is implicit in much other commentary, for example, the *Toronto*

Globe & Mail editorial cited earlier, blustering about the possibility that the USSR might provide Nicaragua with a radar system to monitor its own territory, subjected to US attack. If it is indeed, as alleged, an intolerable threat to world order for the USSR or Cuba to "bolster" a regime attacked by the US in Central America, then evidently the US has a right to impose a blockade to prevent them from doing what they have no right to do. And if a superpower confrontation results, we can blame the Russians as we go up in smoke.

Putting aside its moral level, all of this is the kind of thinking that has led us close to nuclear war in the past, and will again.

In fact, the USSR would very likely back away from a military confrontation with the US in the Caribbean. It has repeatedly done so elsewhere after provocations that the US would not tolerate for a moment, particularly in the Middle East, the most likely location for the outbreak of global war.[3] Nevertheless, Lehman's prognosis cannot be discounted.

Senator Durenberger's proposal illustrates what has been called "the deadly connection": the prospect that Third World intervention will lead to superpower confrontation and nuclear war. This has come close to happening quite a few times in the past, and will again. There is no more urgent issue on the contemporary scene.[4]

One such occasion was the Cuban missile crisis that brought the world ominously close to nuclear war in 1962. At that time, according to testimony of participants, planners considered a nuclear war highly likely if they rejected Khrushchev's offer to resolve the crisis peaceably with complete withdrawal of Soviet missiles from Cuba. They rejected this offer because it entailed simultaneous withdrawal of US missiles from Turkey: obsolete missiles for which a withdrawal order had been issued (but not yet implemented) because they were being replaced by Polaris submarines. "The best and the brightest" decided to face what they took to be a high probability of global destruction to establish the principle that the US alone has the right to keep nuclear weapons on the borders of an enemy, even missiles that it has already replaced with more advanced weapons.

One analyst of the crisis aptly remarks:

> Never before had there been such a high probability that so many lives would end suddenly. Had war come, it could have meant the death of 100 million Americans, more than 100 million Russians, as well as millions of Europeans. Beside it, the natural calamities and in-humanities of earlier history would have faded into insignificance. Given the odds on disaster—which President Kennedy estimated as "between one out of three and even"—our escape seems awesome. This event symbo-

lizes a central, if only partially "thinkable," fact about our existence.

This surely must be one of the low points of human history. It is a fact of some significance for the future that it is generally regarded here as a glorious moment, "one of the finest examples of diplomatic prudence, and perhaps the finest hour of John F. Kennedy's Presidency," in the words of the same respected scholar.[5]

Turkey remains a major US nuclear outpost, aimed in part at the Middle East and in part at the USSR, with a US nuclear combat base and nuclear warheads also stored for the use of the Turkish air force. Turkey is the third-ranking recipient of US military aid, after Israel and Egypt. The priorities indicate the significance for US planners of control of the incomparable energy resources of the Middle East. The major concern is "radical nationalism," which, it is feared, might threaten US control over these resources. "Radical nationalism" is another of those curious terms of US political theology—like "Communism," "stability," "containment," "democracy," "aggression," etc.—with technical meanings only dimly related to their normal sense: in this case, the reference is to nationalist movements that do not obey orders, whatever their political complexion may be, as opposed to "moderate nationalism," properly obedient. US relations with Israel, unique in international affairs, have always been closely related to these concerns. But the structure of military installations designed to deter the indigenous threat also faces the USSR, to ensure that there will be no interference from that direction in a core region of the US global system.[6] A 1983 US Air Force Publication describes the nuclear weapons mission in Turkey as "in an aggressive growth stage," with nuclear-armed aircraft on "alert" status, ready to strike Soviet targets.[7] The same planners who have placed the growing US nuclear arsenal in Turkey on alert warn us that Nicaragua, even Grenada, is a threat to our very existence, compelling us to take aggressive action of a sort that might lead to nuclear war. And their assessment is widely shared, yet another reflection of the paranoid fever of what passes for intellectual life.

The US now has more than 13,000 nuclear weapons capable of striking the USSR, over 11,000 of them classified as "strategic"; the USSR can explode about 8500 nuclear weapons on the United States. The US arsenal rose from about 4000 to 9200 during the 1970s while the Soviet arsenal increased from about 2000 to 6500. France and England have about 1000 additional nuclear weapons targeted against the Soviet Union, and their arsenals are rapidly increasing. NATO has always outspent the Warsaw Pact on armaments by a considerable margin, even by the US government figures, which have a built-in bias to inflate Soviet expenditures. Furthermore, a large component of Soviet weaponry is directed against China. Since 1976, Soviet military spending has slowed to 2% a year, according to the CIA, while US military spending has grown at more than twice that rate over the same period. The US is also well ahead in weapons technology and has consistently led in weapons deployment by several years. The Center for Defense Information, from which these figures are taken, comments aptly that "we are *mutually* inferior because there is no superiority in mutual destruction."[8]

President Reagan has a rather different version of all of this. He informed the country that "we have fewer warheads than we had in 1967...over recent years we've followed a policy of kind of unilaterally disarming and the idea that maybe the others would follow suit."[9] This is a reference to the period when US strategic weapons more than doubled to over 9000 with constant technological improvements, a novel form of unilateral disarmament. One should not, incidentally, accuse the President of lying, just as the term is inappropriate in the case of the random babbling of a young child. To lie requires a certain competence; one must first have mastered the concept of truth.

Sometimes the reports from Washington are quite true, however. Every year, the Pentagon produces a glossy publication designed to terrify the taxpayer who has to bear the costs of these military programs, documenting the Soviet drive for world domination and their immense advantage over us in every conceivable respect. The 1983 volume observed ominously that the USSR had a "superior" capability in liquid-fueled missiles. This is quite accurate. 96% of Soviet missiles are liquid-fueled while 95% of US missiles and all those on submarines are modern solid-fuel missiles, the US having passed beyond the unreliable liquid-fuel technology 20 years ago.[10] The Pentagon report did not comment on the Soviet lead in horse-drawn artillery, which may well be no less awesome.

The incipient anti-nuclear movement of the early 1960s turned to more urgent concerns as the decade progressed: to the actual use of conventional weapons rather than the potential use of nuclear weapons (probably as a result of a Third World conflict such as US aggression in Indochina). As the Indochina war wound down, the arms race became once again a more central concern. The major focus of attention has been on the growth of nuclear arsenals and advanced weapons systems, which has been remarkable. The emphasis is misplaced. The size of nuclear arsenals is a real but secondary consideration, though technological advances may pose an extreme hazard, particularly if they compel resort to computer-based rapid decision systems and launch-on-warning strategies, in which case war is likely if only from error, inadvertence or misjudgment in time of tension; Reagan's Strategic Defense Initiative (SDI: "Star Wars") is particularly dangerous in this respect. Even if nuclear arsenals were vastly reduced, a nuclear interchange would be a devastating catastrophe. In fact, even if they were reduced to zero, the capacity to produce nuclear weapons would not be lost and they would soon be available, and would be used, in the event of superpower conflict.

Furthermore, the relation between the size of nuclear arsenals and the likelihood of the use of nuclear weapons is not a simple one. Recall that on the one occasion when nuclear weapons were used to massacre civilians, exactly two were available—and if two more had been available and deliverable, in the hands of the Japanese enemy, there would have been no atom bombing for fear of retaliation. Nuclear deterrence probably does work, to some extent at least, a fact that cannot be lightly dismissed. Consider, for example, the US terrorist war against Cuba. It is possible that the US was inhibited from escalating its large-scale program of international terrorism to direct invasion by fear of widened, perhaps nuclear conflict, and similar concerns may have inhibited each of the superpowers on other occasions as well. Suppose that reduction of the deterrent capacity would tend to increase the aggressiveness of one or the other of the superpowers, not an unlikely consequence. Then it would increase the likelihood of superpower conflict, and with it, the likelihood of nuclear war. It is not obvious that the prospects for peace and survival are enhanced significantly, or perhaps at all, by efforts to reduce nuclear arsenals if such moves are not an integral part of a more general program to constrain state violence.[11]

It should be mentioned that much of the study of nuclear deterrence in the West is of limited relevance, because it is restricted to the problem of deterring the USSR, omitting as unthinkable the corresponding question that arises with regard to the other superpower. We would doubtless find the mirror image in Soviet books and journals.

The disarmament movement—particularly those elements in it that can gain media attention—has concentrated on demonstrating the awesome consequences of nuclear war and on various plans to halt or reverse the arms race. One might feel that the first of these endeavors is an insult to the intelligence, but perhaps those who judge otherwise are correct. If so, then the task of reiterating the obvious is an important one. The second line of action is also highly important, though not, in my opinion, for the reasons generally adduced; I will return to that. But the most significant issues may well lie elsewhere.

If we are concerned to avert nuclear war, our primary concern should be to lessen tensions and conflicts at the points where superpower confrontation is likely to develop, the Third World posing the greatest threat. There has rarely been a serious likelihood of war breaking out over European issues, though propagandistic exploitation of the superpower conflict to achieve other ends has led to concentration on this prospect, remote with rare exceptions. In a poll of military experts, 55% ranked Middle East conflicts as the most likely cause for nuclear war, with 16% choosing accidental use, a possible consequence of technical advances in weaponry.[12] If we are willing to face the central issue, we will find that there is often a great deal that we can do, since not infrequently US policy has been instrumental in maintaining and enflaming dangerous tensions and conflicts, primarily in the Middle East, particularly since 1967, but also elsewhere, including Central America and the Caribbean.

Until recently, the disarmament movement has tended to ignore this central issue, sometimes in quite shameful ways. The most dramatic example was the huge demonstration in June 1982 in connection with the UN disarmament session. The demonstration took place a week after the US-backed Israeli attack on Lebanon, which—apart from its murderous consequences— brought the superpowers close to nuclear confrontation as Israel attacked the forces of a Soviet ally, Syria, which had not attempted to impede the Israeli onslaught, assuming it to be aimed solely against the Palestinians. Joseph Gerson, peace secretary of the AFSC in New England, comments:[13]

> If the June 12 march was one of the greatest successes of the American peace movement, it was also one of our notable failures. After serious debate, the June 12 Coalition decided not to address questions of intervention in the organizing effort or at the rally in Central Park. On June 12, as people in the Middle East were being torn and seared with American-built cluster bombs, we were silent in New York. While the world lurched toward the nuclear holocaust that we had all come to prevent, we were silent. Only one woman had the insight and courage to speak about the war in Lebanon from the podium. Today it is President Reagan who tells us that an escalation of the war in Lebanon could lead to World War III.

The impassioned denunciations of the Israeli attack by Lebanese UN Ambassador Ghassan Tueni (a conservative Christian, owner of Lebanon's respected newspaper *An-nahar*) at the UN disarmament session were also ignored by the peace movement, and also, naturally, by the *New York Times*, which never mentioned him during those terrible months, while they were applauding the "liberation" of Lebanon. It is remarkable to see that even the peace movement, in this and other ways, registered its commitment to the general principle that the threat of nuclear war is a relatively insignificant matter when measured against the importance of protecting Israel and US relations with it from critical scrutiny. The event also illustrates the unwillingness, until recently, to face the most serious of the threats to survival: the deadly connection.[14]

2 The Nuclear Freeze Campaign: Successes and Failures

The disarmament movement has some real achievements to its credit, the most dramatic being the nuclear freeze campaign, probably the most successful organizing campaign ever carried out in the US peace movement—and the one which has had, perhaps, the most meagre results. Let us ask what is to be learned from its experience.

The campaign succeeded brilliantly in its specific organizing objectives. It succeeded in convincing three-fourths of the population to support a nuclear freeze, a remarkably high figure. Of this number, some were undoubtedly aware that the Soviet Union had introduced a Resolution at the UN General Assembly in October 1983 calling for a comprehensive freeze on the testing, production, and deployment of nuclear weapons, adding that this did not preclude reduction of these weapons. Some no doubt also knew that "on December 15, 1983, the UN General Assembly adopted the Soviet freeze resolution by a vote of 84 in favor, 19 opposed, including the United States."[15] Some may even have known that a year earlier, the US voted against a UN resolution that carried 111 to 1 calling for the outlawing of nuclear tests, and, with its allies, opposed a call for freezing the production and emplacement of nuclear weapons that carried 122 to 16; that a few months earlier, Reagan had announced that the US would not resume negotiations towards a test ban, in violation of its commitments under the 1968 Non-Proliferation Treaty; and that in the opinion of independent experts, verification is quite feasible. The distinguished physicist Hans Bethe, who has long concerned himself with the topic, wrote that even without on-site inspections "we could safely conclude a comprehensive test ban treaty, or a treaty with a very low threshold like two kilotons," leaving only the possibility of tests with "no military significance" for the superpowers. The former director of the respected Swedish Peace Research Institute (SIPRI), Frank Barnaby, stated that "the [US] demand for verification is used to hide the lack of political will."[16] News coverage of these matters has been perfunctory; they are quickly forgotten, and their implications, rarely discussed.

The great success of the freeze campaign, then, was to convince an overwhelming majority of the population to support a proposal that could have had a major effect on limiting the arms race and thereby enhancing American security, a proposal that was furthermore feasible, supported by the superpower enemy and by world opinion fairly generally. The failure was that all of this had essentially zero impact on American politics. The freeze was not an issue in the 1984 presidential campaign apart from some rhetorical flourishes. It is not a live issue in Congress. In fact, virtually the sole impact was to compel the Administration to enter into negotiations for the obvious purpose of pacifying public opinion, here and in Europe, so that it could proceed with the planned arms escalation.

We conclude from this experience that the factors that drive the arms race are powerful, sufficiently so as to render irrelevant both public opinion and the feasibility of programs that would materially enhance the prospects for human survival.

The primary significance of a nuclear freeze is that it would halt the technical advances in weaponry that are the most threatening feature of the arms race, far more so than the mere size of nuclear arsenals. This is also one of the major reasons why it cannot seriously be considered in the US, a matter to which we return in section 5.

The dangers posed by technical advances are evident enough. Highly accurate Pershing II missiles in West Germany or Soviet submarines off the Atlantic coast, with only a few minutes flight time to targets, leave little warning time and force reliance on computers or junior officers. Paul Bracken, a specialist on command-and-control, notes that "they threaten decapitation, and the reaction is likely to be the adoption of a range of extremely dangerous operating policies, such as launch under attack or a more extensive predelegation of firing authority within the military." Former Secretary of Defense Robert McNamara noted that "fear of the Pershings could stimulate a policy of launch on warning" or a policy of "preemption." Warning systems have a poor record, with many false warnings because of misinterpreted signals or computer failure. A congressional committee found 3703 false warnings of Soviet attacks in an 18-month period ending in June 1980, 151 of them relatively serious. Bracken contends that "the chance that you'd get an accidental war out of the blue, in peacetime, because a transistor failed or a major went mad, has been exaggerated," given the elaborate system of human and computer checks. But the main problem, of course, has to do with periods of international tension: "the chances of a war if you've already gotten into a crisis are a lot higher than is thought," he adds, since the system of checks may not function. The dangers are vastly enhanced under SDI, which would further increase the reliance on hazardous quick-response systems.[17]

3 The Lessons to be Drawn

The case of the nuclear freeze is not unique. "In April 1981, the Soviet Union renewed efforts to negotiate an end to the arms race in space, presenting to the United Nations a draft treaty to limit space-based weapons," after having suspended testing for two years. The proposed treaty would have banned the crude Soviet anti-satellite weapon, and Foreign Minister Gromyko stated that "We are prepared to go even further—to agree on banning in general the use of force both in space, and from space against the earth." The Reagan Administration strongly opposed this hopeful development. A leaked 1984-88 DOD directive for national military strategy, "Five Year Defense Guidance," states that provisions should be made to "wage war effectively" from outer space and that the Pentagon will "vigorously pursue" space systems to "project force in and from space," adding that the US "must ensure that treaties and agreement do not foreclose opportunities to develop these [military space] capabilities." "The nation that controls space may control the world," Under-Secretary of the Air Force Edward Aldridge stated in 1983, and the US does not want any impediment to such control, despite the serious threat to survival entailed by extending the arms race to space.[18]

The fall 1985 series of arms talks also "resulted from a Soviet initiative that was accepted almost intact by the United States, according to administration sources," the *Washington Post* reports. The fact that the Soviet initiative was accepted can be largely credited to the freeze campaign, while the lack of results again illustrates its failure. Radio Moscow said the Soviet idea is "to conclude an agreement to prevent militarization of outer space, to freeze nuclear armaments and to fully ban nuclear weapon tests."[19]

In September 1985, the USSR proposed a 50% reduction in the strategic nuclear arsenals of the US and the USSR in exchange for banning of Reagan's SDI.[20] The *Times* reported that Reagan "welcomed" the Soviet proposals and that the Administration responded with "optimism that the Soviet Union was finally weighing in with a serious proposal..." In fact, the proposal led to consternation as to how best to evade it, and it was hardly the first "serious proposal." Only a week before, the majority of the 90-nation conference reviewing the anti-proliferation treaty supported the Soviet position on banning of nuclear weapons testing, following the unilateral Soviet 5-month suspension of weapons testing on August 6, which the US refused to join. UPI reports that "The United States, backed only by Great Britain, became the odd man out by refusing to support a full nuclear test ban—the burning issue in this year's conference," and cited Senator Carl Levin, after visiting the conference: "What struck me the most," he said, "is the nearly unanimous view of US allies that the United States should return to the negotiating table with the Soviets relative to a comprehensive test ban treaty. Repeatedly I was told the United States is hurting itself by refusing to even sit down and negotiate." The evasive *Times* report on this conference is headlined "Parley Criticizes Nuclear Powers." The *Times* commentary on the September proposal also noted, this time accurately, that the Administration was concerned over Soviet "shrewdness and finesse"; the unstated problem is that this "shrewdness" makes it difficult to evade the proposals.[21]

The August 6 announcement of a Soviet test moratorium elicited an effective US government disinformation operation, which virtually eliminated it from awareness. On learning of the proposal, the US moved to undercut its impact before it was made public by announcing an "unconditional" and "unilateral" offer to the USSR to monitor a US nuclear weapons test. The Administration then claimed that the Soviet moratorium was a meaningless charade because they had "accelerated the number of tests that they've had so that they wouldn't need to test for the next five months or so" (National Security Adviser Robert McFarlane). The media accepted this fable. The *New York Times* wrote that the Soviet offer "would ring hollow even if it had not come immediately after an energetic series of Soviet test explosions." Unreported was the fact that the Soviet testing program for 1985 was below the average for preceding years, with seven tests compared with nine for the US, which was testing more sophisticated technologies, and a tenth immediately after the Soviet moratorium. Overall, the US has conducted 754 nuclear explosions as compared to 561 by the USSR and about 200 by other powers. Senator Durenberger had commented earlier that "a Comprehensive Test Ban Treaty would stop menacing Soviet developments while preserving the technological edge the United States enjoys in their nuclear warheads."[22]

Again we see that the US military system is driven by powerful factors, sufficient to override domestic and international opinion and even direct threats to US security. Once again, the complicity of the media is illustrated, this time, in accelerating the race to destruction.

A ban on nuclear weapons testing would halt or at least seriously impede dangerous technical advances. A comprehensive ban on flight testing of missiles would reduce the likelihood of a first strike, the alleged goal of "Star Wars." The reason, as explained by Herbert Lin, Research Fellow in the MIT Defense and Arms Control program, is that "a first strike requires missiles of certifiably high reliability," and "virtually all analysts agree that the lack of flight testing would over time erode confidence in the performance of these missiles." Such a test ban, he notes, would achieve the stated goals of the Star Wars program within even the most optimistic time frame and assessment of SDI and "at much lower cost and technical risk," without affecting deterrent capacity ("since only a fraction of our nuclear arsenal can cause unacceptable damage to the Soviet Union"), and with no problems of verifiability.[23] There is no evidence that this option has been seriously considered, and we may assume with some confidence that it will not be.

Essentially the same argument holds with regard to a nuclear test ban, which would over time "affect the very high level of stockpile confidence required for a nation contemplating a 'first strike' strategy" without significantly affecting the "lesser degree of confidence required for retaliation against attack." Administration officials concede that this is a "weak link in their position" of opposition to a ban.[24] Possibly other forms of testing could confirm warhead reliability, but confirmation of missile reliability requires actual testing. These issues, and the fact that they are not being seriously discussed—or, as far as we know, seriously considered— suggest that the alleged goals of SDI are fraudulent and that security concerns are not what motivate this program.

A further reason to doubt that the alleged goals are intended seriously is that a state possessing such a system could hardly trust it to prevent unacceptable damage from a first strike. James Fletcher, who headed the panel that recommended proceeding with the SDI program, commented that it poses what is "clearly one of the largest software problems ever tackled, requiring an enormous and error-free program on the order of ten million lines of code." "By the fifteenth or sixteenth general nuclear war, we'd probably get the bugs out," Bracken comments.[25] Few people acquainted with computers and software will question this judgment. The only conceivable (semi-rational) military purpose of such a system would be to facilitate a first strike, in the hope (hardly to be taken very seriously by rational planners) that it might provide protection against a retaliatory strike. The state lacking this system would be well-advised to accept the worst-case analysis and take this possibility seriously. This combination of rational expectations may well enhance the probability of a first strike, perhaps by the state possessing the system on the assumption that a retaliatory strike could be blocked, but more likely by the state lacking the system, which might, in a time of crisis, fear the loss of its deterrent capacity. The greater the confidence in the reliability of the system, the greater its contribution to the likelihood of a first strike in times of crisis. Thus the argument against the program on the grounds that it will not work is misconceived. Nor does the system make sense as a way of defending the land-based deterrent, given the fact that the other elements of the "triad" (submarines and bombers) provide more than an adequate deterrent. It is difficult to conceive of any security reason for the system; in fact, it would harm US security, more so to the extent that it appears reliable. We will see directly that there are further compelling reasons to doubt that security concerns were a factor motivating its development.

At the UN, "the United States has been almost alone in opposing successive resolutions calling for a comprehensive test ban— resolutions which have received greater support from the United Nations throughout its history than any other disarmament issue"; "During the 1984 session of the General Assembly the United States and all or several of its NATO allies found themselves in a small minority voting 'no' or abstaining on resolutions calling for a nuclear weapons freeze, prevention of an arms race in outer space, and prohibition of the use of nuclear weapons," among other disarmament proposals, all backed by the USSR, voting with the majority. The result is "a growing alienation of the United States from the mainstream of international opinion."[26] Diana Johnstone, whose in-depth coverage of European affairs is unparalleled in the US press, reports from Geneva that the Swedish chairperson of the first review of the nuclear weapons non-proliferation Treaty told a disarmament conference that there can be "no progress" on a freeze "so long as the present U.S. administration exists," reflecting opinions widely held among knowledgeable Europeans.[27]

In a report on a denunciation of the Reagan Administration by Soviet Foreign minister Gromyko at an East-West conference on European security, which caused "bafflement" because of its "intensity"—obviously another blow to world peace—John Vinocur of the *Times* mentioned Gromyko's proposal of a pledge of no first use of nuclear weapons, a nonaggression pact between the Warsaw Pact and NATO, cuts in military spending, renunciation of chemical weapons and a nuclear-free zone in Northern Europe, along with measures to limit military maneuvers. A year earlier, the USSR had introduced a proposal for NATO and the Warsaw Pact to limit troop strength to 900,000 men until larger reductions can be arranged and for the USSR and the US to begin mutual troops and arms reductions. In September 1985, the USSR announced that it would agree to withdraw chemical weapons from Eastern Europe if the US did the same from Germany, thus creating a chemical arms-free zone in the region; this was rejected by the US. Former SIPRI director Frank Barnaby condemned the "absurd and extravagant [US] verification demands" that have prevented a chemical weapons ban.[28] We learn little about such matters here.

As always, the arms negotiations involve maneuverings by the superpowers to achieve maximal advantage (see note 20), These issues aside, one major US objection to Soviet arms reduction proposals is that they require termination of Reagan's SDI. The White House has stated that this is out of the question. "Officials of the North Atlantic Treaty Organization remain skeptical about President Reagan's Strategic Defense Initiative and anxious about the way it seems to have become a nonnegotiable article of faith within the White House," Steven Erlanger reports from Brussels. They prefer that SDI be "used as a bargaining chip in Geneva to achieve substantial reductions in the Soviet nuclear arsenal"; a curious formulation, given the standing Soviet offer of substantial mutual reductions if the militarization of space is avoided. NATO officials are concerned that the US is "losing the propaganda war in Western Europe," a development with domestic implications that concern them. US NATO commander Bernard Rogers "agreed in an interview that the West is losing the battle for public support to Moscow." Apart from the PR aspect, NATO officials are concerned that preparations to deploy SDI might tempt the Soviet Union to a preemptive first strike, also reiterating the common observation that SDI will drive the USSR to large-scale missile construction to overwhelm it, not armaments reduction.[29]

National Security Adviser Robert McFarlane stated a few days later that testing and development of anti-missile lasers and other such systems is "approved and authorized" under the ABM treaty of 1972, offering a "new interpretation" of the subject, and a dangerous one, which would serve the "more ambitious goal" of removing "all constraints on the nuclear arms race," Anthony Lewis observes.[30] A flurry of protest led to Administration retraction, but this is unlikely to be the last effort to stretch the sense of existing treaties to accommodate SDI.

The US has opposed across-the-board reductions, preferring to focus on land-based missiles, on which the USSR primarily relies, while they constitute only a part of the US triad of land-naval-air nuclear forces. Throughout, the US has feigned surprise that the USSR placed "a greater reliance on the land-based missiles" (Reagan) and therefore rejected US proposals designed to reduce them while leaving the US with its enormous advantages in the other two legs of the triad. Reporting on the Reagan-Mondale TV debate where Reagan made these pronouncements, stating that he had only recently learned that most Soviet nuclear weapons are on land-based missiles, Fred Kaplan comments that

> it could not possibly have been a 'surprise' to anyone but Reagan that the Soviets rely on their land-based missiles above all others. Everyone who deals with nuclear issues knows that 70 percent of Soviet warheads are on land-based missiles, just as every schoolchild knows $2 + 2 = 4$. The fact that Reagan did not know and that he still finds it puzzling, reveals not only that he has no feel for strategic issues, but also that he does not comprehend his own Administration's arms-control record, does not understand why the Soviets found his proposals unacceptable, does not realize that those who made the proposals almost certainly designed them to be unacceptable.

Mondale proceeded "to outflank Reagan on his right wing," Kaplan observes, opposing Reagan's fanciful remarks on transfer of SDI technology to the USSR.[31]

The concentration on land-based missiles is a tactical ploy designed to avoid the danger of a halt in the arms race; rejection of a freeze, a test ban, and other such measures serves the same goal. The US favors an agreement to reduce the number of warheads as long as it does not impede technical advances in weaponry, even though these increase the danger to US security while numerical reductions have only the most limited effects. We return to the reasons, but the tendencies are clear in the negotiating posture.

"Reagan's determination to pursue both anti-satellite weapons and a space-based missile defense seems likely to end" the tacit agreement that space is "more useful as an observation post than as a potential battleground," *Washington Post* military commentator George Wilson observes, thus initiating "a new and expensive competition," and an extremely dangerous one. Current Soviet anti-satellite (ASAT) weapons are "little better than the ASAT weapons the United States deployed in the Pacific in the 1960s and then abandoned," as relatively worthless, but with Reagan's program in operation the USSR will no doubt "intensify work on a new generation of satellite killers," again increasing the threat to US security, given our reliance on satellites. An Air Force officer interviewed by *Science* notes that destruction of early warning satellites would "provide an excellent cover for a limited nuclear strike." The USSR would have less than 15 minutes to prepare for retaliation and would face enormous difficulties in transmitting orders, with satellites destroyed—so that a perceived threat of destruction might well trigger a desperate preemptive strike. Current ASATs are regarded as virtually useless, *Science* notes, citing the chairman of the Joint Chief of Staff and others. Howard Ris, executive director of the Union of Concerned Scientists, observes that the US was the first to deploy an operational ASAT system, dismantled in 1975, and considered the current Soviet system 20 years ago, but rejected it as impractical. "The Soviet ASAT 'threat' is a fiction created by the Reagan administration to justify the U.S. program," he notes, though if no treaty is signed barring future improvements, they will endanger US security.[32]

It is clear enough why the USSR sees SDI as a grave threat. Defense Secretary Caspar Weinberger said in December 1983 that unilateral Soviet development of such a system "would be one of the most frightening prospects I could imagine." A White House document added that under such circumstances, "deterrence would collapse, and we would have no choices between surrender and suicide." Soviet analysts are capable of drawing similar conclusions. Furthermore, though SDI is called a "defense" plan in the US, its offensive potential is quite real; one proponent, a laser expert, says its elements have the capacity to "take an industrialized country back to an 18th-century level in 30 minutes," quite apart from its potential use as a defensive shield supporting a first strike. Robert Bowman, president of the Institute for Space and Security Studies and former director of "Star Wars" programs for the Air Force, adds that these are "*not* purely defensive systems. They're not even *primarily* defensive systems," any more than the battleship New Jersey, cruising the Mediterranean, is a defensive weapon. "They are capable of attacking anything in the no-man's land of space, and possibly even within the sovereign territory of other nations." The US has " 'won' the race to deploy every new weapon, from nukes to MIRVs," he comments, "but the end result has been a net decrease in our security when the Soviets have inevitably matched us, producing a more dangerous stalemate." Former chief SALT negotiator Gerald Smith comments that "if the Soviets announced that their goal was to make American missiles 'impotent and obsolete'," we would increase our missile force; they will respond the same way. The SDI dooms arms control, he comments, reiterating a plausible and widely-held view.[33]

The International Institute of Strategic Studies in London describes SDI as a dangerous risk to peace, noting that "even if strategic defences were to prove feasible, they could damage stability rather than strengthen it." In fact, the system is more dangerous if it appears to be effective. The congressional Office of Technology Assessment concurs that SDI might make nuclear war more likely, encouraging the USSR to increase its nuclear attack forces and threatening "the entire arms control process." It advised that the best course for the US would be "to seek a treaty limiting the testing of such space weapons," the *Times* reports: to rephrase in more accurate terms, deemed improper, the best course would be to accept the Soviet proposals to this effect. The study also concluded that if both the US and USSR possessed such systems there would be "an extremely dangerous possibility" of a nuclear surprise attack, on the assumption that a first strike would so cripple an adversary that the attacker's defenses could ward off most retaliation. Without a comprehensive arms control agreement, "as the United States and the Soviet Union begin to deploy [ballistic missile defense], each might easily suspect the other of attempting to gain military advantage by seeking the ability to destroy most of the opponent's land-based missiles and then use defenses to keep retaliatory damage to a very low level," a perfect recipe for a first strike, the study states, adding that "It is important to note, however, that no one has yet specified just how such an arms control agreement could be formulated"—while many have explained why it is precluded by SDI. An effective US system might decrease the threat of a preemptive Soviet strike, the study argues, but only with "a considerable degree of Soviet cooperation," namely, substantial reduction of Soviet missile forces; exactly the opposite of what is anticipated. Contradicting repeated statements by President Reagan and his associates about a huge Soviet lead in missile defense, the study states that "in terms of basic technological capabilities...the United States remains ahead of the Soviet Union in key areas required for advanced [ballistic missile defense] systems." Few serious observers have many doubts on this score.[34]

Along with many others, Peter Clausen observes that

Through Soviet eyes, however, the SDI offers ample grounds for an alarming worst-case analysis of the U.S. threat. From Moscow's vantage point, a U.S. territorial defense, deployed in combination with new hard-target-kill weapons like the MX, Trident II, and the Pershing II, would look like a first-strike posture. With roughly two-thirds of its warheads on vulnerable land-based missiles, Moscow must worry that the United States could destroy the Soviet Union in a first strike, leaving the heart of its nuclear arsenal with too few surviving warheads to be able to penetrate American defenses. This threat can only strengthen the Soviet predilection to attack preemptively in a severe crisis.

George Ball describes the President's SDI proposal as "one of the most irresponsible acts by any head of state in modern times."[35]

The first strike threat is in my view exaggerated, since, as already noted, no imaginable system would prevent a crippling Soviet response (or conversely), and a first strike might itself have immensely destructive global consequences. But in situations of crisis all bets are off, particularly with reliance on computer-based response systems. And one can hardly have any confidence in the rationality of planners who have repeatedly shown that they are willing to approach the brink on the most astonishing grounds, and who are much honored for this display of courage—in reality, lunacy (see pp. 172-3).

It is a noteworthy fact, not adequately stressed, that SDI was not motivated by military considerations; these were devised after the fact to justify a program undertaken on other grounds. The idea was proposed well before the President's surprise announcement of March 23, 1983, in a privately-funded study initiated by right-wing industrialists associated with the Heritage Foundation, with technical advice from Edward Teller and General Daniel Graham, though Teller (who nonetheless supports SDI) noted that the USSR could overwhelm the proposed system at 1/10 its projected $100 billion cost. A high-level Pentagon review dismissed the project, as did a congressional Office of Technology Assessment, George Ball reports. He comments that the project "was opposed until the last minute by [Reagan's] secretary of defense and other principal members of his government." Top Pentagon specialists were neither consulted nor informed, knew nothing of the proposal until the day before its delivery, and thus "had no major input," in the words of Richard DeLauer, the leading Pentagon expert on missile defense. The foreign affairs and defense spokesman of the British Social Democrat Party, Lord Kennet, notes that "there is no military demand for SDI in Europe, and before the president spoke there was no military demand for it in the United States"; "very senior British defense officials were briefed by very senior U.S. defense officials the day before the speech about its contents, and SDI was not part of it," a significant fact. Informed political circles in Britain, he says, know that the SDI speech was made before Reagan consulted his defense secretary or the Joint Chiefs of Staff. He also notes that previously the US "went to great pains to persuade the Soviet Union" that such a system would be "destabilizing, alarming, and so forth," and that the system will bring about the "absolutely terrifying" prospect of reliance upon computers and automatic decision-making, seriously increasing the likelihood of war. He also suggests that SDI might create the worst crisis in NATO's history because "we know SDI would be terribly damaging to our interests,"[36] though in fact, European governments and corporations will scurry to gain what opportunities for profit they can from this bonanza, with appropriate strategic theories sure to follow.

In fact, European elites tend to be schizophrenic on Reaganite adventurism. On the one hand, they fear it and oppose many of its aspects. Lord Kennet notes that the invitation to Israel to join the Star Wars program "presents a special problem, since Israel's repeated flouting of U.N. resolutions and continued illegal occupation of foreign territory, despite European, and indeed U.S. pleas,[37] makes any military association impossible for us. Like Nicaragua, this is a general problem of European-US relations." Israel was the first country to agree to take part in SDI.[38] Independently of SDI, David Watt, Director of the Royal Institute of International Affairs in London, described "the chasm that lies between current American perceptions of the world and the world's perception of America." He observes that "with the possible exceptions of the Israelis, the South Africans, President Marcos of the Philippines and a few right-wing governments in Central and South America," most of the world believes "that the Reagan administration has vastly overreacted to the Soviet threat, thereby distorting the American (and hence the world) economy, quickening the arms race, warping its own judgment about events in the Third World, and further debasing the language of international intercourse with feverish rhetoric.[39] He adds that "it is in my experience almost impossible to convey even to the most experienced Americans just how deeply rooted and widely spread the critical view has become." As if to confirm this judgment, in the companion article on the current international scene in *Foreign Affairs*, editor William Bundy writes that with regard to the "degree of threat from the Soviet Union...the Reagan administration's broad view seems to this observer nearer to reality than the often excessively sanguine and parochial stated positions of other major nations."[40] Yet at the same time, Europe is eager to gain what profit it can from US enterprises at which it sometimes looks askance, such as SDI, and European intellectuals are often more "colonized" by the US than they like to believe, a fact already illustrated.

As in the case of the nuclear freeze, a majority of the US population opposes "Star Wars," despite the massive PR campaign: in a July 1985 poll, 53% disapproved while 41% approved, and only 26% would approve if the program were to conflict with the ABM treaty, as it surely will.[41]

Again we must conclude that the factors that drive the military system remain uninfluenced by public opinion here and abroad or by the real dangers posed to American security. The lesson of the successes and failures of the nuclear freeze movement, then, is reinforced: the causes of the race to destruction are deeply-rooted in our institutions and their commitments. Alleged security concerns serve as a cover for something else. And tactics must be revised accordingly.

Not everyone has drawn this conclusion. The Institute for Defense & Disarmament Studies sent out a three-page funding letter in March 1985 signed by its director, Randall Forsberg, who deserves much of the credit for the successes of the nuclear freeze campaign. The letter analyzes what has occurred in the following way. The Institute, which "launched the nuclear freeze movement in 1980," accomplished what it set out to do: it educated the public to support a nuclear freeze. But this popular success did not lead to "a *real* electoral choice on the issue in 1984." Why? Because of "expert opposition to the freeze," which prevented Mondale from taking a supportive position. The conclusion, then, is that we must devote our efforts to "building expert support": convincing the experts. This achieved, we will be able to move to a nuclear freeze.[42]

The underlying assumption is that the military system drives forward because political leaders and their expert advisers do not understand some technical points that are clear to us in the peace movement. That is the problem, and we can overcome it by explaining to them that there is a better way to achieve their goal of security and peace.

The consequences of this stand are predictable. Despite the announced commitment to popular activism, the public will be marginalized and quiescent since naturally it cannot be part of this elevated debate. Public apathy and obedience, and faith in alleged "experts," will also extend to other domains. Few will understand the definition of "expert" given by Henry Kissinger in one of his rare moments of lucidity: the "expert has his constituency—those who have a vested interest in commonly held opinions: elaborating and defining its consensus at a high level has, after all, made him an expert."[43] We need only bring to the fore what is presupposed: the "constituency" are those who hold state or private power, two categories that are closely linked.

Meanwhile, debate will be inconclusive. Strategic theories are highly speculative at best; no one can guess what people in command positions will do under this or that critical condition. There is no certainty about crucial facts, for example, whether the Russians can outfox Star Wars. When experts disagree and facts are uncertain, the reasonable thing to do is to try. Meanwhile, the arms race can proceed unencumbered.

The alternative is to tell people the truth: that the security of the US or Western Europe has rarely been a matter of central concern, and that the military system has been driven by different factors, to which we turn in section 5. But those who undertake to do so, and to draw appropriate conclusions for action, will not be too popular among elite groups. They will have to abandon respectability, prestige, institutional funding, media access, and the other perquisites of obedience to the main tenets of the doctrinal system.

4 Defense Against the Great Satan: The Doctrine and the Evidence

4.1 Defending the National Territory

What are the reasons for the dedicated march towards destruction and the irrelevance of public opinion, feasibility of alternatives, or security concerns? There is a conventional answer: We must defend ourselves against what President Kennedy called the "monolithic and ruthless conspiracy"; from "the focus of evil in our time," "the men who say...there is no God" with whom we therefore cannot "compromise," in the words of our own Khomeini, who believes that our generation may see the Day of Judgment prophesied in the Bible.[44] Thus at the two extremes of the spectrum of American politics we have essentially the same answer: we must be very strong to defend ourselves against the Empire of Evil.

This conventional answer is uninformative. In the technical sense of information theory, the claim that we are defending ourselves from some Great Satan conveys no information, because it is entirely predictable: every action of every state is justified in defensive terms, so the fact that these actions of this state are justified in terms of defense tells us no more than that we are listening to the spokesperson for some state. Thus, Hitler took the Sudetenland, invaded Poland and conducted the Holocaust for defensive reasons: Czechoslovakia was a dagger pointed at the heart of Germany, terrorists were killing innocent Germans, the Poles stubbornly refused to make peace, Germany had to defend itself against the Jews conspiring with the Bolsheviks and Western capitalism, and so on. There is virtually nothing that has not been rationalized in the name of security and defense.

To evaluate the defensive rhetoric of some state, we must turn to the historical record. Let us consider, then, a few significant moments, keeping to the post-World War II period.

As discussed in chapter 2, the US emerged from the war in a position of world dominance with few parallels in history, and with a firm determination to keep things that way. The geopolitical framework developed by planners, which has earlier precedents as noted, persists unchanged, including the sanctity of the Fifth Freedom and the commitment to "maintain the disparity" by harsh measures if necessary, preventing the "contagion" of independent development from "infecting" other regions, to the extent feasible.

In terms of security from threat, the US was also in an unparalleled position. There were no threats in the Western Hemisphere and the US controlled both oceans. No enemy could possibly reach us. There was, however, one potential threat: the development of ICBMs that could reach the US, fitted with highly destructive hydrogen bomb warheads. It is useful, then, to consider what efforts were undertaken to prevent the development of ICBMs or the hydrogen bomb. The record shows no serious effort to avert the sole potential threat to the security of the United States, indeed, little concern about the matter in the first postwar decade when progress might have been made in this direction. These facts do not comport well with the thesis that security considerations guided US policy.

In fact, Stalin's "peace offensives" were regarded as a serious threat that must be resisted, as this conventional terminology indicates. A *Business Week* analysis of 1949 noted that so far "Stalin's 'peace feelers' have been brushed aside" by Washington, but there is evidence that this "peace offensive" is serious, a prospect that they regarded with some concern, for reasons to which we turn in section 5. The same concerns are felt today. The cover of the London *Economist* (which generally supports Reagan's programs) shows the President clad in military garb speaking to armed troops, with the caption: "Right, men, are we ready for their peace offensive?"; caricaturists are granted latitude beyond the norm, not only in the West.[45] Stalin's 1952 proposal for a unified demilitarized Germany under internationally supervised elections (which the Communists were sure to lose) was rebuffed in favor of the rearmament of Germany within a Western military alliance,[46] a guarantee that the Soviet grip over its European satellites would not relax, whatever internal changes take place in the USSR; given recent history and security considerations, no Russian government would permit erosion of its control over this region in the face of a rearmed Germany allied to the United States. The possibility of

reducing tension and conflict was dismissed in favor of the imperatives of confrontation and military build-up. The security of the
United States was again a secondary concern.

4.2 The Defense of Western Europe

Perhaps, then, it was the fear of a Soviet attack on Western
Europe that motivated US militarism. This thesis is also not easy
to defend, quite apart from the fact that opportunities for relaxa-
tion of European tensions have hardly been vigorously pursued by
US planners. The US never seriously anticipated a Soviet attack on
Western Europe, despite the familiar public stance concerning the
Russian hordes poised to take this defenseless prize. In his very
important study of this question, already cited in connection with
US plans for Latin America, Melvyn Leffler argues persuasively
that "while civilian officials and military strategists feared the
loss of Eurasia, they did not expect the Soviet Union to attempt its
military conquest. In the early Cold War years, there was nearly
universal agreement that the Soviets, while eager to expand their
influence, desired to avoid a military engagement."[47] "American
military analysts were most impressed with Soviet weaknesses
and vulnerabilities," and estimated that it would take 15 years for
the USSR to overcome wartime losses in manpower and industry.
Even with "Herculean efforts," American intelligence did not
expect the USSR to reach the pre-World War II levels of the US
within 15 to 20 years. As Cold War conflicts intensified, US military officials anticipated "hostile and defensive Soviet reactions"
to American initiatives such as fortifying Turkey as an offensive
base against the USSR or during the Berlin crisis, attributed by US
army planners to "actions on the part of the Western Powers" (their
phrase, in a report to Eisenhower).

The fear on the part of US planners of "losing control of Eurasia" lay "less in American assessments of Soviet military capabilities and short-term military intentions than in appraisals of economic and political conditions throughout Europe and Asia,"
Leffler concludes. The CIA warned in 1947 that "The greatest
danger to the security of the United States is the possibility of
economic collapse in Western Europe and the consequent accession
to power of Communist elements." Assistant Secretary of War
Howard Peterson urged "emphasis on strengthening the economic
and social dikes against Soviet communism" rather than preparation for war. We have already noted Dean Acheson's expressed
concern over the dangers of democratic politics in France and
Italy, as he browbeat congressional leaders into accepting the
Truman Doctrine in 1947. In 1948, the National Security Council
reiterated the longstanding estimate that the USSR was unlikely
to resort to war, while warning that "Soviet domination of the
potential power of Eurasia, whether achieved by armed aggression
or by political and subversive means, would be strategically and

politically unacceptable to the United States" (my emphasis). Leffler observes that "American assessments of the Soviet threat were less a consequence of expanding Soviet military capabilities and of Soviet diplomatic demands than a result of growing apprehension about the vulnerability of American strategic and economic interests in a world of unprecedented turmoil and upheaval." A prime concern was indigenous unrest, on the assumption that US national security required "access to the resources of Eurasia outside the Soviet sphere."

Leffler notes that the dynamics of the Cold War become more clear "when one grasps the breadth of the American conception of national security," which "included a strategic sphere of influence within the Western Hemisphere, domination of the Atlantic and Pacific oceans, an extensive system of outlying bases to enlarge the strategic frontier and project American power, an even more extensive system of transit rights to facilitate the conversion of commercial air bases to military use, access to the resources and markets of most of Eurasia, denial of those resources to a prospective enemy, and the maintenance of nuclear superiority." In particular, the US commitment to the rebuilding of Russia's traditional enemies Japan and Germany within the US system, and the maintenance of air power, atomic weapons and bases on the periphery of the Soviet Union, virtually guaranteed continued tension.

The concerns throughout fell within the reigning geopolitical conceptions already discussed, with aggression on the part of a severely weakened Soviet Union faced with overwhelming US power a remote contingency.

In the most detailed current study of the postwar Soviet army, Michael Evangelista cites an intelligence estimate of 1945 that concluded that Soviet weakness made it unlikely that they would risk a major war for at least 15 years, and notes that similar assessments were made by the CIA well into 1949 and were supported by foreign observers. Subsequent intelligence estimates "exaggerated Soviet capabilities and intentions to such a great extent," he notes, "that it is surprising that anyone took them seriously." In fact, it is not surprising when one considers their utility in justifying US policies that were motivated on quite different grounds but justified in these terms; see section 5, below. Evangelista's study indicates that even in numerical terms, Western forces matched those of the Soviet Union in Europe, putting aside their much higher cohesion and morale, technical level and economic base, and the fact that Soviet forces were engaged in such tasks as reconstruction of large areas devastated by the German attack, which had concentrated the bulk of its fury on the Eastern front.[48]

We forget much too easily that "until mid-1944, almost 95% of all Nazi ground forces were engaged on the Eastern Front, where

Germany suffered 10 million of its total 13.6 [million] casualties; and that 50 Soviet citizens died for every one American. Even after 40 years, no 'historical truth' is more important in Soviet minds," Stephen Cohen observes, however insignificant all this may seem to American commentators who urge us to dismiss "the pretense that the Soviet Union helped us to liberate Europe" and the idea that "we could not have won the war without the help of the Soviet Union."[49]

In short, fear of a Soviet attack on Western Europe was not a dominant concern. At some level, Western European planners must recognize this. Western Europe has an economy far larger than that of the Soviet bloc, a much higher technical and educational level, a population of comparable size and much greater internal cohesion. If they really took the Soviet threat seriously, they could build a military system that would overwhelm that of the USSR. The fact that they do not is not without significance.

4.3 The Containment Doctrine

While security concerns dominated early postwar thinking, these had more to do with the Fifth Freedom than with any potential military threat to the US or its allies. Neither in its near-impregnable Western Hemisphere fortress nor in Europe nor in other spheres of expanding US influence did the US adopt a defensive stance, despite conventional rhetoric about "containment of the Soviet threat" that dominates scholarship and other commentary. "To a remarkable degree," John Lewis Gaddis comments in summarizing his major scholarly study of so-called "containment" doctrine, "containment has been the product, not so much of what the Russians have done, or of what has happened elsewhere in the world, but of internal forces operating within the United States." He is referring specifically to variations in the way the policy of "containment" is pursued, not the persistent regularities, which he ignores, or the causes for them. Within this narrow framework, he notes that "What is surprising is the *primacy* that has been accorded economic considerations in shaping strategies of containment, *to the exclusion of other considerations*," referring to state economic management.[50] The same observation holds when we generalize to broader considerations, including the crucial commitment to the Fifth Freedom.

In fact, the very term "containment" begs numerous questions and tends to undercut rational understanding of contemporary history. US policy is conventionally described in a framework of containment, détente, and return to containment in response to Soviet transgressions. The framework of discussion presupposes, as given, that the US stance is defensive throughout, that the US is not an active agent in world affairs pursuing its own objectives, but only responds to the acts of evil adversaries. The claim is often quite explicit, sometimes in the most astonishing forms, for example, when Henry Kissinger anguishes over the fact that in the 1960s "European intellectuals began to argue that the Cold War was caused by American as well as by Soviet policies" while "a vocal and at times violent minority" in the US dared to challenge "the hitherto almost unanimous conviction that the Cold War had been caused by Soviet intransigence" alone.[51]

The framework is a convenient one for Americans to adopt, but it has to be argued, not presupposed as is the convention. Thus, in one of the more critical studies within the mainstream, Gaddis explains that he adopts the conventional framework while recognizing (which is rare) that "the term 'containment' poses certain problems, implying as it does a consistently defensive orientation in American policy." He believes that the implied premise is correct but does not argue the point, dismissing it as "irrelevant for the purposes" of his study of US postwar strategy. The reason for this remarkable judgment is that "American leaders consistently *perceived* themselves as responding to rather than initiating challenges to the existing international order," so that it seems to him "valid to treat the idea of containment as the central theme of postwar national security policy."[52] By the same logic, we should treat containment of the US as the central theme of postwar Soviet policy, and containment of the West, the USSR, and the Jewish challenge as the central themes of Hitler's policy, since Hitler as well as Stalin and his successors perceived themselves as responding to challenges to the health and integrity of the societies they ruled. We expect state managers to perceive their role as defensive; the beginning of serious inquiry is an investigation into whether this perception is based on fact or convenience.

4.4 Containing the anti-Fascist Resistance: From Death Camps to Death Squads

In pursuit of its actual global geopolitical objectives, the US turned at once to a major post-liberation task: dispersing or destroying the anti-fascist resistance in favor of more trustworthy elements, often fascist collaborators. The victors in World War II had plans for the postwar world that conflicted with the vision of leading forces in the countries they were liberating from the Axis yoke. We easily recognize this in the domains conquered by the Red Army, but our ideological institutions, once again, protect us from perceiving the systematic pattern of US behavior in the regions it controlled, or comprehending the reasons for it.

One of Churchill's most trusted advisers, South African Prime Minister Jan Christiaan Smuts, warned him in August 1943, with regard to southern Europe, that "with politics let loose among those peoples, we may have a wave of disorder and wholesale Communism set going all over those parts of Europe." The reason, as British historian Basil Davidson comments, was that with the collapse of traditional ruling classes or their collaboration with the Nazis, "large and serious resistance came and could only come under left-wing leadership and inspiration": "the self-sacrifice and vision required to begin an effective resistance, and then rally others to the same cause, were found only among radicals and revolutionaries," most of them men and women who "followed the hope and vision of a radical democracy."[53] Plainly the US would have none of that. It took serious efforts to reverse the trend.

The pattern was set in the first area liberated by US forces, North Africa, where in 1942 the US placed in power Admiral Jean Darlan, a leading Nazi collaborator who was the author of the Vichy regime's anti-Semitic laws. Stephen Ambrose comments:[54]

> The result was that in its first major foreign-policy venture in World War II, the United States gave its support to a man who stood for everything Roosevelt and Churchill had spoken out against in the Atlantic Charter. As much as Goering or Goebbels, Darlan was the antithesis of the principles the Allies said they were struggling to establish.

The American army next drove up the Italian peninsula, restoring the rule of fascist collaborators while dispersing the Italian resistance, which had fought courageously against up to six German divisions, after it had liberated much of Northern Italy. "Italian committees of liberation might stimulate partisan warfare and continue to help in destroying the enemy," Davidson writes, "but they were not going to be allowed to govern Italy afterwards, being all too obviously the fruit of letting politics loose among people who could not be trusted"; the partisans were in effect told "to pack up and go home." From 1948, the CIA undertook large-scale clandestine intervention in Italian politics, labor and social life, spending over $65 million in such projects (which continued at least until 1975) by 1968, part of a more general European program in which US labor leadership also played a significant role, contributing effectively to the weakening of the labor movements.[55]

In Greece, the British army took over after the Nazis had withdrawn, displacing the Greek guerrillas and imposing a brutal and corrupt regime, which evoked renewed resistance that Britain was unable to control in its postwar decline. The US stepped into the breach under the Truman Doctrine in 1947, launching a murderous counterinsurgency war, complete with the full panoply of devices soon to be employed elsewhere: massacre, torture, expulsion, reeducation camps, and so on. The US-organized war was in support of such figures as King Paul and Queen Frederika, whose background was in the fascist movements, along with outright Nazi collaborators such as the Minister of Interior of the US-backed regime. The US succeeded in crushing labor unions and the former anti-Nazi resistance based among the peasantry and working classes and led by Greek Communists, eliminating even mild socialists with blatant interference in the political process, and creating a society in which US corporations and the Greek business elites prospered while much of the working population was forced to emigrate to survive.

Twenty years later, the US supported the first fascist restoration in Europe (also, the first government headed by a CIA agent, Colonel Papadopoulos, who was the liaison between the CIA and its Greek counterpart, virtually a subsidiary). This was shortly after President Lyndon Johnson had delivered an important lesson in political science, more enlightening than many weighty tomes, to the Greek Ambassador. When the Ambassador objected to US plans to partition the independent Republic of Cyprus between Greece and Turkey, saying that "no Greek parliament could accept such a plan," Johnson responded:

> Fuck your parliament and your constitution. America is an elephant, Cyprus is a flea. Greece is a flea. If these two fellows continue itching the elephant, they may just get whacked by the elephant's trunk, whacked good... If your Prime Minister gives me talk about democracy, parliament and constitution, he, his parliament and his constitution may not last very long.

For good measure, he added: "maybe Greece should rethink the value of a parliament which could not take the right decision," where "right" has its usual meaning. Greece was "whacked good" shortly after under the US-backed fascist regime, and the second flea, Cyprus, received the same treatment a few years later, with US and British support.[56]

Much the same was true in Asia, including Vietnam, Thailand, the Philippines, and Korea, while in Europe the US moved to abort steps towards any form of "national capitalism" (let alone socialism) that might have led to independence from the US-controlled global order. US influence and control expanded, in part by design, in part as a reflection of the objective power balance, at the expense of France and England (not to speak of indigenous populations), in the Middle East and Latin America.

The US attitude towards fascist restoration was hardly different in Latin America. The US showed little concern when pro-Franco, pro-German elements overturned Colombian democracy in 1949 creating what the *New York Times* described as "a totalitarian state, directly instigated by the [fascist] Government of Spain on the very frontiers of the Panama canal," with hundreds of people killed.[57] "The fascist seizure of Colombia was far more brutal" than the Communist takeover in Czechoslovakia in 1948, Fleming writes: "But the advance of fascism to the Panama Canal itself did not cause a wave of anger and fear to sweep through Washington and the West. This was due to two reasons: fascism was not then led by a great power; and, in the main, it preserves the privileges of the upper classes, instead of turning the social structure upside down." Panama itself was taken over in the same month by another supporter of Franco and Mussolini, who was so pro-Axis that he had been deposed in 1941, while the year before, Venezuelan democracy had been destroyed by a military coup, again raising no great concern in the US.

One aspect of the postwar project was the recruitment and protection of Nazi war criminals in the service of the war against the anti-fascist resistance and the Soviet bloc. In Asia, collaborators with Japanese fascism were often favored, as in Korea, where even the Japanese police were used as the US "liberated" the southern part of the peninsula from its own population with violence, bloodshed and destruction of the indigenous sociopolitical system that sprang into existence as the brutal Japanese occupation was terminated. As the end drew near for Nazi Germany, leading Nazis began to prepare for the postwar period, perceiving that in alliance with the US they could resurrect their anti-Bolshevik crusade while saving their skins and fortunes, and perhaps, some hoped, restoring fascism on a global scale. Their plans generally accommodated to US intentions. Nazi war criminals were quickly incorporated into the US intelligence apparatus in Europe; some mysteriously "escaped" from Western custody or were released "for good behavior," or were simply concealed by US agencies. German funds were transferred to Latin America, which became the center of a "Black International," particularly in the 1960s and 1970s, as the US supported National Security States on the Nazi model throughout the region, using Italian fascists as well as Nazi war criminals who had been spirited out of Europe by US intelligence with the assistance of the Vatican and a network of fascist priests when it became impossible to protect them from retribution there; many were brought to the US. The most important of the networks founded by the Nazi-US alliance was the Gehlen organization, constructed under US auspices by General Reinhard Gehlen, who had headed Nazi military intelligence on the Eastern Front; "in 1949, Gehlen's team became the official espionage and counter-espionage service of the new West German state, under close CIA supervision."[58]

Among those eagerly snapped up by US intelligence were Franz Six and his subordinates, Emil Augsburg (who became Gehlen's senior evaluator on Soviet affairs), Horst Mahnke (who went on to a distinguished publishing career in Germany) and Stanislaw Stankievich (who worked for Radio Free Europe until his retirement), all of them prominent Nazi gangsters who had been involved in horrifying massacres of Jews and others on the Eastern front. There were problems in employing Dr. Six, who was on trial for war crimes at Nuremberg, but his sentence was quickly commuted by High Commissioner John J. McCloy and he went to work for Gehlen, with special responsibility for developing a "secret army" under US auspices, with instruction and guidance by US, former Waffen-SS and Wehrmacht specialists, to be parachuted into the Soviet Union to make contact with forces left behind there by the Nazis after the German retreat. The operation was carried out, but without success, since the organization had been penetrated by Soviet agents.

According to John Loftus, who investigated these matters for the US Justice Department, these "rollback" operations were advocated by the Dulles brothers, Nelson Rockefeller, and George Kennan, among others, and run from Kennan's office under the direction of Frank Wisner, whose goal was to continue "the fight against communism by recruiting guerrilla bands of former SS men" in accord with State Department plans "to overthrow the governments of several Eastern European countries." Wisner also planned to have these SS underground armies help overthrow the Soviet regime from within, operating within the USSR in Byelorussia and the Ukraine as well as Eastern Europe. In 1949, the CIA initiated a three-year program to establish a network of active resistance movements behind Soviet lines, and US aircraft stripped of identifying marks dropped CIA-trained Ukrainian operatives to join a partisan army, formerly encouraged by Hitler, which was fighting in the Carpathian mountains, along with hundreds of other agents and military supplies. These efforts continued at least until the early 1950s. The "rollback strategy" was made official in NSC 68, just prior to the Korean war, which urged a vast US military buildup and efforts aimed at "fomenting and supporting unrest and revolt in selected strategic satellite countries" and "foster[ing] the seeds of destruction within the Soviet system," in the hope that the US might eventually "negotiate a settlement with the Soviet Union (or a successor state or states)."[59]

The USSR presumably did not take kindly to the reconstruction of the Nazi apparatus in Germany, which had virtually demolished the country and massacred millions of its citizens, or US support for Hitler's allies who continued fighting within the USSR with CIA support. But all of this is passed over lightly here; we prefer to see ourselves at the mercy of Soviet aggressors. One might ask what the reaction would be if the situation were reversed.

Perhaps the best-known of the Nazi war criminals incorporated into US operations in Europe was Klaus Barbie, "the Butcher of Lyon," who was responsible for numerous crimes in France and was duly placed in charge of spying on the French by US intelligence. When he could no longer be protected in Europe, he was sent by the US to Bolivia, where he became a central figure in the fascist network there, his best-known achievement being his role in organizing a murderous coup in Bolivia in 1980 with the assistance of

Italian fascists, Argentine intelligence agents who allege that they were trained by US and Israeli specialists and that Barbie was in close contact throughout with US intelligence, the Moon cult (working with US intelligence), and with a foreign mercenary army recruited for the fascist coup, including Germans and two Israeli agents, according to Hermann. The US subsequently turned against the coup regime when it became clear that the generals were more interested in cocaine profits than in the anti-Communist crusade, and the Argentine intelligence agents went on to Central America. One, who also claims to have been involved in the Pinochet coup in Chile in 1973, says that in 1982 he went to Guatemala where he "worked primarily with the North Americans. That was the best time"—during the Ríos Montt massacres, already discussed.[60]

According to Hermann, the "Black International" in Latin America, in which Barbie was a leading figure, included Dutch Nazi Alfons Sassen (who "escaped" from Holland after working with US intelligence) in Ecuador, Friedrich Schwend (who worked with US intelligence in Austria and Italy and was sent to Latin America under false identity papers supplied by US intelligence when he was wanted for murder in Italy) in Peru, Wim Sassen (who "escaped" from US custody in Holland) in Argentina, and Walter Rauff (the inventor of the first gas chambers) in Chile. One of its leading figures was SS Obersturmfuehrer Otto Skorzeny, who had rescued Mussolini and whose last assignment for Hitler was to train the "Werewolves," who were to fight to the death after the allied victory. He developed plans for a partisan war against the Soviet Union (sent on to Eisenhower), then was released by a US military court, then "escaped" from US custody after he had been jailed by the Germans. He worked as coordinator of the Latin American-based Black International from fascist Spain, where his US advisor described him with great admiration as "a gentleman of Victorian knighthood." The top figure was Hans Ulrich Rudel, former Luftwaffe air ace, who had close personal and business relations with dictators Stroessner in Paraguay and Pinochet in Chile.

In 1982 a new Bolivian government sent Barbie back to France, where he will come to trial unless he mysteriously dies in prison; collaboration with the Nazis was so widespread in France that many would prefer that his stories not be told. A flurry of interest was aroused here as the unsavory US role in his career was partially revealed. This elicited a letter to the *New York Times* by Col. (ret.) Eugene Kolb, identified as a former Counterintelligence Corps officer who was chief of operations in the Augsburg region. Kolb defends the use of Barbie as an agent, noting that his "skills were badly needed": "To our knowledge, his activities had been directed against the underground French Communist Party and

Resistance, just as we in the postwar era were concerned with the German Communist Party and activities inimical to American policies in Germany."[61]

Kolb's comment is apt. The US was picking up where the Nazis had left off, and it was therefore entirely natural that they should employ specialists in anti-resistance activities, whose "atrocities" were not considered real atrocities, given the nature of the targets.

Kolb does not mention that he was in fact Barbie's superior and had vigorously defended Barbie when the French finally attempted to extradite him. He wrote in a secret memorandum at the time that "while charges against subject may possibly be true, they are probably not true... Subject is now considered to be the most reliable informant this headquarters has."[62] It surpasses belief that US intelligence was unfamiliar with the record of this leading Nazi torturer and assassin.

There should have been little surprise, then, when in the context of President Reagan's visit to the Bitburg cemetery, where SS veterans were buried, it was revealed that a few months earlier he had criticized Americans who fought for the Spanish Republic, stating that "I would say that the individuals that went over there were in the opinions of most Americans fighting on the wrong side." They should have been fighting *for* the fascists, not against them, in his view. Reagan is simply more honest than most of his cohorts.[63]

The postwar US project of crushing the anti-fascist resistance with Nazi assistance establishes a direct link between Nazi Germany and the killing fields in Central America. Linklater, Hilton and Ascherson observe accurately that the "ideals and methods" of fascism found "fertile soil" as they were transplanted to the Western Hemisphere: "The right-wing dictatorships of Argentina, Bolivia and Chile and the secret police they employed, adopted and exported [these ideals and methods] to Central America—to El Salvador and Guatemala, where the death squads which are the weapons of dictatorship can be seen in operation today. That is the true legacy of Fascism." Klaus Barbie's group in Bolivia included "some of the most savage and professional killers of the Italian ultra-right, accompanied by romantic worshippers of the swastika from Germany, France and even Switzerland." They brought with them the "technologies of repression" designed by the Nazis:

> Barbie introduced the fully-developed concentration camp to Bolivia, and lectured on the use of electrodes applied to the human body to extract confessions, a technique first developed by Gestapo interrogators in France. Together with the Italian terrorist Stefano delle Chiaie, he organised the squads of mercenary thugs which held down Bolivia by murder and intimidation, and which are seen performing the same task in El Salvador today. Not

only the Bolivian dictatorship but General Pinochet in Chile, the officers who directed the 'dirty war' in Argentina in the 1970s, and today's exponents of counter-terror in Central America have drawn deeply on the skills and services of this very special immigration from Europe.

The Barbie story, they write, "connects the Third Reich in Germany to the military regimes of South and Central America, which leads from one age of Fascism to another." El Salvador recruited "the men and expertise for its death squads among those who had learnt their trade" from their Nazi tutors in Argentina, Chile and Bolivia. The Italian fascist murderer Stefano delle Chiaie—who is suspected of engineering the worst terrorist atrocity in Europe since World War II, the bombing at a Bologna railroad station in August 1980 in which 84 people were killed—advised Major Roberto d'Aubuisson on anti-subversive tactics for the Salvadoran army in 1980. He and his terrorist associates, holding Argentine passports, transmitted information to the Argentine neo-Nazi generals on left-wing exiles and passed on "arms, equipment, and finally men for the Salvadoran death squads."[64]

Surely all of this was well-known to the US government. As noted earlier, Rand Corporation terrorism expert Brian Jenkins notes blandly that "Argentina acted as a proxy for the United States in Central America," referring to Argentina under the murderous neo-Nazi generals, now on trial for massive crimes; he adds that the US "provides military assistance and training to the Honduran armed forces, while Argentinian advisers until recently provided training and management support to the Nicaraguan guerrillas,"[65] a well-coordinated joint operation, terminated when the military dictatorship in Argentina was overthrown. The operations in El Salvador and Guatemala are another facet of these joint enterprises, which trace directly back to US solicitude and care for useful Nazi gangsters as Europe was liberated from Hitler.

These are a few glimpses into what Edward Herman properly calls "The Real Terror Network." We may recall Juan José Arévalo's sorrowful comment in 1951 that "The arms of the Third Reich were broken and conquered...but in the ideological dialogue... Roosevelt lost the war. The real winner was Hitler."[66]

This chapter of postwar history adds another facet to the story. In accordance with the guiding geopolitical conceptions already discussed and illustrated, it was essential to destroy the popular anti-fascist resistance in much of the world, and the US quite reasonably turned to specialists in the task, drawn from the ranks of leading Nazis. These useful folk were then sent on to safer climes when their task was done and they could no longer be protected, and there they continued their work, which happened to integrate quite well with other US enterprises in defense of the Fifth Freedom, specifically, those with which we have been primarily concerned. Meanwhile the CIA was directed to covert operations, including "the support of terrorism around the world," in the words of the document that launched these operations,[67] but primarily subversion, some of the main targets being democratic governments that appeared to be drifting out of US control. The pattern of intervention of earlier years expanded worldwide and intensified in scale. Throughout, the project in which the US-SS alliance has been engaged, from early postwar Europe to contemporary El Salvador and Nicaragua—with some important stops in Latin America in between—has been described, when it is noted at all, in the conventional rhetoric of containment, defense against the Empire of Evil. A closer look shows something quite different: additional evidence for the general thesis that the US has felt it necessary to defend large parts of the world from "internal aggression" by their own populations, but little support for the idea that the growth of the US system of international security—with strategic armaments as a crucial element—was driven by the need to defend ourselves against the encroachments of the Great Satan.

4.5 Escalation of the Pentagon System: The Pretexts and the Evidence

Another way to examine the plausibility of the defensive rhetoric of US diplomacy and scholarship is to consider the moments when the regular growth of the military system sharply escalated. There are three crucial periods: the early 1950s, the early 60s, and today, with Reagan's unprecedented military build-up, extending steps initiated during the final period of the Carter presidency. We may ask, then, what new dangers required a major expansion of US military force in these three periods.

We discover that in each case, though the threat of the Great Satan was invoked to frighten the taxpayer into paying the bill, the real reasons were quite different and the pretexts offered were a fraud, a fact that poses yet another challenge to conventional doctrine.

In the early 50s, the official reason for the near quadrupling of the military budget was the Korean war, presented as firm evidence of the Soviet drive for world conquest. In fact, there was little reason then, nor is there now, to suppose that the North Korean invasion was Soviet-inspired, and the background circumstances are rather different from what has generally been assumed. Bruce Cumings, in the major scholarly study of the pre-war period, observes that fighting had "claimed more than one hundred thousand lives in peasant rebellion, labor strife, guerrilla warfare, and open fighting along the thirty-eighth parallel [only the latter involving North Korea]—all this before the ostensible Korean War began." This toll includes some 30,000-40,000 killed in Cheju Island alone in 1948 in the course of "one of the most brutal, sustained and intensive counterinsurgency campaigns in postwar Asia," one phase of the US effort to destroy the popular regime that had taken over most of Korea before the US forces landed in 1945. This rather significant US-organized massacre is known only to specialists. It should also not be overlooked that fighting on the border had been constant, primarily provoked from the south, after the US succeeded in imposing a regime that had little domestic support and overcoming a large-scale popular revolution.[68] But the question of the origins of the phase of the war that began in 1950 is academic in the present context, since the US plans for massive increase in the military budget had already been laid and are outlined in NSC 68, well before the outbreak of the war, which was simply exploited to justify plans that had been put forth on entirely different grounds.

The future of Korea had been discussed in the War and Peace Studies groups of the Council on Foreign Relations and State Department, discussed earlier. In May 1944, David Rowe submitted a study in which he dismissed proposals for quick Korean independence as unrealistic, urging rather that Koreans "pass through a period of political education if they are to attempt self-government on an independent basis," this education to be carried out under US tutelage within a UN framework.[69] The methods used by the US occupation forces are often described as unwise, the result of lack of familiarity with Korea and Cold War tensions; partly true, but such accounts fail to observe how well this particular case fits into the general worldwide picture.

Rowe incidentally continued to offer advice to the government. In 1966, when he was director of graduate studies in international relations at Yale, he proposed to Congress that the US buy up all surplus Australian and Canadian wheat so that there would be mass starvation in China: "Mind you, I'm not talking about this as a weapon against the Chinese people," he said. "It will be. But that is only incidental. The weapon will be a weapon against the Government because the internal stability of that country cannot be sustained by an unfriendly Government in the face of general starvation." This suggestion, which merits comparison to the *New Republic* advice that we proceed "regardless of how many are murdered" in El Salvador, has much earlier antecedents in American history, from 1622, when Virginians destroyed Indian crops; this was an early phase in "the strategy universally adopted by European troop commanders," one aspect of the concept of total war taught by the European invaders, and again, a technique that had been pioneered in Ireland.[70]

Turning to the second case, the Kennedy military build-up was justified on the basis of an alleged "missile gap," which President Eisenhower correctly maintained did not exist; the origins of the "missile gap" lie in the failure of an earlier "bomber gap" to materialize. The Russians in fact had *four* operational ICBMs, located at a single missile-testing site, when the Kennedy Administration undertook the construction of 1000 Minuteman missiles to compensate for the "gap" which it knew to be fraudulent, setting off the current phase of the strategic arms race. At the time, Fred Kaplan observes, "there *was* a missile gap, even a deterrent gap, and the ratio in forces was nearly ten to one—but the gap was in *our* favor." Kennedy's adviser for National Security Affairs, McGeorge Bundy, noted in an internal memo that the phrase "missile gap" had had a "useful shorthand effect of calling attention to...our basic military posture"; the facts were therefore a marginal issue. The arms build-up proceeded, independently of the alleged motive.[71]

The third major build-up under Reagan was justified to the public by an alleged "window of vulnerability," which would make it possible for the USSR to knock out 90% of the US ICBMs with only one fifth to one third of their long-range missiles, so Paul Nitze and other Reagan advisers argued. "This wonderful phrase," Walter Pincus observes, "emerged during the attack on former President Carter's strategic arms limitation talks with the Russians... The 'window' was supposed to open in the early 1980s and close only when U.S. deployment of substantial MX missiles was underway... While the 'window' was open, however, the alleged Soviet advantage in ICBM power was going to encourage Moscow to undertake all sorts of aggressive adventures around the world, unafraid of any Washington response." But, Pincus continues, the "window" opened even wider under Reagan, with the phasing out of old systems before new ones come into operation, and somehow the Russians did not rampage, though according to official theology the entire world was at their feet; they must be very considerate folks. The idea has "faded into thin air," Pincus comments. By the end of 1984, the nuclear balance remained about as it was when Reagan came into office, with no noticeable Russian moves to take over the world despite their alleged capacity to do so with ease. Once again, the wailing over our "vulnerability" and the striking of heroic poses serves quite different ends.[72]

It was always apparent that the concept was fraudulent, and the point is now hardly contested. In testimony before Congress, General Benny Davis, the head of the Strategic Air Command, stated that MX vulnerability was "no longer an issue," because "we have discovered that existing silos are harder than originally thought." This fortuitous discovery, it is hoped, will help counter critics who ask why the missile should be deployed if it is vulnerable. Furthermore, he continued, there never was any such vulnerability, because a successful simultaneous attack against all three legs of the triad — bombers, submarines, and land-based missiles— is plainly impossible, exactly as pointed out from the start by critics of Administration rhetoric, who also added the obvious point that a small subpart of any of these forces would more than suffice as a deterrent. Gen. Davis also stated that "The whole question of a window of vulnerability that was raised some years ago did not relate specifically to the vulnerability of missile silos," an obvious falsehood as noted by Senator Hart, who responded: "The history of the 'window of vulnerability' is silo vulnerability, and any effort to portray it as something else is a blatant attempt at revisionism." Hart is correct, Fred Kaplan observes, citing earlier explicit statements to this effect. The point is that the "window of vulnerability" has outlived its usefulness as a technique for accelerating military production, and is now in fact an impediment to this program because of fears of survivability of the missiles Reagan wants to produce. Therefore, the "window" has conveniently closed.[73]

In fact, the President's own Scowcroft Commission had closed the window in April 1983. A meeting of the National Security Council, Leslie Gelb reports, was devoted to the "overriding issue" of how to respond to the Scowcroft Commission report and congressional pressures on arms control, "and how to restore some credibility to the Administration's negotiating position and maintain the consensus for increased military spending."[74]

The "window of vulnerability" was as serious an issue as the "missile gap." As in the case of the first major postwar military buildup, the plans for military expansion preceded the events used to justify them; the Carter Administration initiated plans to sharply increase military expenditures and cut back social programs in 1978, and then exploited the subsequent Iran hostage crisis and Soviet invasion of Afghanistan to demonstrate the need for these programs, with the "window of vulnerability" coming later to foster appropriate fears among the population. The rate of production of warheads was low in 1976-8; it increased in 1980 and 1981 and accelerated in Fiscal Year 1982 in accordance with Carter's programs. The Nuclear Weapons Stockpile Memorandum signed by President Carter in October 1980 (for 1981-3) called for a further "dramatic increase in warhead production," "a very sharp increase." Reagan's first Stockpile Memorandum in March 1982 authorized only a slight increase over the Carter plans, though the entire military system vastly expanded under Reagan. Robert Komer, Under-Secretary of Defense in 1979-80, notes that "Actual defense outlays went up in every Carter year, in strong contrast to the declines characteristic of every Nixon-Ford year from FY1969 through FY1976" (resulting from the end of the Vietnam War), with a "substantial increase" in FY1981 (under Carter). The actual military outlays for the early 1980s "average slightly lower than the Carter projections... Almost every Reagan equipment program to date was begun under Carter, or even before, with the notable exception of SDI." At the same time, Soviet increases in spending, which accelerated after the Cuban missile crisis, tapered off to about 2% a year from 1976.[75]

In fact, the whole charade is farcical. Windows and gaps appear when they are needed to justify escalation of military spending; they close when they no longer contribute to this end, or when other concerns require reduction of military programs. In none of the three crucial cases was there any significant change in the international environment, any new threat to the US or its allies, to justify the military programs undertaken. In each case, a threat was fabricated. In the latter two, the arms buildup proceeded while its purported motivation was conceded to be a fabrication; the first case differs only in that the fraud was not conceded.

The similarities between the Reagan and Kennedy programs go beyond the exploitation of fabricated crises. During the 1960 presidential campaign, Democratic liberals denounced the Eisenhower Administration for frittering away American affluence in "indulgences, luxuries, and frivolities" while the United States faced "the possibility of annihilation or humiliation," calling for "accelerating and enlarging our defense effort" rather than diverting resources to consumer goods for people who already enjoy a "frivolous standard of living," while our global enemy marches from strength to strength.[76]

The story was re-enacted in 1980, with the tables turned. President Reagan likes to say that he is following in the footsteps of John F. Kennedy, a claim that the Democrats indignantly reject though it has more than a little merit. Reagan's programs are in several important respects close to Kennedy's, and the 1980 campaign rhetoric was reminiscent of 1960. Like Eisenhower in the eyes of the Kennedy liberals, Carter was portrayed by the Reaganites as not sufficiently militant and activist, a "wimp" standing by helplessly while the Russians take over the world. The major domestic programs of the Kennedy and Reagan Administrations were a huge military build-up and regressive fiscal measures to stimulate investment. The "monolithic and ruthless conspiracy" of Kennedy has become Reagan's Empire of Evil. The similarities of program and rhetoric tell us something about the real spectrum of American politics.

There are also some differences; there was nothing in the Kennedy period to match the mean-spirited attack on the poor undertaken by Reagan, though one must bear in mind the decline in relative US power in the interim and the corresponding reduction of means to achieve domestic and international ends. Kennedy could envision "great societies at home and grand designs abroad," in the words of presidential adviser Walter Heller,[77] but now the hungry and destitute must sacrifice for the "grand designs," as is recognized, in their own style, by Kennedy's "neo-liberal" descendants.

There are other striking differences. The Kennedy Administration evoked much enthusiasm and admiration among the liberal intelligentsia, but there is no Camelot today. In part, this difference reflects the fact that the Reaganites dismiss the intelligentsia with contempt while Kennedy offered them a place in the sun, a chance to rub shoulders with the great and even to share in the exercise of power. Furthermore, Kennedy's programs seemed to promise success, in part achieved, while Reagan's successes lie primarily in mortgaging the country's future while overseeing a vast transfer of resources from the poor to the wealthy, as statistics on real disposable income demonstrate, if the homeless in the street do not suffice.

These differences reflect in part the social base of the Reagan Administration, in part the decline in American global hegemony, a decline that has also affected the superpower enemy despite much frenzied rhetoric.[78] To mention only the most striking example, the Kennedy Administration was concerned over the viability of the Japanese economy.[79] This is hardly the concern of planners today. There are also domestic problems that the Kennedy planners did not have to face, though Reagan does. We turn to these matters in the next chapter.

Returning to the main theme, as this discussion indicates, the defensive rhetoric is not to be taken seriously. Other factors are operative, not those adduced to frighten the citizenry into bearing the costs of the arms race.

5 The Roots of the Pentagon System

Despite its generally frivolous character, there is a sense in which the defensive rhetoric is appropriate: we must defend the Grand Area from its own populations—from "internal aggression" which threatens the Fifth Freedom. But why do we need strategic weapons to guarantee the right to intervene in our vast domains?

There is a reason. Strategic weapons provide an "umbrella" for intervention and aggression with impunity. The argument has been developed in various forms by planners. Carter's Secretary of Defense Harold Brown reported to Congress that with our strategic nuclear capabilities in place, "our other forces become meaningful instruments of military and political power," a sound observation. Paul Nitze made a similar point in NSC 141 in January, 1953. He argued that a civil defense program was necessary for two basic reasons: (1) to make a first strike against the USSR a feasible prospect, and (2) to guarantee "the freedom of the United States Government to take strong actions in the cold war" without too much concern over Soviet retaliation: Soviet advances in nuclear weaponry "would present an extremely grave threat to the United

States" because they "would tend to impose greater caution in our cold war policies to the extent that these policies involve significant threat of general war." Our "cold war policies" are the regular policies of intervention, and it is important to maintain our freedom to carry them out. The argument carries over to the development of strategic weapons, for the reasons given by Harold Brown.[80]

Notice that what concerned Nitze in 1953 was the "deadly connection": the fear that intervention might lead to nuclear war. Civil defense being inconceivable, an intimidating posture is therefore required so that we need not be overly cautious in our Cold War policies of intervention. Notice further that Nitze's two arguments for civil defense—facilitating a first strike and interventionist policies—carry over directly to Star Wars, which, Reagan argues (and some of his more fanatic cohorts apparently believe), would protect the US population. Nitze remains today a leading adviser on National Security issues, though he is considered insufficiently militant —a measure of our progress in the past 30 years; he has been described in the press as a proponent of flexibility and "it's affected his credibility" with the President, one of his subordinates commented.[81]

Here we see the first real reason for the vast and constantly expanding military system: to permit free exercise of our Cold War policies of intervention and subversion, in accord with the overriding geopolitical conception. There is also a second good reason. The Pentagon system has become our system of state intervention in the economy. The state quite naturally turns to this method when it is necessary to "get the country moving again," to "reindustrialize," in Kennedy-Reagan rhetoric.

In each of the three periods of major military expansion just reviewed, there was concern over domestic economic stagnation. In a modern industrial society, there is one primary idea as to how to deal with this problem: state intervention to stimulate the economy. This was the lesson taught by the failure of the New Deal and the success of the wartime mobilization in overcoming the depression. The war, business historian Alfred Chandler observed, "brought corporate managers to Washington to carry out one of the most complex pieces of economic planning in history," thus lessening "the ideological fears over the government's role in stabilizing the economy." The vast government expenditures, dwarfing the ineffectual New Deal, laid the basis for "a period of prosperity the like of which had never before been seen," teaching the Keynesian lesson that the government should act as a "coordinator of last resort" when "managers are unable to maintain a high level of aggregate demand." The wartime experience led General Electric president Charles E. Wilson to propose a "permanent war economy" in 1944. Another business historian, Joseph Monsen, notes that enlightened corporate managers, far from fearing government intervention in the economy, view "the New Economics as a technique for increasing corporate viability."[82]

For a variety of reasons, the device that best serves the needs of existing power and privilege is what is sometimes called "military Keynesianism": the creation of a state-guaranteed market for high technology rapidly-obsolescing waste production, meaning armaments. Their Keynesian advisers assured Truman and Kennedy that military production was unproblematic. Leon Keyserling endorsed the warlike—in fact, rather hysterical—conclusions of NSC 68, and Paul Samuelson informed President Kennedy that military spending, "if deemed desirable for its own sake can only help rather than hinder the health of our economy in the period immediately ahead."[83] Although Reagan professes a "conservative" ideology, in fact he and his advisers are committed partisans of Keynesian methods to stimulate production through the military system and to increase demand by cutting taxes. The recovery from the deep recession induced by the Reagan Administration was "a classical Keynesian recovery," investment banker Felix Rohatyn observes, "stimulated by tax cuts and huge amounts of government spending—especially in the military area..."[84]

There are surely more efficient and less dangerous techniques of economic management than military spending. Why, then, the regular recourse to this device? The basic reason is that the theoretical alternatives do not serve to enhance existing privilege and power as does the creation of a state-guaranteed market for high technology production—that is, the military system—which is why the latter measures regularly elicit business support. The point was explained in the *Business Week* article of 1949, cited earlier, expressing concern over Stalin's "peace offensive."[85] The problem posed by this "offensive" was that it might interfere with "the prospect of ever-rising military spending," with deleterious effects. The background assumption is that substantial government spending must continue. The question is: for what? The article goes on to extol the advantages of military Keynesianism over other measures that would suffice to deal with the domestic problems at hand:

> But there's a tremendous social and economic difference between welfare pump-priming and military pump-priming. It makes the government's role in the economy—its importance to business—greater than ever. Military spending doesn't really alter the structure of the economy. It goes through the regular channels. As far as a businessman is concerned, a munitions order from the government is much like an order from a private customer. But the kind of welfare and public works spending that Truman plans does alter the economy. It makes new

channels of its own. It creates new institutions. It redis-
tributes income. It shifts demand from one industry to
another. It changes the whole economic pattern.

The transition to a peacetime economy could be easily managed, the editors argue, but the impact on the society would be
unacceptable, weakening the dominant role of business interests
and permitting other forces to develop as "the Truman Administration would get its chance to go ahead with civilian spending
programs that the big military budget has kept under wraps,"
including "elaborate plans for development of natural resources,
expansion of public works, broadening of social welfare programs." These would be "Truman's answer to a fundamental problem that would emerge as soon as military spending slacked off—
the problem of making the business boom go on indefinitely under
its own steam."[86] As income is redistributed, new popular elements
enter into the formation of policy and new social and economic
structures arise. This outcome being intolerable, the state must
confine its intervention in the economy to subsidizing military
production. In short, state intervention in the economy is fine, even
necessary, but only if it is conducted in such a way as to enhance
existing power and privilege, hence through the military system.

This analysis in fact understates the businessman's case for
military spending, which is not simply a matter of arms production, but of support for the advanced sectors of the economy quite
generally. The development of computers, for example, has largely
been a product of state intervention through the military system,
and remains so today; development of the current "fifth generation" computers is financed by the Pentagon, the Department of
Energy (which is responsible for nuclear weapons) and NASA,
largely a military-related enterprise, and these will be the prime
users in the early phases at least. The military system provides an
optimal means to compel the public to subsidize the costly programs of research and development, leaving private industry to
reap the profits during this phase and later, if commercial applications become possible. It amounts to a system of forced public
investment, of public subsidy and private profit, with little interference with the businessman's prerogatives.

The SDI program is a dramatic example. "The real importance
of Star Wars is only tangentially related to national defense,"
Robert Reich observes, "But the consequences for national economic development will be profound." In fact, the system is likely
to be harmful to national security, as noted earlier, a matter of little
concern to planners. "The Pentagon appears to understand the
true implications," Reich continues: "The campaign has been
touted in Congressional hearings as a path to competiveness in
advanced technologies." National economic policy management
and subsidy to advanced technology through the Pentagon is of

course nothing new, he notes, but "the problem is never before have we entrusted so much technological development to the Pentagon in so short a time," raising questions about allocation of scientific resources, secrecy which will limit development and commercial applications, and so on.[87] Business leaders understand the true implications no less than the Pentagon, and those who hope to be in on the take have correspondingly expressed much enthusiasm for Star Wars.

The director of resource management at SDI's Pentagon office notes that "80% of our money is going to the private sector," a fact appreciated by business at home and abroad. "Almost no cutting-edge technology will go without a shot of new research funds" in this vast program of state subsidy to private enterprise, *Business Week* observes cheerily.[88] Business enthusiasm for the Star Wars program is therefore quite understandable, as is the fact that SDI did not arise from military demands.

Nor is it surprising that the SDI program is pursued regardless of the threats it poses to survival. Planning in business and government is short-range; the long-term threats are someone else's concern. This is to be expected in a competitive society where those who do not devote themselves to short-term advantage are unlikely to be in the competition in the long run. The widely-heard argument that Star Wars and other advanced weapons programs are irrational, even lunatic, may be correct from the point of view of people concerned with survival, but in the framework of business and state managers, they are quite rational.

There has always been a kind of love-hate relation between business interests and the capitalist state. On the one hand, business wants a powerful state to regulate disorderly markets, provide services and subsidies to business, enhance and protect access to foreign markets and resources, and so on. On the other hand, business does not want a powerful competitor, in particular, one that might respond to different interests, popular interests, and conduct policies with a redistributive effect, with regard to income or power. It has never been an easy problem to solve. It is difficult to imagine a system better designed for the benefit of the privileged than the military system.

The system has had many successes over the years, and still does, despite the increasing economic problems it produces in an era where relative US power has diminished. As I write, *Business Week* reports that "key statistical indicators have been flashing mixed signals" about the future of the economy, "but economists are counting on one constant to keep the economy growing [and profits flowing]: defense spending." The chief economist for US studies at Wharton Econometrics observes that "Defense spending increases probably provided the greatest momentum to growth in recent years." Furthermore, "since a growing share of defense spending is going for hardware, it is supporting the economy by giving the import-battered manufacturing sector a shot in the arm." This is one area where US industry has the field pretty much to itself—so far; the Japanese have their eye on this huge market. Faith in this perpetual public subsidy allows corporations "to fill nondefense orders first," relying on "defense spending as a cushion for those times when other business gets weak."[89] Again, it would be hard to design a system more conducive to business needs. Much the same has been true at crucial moments throughout the postwar period.

It is commonly observed that these methods are less satisfactory than the Japanese system of state-coordinated production geared to the commercial market, but there are many qualifications necessary, in part based on cultural factors and historical contingencies and in part on a kind of international division of labor in the state capitalist economies, with the US taking the lead in the costly enterprise of innovation and development, leaving the Japanese more free to occupy themselves with the profitable task of application and commercial sale. Some years ago, this was satisfactory. At a time of US dominance over the global economy, military Keynesianism could be adopted as a program of state industrial management without undue concern for our rivals in the world economy, but that is no longer true. By now, this is leading to internal conflict in the global state capitalist system, a matter of serious import that I cannot pursue here.

Though the difference between the US Pentagon system of industrial policy and the Japanese system is significant, still it should not be exaggerated. The Pentagon and Japan's Ministry of International Trade and Industry (MITI) "are putting their money into very similar kinds of R&D," the London *Economist* observes, citing an OECD study. These constitute the leading edge of current technology, with the US effort falling largely under Reagan's SDI. The Eureka project, designed as a European alternative to Star Wars, is focusing on the same areas, which are expected to be "the 21st century's high-tech sectors.[90]

A further reason for the attractiveness of military Keynesianism is that the ordinary citizen has to be willing to pay the costs of subsidizing advanced sectors of industry, a fact also appreciated by business leaders. An LTV Aerospace Corporation executive made the point clearly while explaining why the post-Vietnam world "must be bolstered with military orders":[91]

> It's basic. Its selling appeal is defense of the home. This is one of the greatest appeals the politicians have to adjusting the system. If you're the President and you need a control factor in the economy, and you need to sell this factor, you can't sell Harlem and Watts but you can sell self-preservation, a new environment. We're going to

increase defense budgets as long as those bastards in Russia are ahead of us. The American people understand that.

This was in 1968, when "those bastards" were no more ahead of us than they are now. But that is beside the point. With a properly functioning propaganda system, the American people can be made to "understand" what is plainly false, and the system of public subsidy, private profit, can march onward.

The method is constantly employed, with great skill. As the press loyally played its assigned role in whipping up hysteria and indignation after the Soviet Union shot down a South Korean civilian airliner—a reaction radically at variance with its behavior in many similar cases when "our side" was implicated, some at exactly the same time—the *New York Times* business pages noted that the event "has helped heat up the sluggish stocks of military contractors" and strengthened Reagan's hand in pressing for military spending, quoting an aerospace analyst who said: "The Korean jetliner incident provided a spark for a more positive reappraisal of the defense industry... And virtually all defense stocks have gone up."[92] As noted, far more than the "defense industry" is at stake.

It is a rare political leader who can face the public with the news that it is necessary for the poor to bribe the rich, who control investment, for the ultimate benefit of the economy. The citizen can, however, be mobilized to this effort in fear of the great enemy about to destroy us. Kennedy did attempt another method, the man-in-space program, presented in quasi-military terms of national grandeur, but people soon became bored at the sight of heroic figures walking on the moon and this device had to be abandoned. Military spending does not have this defect, if the public can be sufficiently terrorized. As the American satirist H. L. Mencken once observed, "The whole aim of practical politics is to keep the populace alarmed (and hence clamorous to be led to safety) by menacing it with an endless series of hobgoblins, all of them imaginary," a lesson that leaders of both superpowers, and many others, understand very well, and that plays its part in the regular recourse to military Keynesianism and in the fostering of national hysteria over the enemy's crimes.

For such reasons, the Pentagon system has become the American system of industrial policy. Once this system of state management of the economy is established, it is exceedingly difficult to dismantle as powerful vested interests add their weight to the persistent advantages already noted. It is no surprise that Reaganomics was largely a system of "military Keynesianism gone wild," leading predictably to a huge deficit, deterioriation of the ability to compete in international trade and other deleterious consequences that are ignored in short-term planning or dismissed on mystical grounds.

One might ask whether reliance on the Pentagon system of economic management might not be able to function even with a ban on development or testing of nuclear weapons and missiles. A former government official who has been a strong advocate of arms control once remarked, only semi-jocularly, that arms control agreements might become truly effective if the technology of arms control and its spin-offs became more advanced and profitable than the technology to which weapons production contributes. None of this seems feasible, in part for technical reasons (thus, advanced nuclear warheads and missiles are a central component of the SDI program of high tech subsidy), in part for reasons of propaganda: it would be quite a trick to menace the public by an endless series of hobgoblins while holding back on development and deployment of advanced weapons systems to defend against them.

Reagan's domestic programs involved a substantial transfer of wealth from the poor to the rich and huge state intervention in the economy through the military system. It was evident, and predicted, that the political leadership would therefore be compelled to seek international confrontation and to devise a series of threats, which have ranged from Libyan hit-men stalking Washington to assassinate Our Leader,[93] to the military threat posed by Grenada, to the "window of vulnerability." The accompanying rhetoric is reminiscent of NSC 68 and the exploitation of the Korean war as proof of Soviet intentions, and of the Kennedy days. In El Salvador, for example, the Carter Administration viewed the problem as a local one: its task was to conduct a massacre of sufficient scale to guarantee the rule of the gangsters of its choice. Reagan took up and extended this challenge, but presented it as a battle against "the focus of evil in our time," the source of all turmoil in the world, a change in format that is the natural concomitant of the shift in domestic programs.[94] There are many other examples.

It was also predictable, and predicted, that the second Reagan term would see a diminution in hysterical rhetoric and the desperate search for international confrontation. The reason that will be proffered is that the Russians have been tamed by Reagan's stern display of manliness; the real reason is that it is becoming necessary to face the costs of Reagan's Keynesian excesses, and boundless military spending will not serve this end. Hence the Soviet threat of global conquest will somewhat dissipate—this, of course, on the assumption that no major challenge arises to American domination. If, say, Marcos goes the way of the Shah or Somoza, then the Russians will once again be on the march.

For similar reasons, one may anticipate that the US will show some interest in arms negotiations, and may even accept an agreement as long as it satisfies certain basic conditions. The comparative advantage of the US is no longer in production, so limits on scale of weaponry are tolerable, even desirable. But the state role in development of advanced technology must be preserved, so no limits can be accepted on research, development and deployment of new and more advanced weapons systems in conformity with the now well-established system of state industrial policy. Build-down combined with Star Wars is a natural posture for the US, though there are problems, since the allegedly "defensive" systems compel the USSR to enhance its offensive capacity. Meanwhile the debates will proceed in their largely irrelevant terms.

One can see why the substantial popular support for a nuclear freeze had no effect. A nuclear freeze would place limits on the creation of an ever-more intimidating posture in which our conventional weapons become "meaningful instruments of military and political power" (Harold Brown), and on the crucial state role in high technology development and production. It is therefore unacceptable. In particular, in the absence of any realistic alternative system of state capitalist industrial management, the nuclear freeze cannot arise as a serious issue within the political system, whatever popular attitudes may be. As Seymour Melman has emphasized for many years, the disarmament movement must assign the issue of economic conversion a central place on its agenda, or it will achieve very little. And this is no simple matter, because it bears on the institutional structure of power and privilege, as the owners and managers of the society are well aware.

Adopting the point of view of the dominant elites, one can see why "peace" has become a dirty word, some kind of Russian plot; the common term "peacenik," with its intended connotations, is a case in point. There is no term "warnik"; advocacy of militarism is the domain of the "good guys," not deviants of one or another sort—it is furthermore the norm, so no term for this stance is required.

6 The Consequences

It is to be expected that domestic militarization will be accompanied by an "activist" (i.e., aggressive) foreign policy. One reason, already mentioned, is that the population must be mobilized to pay the costs and must therefore be convinced that it faces a terrible threat. A domestic program of military Keynesianism thus fosters a search for confrontation and military adventures abroad. The relation may also arise in the opposite direction. Concern over a loss of hegemony abroad requires intervention, hence reinforcement of the nuclear umbrella under which it may proceed effectively. An ideology of assertiveness, mock heroics and machismo fosters both domestic militarization and foreign adventures. These processes quite generally develop in parallel. We observe them today in the idiocies of the Rambo cult and the equivalent among the jingoist intellectuals, who, mimicking Goebbels, speak of "the sickly inhibitions against the use of military force" of earlier years, now happily overcome with such "inspiriting" acts as the invasion of Grenada, a fabulous triumph of American arms.[95]

The correlation between domestic militarization and foreign "activism" held in the three periods of military expansion mentioned earlier, notably the latter two. Consider just Latin America. In 1951, "in a historic turn," Congress passed the Military Defense Assistance Act "that created new ties between Washington and Latin American armed forces," and the US undertook training of Latin American officers at the School of the Americas in the Panama Canal Zone. "By the end of 1954," not merely coincidentally, "military dictators ruled thirteen of the twenty Latin American nations," "a new high for the twentieth century," including all Central American nations except Costa Rica.[96] The Kennedy Administration changed the emphasis of the military assistance program from "hemispheric defense" to "internal security"— meaning war against their own populations. Given the realities of US dominance, this meant, in effect, that "the Latin American military role was changed from 'hemispheric defense' to 'internal security'," in the words of Charles Maechling, who led counterinsurgency and internal defense planning from 1961 to 1966.[97] In the light of its consequences, this was one of the most significant decisions of recent history, one little noted here. This decision, Maechling notes, represented a change from toleration "of the rapacity and cruelty of the Latin American military" to "direct complicity" in their crimes, to US support of "the methods of Heinrich Himmler's extermination squads." The consequences, as we have seen, were horrendous, as much of Latin America was turned into a torture chamber under a rash of National Security States as a result, in significant measure, of US policy initiatives. The same phenomenon is notable in the current phase of military expansion.

Elsewhere too, the consequences of the interventionism that goes hand-in-hand with militarization of the domestic economy have been grim. Ruth Sivard counts up 125 or more military conflicts since World War II, 95% in the Third World, in most cases involving foreign forces, with "western powers accounting for 79 percent of the interventions, communist for 6 percent." Even if not taken too literally, such figures should give us pause. The toll is incalculable. In Indochina alone, a standard Western estimate is that about 500,000 were killed by the French in their US-backed war, and one recent estimate is that deaths from 1965 may have been 3 million or more. Add to this perhaps 170,000 killed in the previous ten years of US terror and some 1/2 million to 1 million killed during the US wars in Laos and Cambodia, and we have perhaps 4 million or more killed, a respectable achievement in the days before we fell victim to the "sickly inhibitions against the use of military force." Such figures do not register the full toll by any means: the millions of war invalids and orphans (the "most disadvantaged" orphans are estimated at 700,000), the destruction of the land, the psychic injuries of one of the major catastrophes of the modern era.[98] All of this proceeds as we "defend ourselves from the Soviet threat," just as the horrors of Hungary and Afghanistan are part of the Soviet "defense against the American threat."

Other consequences of the system include the enormous waste of scarce human and material resources and the constant threat of nuclear war, points too obvious to take the space to dwell on here.

7 Cold War Realities

In the United States, the role of the state in stimulating and organizing the economy and the concern to maintain order and discipline within our broad domains, often operating in parallel, regularly spur domestic militarization and fuel the arms race under the propaganda cover of defense against Soviet aggression, with further interactions as already discussed. Our superpower enemy behaves in much the same way, though the sources of its conduct differ. The prime concern of its military-bureaucratic elite is to run their dungeon without interference and to control the satellites, while seeking targets of opportunity elsewhere. Since their rule is based on violence, they also naturally turn to domestic militarization as their essential policy, and they too require the measures described by Harold Brown, cited earlier, to ensure the freedom to pursue their goals within their own domains. The two superpowers are locked into military systems of domestic social and economic management and global domination.

They are also locked in a deadly embrace, as the dynamics of the Cold War reveal. There is no doubt that each of the superpowers would prefer to have the other disappear, and as noted, the US did for a time toy with rollback as a strategy; one hears echoes of such plans among the more fanatic Reaganites today. But these have not been the operative policies. Whatever the leadership may wish, each superpower has long come to recognize that the other is there to stay, short of mutual annihilation, and they have settled into a tacit partnership in global management: the Cold War system, in which each superpower exploits the threat of its Great Satan to mobilize its own population and often recalcitrant allies to support brutal and violent measures in its own domain. The Cold War long ago came to have a certain functional utility for the superpowers, one reason why it persists. At the same time each superpower expands its own deterrent force, to guarantee a space within which it is free to resort to violence; for us, much of the world.

The picture comes into focus with relative clarity if we consider the actual events of the Cold War, putting the rhetoric aside. The typical event of the Cold War is an act of aggression or subversion by one of the superpowers against an enemy within its own domains: East Berlin, Hungary, Czechoslovakia, Poland, Afghanistan—Greece, the Philippines, Iran, Guatemala, the Congo, Indochina, the Dominican Republic, Chile, El Salvador—and all too many others. In each case, intervention within the system is justified at home by appeal to the threat of the Great Satan. Such events constitute the major substance of the Cold War, behind the rhetoric of superpower conflict. The latter conflict is real, in that each superpower provides barriers to the ambitions of the other; and latent, in that the system will eventually explode. But behind these realities lies a good measure of tacit complicity in global management, and deception about the reality of the modern world.

The point has been understood well enough by Third World victims of the Cold War system, for example, Foreign Minister Toriello of Guatemala, who pointed out, just prior to the CIA coup in 1954, that the US exploits fears of Communist expansionism to prevent threats to the Fifth Freedom; he was "voicing the thoughts of many of his (Latin American) listeners," Connell-Smith observes; hence the ovation he received.[99] At home, reality has been successfully obscured, but there are occasional glimmerings of insight. In 1951, Hans Morgenthau wrote that "the forces that in the interwar period erected the specter of Communist revolution into a symbol of all social reform and social change itself are at work again...":[100]

> In embarking upon a holy crusade to extirpate the evil of Bolshevism these forces embarked, as they do now, in actuality upon a campaign to outlaw morally and legally all popular movements favoring social reform and in that fashion to make the status quo impregnable to change. The symbol of the threat of a non-existent Communist revolution becomes a convenient cloak, as it was for German and Italian fascism, behind which a confused and patriotic citizenry can be rallied to the defense of what seems to be the security of the United States, but what actually is the security of the status quo.

There was much truth in this description then, as there is today.

In fact, the Great Satan is there, surely enough. Reagan's Evil Empire is exactly that, as is its American counterpart. The enemy is indeed ugly and threatening, with an ample record of brutality and atrocities, brandishing means of destruction that can scarcely be ignored, so there is at least a modicum of plausibility when the

Soviet Union appeals to its population to rally to the "defense of Afghanistan" against bandits supported by the CIA and other warmongers, or when the US does the same while defending South Vietnam by armed attack against its population. In short, the system works, often with spectacular success. Thus, in our highly ideological and deeply-indoctrinated society, the US attack against South Vietnam in 1962, expanding in later years, simply does not exist as an event of history. I do not know of even one case where it was described as such in the media or establishment scholarship, quite a remarkable achievement of propaganda, one that any dictator would envy.[101]

For us, the Cold War has been a war against much of the Third World, while for the USSR, it has been a war against their subject populations. This is the real meaning of the Cold War, and we should not forget it, when we turn our attention to the fact that this system of massacre, torture and oppression may, in the end, engulf us as well.

The Cold War system of global management is highly unstable, and sooner or later it will break down, as has come close to happening often in the past. Those who value their reputation as good prophets should predict that the system will remain stable. As long as it persists, they will be right, and they can scoff at those who, "driven by vague fears of the end of the world," have taken part in such "quasi-religious rituals" as arms control talks, and at the doomsayers overcome by "Protestant angst" or other psychic disorders.[102] And when it breaks down, there will be no one left to prove them wrong.

The system has a certain inner rationality in the short term, within the framework of state and private planning. In the longer term, it is a system of mutual suicide, but it is far from easy to see how we can extricate ourselves from it, because core institutional factors are involved.

Until major institutional changes become possible, we are limited to a holding action, rather like putting a band-aid on a cancer, in an effort to avert imminent catastrophe. Such actions, however frustrating and often futile they seem, must not be abandoned. It is necessary to oppose the next fantastic military system that will be concocted, the next intervention, the next attack on a potential rotten apple. We have a responsibility to try to protect people who are being viciously oppressed, and we may also hope to create a certain space in which, perhaps, there will be a way to work for more substantial institutional changes that will get to the roots of the problem.

Not all the problems of international society result from US initiatives, but we have an ample share. In a sense, this is a hopeful sign, since it means there is much that can be done by people who can muster the courage and integrity to face the facts honestly and with determination.

5 The Challenge Ahead

1 The "Conservative" Counterattack

1.1 Confronting the Threat of Democracy at Home

Of the various reasons advanced for the unwillingness of the "true democrats" to take part in the political system in Nicaragua, one has a ring of credibility: their allegation that the Sandinistas exerted too much control over domestic institutions for them to have a fair chance. There is merit in this argument, despite the access to the public granted them by electoral law and the advantages resulting from their private power and external support. Correspondingly, there is merit in the argument that principled critics of public or private state capitalist institutions are effectively excluded from the political system when control over the economy and communications is concentrated in the hands of a small elite of owners and managers with essentially shared interests, as in the United States. Under these conditions, the bounds of political action are narrow, even when there is no resort to state violence to ensure that they are not transgressed.

It has long been understood that democratic forms are of limited significance (and are therefore quite safe) when isolated individuals confront systems of concentrated power alone. Meaningful democracy presupposes the ability of ordinary people to pool their limited resources, to form and develop ideas and programs, put them on the political agenda, and act to support them. In the absence of organizational structures and resources that make this possible, democracy amounts to the option of choosing among candidates who represent the interests of one or another group that has an independent power base, generally in the private economy.

The conclusion is all the more valid when central areas of decision-making are excluded in principle from the domain of democratic participation and public control: decisions about investment, the nature and conditions of productive work, and so on. These are among the reasons why capitalism and democracy are incompatible, if by "democracy" we mean a system of genuine popular participation in determining the conditions of social life.

In an important study of American political history, Thomas Ferguson observes that

> The prerequisites for effective democracy are not really automatic voter registration or even Sunday voting, though these would help. Rather, deeper institutional forces—flourishing unions, readily accessible third parties, inexpensive media, and a thriving network of cooperatives and community organizations—are the real basis of effective democracy.

Even high voter turnout, which does not exist in the US, would mean very little in itself: "To assess the meaning of voting in such situations, a hard look is vital at the resources available to individual voters to form and express an opinion—and above all to participate in secondary organizations." In these respects, he notes, "the American experience has been less than edifying."[1] Once again, the point is simply fortified when we consider the vast range of essential decision-making over general social life that is excluded in principle from the system of formal democracy.

Business and the political system it has controlled since the earliest days is, not surprisingly, hostile to meaningful democracy; in fact, any such prospect has regularly been regarded as a serious danger by US elites, either in the US itself or in its dependencies.

In the dependencies, the threat of meaningful democracy can be suppressed by violence, and often is. El Salvador is a case in point. As discussed in chapter 3, the growth of an extensive network of secondary organizations that offered some hope to the large majority of the population, traditionally marginalized, led to Carter's terrorist war in 1980. The concern was that these popular organizations might "shoulder the responsibility for the future of El Salvador," in the words of the assassinated Archbishop as he vainly pleaded with President Carter to refrain from backing the armed forces, which "know only how to repress the people and defend the interests of the Salvadorean oligarchy." Carter's war succeeded in demolishing the popular organizations and guaranteeing the rule of the armed forces and the oligarchy, with a subsequent facade of "elections" added under Reagan to appease the home front once the danger of meaningful democracy was overcome. These successes removed the internal struggle from the political to the military arena, a replay of the US achievement in South Vietnam two decades earlier, as already discussed. The

THE CHALLENGE AHEAD 223

example of El Salvador and many others illustrate the loathing for democracy on the part of dominant US elites and the fear that it inspires, and the capacity of a great power to remove issues from the domain of political struggle, where it is weak, to the preferred domain of violent conflict. These and other examples discussed earlier also illustrate the impressive ability of our ideological institutions to eliminate inconvenient truths from history.

At home, the problem of blocking the threat of meaningful democracy is more complex, death squads, torture, and army massacres not being feasible options, so the enterprise takes different forms. But the concern is no less real. It was voiced, for example, in the 1975 Trilateral Commission report mentioned earlier.[2] The American contributor, Harvard political scientist Samuel Huntington, refers nostalgically to the days when "Truman had been able to govern the country with the cooperation of a relatively small number of Wall Street lawyers and bankers"; under these circumstances, there was no "Crisis of Democracy." But the turbulent 1960s disturbed this pleasant arrangement, as segments of the normally quiescent population became organized and began to press their demands, which cannot be met without redistribution of wealth and power, not to be contemplated. The crisis was compounded by "value-oriented intellectuals" whose critical analysis endangers the institutions that are responsible for "the indoctrination of young," the report warns, and by the media, which may have to be muzzled, it suggests, if they persist in their adversarial stance (vastly exaggerated, in their paranoid vision). These beginnings of popular engagement in democratic politics constitute the Crisis of Democracy that threatens the West, and the Trilateral scholars therefore urge more "moderation in democracy," measures to return the population to a more becoming state of apathy and passivity, so that "democracy," in the preferred sense, can survive.

Recall that these are the views of the liberal and moderate segment of dominant elites, the groups that took the leading role in the Carter Administration shortly after.

Recourse to state violence being limited, particularly against people who have a share in wealth and privilege, those who wield private and state power must turn to other means. It becomes crucially important to follow the advice of the US Operations Mission in Vietnam, already quoted (p. 30):

> The ultimate target is the human mind. It may be 'changed,' it may be rendered impotent for expression or it may be extinguished, but it still remains the critical target.

In such places as South Vietnam and El Salvador, the human mind may simply be extinguished, but at home it must be rendered impotent in other ways. The past decade has, accordingly, been a period of dedicated efforts to overcome the "Vietnam syndrome"— a fearsome plague that spread during the terrible sixties, with such symptoms as insight into the real world and accompanying feelings of sympathy and concern for the victims of aggression and massacre. The Vietnam syndrome, along with the incipient attempts of large parts of the population to enter the political system, to organize, to act to achieve social goals—these were the various forms of insubordination that constituted the Crisis of Democracy.

These intolerable departures from the approved moral code were not the first to evoke the fear of democracy at home. The rise of Populism in the Midwest and South in the late 19th century was another case. Long depicted in scholarship as a primitive, proto-fascist and anti-Semitic movement, Populism is more accurately construed as "the most truly libertarian social force relative to both the regions in which it temporarily emerged as a factor...," Gabriel Kolko writes, as more recent work has shown. Populism was quickly suppressed, leading to a huge migration to Canada from the states with large agrarian radical movements, "an important strand in the Canadian social democratic movement," absent here.[3] The quick demise of Populism under assault from a small component of business shows that "*The largest, best-organized, and most cohesive mass political movement in American history could not compete with even a part of the business community.*"[4] These events provide some insight into the limitations upon democracy (in other than a formal sense) when real power is narrowly concentrated.

Similar concerns arose after World War I. Exploiting his doctrine that the recent great wave of immigration had brought people "who have poured the poison of disloyalty into the very arteries of our national life," President Wilson turned to direct state repression, including mass expulsion of those whom Attorney-General Palmer, a liberal and progressive, called "alien filth."[5] Wilson's Red Scare, which established the FBI under J. Edgar Hoover as the national political police, succeeded in severely weakening the labor movement and undermining democratic politics. Promoted by business and proceeding with the enthusiastic support of the press, the repression wound down when it had achieved its ends and when elites began to fear that the anti-immigrant hysteria they had evoked might deplete the best reserve of cheap labor.[6]

The story was reenacted after World War II. NSC 68 in 1950, while proposing a vast military build-up and a rollback strategy, warned that our society would be "vulnerable" if dissent were too freely tolerated and that "a large measure of sacrifice and discipline will be demanded of the American people." The alleged Communist threat to our survival was skillfully manipulated to induce conformism and passivity. The antics of Joe McCarthy were one variant, quickly terminated when they passed beyond helpless victims and extended to such powerful institutions as the US Army. But "McCarthyism"—the campaign to reduce the population to apathy and obedience and eliminate independent thought —was far broader, and was eminently successful for some years; its effects have yet to be overcome.

With the democratic revival of the sixties, US elites recognized the threat and dedicated substantial resources to assuring that the Crisis of Democracy would be overcome.[7]

In the years since, Thomas Edsall observes, there has been "a major shift in the balance of power in the United States" with "a significant erosion of the power of those on the bottom half of the economic spectrum, an erosion of the power not only of the poor but of those in the working and middle classes" and a corresponding "sharp increase in the power of economic elites." The process culminated in the Reagan programs that reshaped government, even more than before, into a welfare system for corporate power and wealthy sectors. As discussed in chapter 4, the military system is one of the devices used effectively to this end, as in the past. In the Democratic Party, early 70s reforms in fact transferred power "to a new, and affluent, elite," while the Republicans became a true class party, the party of business and wealthy professionals, to an unprecedented extent. Furthermore, "during the 1970s, the political wing of the nation's corporate sector staged one of the most remarkable campaigns in the pursuit of political power in recent history," establishing a network of over 150,000 professionals in Washington who are engaged not only in securing defeat or passage of bills that concern them but also "in a much more complex process, the shaping of the precise language of legislation and of the committee reports that accompany legislation." Business also established an elaborate system of private institutions engaged in research, scholarship and ideological pronouncements, dwarfing in scale anything that had existed before, with the goal of "altering the terms of the policy debate" by sheer mass to a new "conservative" consensus.[8]

The concept of "conservatism" in its contemporary Orwellian usage is illuminated in a position paper of one of the most influential of these new institutions, the Heritage Foundation, presented to Ronald Reagan in November 1980 as "a blueprint for conservative government." The study advised Reagan to recognize "the reality of subversion and [to put] emphasis on the un-American nature of much so-called dissidence," adding that "It is axiomatic that individual liberties are secondary to the requirement of national security and internal civil order."[9] Fascists and Stalinists everywhere would applaud these sentiments. Not only in its doctrines, but more crucially in its behavior, modern "conservatism" reveals itself to be a form of advocacy of state power and state violence committed to securing the privileged position of business elites; what Bertram Gross has called "friendly fascism."[10]

1.2 The Attack against Labor

A counterpart to the campaign to stamp out heresy was a sharp attack against labor. Edsall observes that

> In advanced Western democracies both on this continent and in Europe there is a direct and demonstrable correlation between government commitment to domestic social spending and the strength of the trade union movement. There exists in no Western democracy any other major organization cutting across racial and ethnic lines that can defend progressive distributional policies of both taxation and spending... Without a strong labor movement, there is no broad-based institution in American society equipped to represent the interests of those in the working and lower-middle classes in the formulation of economic policy.

In short, unions are unique within capitalist democracy in providing some way for people of limited resources to enter meaningfully into the political system, and therefore they too must be "rendered impotent" to guard against the threat of democracy. The attack on labor involved a variety of means, including illegal firings to undercut free union elections (business "found the sanctions for fighting unions through illegal tactics worth the price") and other measures, with considerable assistance from the labor bureaucracy. Reagan's 1981-82 recession had a notable impact in this regard. Like the revival of military escalation, the attack on social legislation began in the latter part of the Carter presidency, taking flight under Reagan along with the assault against the labor movement.[11]

Thomas Ferguson and Joel Rogers review the effects of the first four years of these endeavors. Average first-year wage increases in major collective bargaining agreements set a record low in 1984, lagging significantly behind inflation for the third year running. "This dismal bargaining record," they note, "reflects the spectacular decline in union membership over the Reagan years," with a 22.4% drop in unionization rates for the private sector. Anti-union decisions of the National Labor Relations Board more than tripled, to 57% of contested cases, since the last Republican-dominated board under the Ford Administration. Unions lost 86% of the cases brought against them. OSHA, which is in charge of worker health and safety, has virtually ceased to function. The Office of Technology Assessment confirms that enforcement levels are so low as to provide virtually no deterrent to violation of legislation on occupational health and safety—a fact that is not surprising, considering the President's stand on the matter: "My idea of an OSHA would be if government set up an agency that would do research and study how things could be improved, and industry could go to it and say, we have a problem here and seem to lose more people by accidents in this particular function. Would you look at our plant, and then come back and give us a survey?"[12] The system of private privilege for which Reagan serves as figurehead demands a powerful state, protected from scrutiny by citizens,[13] and untroubled by democratic participation, ruling by violence abroad and intervening massively in the economy at home, but restricting itself to service to wealth and privilege: modern "conservatism." Certainly it cannot be expected to enforce the laws dealing with health and safety of workers.

1.3 The Attack against Rights

The refusal to enforce the law extends to other domains as well. The Administration systematically refuses to carry out statutory mandates established by Congress in such areas as civil rights of institutionalized persons, voting rights, fair housing, and sex discrimination. The American Civil Liberties Union reports that as a result of the Administration's refusal to adhere to "the constitutional requirement to enforce civil rights laws," the ACLU has been forced to handle about 80% of all voting rights cases in the deep South," acting in effect as a "private attorney general," an impossible burden. This "conservative" Administration posture guarantees, as intended, that the laws will not be enforced."[14] "Conservative" lawlessness is not limited to international affairs.

The Administration is, however, not entirely inactive in the matter of voting rights. It is conducting extensive investigations of voting fraud in Alabama, all in the "Black Belt" where blacks have recently gained local political power as a result of their enfranchisement a mere two centuries after the American revolution. These actions are placing the area in "a state of political siege and almost legal tyranny," in the words of Lawrence Wofford of the Campaign for a New South, an organization devoted to promoting black voting strength. The government had at this point lost all its cases,[15] but this hardly matters, since the assault on black politics will serve its purpose of discouraging black voters and undermining activists. Democratic Representative Don Edwards of California suggested that government officials "have been misused by whites attempting to thwart black political advances"—a far too charitable interpretation. One can imagine what the Justice Department would find if it were to carry out comparable investigations of white-run counties in that region or elsewhere.[16]

The attack on civil liberties is one facet of a broad campaign to restore inequity and discrimination overcome to a degree in the past generation. The attack on labor also renews major themes of

US history, which have been replayed over and over since President Andrew Jackson "became the first U.S. President to send troops to break a strike, while all levels of government largely declined to interfere with employers 'rights' to dismiss, spy upon, or blacklist any worker they chose... American history is replete with examples of business groups and individual firms retaining vast arrays of military and paramilitary forces for long periods of time."[17] The significant point, Ferguson continues, is that

> In industrial societies perhaps the single most important and obvious dimension to examine [in respect to the interests served by public policy] is state policy toward the "secondary" organizations of the citizenry. By far the most important of such organizations, of course, are labor unions. Though most discussions of American "democracy" elide the often ugly facts, the truth is that if employers are allowed untrammelled rights to destroy organizations created by their laborers then claims about "citizen sovereignty" are merely cynical rationalizations for elite investor dominance whether in Poland in the 1980s, Massachusetts in the 1850s, Pennsylvania before the New Deal, or much of the South and West today.

One expression of the current phase of the attack on democracy is a form of Newspeak devised for the 1980 and 1984 elections: the use of the term "special interests" with reference to working people, women, the aged, the handicapped, ethnic groups, etc.; in short, the population at large. Only one group does not achieve the rank of "special interests": the corporate elite. The Democrats are the party of the "special interests," the Reaganites charged, while the Republicans had no such commitment. In fact, the Democrats are only marginally more responsive to such "special interests" than the Republicans; rather, the party is dominated by other sectors of the business and financial communities. But their slightly greater responsiveness to the population at large makes them the party of the "special interests."

Notice that the terminology makes a good deal of sense in a capitalist democracy, where the interests of owners and managers are indeed "general interests" that must be satisfied or the society will grind to a halt. The general population, however, is irrelevant except insofar as it serves the needs of private power, and therefore constitutes "special interests."[18]

1.4 The Attack against Independent Thought

The business classes also moved effectively to extend their already massive dominance over universities and the media—always deemed inadequate, as business constantly complains. This phase of the campaign included publications for the general public and in universities, where well-funded reactionary jingoist ("conservative") journals are now widespread in an effort to counter threats of intellectual independence at the source. The general idea was succinctly expressed by Walter Wriston, chairman of Citicorp and a fund-raiser for the American Enterprise Institute: "I write the songs the world sings."[19] No other melodies are to be heard.

At the lunatic fringe we have such organizations as Accuracy in Academia, a spinoff of the reactionary thought-control organization Accuracy in Media (AIM), which monitors the media for deviations from the Party Line. The new offshoot alleges that there are 10,000 Marxist professors on campus (where "Marxist," in their terms, includes people who would be regarded as mainstream moderates in European industrial democracies) out of a total number of 600,000 professors. To combat this threat, they propose to monitor these dangerous creatures, using student spies, the aim being "to promote greater balance," according to director Laslo Csorba.[20] The idea that an advantage of 60 to 1 does not suffice for "balance" captures well the totalitarian mentality of these elements, as does the very idea, which would be abhorrent to people who had even the most remote conception of the notion of a free society.

One might observe, however, that the paranoid vision of Marxist-controlled universities, which barely merits the term "comical," is not limited to the totalitarian right. One can read in the *New York Times Book Review* that Marxism "has come close to being the dominant ideology in the academic world"; this, from a respected liberal intellectual historian who has surely set foot in American universities more than once.[21] The concept is so remote from reality as to defy rational discussion. It can only be understood as a reflection of the fear that if heresy is granted even a tiny opening, then all is lost.

Such groups as AIM and its offshoots, however ludicrous their antics, have an effect. Consider the question of critique of the media, a crucial activity in a free society. There are, in fact, two forms of such critical analysis. One is lacking in factual substance, ridiculous in its parody of argument, and extremely significant: the "conservative" critique, of which the activities of AIM provide an instructive example. The other is based on extensive factual analysis, carefully argued, often devastating, and wholly without influence: for example, Edward Herman's study of *Times* coverage of the Central American elections (p. 140). There are thousands of pages of similar material. The "conservative" critique is "on the agenda"; the "left-wing" critique is not. Thus, when Public Television produced a series on the Vietnam war, it was subjected to both kinds of critique, one absurd, the other serious, the first influential, the second non-existent, except for readers of marginal journals. PBS was compelled to acknowledge the first kind of critique and even to run a program expounding it. The second kind, whatever its merit, can be safely ignored. The difference lies not in intellectual content, but simply in clout. There are no takeover bids or pressures in Washington coming from the "left."[22] The net effect is to entrench the spectrum of discussion well within the framework of the state propaganda system, with significant effects for the functioning of democracy.

The ignored and irrelevant critique is called "left-wing" or "radical" or "Marxist" in US political theology, as is critical discussion of state and private power generally, terms virtually without meaning in this context except as a form of generalized abuse and a device for avoiding the need to attend to heresy. It is worthy of mention that the highly indoctrinated modern techno-logical societies have taken a long step backwards in these respects from the medieval period, when it was taken for granted by theologians that heresy must be carefully considered and refuted; now it is sufficient merely to label it as such, with some appropriate "scare word."[23]

We might pursue this matter slightly further. The media are constantly criticized as dissident and antagonistic to established power, so much so that they constitute a threat to the survival of American institutions, some allege; for example, the authors of the Trilateral Commission study *Crisis of Democracy*. The "left-wing" critique holds (and I believe, demonstrates) that the media tend overwhelmingly to be subordinated to state and private power. Are these two claims contradictory? Not really, when we look more closely. We might make a distinction between the state and the government, where the state is a system of institutions, including private institutions that set conditions for public policy, which are relatively stable, changing slowly if at all. These constitute the actual nexus of decision-making power in the society, including investment and political decisions, setting the framework within which public policy can be discussed and is determined. The government consists of whatever groups happen to control the political system, one component of the state system, at a particular moment.

In these terms, the "left-wing" critique holds that the media may well be critical of the government while they remain obedient to the state. The "conservative" critique agrees that the media are often critical of the government—this is their great crime; their obedience to the state is assumed. "Conservatism" of the contem-porary variety demands total servility, not mere obedience. Thus the two forms of critique are not, in reality, contradictory, quite often. One might add that obedience of the corporate media to the state is hardly noteworthy or surprising; they serve quite generally as ideological institutions of the state.

The enormous evangelical movement and its media have also become a powerful factor in imposing the "conservative" consensus. The United States is unique among industrial democracies in the allegiance of the population to religious doctrines and institutions, often of a fanatical variety; it is a dramatic exception to the general rule that such allegiance declines with industrialization. It may be that this departure reflects the more limited opportunities for political participation beyond the local level in a society with a highly class conscious business class and few politically-relevant secondary organizations. Ferguson notes "the overwhelming importance of manufacturers in launching the great revivals and temperance crusaders of the 1830s," and the fact that "while business elites almost always protected (and often encouraged) immigrant churches, they spared no expense to destroy unions."[24] This makes good sense. People will seek some form of association, and if meaningful participation in democratic politics is to be excluded, other forms, less threatening to privilege, should be fostered. It is also useful to maintain the population at a low cultural level, a result that has been achieved with much success in the United States, where 39% of the population believe in the Biblical prediction of Armageddon "and accept it with a certain fatalism" (a belief shared by the President, and one that is advantageous for policy-makers intent on increasing the dangers of nuclear war), a mere 9% of the population accept Darwinian evolution while 44% believe that "God created man pretty much in his present form at one time within the last 10,000 years," and so on.[25]

Such successes also have their problems, however. Doctrinal fanaticism may retard scientific progress, as the Soviet experience illustrates, and segments of the churches have become central elements in the movements for peace and social justice, a fact that has caused them to be subjected to unremitting criticism for their "radicalism" if not "anti-Americanism." The very existence of the latter phrase, incidentally, is a reflection of the ideological fanaticism that protects private and state power; a corresponding concept exists in the USSR and some other societies, but would be considered laughable in many, as it should be. Another natural feature of contemporary "conservatism" is, predictably, an attack on independence of religious institutions. The government is now engaged in undercover infiltration of churches and worship sessions, using informants and undercover agents to make tape recordings of conversations and prayer meetings, apparently an innovation in American history though familiar practice in the totalitarian societies that the "conservatives" have taken as their models.[26] The practice was revealed in the course of a trial of two Roman Catholic priests, a nun, a Presbyterian minister, a Quaker activist and six others accused of the crime of offering sanctuary to Salvadoran refugees whom the government is determined to send back to the fate it has arranged for them at home. No doubt AIM will soon be sending spies to monitor sermons to ensure that they are "politically correct."

1.5 Investing to Control the State: the Political System of Capitalist Democracy

Saloma observes that so-called "conservatives" have "largely succeeded in building institutions that incorporate a new long-term strategic dimension into American politics." In the introduction to his book, Henry Steele Commager terms the system Saloma describes not so much a "new political order" as a "new political disorder," which is, "quite simply, the product of money in politics."[27] There is much truth to these assessments. All of this is to be understood as the response by a highly class conscious business community to the Crisis of Democracy perceived by the liberal wing of the groups that rule the capitalist democracies. It is the domestic counterpart to the violent destruction of the "popular organizations" in El Salvador, a prerequisite for what is called "democracy" in the US ideological system.

Again, the continuity with earlier American history should be stressed. Ferguson observes that throughout this history—and notably again in the contemporary period—"As whole sections of the population begin investing massively in political action, elites become terrified and counterorganize on a stupendous scale... And invariably, elites openly begin discussing antidemocratic policy measures and more than usually exalt order and discipline as social goals." The current era exemplifies the pattern, as do the earlier cases mentioned above.

Ferguson concludes from his review of American political history that "the fundamental market for political parties usually is not voters." Rather, "The real market for political parties is defined by major investors, who generally have good and clear reasons for investing to control the state... Blocs of major investors define the core of political parties and are responsible for most of the signals the party sends to the electorate." Periods of political compromise reflect consensus among major blocs of investors, as in the "era of good feeling" after the War of 1812, when "Quite like Mexican elites a hundred years later, American investors for a time enjoyed the luxury of ruling an essentially one-party state under the banner of revolutionary democracy" as "party competition (and voter turnout) virtually disappeared"; one of many such periods, including the present to a significant degree. Party realignments, he argues, reflect basic changes "in the core investment blocs which constitute parties." This "investment theory of politics," which explains a good deal of American political history, regards political parties as *blocs of major investors who coalesce to advance candidates representing their interests*," interpreted not as special interests but as the general interest, while "on all issues affecting the vital interests that major investors have in common no party competition will take place." One aspect of the process is "the interaction of high business figures and the press," which "has frequently been pivotal for American politics."[28]

The New Deal period represented a limited departure from this system: "for the first time in American history, masses of ordinary voters organized themselves and succeeded in pooling resources to become major independent investors in a Party System." But even in this case, at the center of Roosevelt's new political coalition "are not the workers, blacks, and poor that have preoccupied liberal commentators, but something else: a new 'historical bloc' (in Gramsci's phrase) of high-technology industries, investment banks, and internationally oriented commercial banks."[29] The Reagan program is often described as instituting a "revolution" that may overturn the New Deal. The purpose of this coordinated and wide-ranging campaign, as noted, is not merely to concentrate state resources on service to private power, but also to overcome the Crisis of Democracy, the threat of democracy inherent in the engagement of ordinary people in the political system. That is one reason why a large part of the Reagan program is also supported by the political opposition, representing other segments of dominant elites.

Ferguson notes further that "In a political system like that of the United States, the costs associated with control of the state effectively screen out the bulk of the electorate from sustained political intervention." This crucial point is developed further in a very illuminating study by Joshua Cohen and Joel Rogers.[30] They identify two major factors that constrain the political process in a capitalist democracy: the "resource constraint" and the "demand constraint." The former is straightforward enough: groups that command substantial resources can use them to advance their ends through the political system, those who do not—the large majority—may passively observe, with regard to central issues of public policy.

The more subtle "demand constraint" has to do with the factors that "direct the exercise of political rights toward the satisfaction of certain interests." In capitalist democracy, the interests that must be satisfied are those of capitalists: otherwise, there is no investment, no production, no work, no resources to be devoted, however marginally, to the needs of the general population. Therefore, it makes good sense for workers to subordinate their needs to the interests of capitalists, which constitute "a necessary condition for the satisfaction of all other interests within the system... The interests of capitalists appear as general interests of the society as a whole, the interests of everyone else appear as merely particular, or 'special'," as in the Reaganite rhetoric noted earlier. This must be the case when "investment decisions remain out of the reach of social control." Short of the revolutionary step of organizing to place investment decisions under democratic control, workers may rationally choose to avoid politics altogether (as they do, to a great extent, in the US) or limit their engagement to the satisfaction of narrow demands, avoiding larger issues. The process is further advanced by the controls of the ideological system—the hobgoblins regularly brought forth, the jingoist propaganda, the unremitting propaganda about "free enterprise" which must receive massive public subsidy, etc.—and by the fact that the mere effort to gain information and understanding represents a significant investment, worthwhile for business interests and others that command the resources to use them for their own purposes, a mere luxury for people who lack secondary organizations in which they can pool their resources to put what they discover to some use. The policy of "rational ignorance" thus makes sense, in a society where true power is narrowly concentrated and popular organizations barely exist. What is called "public debate," Cohen and Rogers comment, thus reduces to a game in which "different producer groups take turns bombarding the public with misleading information." And there are few resources available to the public to allow them to inquire further, and little for them to gain by expending the quite considerable effort to do so. The public rationally turns to pursuit of personal gain and "private forms of satisfaction," serious engagement in the formation of public policy not being a realistic option.

Further questions also arise, though they are secondary to these essential features of the system of capitalist democracy. Suppose we ask what some government official will do upon leaving office: will he or she join a corporate law firm, a millionaires club, an investment bank, a board of directors—or rather become a unskilled laborer, machinist, clerk, or service worker? The answer provides a certain insight as to which group the person really represents. The class background and associations of elected and appointed officials, and their private aspirations and expectations, are of no small significance.[31] They reflect the concentration of real power, and are factors influencing the stand that elected officials take on public issues.

1.6 "The Ultimate Target": the Public Mind

The task of rendering the human mind "impotent for expression" (see p. 223) nevertheless must be diligently pursued, as illustrated by recurrent Crises of Democracy. This point too has been clearly understood in the business community. An AT&T executive observed in 1909 that "the public mind...is in my judgment the only serious danger confronting the company." "From the turn of the century until this day," Gabriel Kolko comments, "it was the object of a cultural and ideological industry that was as unrelenting as it was diverse: ranging from the school to the press to mass culture in its multitudinous dimensions."[32] The success of government propaganda during World War II helped inspire the growth of the US public relations industry, a unique and highly significant institution. Its patron saint, Edward Bernays, who served on the government propaganda commission during World War I, wrote in the 1920s that[33]

> The conscious and intelligent manipulation of the organized habits and opinions of the masses is an important element in democratic society...it is the intelligent minorities which need to make use of propaganda continuously and systematically. In the active proselytizing of minorities in whom selfish interests and public interests coincide lie the progress and development of America.

The alleged "coincidence" is a widely-held dogma, traceable in one form to early liberal theorists, with "scientific" contributions by the noted psychologist Edward Thorndike and others in the modern period.[34]

In one of his later efforts, Bernays achieved great success in preparing the "public mind" for the overthrow of Guatemalan democracy in 1954, including the "first-class public relations" coups involving the *New York Times* described by the United Fruit PR director (see p. 165). Shortly after World War I, America's leading journalist, Walter Lippmann, devised the term "manufacture of consent" for this new and essential "art" in "the practice of democracy." Leading intellectuals, social scientists and psychologists extolled the virtues of manipulating the public mind to achieve the goals of enlightened leadership, observing that this was a necessity in a stage of history when violence could not be used to control a population that has a theoretical voice in public affairs. We must not succumb to "democratic dogmatisms" about "men being the best judges of their own interests," the influential political scientist Harold Lasswell warned. A system of thought control with few parallels and remarkable successes has been devised, with a good deal of conscious thought and planning throughout.[35] It is reinforced by the "resource constraint" and the "demand constraint," which help explain why political life tends to become the province of blocs of investors who find it worthwhile to invest to control the state.

Returning to the elections in Nicaragua, the Independent Liberal Party, which withdrew two weeks before the elections (apparently under intensive US pressure and possible bribery that was barely reported here[36]), objected that elections could not be held freely while the state-run television network broadcast "programs that promote hatred and class struggle" and while students were subject to "an ideological campaign in favor of the Sandinista front."[37] As noted, the point is not to be dismissed, even putting aside the public and private resources at the hands of the opposition, including inherited wealth, control over much of the economy, support from the influential Church hierarchy strongly backed by the Vatican in a predominantly Catholic country and from the nation's largest newspaper, subsidized by the country organizing the ongoing military attack against Nicaragua, and the backing of the long-term master of the region. But whatever merit the charge has, it is clear enough that the Sandinistas are the rankest amateurs in this regard, restricted to crude and sometimes ugly devices of control long surpassed by more sophisticated practitioners of the art.

1.7 The Domestic Successes of "Conservatism"

The business-organized counterattack against the Crisis of Democracy has had many domestic successes: weakening the labor movement, increasing the state role in the economy to the benefit of advanced sectors of industry, undermining health, safety, civil rights and environmental protection, extending business control over the ideological system and reversing the weak steps towards a more open society taken during "the time of troubles," and so on. Its economic consequences include the deepest recession since the war followed by "a classical Keynesian recovery" (see p. 209), nicely timed to create the impression during the 1984 election that things were looking up under "Reagan-omics." During Reagan's first term, the average annual growth rate fell by 25% from the rate during the Carter years while Reagan's "conservatism" brought productive investment and the US position in international trade to record lows and the Federal deficit to record heights as the ratio of state spending to GNP rose more rapidly than at any time since World War II. Growth in nonagricultural employment fell from 3.3% under Carter to 1%. Employment in manufacturing fell by 0.7 million in contrast to an increase of 1.3 million under Carter. The unemployment rate in 1984 was higher than the average for any year of the Carter Administration, and would have been higher still had the growth in the labor force not declined. Real wages continued their decline at a rate faster than in the Carter years while the share of government spending in the national product rose. Inflation dropped, with about one-third to one-half of the reduction a result of the leveling off of petroleum prices, much of the rest attributable to the assault on labor and the Reagan-induced recession, which had a serious impact elsewhere as well, particularly for the "developing countries." The change in real disposable income during the Reagan years was as follows, by quintiles of the population (rounded figures): bottom quintile, -8%; second quintile, -2%, third quintile, +1%, fourth quintile, +4%, top quintile, +8%—a striking reflection of the policy of shifting resources from the poor to the wealthy.[38] Some additional successes of Reagan-style Keynesianism, implemented via the Pentagon and aimed at enriching the wealthy, are revealed by a study of a Harvard Task force on Hunger, which estimates that 20 million Americans are hungry, with gains of the late 1970s reversed by cuts in federal food aid. A mayoral Task Force on Hunger estimated that close to 900,000 Chicagoans (one in four persons) are malnourished or undergo frequent periods of inadequate food; one Catholic shelter in Chicago with 75 beds for women and children turned away more than 14,000 people in 1983-84. The government pointed with pride to a drop in poverty in 1984, failing to add that according to its own statistics, the poverty levels were higher than before the Reagan-induced recession, in fact higher than at any time since the mid-60s. In September 1985, the civilian unemployment rate stood at 7.3%, the highest on record for this stage in an economic recovery. In the preceding two years the average period of unemployment was higher than for any two-year period since World War II, with less than a third of the unemployed receiving benefits as compared with about 1/2 during the 1970s. Average gross weekly earnings for 1984 were below the 1972 peak. Close to 34 million Americans are living below the poverty line, with 100 million below the Bureau of Labor Statistics' "low standard city budget for a family of four." Furthermore, the future prospects are dim, as poverty is increasingly concentrated among the young, who are locked into a system with no escape. 22.2% of Americans under 18 (48% of black children) live in poverty as compared with 14.3% in 1969-70, a tendency that has accelerated rapidly since 1979. All noteworthy achievements, which are hardly likely to be overcome with the rapidly mounting federal and trade deficits of "Reaganomics'," meaning that future production will increasingly go to paying debts.[39]

The situation of the hungry, poor and homeless reflects the historical inability of the American economy to provide a decent life for much of the population. With its unparalleled advantages—vast internal resources, no external enemies, a huge flow of cheap labor and capital when needed, an empty continent once the land was cleared of the native population, and so on—the United States should by far surpass all other countries in such measures as infant mortality, life expectancy, and other indicators of "quality of life." In fact, it is well down the list, a catastrophic failure of American state capitalism.

2 The Opportunities for Constructive Action

2.1 The System of Control: its Points of Weakness

In earlier chapters we have reviewed some of the achievements of the revival of "conservatism," Reagan-style, in foreign policy and national security affairs, placing them in their historical context; we have now considered some of the domestic results of the concerted campaign by business sectors to reverse the advances of the preceding years in economic welfare, civil rights, intellectual freedom, and democratic politics. The Crisis of Democracy and related progress of the recent past were taken quite seriously by those whose privilege was threatened, and they have once again demonstrated their mastery of the machinery of state in this impressive counterattack.

The weapons at the hands of the state managers and the closely associated blocs of investors whose agendas determine "public debate" are substantial and should not be underestimated. Some tend to disparage the current wave of reactionary jingoism on grounds of its intellectual bankruptcy and often sheer silliness, typified by the titular leadership. That is a mistake; Tyrannosaurus also had a small brain, but one wouldn't want to get in its way. Furthermore, despite the choice of political figurehead, there was nothing foolish—in short-run terms at least—about the methods employed to restore domestic and international order.

Nevertheless, despite the enormous power of the system of control and coercion, it has notable points of weakness. There remains a strong residue of resiliency and independent-mindedness on the part of much of the population, and it is fortified by a tradition of individual civil liberties, an extremely important fact. This tradition is under such severe attack by the Reaganites that the—hardly radical—American Civil Liberties Union has felt it necessary to launch a Bill of Rights Campaign in an effort to maintain the nation's heritage against the onslaught of today's "conservatives," but it is still vibrant. Furthermore, it will be defended by powerful groups, for one reason, because they are its major beneficiaries. Though it has never been a pure capitalist society—nor has any other, for the simple reason that such a society could not long survive—the United States approaches this status as closely as any in the contemporary world. In such a society, everything becomes a commodity, including freedom: you have about as much as you can purchase—for many of us, quite a lot, in a relatively wealthy society such as ours. For a black teenager in the ghetto subjected to police harassment or sometimes direct state violence, the guarantees of civil rights often amount to little. However, those who have some degree of privilege and wealth can act to defend their rights, making use of the legal mechanisms that exist. The same is true of other rights, such as freedom of speech and association. These become meaningful to the extent that one has the resources to exercise them. We can expect these rights to be defended by people who benefit by them, so that dissidents also have a space in which to operate that is often lacking elsewhere, and in much of the world is close to zero.

Furthermore, as noted, the general obedience of the media does not approach full subservience, much to the distress of "conservatives," and there is a tradition of professionalism of reporting that is also lacking in much of the world. An American journalist is as likely to give an accurate account of what he or she sees as any in the world, far more than most; though what they look for, and how they perceive it given a background of indoctrination, and what the editors will tolerate or select, are different matters. The very opulence of the society, combined with this professionalism and the unusual openness of the government to scrutiny—also under attack by "conservatives"—make it possible to obtain a good deal of relevant information and understanding of the contemporary world, for those who are willing to make the effort to escape the doctrinal confines and have the commitment to persist in this course. Opportunities for organizing are available, with difficulty but not with the barriers posed elsewhere, and even the important option of civil disobedience remains when the state has limited resources of violence to employ against relatively privileged groups.

These persistent elements of a society far more free than most made it possible for the Crisis of Democracy to develop during the sixties, as it had before. It was widely believed that the crisis had been resolved by the measures undertaken in subsequent years, that the dread Vietnam syndrome had been cured. The hope that all of this had been put to rest in the "quiescent 70s" was quickly shattered by the popular response to Reagan's attempt to rekindle the aggressive enthusiasms of Kennedy's New Frontier. It is, in fact, remarkable that the 70s have so commonly been described as a period when popular movements were tamed. As many people know from their own experience, this allegedly quiescent period was one of wide-ranging activism; it was precisely in this period that the feminist movement became a vital force, with a far-reaching impact on social life, along with the environmental movement and much else. The growth of the disarmament and solidarity movements in response to the "Resurgent America" programs of the later Carter and Reagan Administrations should have come as no real surprise.

The fashionable talk about the "me generation" and the growth of narcissism may have some basis in reality, but it reflects more than a little wishful thinking and conscious propaganda as well. If people, particularly young people, can be persuaded that their contemporaries are fixated solely upon their own interests and pleasures, then human concerns will abate and the threat of democracy will be stilled, or so it is hoped. Each individual may know that this description is not true of himself or herself. But if, as alleged, that is the "in thing," then perhaps one's natural inclinations can be suppressed under pressure of conformity to what is heralded as the group norm. It is far from clear that this aspect of the propaganda campaign has had very great success.

2.2 The "Shift to the Right": Rhetoric and Reality

It is commonly argued that there has been a great "shift to the right" from the Kennedy to the Reagan years. There has indeed been a major mobilization of the powerful forces of the class conscious business and professional communities, and a shift to the right among the articulate intelligentsia who increasingly associate themselves to these elites. But the evidence hardly shows that the population has adopted the ideology of reactionary jingoism, enhancement of state power and its role in international violence and intervention in the economy, and enrichment of the wealthy at the expense of the disadvantaged: the basic components of contemporary "conservatism."

The "Reagan landslide" is often cited as support for the alleged shift, even on the left. But this is most misleading. In the first place, there was no Reagan landslide. In his 1980 victory, Cohen and Rogers comment, Reagan "gained a smaller percentage of the eligible electorate than Wendell Willkie did in his decisive 1940 loss to Roosevelt"; the turnout was "the third lowest in American history, higher only than the 1920 and 1924 elections that followed the abrupt swelling of the eligibility rolls resulting from the enfranchisement of women." Presidential historian William Leuchtenburg comments that "Reagan, far from having won in a landslide, got little more than a bare majority of the popular vote and only 28 percent of the potential electorate." Furthermore, he adds, "exit polls found that voters backed Reagan less because they shared his outlook than because they wanted an alternative to Carter." A *New York Times*/CBS poll found that only 11% of Reagan voters (hence, 3% of the electorate) chose him on grounds that "he's a real conservative," and other studies showed that degree of liberalism accounted for less than 1% of the loss of electoral support for House Democrats.[40]

Despite unprecedented efforts to bring out the vote, the 1984 returns were similar. Registration increased substantially: by 20% in Texas, by 13% in California, etc. But actual voting increased by only 1%, to 53% of the electorate. Again, Reagan's stand on issues was a minor factor in the vote. The percentage of his supporters who voted for him because he was a "real conservative" went down to 4%. Since Reagan received just under 30% of the electoral vote, this means that about 1% of the electorate voted for a "real conservative." Hardly a landslide victory for "conservatism," with one qualification: those whose voices matter did prefer Reagan's program, which benefits them in the short run at least.

In general, polls showed, issues of any sort were a marginal element in the campaign. To the extent that they were, voters opposed Reagan. A Harris poll reported that by 55 to 38 percent, voters said the country would be worse off with a Republican-controlled Congress that would pass Reagan's proposed legislation.[41]

Such results on voter participation and attitudes would have been regarded as a disaster for the political system in other industrial democracies.

A further reason to doubt the conventional wisdom, Vicente Navarro points out, is that just a year and a half before the election, Reagan was the most unpopular of the last five presidents, and even in 1984, nearly 2/3 of all elective positions were won by Democrats; the London *Economist* observed that Congress turned out to be "a bit more liberal" instead of becoming more "conservative." The well-timed recovery from the Reagan-induced recession was one major factor in Reagan's personal victory, assisted by Mondale's lackluster performance and mimicry of Reagan and the fact that only 5% of the public regarded the central problem Mondale stressed, reduction of the deficit, as a major issue. This was no doubt a major issue for Mondale's backers in the financial community, and the light-hearted "après moi, le déluge" abandon of the Reaganites can hardly cheer rational minds. But as Navarro comments, few people are "willing to pay extra taxes to cover an abstract category called 'the deficit'."[42]

However, polls do indicate regularly that the public would support a tax increase devoted to New Deal and Great Society programs, contrary to widespread beliefs. Support for equal or greater social expenditures was about 80% in 1980, and increased by 1984. The public opposes cuts in Social Security with near unanimity, prefers cuts in military spending to cuts in health programs by about 2 to 1, supports the Clean Air Act by 7 to 1, opposes cuts in Medicare or Medicaid by well over 3 to 1, prefers defense cuts over cuts in these medical aid programs by 3-4 to 1, and opposes a ban on abortions by over 2 to 1. Three-fourths of the population support government regulations to protect worker health and safety, and similar levels support protection of consumer interests and other social expenditures, including help for the elderly, the poor and the needy. Navarro observes that "the majority of Americans favor *more*, not less, government intervention in supporting people's lives and welfare," and would be willing to pay higher taxes if these were spent for such purposes. When asked if they support welfare, the public—properly brainwashed by propaganda about "welfare cheats"—registers opposition, but when asked about specific social programs, they express overwhelming support. Similarly, the public backs military spending to defend ourselves from the threat to our existence posed by the Evil Empire and its outposts in Grenada and South Yemen—though not when the choice is between this and social programs. Still more strikingly, Gary Hart's pollsters found in 1975 that the overwhelming majority believe that workers and the community should control business enterprises, though "socialism" is advocated by virtually no one.

Like Mondale, Hart opposed the public on all these issues, under the slogan: "To get the government off your back, [you have to] get your hands out of the government's pocket." Only high technology industry is to keep its hands in this rapidly filling pocket. After the 1980 election, Hart joined in a unanimous Senate Budget Committee vote to undermine social legislation that is overwhelmingly supported by the public, undoing "thirty years of social legislation in three days," in Senator Moynihan's words.[43] The fact that Congress overwhelmingly voted against the policies supported by the public is informative, with regard to the factors that determine public policy.

Again, the shift began under Carter. Navarro observes that Carter was elected in 1976 on a platform that included expansion of New Deal programs, but enacted none of these proposals. The growth rate in social spending dropped from about 8% under Nixon and Ford to 4% under Carter, and was then reversed by Congress under Reagan while government spending radically increased— for the military system of subsidy to advanced industry. As noted earlier, the plans to reduce social spending in favor of the military system were advanced by Carter in late 1978, then implemented under the pretext offered by the Iranian hostage crisis and the Soviet invasion of Afghanistan, then the "window of vulnerability" and other fantasies. The choice of military over social programs ran exactly counter to the public will, but the public was never offered a choice on these matters in the political system, and the ideological institutions prefer tales about a shift to the right that is more congenial to their own perceived interests and their conception of the proper government role in economic and global management.

In the case of military spending, the reasons diverge sharply from the pretexts, as we have seen. The same is true of the other side of today's coin: the attack on the working class and the poor. The pretext is an alleged popular shift towards "conservatism." The reasons are basically two: first, the real decline in US hegemony which makes it impossible to pursue simultaneously the "great societies at home and grand designs abroad" of Kennedy-style rhetoric, requiring a sacrifice of the former since the latter are a *sine qua non* of policy for elite groups; and second, the deep concern felt across the spectrum of elite opinion over the Crisis of Democracy in its various manifestations, a crisis that demands a return to obedience and austerity, to the "sacrifice and discipline" called for in the halcyon days when business could control the state without interference from the lower orders.

But the real issues do not arise for the electorate. On these, the public is granted no voice, in accordance with the workings of capitalist democracy in the United States, as already discussed. The reasons why voters paid little attention to issues as they voted, or did not even take the trouble to show up at the polls, are not obscure. It took a discerning eye to perceive a difference between the candidates, and history offers few reasons to believe campaign promises in any event. The campaign was, as always, a major media event, part of the hoopla designed to show how marvellously democracy works. But commentators on the TV debates reflected a sharper insight when they chose to discourse learnedly on Mondale's choice of a necktie, or debated whether Geraldine Ferraro looked down too much at her notes, or waited to see if Reagan could weather a TV performance without some incredible blooper. Others labored mightily to lend some seriousness to the affair, but theirs was no easy task. It is not too suprising that most people who didn't just stay home appeared to vote for the guy with the nicest smile, who made them feel good, who happened to be running while the economy was temporarily recovering from the depths to which his advisers had reduced it.

Despite all this, it could be argued that the marginal differences between the elite groups that backed the two candidates might yield a major difference in consequences for victims of US state power at home and abroad. Sometimes it is worthwhile to make even decisions of third-order importance. On this matter, it is also arguable that the significance of voting varies with the office; members of the House are likely to be more responsive to their constituents than Senators, and the latter more responsive to the electorate than the President. As we move up the hierarchy and relations become more remote, the incumbent tends more to cater to the needs of those who control the private economy, who are also more concerned with domestic and international policy at that level.

As always in US politics, voting remained largely an elite affair in the Reagan years. Barely 1/3 of the unemployed voted in 1980. Working class turnouts in the US are roughly 30% lower than middle class turnouts; blacks vote 20% less than whites. "If we concentrate on people with less than five years of formal education, a sure sign of class, we find that in Italy, 75% vote, in America, 8%," Leuchtenberg comments. In the 1980 elections, 49% of eligible voters with family incomes of $5000-$10,000 voted, compared with 74% of those with incomes over $25,000. 71% of white collar workers and 48% of blue collar workers voted. An analysis of 30 democracies showed "a significant correlation between high voter turnout and the presence of political parties representing clearly defined strata of society—that is, parties strongly tied to specific income classes, religious groups, or language groups," Edsall observes. In the US, where the choice is between two factions of the Property Party, many see no point in voting at all. The past decade, Edsall concludes, has seen "a growing inability of the political system to represent, in the highly complex process of developing economic policy, the interests of the bottom three-fifths of society."[44] In general, there is ample reason to accept Walter Dean Burnham's conclusion that the class pattern of abstention "seems inseparably linked to another crucial comparative peculiarity of the American political system: the total absence of a socialist or laborite mass party as an organized competitor in the electoral market."[45] Along with the increasing weakness of unions and the lack of other politically-relevant popular organizations or political parties structured to permit popular participation, this contributes to the elimination of issues relevant to much of the population from the electoral system, and doubtless accounts in significant measure for their lack of interest in a game played among elite groups. The class character of abstention adds another element to the interpretation of the alleged "landslide."

Polls reveal awareness of the way the political system actually functions, despite massive propaganda efforts. A *Times*/CBS poll after the 1984 election showed that 49% of the public thought the government was run "by a few big interests looking out for themselves," while 40% believed that government is run for the benefit of all the people, as official doctrine holds.[46] The headline of the article reporting these figures reads: "Americans in Poll View Government More Confidently." There was, indeed, an increase in the low level of expression of confidence in government. The fact that half the population holds beliefs that are regularly castigated as "Marxist" or "left-wing" in mainstream media and scholarship—beliefs that appear quite accurate, it seems, and relate to questions of fact rather than ideology in any event—is somewhat more noteworthy, one might think.

The minds may have been "rendered impotent," but not by persuasion, it appears.

There are other respects in which the "shift to the right" among the population proves to be a myth. Unlike the Kennedy years, the general public no longer easily tolerates militarism and aggression. When Kennedy attacked South Vietnam in 1962, there was no public outcry; as noted earlier, the event does not even exist in US history, so profoundly indoctrinated are the intellectual elites, as was the general public at the time. As late as 1965, anti-war activists felt lucky to be able to speak to groups of neighbors in private homes or to address meetings in colleges where the organizers outnumbered the audience, and public meetings were broken up by militant counter-demonstrators, many of them students. Even in Spring 1966 it was impossible in Boston, a center of liberalism, to run an open-air public anti-war meeting, and a church to which it was moved was defaced with tomatos and other projectiles by an angry crowd—all of this arousing no notice among people who later were to be outraged by heckling of war criminals at public meetings and by "student violence," much of it mythical, apart from what was instigated by government provocateurs. But when Reagan attempted to mobilize public opinion in support of direct military intervention in El Salvador, he succeeded only in organizing a large-scale and spontaneous popular movement of protest, and was forced to back down from more ambitious plans and limit himself to an extension and escalation of Carter's murderous war. Kennedy's brinkmanship and nuclear adventurism aroused much admiration, while Reagan's rhetoric—which so far falls short of Kennedy's actions—has, in contrast, provided a major impetus for an international disarmament movement. Case by case, much the same comparison holds.

High-level Pentagon planners may believe that "The U.S. is going back to becoming the world's policeman,"[47] but their joy in this prospect is overly optimistic. It is doubtful that the US can return to those wonderful days when intervention, subversion and direct aggression could be freely undertaken with much success throughout a large part of the world while the public acquiesced and the intelligentsia lauded our noble commitment to Wilsonian principles of freedom and self-determination and the inspiring humanitarianism that distinguishes the US from all other powers in history. The economic consequences of the Pentagon system of national industrial policy can also not be long ignored. It is likely that there will be significant conflict within business circles over the coming years between those who hope to retain the traditional military Keynesian methods and others who believe that they will no longer serve in an era of decline of US hegemony, when industrial rivals can no longer be controlled or dismissed and the domestic population is not so malleable as before.

2.3 Turning the Tide

Such features of the contemporary world and our own society leave ample openings for those concerned to alleviate current suffering or to prepare the ground for substantive social change. Such efforts are perhaps more feasible today than they were in earlier years. The "conservative" mood among elites reflects an understanding of such potential, and its temporary successes should not blind us to the basic weaknesses of the "conservative" program. Even in these years of coordinated elite campaigns and chaos and disorientation among dissident forces there have been some real achievements and some "near misses" where a little more work could have made a large difference. The US wars in Central America are bad enough, but could be worse, as they were in Indochina. The congressional vote on aid to the *contras* in June 1985 was not a "sure thing." Had it gone differently, the Administration would have found more devious means to pursue its war against Nicaragua but the dynamics would have changed considerably, with effects in Honduras and Costa Rica and a chance for a peaceful settlement. The scandalous tolerance of the far worse US-backed atrocities in El Salvador was not inevitable, but rather reflects the failings of people who could have done far more to awaken the public to them. How many of us can reflect with pride and equanimity on what we have done in this case and many others?

Indoctrination is undoubtedly effective, particularly among the educated part of the population, but the system of thought control is based on principles that are flimsy and dishonest and it can collapse very quickly, as happened during the Vietnam war with consequences that persist today. As mentioned earlier, those who labor to rescue the fact that $2 + 2 = 4$ from the commissars who insist that $2 + 2 = 7$ when it suits their needs will not suffer the fate of Orwell's Winston Smith or his real life counterparts in much of the world. They will face unpleasantness, vilification, a degree of risk, sometimes loss of substantial privilege, but not torture, decapitation or psychiatric prison. It is possible even for those who are not saints or heroes to come to understand the world in which we live, and to act to stop the terror and violence for which we share responsibility by turning the other way.

It can be done. Our own recent history shows that, and we need not pretend to ourselves that we do not know the way. The mass popular movement against the war in Indochina undoubtedly had significant effects. It raised the costs to the war criminals who conducted it. It prevented the state from declaring a true national mobilization, so that the war had to be fought on deficit financing, with guns and butter, leading to serious economic problems that finally impelled elite groups to turn against it as an investment that should be liquidated. Anti-war sentiment at home fueled dissidence within the military, which began to collapse, much to its credit. US elite groups learned a lesson familiar to their imperial predecessors: a citizen's army is unable to fight a war against a civilian population. That task requires professional murderers. Principled opposition to the war was minimal among elite groups, but became widespread among the population. As late as 1982, after years of dedicated brainwashing with no audible response, over 70% of the general public regarded the war as not merely a "mistake" but "fundamentally wrong and immoral," a position held by only 45% of "opinion makers" (including clergy, etc.) and by a far smaller proportion of elite intellectuals, to judge by earlier studies that showed that even at the height of anti-war activism after the Cambodia invasion of 1970, only a tiny fraction of them opposed the war on principled grounds.[48]

None of this "just happened." It was the product of dedicated and committed efforts over many years by innumerable people, the most important of them unknown outside of the small circles in which they worked. The same is true of every form of social struggle, whether narrowly focused on some particular atrocity, or devoted to enlarging the domain of freedom and justice.

The consequences of the American war were terrible enough. They could have been worse yet, and would have been had it not been for the mass popular anti-war movement, spontaneous and with little leadership, spearheaded primarily by courageous young people whose achievement is measured by the hatred and contempt they inspired among the commissars who trembled with fear and indignation at the sight of young men and women who dared to defy the Holy State in one of the finest moments of American history, a real achievement by people who cared about their country and are thus condemned as unpatriotic scum by those who prefer to march in parades singing the praises of their leaders.

A standard argument of the reactionary jingoists who dominate discussion of the matter today is that Hanoi (always taken to be The Enemy, since the existence of our attack against South Vietnam cannot be conceded) expected the war to be won on the streets of America, and was proven right, sure proof that the protestors were an evil lot. A more accurate perception was received by a delegation of peace movement activists visiting Hanoi in 1970, who were told by high officials that what impressed them most was something they had read in the press about people in a Midwestern town who had visited a cemetery to place wreaths on the graves of fallen soldiers in a silent protest against the war. But the state worshippers nevertheless have a point. Had it not been for the public opposition that became quite a remarkable force, the government could have moved on without needless distraction to a total victory instead of the partial one they achieved, much as the Nazis won a total victory over the Jews of Europe in a campaign that they too described as "self-defense."

The limited successes of the peace movement are now often heralded as a triumph of American democracy. That is hardly accurate, for two basic reasons. First, consider what was not achieved. There was barely a peep of protest when the US provided the essential means for the French war of conquest, finally coming close to using nuclear weapons, then undermined the political accords and launched a campaign of violent terrorism while blocking the political settlement sought on all sides. By the time protest reached a noticeable level, perhaps a million Vietnamese had already been killed in almost two decades of US-organized terror and violence. That protest, furthermore, was largely directed against the attack on North Vietnam, which carried risks of international war, hence a threat to us. The true nature of the US war against South Vietnam was never widely understood, a crucial fact with implications that persist, playing their part in facilitating the cruel postwar policies aimed at maximizing suffering and repression in the countries we devastated. Protest reached a truly significant level when the US had expanded its aggression to all of Indochina, with ½ million troops fighting in South Vietnam. While the popular movement that escaped the bounds of the doctrinal system was effective, this alleged "triumph of democracy" nevertheless left three countries utterly in ruins with many millions dead, hardly an occasion for great self-congratulation.

Secondly, the successes of the peace movement were largely achieved outside of the system of formal political democracy, by direct action, which raised the cost of aggression. Without these actions, lobbying of Congress, letter writing, political campaigning and the like would have proceeded endlessly with as much effect as they had in 1964, when the American people voted overwhelmingly against escalation of the war in Vietnam, voting for the candidate who at that time was secretly preparing the escalation that he publicly opposed. There was, indeed, a feature of American democracy that made these limited successes possible: the inability of the state to use massive violence against its own citizens. This permitted the public to make a rare and indirect contribution to decision-making, by affecting the calculus of costs of the planners. As I have emphasized throughout, this feature of American democracy is not to be lightly dismissed. Nevertheless, we may note that even the most violent totalitarian state is not free from such calculations of cost. The leading Nazi planner Albert Speer writes in his memoirs that "it remains one of the oddities of [World War II] that Hitler demanded far less from his people than Churchill and Roosevelt did from their respective nations." Hitler was never able to carry out "the total mobilization of labor forces" and other measures of mass mobilization that could be undertaken in the democracies, because of "the regime's anxiety not to risk any shift in the popular mood." This necessity to pacify the domestic population severely hampered the Nazi war effort, he points out, setting back armaments production by several years, according to his estimate.[49]

Consider a more recent and much different example, the case of East Timor, where a huge massacre proceeded under Ford and particularly Carter, with a death toll of 1-200,000, perhaps more, roughly a quarter of the population by fairly conservative estimate, thanks to the support of the US and its allies and the servility of the media and the intellectuals—who, meanwhile, feigned great agony about the simultaneous and in many ways comparable atrocities of Pol Pot, which they had no way to alleviate, in sharp contrast to the Timor massacre, which they could have terminated at once by pressure to withdraw the crucial US support for the Indonesian aggressors. The Timorese remnants were reduced to the level of Biafra and Cambodia, as was finally conceded after the fact, and the killing and subjugation still go on under the cover of Western silence or deception. But some barriers were placed in the way of the consummation of genocide. The Red Cross was finally permitted to enter—intermittently—after four years, and some relief flowed. The murderous assault was limited though not ended. Tens if not hundreds of thousands of people were saved. This was the result of the dedicated work of—literally—a handful of young people, who devoted their lives to bringing the facts to the public, ultimately reaching parts of the government and the press. The personal costs have not been trivial. They will receive no notice or thanks, any more than the courageous war resisters of Vietnam days, certainly not the Nobel Peace Prize they richly deserve. But they have a different reward, the knowledge of what they have accomplished. Many of us can share in such rewards, if we choose to do so.

Intervention in Timor, or even in Indochina or Central America, is a rather peripheral concern of the managers of the US global system, despite the enormous resources sometimes devoted to such enterprises and the genuine fears of "contagion" and "rotten apples." Liquidation of these projects of terror and coercion will not seriously affect the domestic order or the Fifth Freedom, and therefore committed popular efforts can make a real difference. Other tasks are much harder, those that begin to touch the structure of power and privilege; serious efforts to confront the military system are a case in point.

The drift towards mutual annihilation has a seemingly inexorable quality. The factors that impel it forward appear to be out of control, beyond our ability to influence or constrain them. We can only hope that this perception is false. Whether the tide can be turned in this case is not clear, though it is plain enough that it will not long flow on its present course. One effect of the development of nuclear weapons has been to induce a feeling of powerlessness on the part of much of the population, and at the same time, to reinforce the doctrine that the state must be free to conduct its affairs without popular interference or even scrutiny, given the awesome forces that it and its enemy command. These, no doubt, are among the reasons that induce planners to expand their nuclear arsenals and refine the systems of destruction in ever more exotic ways: apart from everything else, they serve as a means of strengthening state power and domestic social control, one reason why they have such appeal to "conservatives" of the modern variety. Another effect of these developments has been a tendency to stare at apocalyptic visions, dismissing political analysis and past approaches to action as now irrelevant in the face of imminent total destruction. While understandable, this is a most serious error. The primary threats—the "deadly connection" and technical advances in weaponry—can be addressed, and must be if we are to survive. What is needed is clear-headed analysis and action over a broad range, often with quite specific and limited goals, not the paralysis that results from contemplation of awesome visions of destruction.

The threat of nuclear war is real enough. There is much that can be done to reduce the threat, and it would be wrong, even criminal, to fail to do what can be done to constrain the military system and to reduce the tensions and conflicts that may lead to its employment, terminating history. Nevertheless, to concentrate all energies on delaying an eventual catastrophe while ignoring the causal factors that lie behind it is simply to guarantee that sooner or later it will occur. There are reasons why states devote their resources to improving the technology of destruction, why they seek international confrontation and undertake violent intervention. If these reasons are not addressed, a terminal conflict is a likely eventuality; only the timing is in doubt. It is suicidal to concentrate solely on plugging holes in the dike without trying to stem the flood at its source. For us, that means changing the structures of power and dominance that impel the state to crush moves towards independence and social justice within our vast domains and that constantly drive it towards militarization of the economy. There is no simple formula to determine how limited energies should be distributed among these many tasks; all must be addressed if there is to be a chance of survival in a world in which a decent person would want to live.

As our society is constituted, public policy will be guided by the imperatives of intervention and military Keynesianism; protests against particular excrescences, however successful, will lead to pursuit of the same objectives by similar means along other paths, since the state—in the broad sense of earlier discussion—relies on them for its survival *in its present form*. Alternatives to existing forms of hierarchy, domination, private power and social control certainly exist in principle, and are well-known, and even supported by much of the population despite their remoteness from the intellectual scene, as already briefly noted. But to make them realistic will require a great deal of committed work, including the work of articulating them clearly.[50] Similarly, opposition to slavery would have failed if no realistic alternative had been advanced: rental rather than ownership of labor, in our own history, not the end to which we should strive, but a major advance nonetheless. Determined opposition to the latest lunacies and atrocities must continue, for the sake of the victims as well as our own ultimate survival. But it should be understood as a poor substitute for a challenge to the deeper causes, a challenge that we are, unfortunately, in no position to mount at present though the groundwork can and must be laid. Protest over Star Wars, massacre in El Salvador, and so on, is a sign of our weakness. A strong peace movement would be challenging military-based state capitalism and the world system it dominates while seeking to support similar forces to the extent that they can survive in the so-called "socialist world."

The latter phrase, incidentally, should be recognized as a joint contribution of the two major world propaganda systems to social control. For the US, it serves as a means to discredit socialism by associating it with totalitarian cruelty; for the taskmasters of the Soviet Union, as a means to gain legitimacy and support by exploiting the aura of socialist ideals and the respect that is rightly accorded them, in an effort to conceal their own brutal practice as they have destroyed every vestige of socialism, from the first moments of their bloody rule.[51]

Unless the various strands of the movements for peace and social justice can develop and sustain a vision of an attainable future that expresses the felt needs of the overwhelming mass of the population for freedom, justice, decency, solidarity and meaningful democracy, and unless they can find a way to follow Bakunin's advice to construct the "facts" of this future within existing society, there will be no way to proceed beyond attempts to mitigate the worst atrocities and to delay the final catastrophe. Plainly, this has not yet happened. The Soviet-Western fraud about "socialism" is one of many mechanisms that have served effectively to undermine any such endeavor. Western-style capitalist democracy, as already observed, aims at a condition in which each individual confronts the organized power of highly self-conscious ruling groups in isolation, flipping a lever every few years but with no means to go further to join with others to gain information and understanding, to raise and consider questions about the nature and functioning of economic and political institutions, to develop concepts and programs of social change, or even to enter or influence the relatively narrow arena of decision-making in the political system in a meaningful way. This must be changed, and only patient efforts among people with whom one lives and works will make such change a reality in the longer term. Separatism, subcultures or actions that remain meaningless or offensive to much of the population, lack of an articulated vision of the future, acceptance without awareness of the doctrines of the state religion—these are among the many reflections of the enormous power of the Western system of fragmentation and ideological control, and of our inability, so far, to combat it, except sporadically.

US foreign and domestic policy has roots in institutional structures; only in a limited way does it reflect the personal preferences and commitments of particular individuals who happen to hold office. The institutional structures fix these policies within certain bounds, leading to ceaseless efforts to maintain or enlarge the Fifth Freedom, reliance on the Pentagon system of state economic management, concerted measures to limit democracy at home and destroy it in the dependencies, a persistent assault on human rights and social justice, construction of a vast system of social control and indoctrination. Within the constraints of existing state institutions, policies will be determined by people representing centers of concentrated power in the private economy, people who, in their institutional roles, will not be swayed by moral appeals but by the costs consequent upon the decisions they make—not because they are "bad people," but because that is what the institutional roles demand; if current incumbents do not perform these tasks, they will be removed in favor of others who will. The closer to the centers of power one stands, the more these factors operate. Those who are serious about inducing changes in public policy will therefore consider ways to modify this calculus of costs.

For elite groups who control capital and investment decisions, the means are direct, well-understood, and constantly pursued. The ordinary citizen who is excluded from the private system of domination and control can resort to other means. Those who own and manage the society want a disciplined, apathetic and submissive public that will not challenge their privilege and the orderly world in which it thrives. The ordinary citizen need not grant them this gift. Enhancing the Crisis of Democracy by organization and political engagement is itself a threat to power, a reason to undertake it quite apart from its crucial importance in itself as an essential step towards social change.

We can also learn from history. There is substantial evidence that the fear of domestic disruption has inhibited murderous plans. One documented case concerns Vietnam. The Joint Chiefs of Staff recognized the need that "sufficient forces would still be available for civil disorder control" if they sent more troops to Vietnam after the Tet Offensive, and Pentagon officials feared that escalation might lead to massive civil disobedience, in view of the large-scale popular opposition to the war, running the risk of "provoking a domestic crisis of unprecedented proportions." A review of the internal documents released in the *Pentagon Papers* shows that considerations of cost were the sole factor inhibiting planners, a fact that should be noted by citizens concerned to restrain the violence of the state.[52] In such cases as these, and many others, popular demonstrations and civil disobedience may, under appropriate circumstances, encourage others to undertake a broader range of conventional action by extending the range of the thinkable, and where there is real popular understanding of the legitimacy of direct action to confront institutional violence, may serve as a catalyst to constructive organization and action that will pave the way to more fundamental change. In contrast, without a background of popular understanding, it may be only a form of self-indulgent and possibly quite harmful adventurism.[53]

Looking beyond the ever-present need to deter particular crimes of state, there is little reason to accept the doctrine that existing institutional structures represent the terminus of historical social evolution, that their principles are graven in stone. There is no need for people to accept as a permanent condition that the vast majority of the population, in order to survive, must rent themselves to those who control capital and resources, means of production and distribution, while decisions over investment and other crucial matters are removed in principle from democratic control, with the further consequence that democratic politics includes a very limited range of social choices, operating within parameters set elsewhere in the state system. The groundwork for great social movements of the past was laid through many years of searching, intellectual interchange, social experimentation and collective action, organization and struggle. The same will be true of the coming stages of social change.

Those who wish to play a meaningful role in influencing public policy or changing its institutional base must begin with honest inquiry, in community with others if it is to be effective. Whether one sees oneself as dedicated to reform or revolution, the first steps are education of oneself and others. There will be little hope for further progress unless the means to carry out these first steps are preserved and enhanced: networks of local organizations, media and publishers who do not bend to state and private power, and so on. These first steps interact: the organizations will not function without access to information and analysis, independent media and publishing will not survive without the participation and intellectual and financial contributions of popular organizations that grow and develop on the basis of shared concerns, optimally based in the community, workplace, or other points of social interaction. To the extent that such a basis exists, a range of possible actions become available: political pressure within the system, community organizing, civil disobedience, constructive efforts to create wholly new institutions such as worker-managed industry, and much else. As activity undertaken in such domains, including conventional political action, extends in scale, effectiveness, and popular engagement, it may well evoke state violence, one sign that it is becoming truly significant.

There are no magic answers, no miraculous methods to overcome the problems we face, just the familiar ones: honest search for understanding, education, organization, action that raises the cost of state violence for its perpetrators or that lays the basis for institutional change—and the kind of commitment that will persist despite the temptations of disillusionment, despite many failures and only limited successes, inspired by the hope of a brighter future.

Footnotes

Introduction

1. For many examples, see my *Towards a New Cold War* (Pantheon, 1982; henceforth, *TNCW*) , and work cited there.

2. See *TNCW* and earlier publications cited, among them, Chomsky and Edward Herman, *The Political Economy of Human Rights* (henceforth, *PEHR*) (South End, 1979), for my own views on the matter. On related issues concerning the Middle East, see also my *Fateful Triangle* (South End, 1983).

Chapter 1

1. Frank Monaghan, *John Jay* (Bobbs-Merrill 1935), 323; this was "one of his favorite maxims," Monaghan notes.

2. David Brion Davis, *Slavery and Human Progress* (Oxford, 1984), 151.

3. David Bain, *Sitting in Darkness* (Houghton Mifflin, 1984), 2.

4. Leon Higginbotham, *In the Matter of Color* (Oxford, 1978), 372; John Booth, *The End and The Beginning* (Westview, 1985), 17.

5. Booth, *End and Beginning*, 32-3; Walter LaFeber, *Inevitable Revolutions* (Norton, 1983), 62.

6. For informative surveys, see LaFeber, *Inevitable Revolutions*; Jenny Pearce, *Under the Eagle* (Latin American Bureau, London, 1981; South End, 1982). On the US role in Guatemala and El Salvador, particularly since the Kennedy Administration raised the level of savagery to unprecedented heights, see Michael McClintock, *The American Connection*, two volumes (Zed, 1985). On the more general picture, see *PEHR*.

7. Bruce Calder, *The Impact of Intervention* (Texas, 1984).

8. William Krehm, *Democracies and Tyrannies of the Caribbean* (Lawrence Hill, 1984).

9. We return to the cases; only in the last was the matter incidental rather than central to US concerns.

10. Charles Clements, *Witness to War* (Bantam, 1984); preface by Murat Williams.

11. Tom Buckley, *Violent Neighbors* (*Times* Books, 1984), 122-3.

12. *Commentary*, November 1979.

13. Tom Barry, Beth Wood, and Deb Preusch, *The Other Side of Paradise* (Grove, 1984); Edward Herman, *The Real Terror Network* (South End, 1982); *PEHR*, II, chapter 3; see chapter 2 on the flight of refugees from the American colonies, one of the richest areas in the world, in fear of the victorious rebels, including boat people who fled in terror to Nova Scotia where they died in misery in the winter cold, perhaps some 4% of the population—the equivalent of over 2 million refugees from Vietnam, a country ravaged and destroyed by vicious aggression.

14. *Draining the Sea...*, Americas Watch (March 1985), ii; Arthur Helton, op-ed, *NYT*, April 2, 1985.

15. *The Electoral Process in Nicaragua*, Latin American Studies Association (LASA) official publication, Nov. 19, 1984, Report of a Delegation of LASA to observe the Nov. 1984 elections. The delegation was headed by LASA President-elect Wayne Cornelius and included a former LASA president, members of the executive council, members of the Association with special expertise on Central America, and scholars (half the delegation) with substantial field research experience in Nicaragua.

16. *Oxfam America Special Report 7*, Jan. 1985.

17. On Nicaragua, see Joseph Collins et al., *What Difference Could a Revolution Make?* (Institute for Food and Development Policy), 1982; Booth, *End and Beginning*.

18. Reed Brody, *Contra Terror in Nicaragua* (South End, 1985). The report of this fact-finding mission includes 140 pages of similar testimony, with some 150 affidavits. The mission, undertaken at the initiative of a New York law firm representing Nicaraguan interests, consisted of Brody, former Assistant Attorney General of New York State, Sister Sandra Price, who has worked in Nicaragua since 1981, and James Bordelon, a law student.

19. *NYT*, Nov. 23, 1984; worse still, Calero added that "we are not killing civilians. We are fighting armed people and returning fire when fire is directed against us" from cooperatives—which, most surprisingly, have armed guards, justifying the massacre of civilians who are not civilians when *contra* soldiers, walking by to enjoy the scenery, are inexplicably fired upon by these terrorists.

See the full-page ad supporting aid to the "democratic resistance" led by Calero in the *NYT*, June 2, 1985, signed by Martin Peretz and Leon Wieseltier of the *New Republic*, along with such regular apologists for US atrocities as Sidney Hook and John Silber and numerous other luminaries: Morris Abram, Hyman Bookbinder, Penn Kemble, Samuel Huntington, Seymour Martin Lipset, Michael Novak, Albert Shanker, Allen Weinstein, Ben Wattenberg, etc.

20. *Boston Globe*, Sept. 18, 1985. The *Globe* devoted 100 words to the priest's report; the *Times*, none.

21. *NYT*, Sept. 15, 1985, datelined Honduras; Shirley Christian, "Anti-Sandinistas vow to cut abuses," *NYT*, Washington, Aug. 24, 1985. Cruz cites scarcity of medical facilities and transportation as reasons for the "delicate thing."

22. Jonathan Steele and Tony Jenkins, *Manchester Guardian Weekly*, Nov. 25, 1984.

23. Marian Wilkinson, *National Times* (Australia), Nov. 30, 1984; Gavin Macfadyen and Joanna Rollo, *New Statesman* (London), Aug. 31, 1984.

24. Orville Schell and Robert Bernstein, *Wall St. Journal*, April 23, 1985.

25. Editorial, *Christian Science Monitor*, Aug. 16, 1985; the editors are noted for the high moral sentiments eloquently proclaimed on suitable occasions.

26. Bill Keller, *NYT*, June 4, 1985.

27. Karl Marx, *The Civil War in France* (1871; International Publishers, 1941).

28. *NYT*, Nov. 23, 1984; Pamela Constable, *Boston Globe*, April 24, 1985; Cruz, *Foreign Affairs*, Summer, 1983; Cruz, op-ed, *NYT*, Dec. 6, 1984; Edgar Chamorro, *In These Times*, Sept. 4, 1985; Dennis Volman, *CSM*, Oct. 15, 1985. We return to the *contra* programs, as the functioning leadership sees them.

29. *In These Times*, Sept. 4, 1985; *NYT*, July 18, 1985; editorial, *BG*, Sept. 14, 1985; *Latinamerica Press*, Oct. 3, 1985, a Church-based publication in Peru.

30. *Country Reports on Human Rights Practices*, Dept. of State, Feb. 2, 1981, 427.

31. *El Salvador: One Year of Repression*, Legal Aid Service of the Archdiocese of San Salvador, World Council of Churches, 1981.

32. *Country Reports*, 1981, 427-8.

33. Alan Riding, *NYT*, Sept. 27, 1981.

34. Editorial, "Reform in El Salvador," *WP-MG Weekly*, Feb. 22, 1981; *NYT*, Dec. 7, 1980. On the media suppression, see *TNCW*, 37, 389, 392, 429-30. For extensive documentation of the pervasive double standard, which is extraordinary in scale, see the references of note 2 in the Introduction, and Herman, *Real Terror Network*.

35. Reuters, *NYT*, Aug. 22, 1985.

36. "Recent Political Violence in El Salvador," Senate Select

Committee on Intelligence, Oct. 5, 1984; Álvaro Magaña, March 1982. Cited by Central America Crisis Monitoring Team, *In Contempt of Congress* (Institute for Policy Studies, 1985).

37. Aryeh Neier, "Exporting Persecution," *Nation*, Sept. 7, 1985.

38. McClintock, *American Connection*, II, 280, citing a Reuters report. See *PEHR*, I; *TNCW*, introduction.

39. Stephen Kinzer, *NYT*, June 30, 1985; *Economist*, July 27, 1985.

40. Barbara Crossette, *NYT*, July 8, 1985; as for the coup, the official claim of Communist Party involvement is dubious at best, a matter discussed in important forthcoming work by Peter Dale Scott.

41. Philip Windsor, *The Listener* (BBC, London), July 11, 1985. See Michael Vickery, *Cambodia* (South End, 1983), the major scholarly study of the period, widely and favorably reviewed in England, Australia and elsewhere but totally ignored in the press here because the conclusions—that the total population decline through 1978 (when the worst massacres took place) was over 400,000, from all causes, with wide variations from place to place— are unacceptable; see also Vickery, letter, *Far Eastern Economic Review*, Feb. 7, 1985. On the media fabrications at the time, including Lacouture's in the *New York Review of Books*, the ignored US intelligence estimates, and the scandalous avoidance of the US role, see *PEHR*, II.

42. Rep. Gerry Studds, *Central America, 1981*, Report to the Committee on Foreign Affairs, US House of Representatives, March 1981; report of a three-person congressional delegation.

43. David Blundy, *Sunday Times* (London), April 26, 1981; Édouard Bailby, *Le Monde diplomatique* (Jan. 1981).

44. *Report on Human Rights in El Salvador*, compiled by Americas Watch and the American Civil Liberties Union, Jan. 26, 1982 (Vintage, 1982).

45. *New England Journal of Medicine*, April 28, 1983. Capital flight is estimated at $1 billion as compared with total US aid of $1.7 billion; see the bipartisan report by Representatives Jim Leach and George Miller and Senator Mark Hatfield, "U.S. Aid to El Salvador," Feb. 1985.

46. Ross Gelbspan, *BG*, Sept. 23, 1985.

47. Moe Snell, *In These Times*, Oct. 2, 1985; George Will, "ACLU swerve to the left," *BG*, Sept. 28, 1985; *NYT* Oct 23, 1985.

48. John Loftus, "Secrets of State," *Boston Review*, July, 1985; William Doherty, *BG*, Feb. 19, 1985.

49. William Shannon, *BG*, Feb. 2, 1983.

50. Ambrose Evans-Pritchard, *St. Louis Post-Dispatch*, May 12, 1985; Mary Jo McConahay, Pacific News Service, Feb. 25-March 1, 1985.

51. Elizabeth Hanly, *In These Times*, April 17, 1985.

52. Alexander Cockburn, *Nation*, June 1, 1985. See *Draining the Sea...* (Americas Watch, March 1985), *Free Fire* (Americas Watch, Aug. 1984), and earlier reports. On Operation Speedy Express, one of the many US Vietnam atrocities beside which My Lai pales into insignificance, see *PEHR*, I, 5.1.3. See *TNCW*, chap. 5, for discussion of the treatment of this and other atrocities by Guenter Lewy, an American scholar whose falsifications and vulgar apologetics for mass murder are highly regarded in the US and England.

53. Philip Taubman, *NYT*, Dec. 4, 1984; Jonathan Kwitny, *Nation*, April 20, 1985.

54. *New Statesman*, April 19, 1985; Amnesty Action (AI), April 1985; Robert Healy, *BG*, Nov. 26, 1985.

55, *CSM*, Nov. 18, 21, Dec. 11; *BG*, Nov. 13, 26, 29, 1984; in the Dec. 11 report, Robert Press of the *CSM* devotes a few sentences to the content of a talk by Mrs. Garcia, who accepted the prize here, noting her charge that members of her family were apprehended and killed and adding portentously that "she did not say why they had been apprehended."

56. Marlise Simons, *NYT*, Sept. 29, 1985.

57. *In Contempt of Congress*; Ray Bonner, *Weakness and Deceit* (*Times* Books, 1984), 353; Australian Labor MP Joan Coxsedge, *Melbourne Sun* (April 20, 1985), reporting on the first Human Rights Congress in El Salvador.

58. *Draining the Sea...*; the reporter cited is Chris Hedges, *Dallas Morning News*, Jan. 21, 1985; Chris Norton, *CSM*, March 21, 1985; two of the few US journalists in Central America who merit the title.

59. James LeMoyne, *NYT*, Sept. 9, 1984.

60. Testimony before the Subcommittee on the Western Hemisphere, Feb. 2, 1984; released by Americas Watch.

61. Quoted by Howard Zinn, *Disobedience and Democracy* (Vintage, 1968), 75.

62. Julia Preston, *BG*, Aug. 15, 1985.

63. COHA News Release, Aug. 3, 1985.

64. Cynthia Brown, ed., *With Friends Like These*, Americas Watch Report on Human Rights and US Policy in Latin America (Pantheon, 1985), 194, 180ff.

65. AI News release, 11 October, 1982, cited by Lars Schoultz, in Martin Diskin, ed., *Trouble in Our Backyard* (Pantheon, 1983), 186.

66. Craig Nelson and Kenneth Taylor, *Witness to Genocide* (Survival International, 1983). The interviewers were Nelson and Central America historian Thomas Anderson.

67. *Voices of the Survivors*, Cultural Survival and Anthropology Resource Center, 1983); the testimony is reported by a Jesuit anthropologist.

68. *Latin America Regional Reports*, May 7, 1982; cited by McClintock, *American Connection*, II, 232-3.

69. *'Bitter & Cruel...'*, British Parliamentary Human Rights Group, October 1984; *WSJ*, Sept. 20, 1985. See also *Guatemala: A Nation of Prisoners* (Americas Watch, Jan. 1984), and numerous other reports by human rights groups documenting atrocities and government responsibility.

70. *Notes on Strategic Hamlets*, USOM, Saigon, Office of Rural Affairs, May 1963; cited by Richard White, *The Morass* (Harper & Row, 1984), 114.

71. *Economist*, May 28, Jan. 15, 1983.

72. Chris Hedges, *Dallas Morning News*, Jan. 21, 1985; cited in *Draining the Sea*...; on Ochoa's Israeli training, see Steve Goldfield, *Garrison State* (*Palestine Focus* Publications, 1985), 41, citing *WP*, Jan. 8, 1983, and *CSM*, Jan. 13, 1983.

73. Brown, *With Friends*; Holly Burkhalter of Americas Watch, "Guatemala Revised"; Christopher Hitchens, *Nation,* October 12, 1985; Abrams on Ríos Montt cited in *In Contempt of Congress;* for Abrams on refugees, also *NYT*, May 5, 1983. On the 1982 massacres, see *Economist,* Dec. 18, 1982, Feb. 19, 1983; *Human Rights in Guatemala: No Neutrals Allowed,* Americas Watch, 1982; and other human rights reports.

74. *BG*, Nov. 29, 1983.

75. "Nightline," ABC television, Feb. 13, 1985, cited in *Draining the Sea*....

76. *BG*, Nov. 29, 1983; *Failure: The Reagan Administration's Human Rights Policy in 1983* (Americas Watch, Helsinki Watch, Lawyers Committee for International Human Rights, Jan. 1984), 34. See the Americas Watch report "*...in the face of cruelty*", Jan. 1985, documenting the dismal story for another year.

77. On Abrams's lies concerning El Salvador, see also Bonner, *Weakness and Deceit*, 250, 326, 355; on Turkey, see "*...in the face of cruelty*", and Brown, *With Friends*.

78. Douglas Foster, *Mother Jones*, Feb./March 1985.

79. White, *Morass*; George Black et al., *Garrison Guatemala* (Monthly Review, 1984), 150f.; Brown, *With Friends*, 196f; Schoultz, in Diskin, *Trouble*, 187-9.

80. E.g., the *New Republic* has carried excellent articles on the continuing atrocities in Guatemala (Allan Nairn, April 11, 1983; Piero Gleijeses, June 10, 1985) with not a word on Israel's crucial contribution. The practice is common even apart from such extreme Party Line journals. On Israel's role in Guatemala, see *Fateful Triangle* and sources cited there; also Black, *Garrison Guatemala*, 154f.; McClintock, *American Connection*, II, 192f., 219; Cynthia Arnson, *New Outlook* (Tel Aviv), March 1984; Victor Perera, *Mother Jones*, July 1985. On the more general picture, see also Israel Shahak, *Israel's Global Role* (Association of Arab-

American University Graduates, Belmont, 1982); Eric Hooglund, *Israel's Arm's Exports: Proxy Merchant for the U.S.* (American-Arab Anti-Discrimination Committee, 1982); Aharon Kleiman, *Israeli Arms Sales* (Jaffee Center for Strategic Studies, Tel Aviv, 1984); Goldfield, *Garrison State.*

81. The same is true of much of scholarship. Thus, in his standard work on militarism in Latin America, Edwin Lieuwen reviews the CIA coup in 1954 with not a mention of the United States; *Generals vs. Presidents* (Praeger, 1964), 41.

82. On these matters, see *PEHR,* I.

83. Yoav Karni, *Yediot Ahronot,* quoted by Goldfield, *Garrison State,* 36; Gidon Samet, "Strategic cooperation: the real reason," *Ha'aretz,* Nov. 6, 1983; see also Wolf Blitzer, *Jerusalem Post* (April 22, 1984), generally confirming the picture. On this and other factors in the "special relationship" between Israel and the US, see *Fateful Triangle.*

84. Wolf Blitzer, *Jerusalem Post,* June 17, 1983.

85. Yosef Priel, *Davar,* July 19, 1983, datelined Washington; Kleiner quoted in *Hadashot,* Aug. 9, 1985.

86. McClintock, *American Connection,* II, 194-5; *Ma'ariv,* March 25, 1982.

87. Magnus Linklater, Isabel Hilton and Neal Ascherson, *The Fourth Reich* (Hodder & Stoughton, London, 1984), 229; *Hadashot,* Aug. 22, 1984. On Israel and the Argentine anti-Semitic generals, see *TNCW.*

88. *Ha'aretz,* Aug. 23, 1983.

89. Yoav Karni, "The Prophet from New York," *Ha'aretz,* June 27, 1985. See *Fateful Triangle,* 16, 386-7, on Wiesel's explicit refusal to condemn Israeli atrocities and his principle that only those "in a position of power" have sufficient information to render critical judgment on the Holy State; accolades are always permissible. Wiesel, regularly nominated for the Nobel Peace Prize, is the author of a work entitled *Against Silence.*

90. Office of Public Safety, USAID Report on a study of AID Public Safety programs, 1967; cited in *Report on Human Rights,* 8.

91. LaFeber, *Inevitable Revolutions,* 169, 132; Brown, *With Friends,* 190f. Also White, *Morass;* McClintock, *American Connection;* Barry, *Dollars and Dictators,* 97-8; Pearce, *Under the Eagle,* 51f.; and for the more general picture, Miles Wolpin, *Military Aid and Counterrevolution in the Third World* (Heath, 1972) and PEHR, I.

92. Richard Millett, *Guardians of the Dynasty* (Orbis, 1977), 251. We return to the US stand in 1978-9.

93. Lester Langley, *Central America: the Real Stakes* (Crown, 1985), 108.

94. Roger Lowenstein, *WSJ,* Sept. 19, 1985.

95. John Kelly, *AfricAsia,* June 1985; citing *WP,* May 10, 1984.

96. "Why Farmers Go Hungry," Oxfam America Educational Publication #12, 1985; Norma Stoltz Chinchilla and Nora Hamilton, in Roger Burbach and Patricia Flynn, eds., *The Politics of Intervention* (Monthly Review, 1984), 228.

97. J.H. Parry, *The Spanish Seaborne Empire* (Hutchison, 1966), chapter 11.

98. Roger Burbach and Patricia Flynn, *Agribusiness in the Americas* (Monthly Review, 1980), 104.

99. Langley, *Central America*, 128-9; Susan George, *How the Other Half Dies* (Allanheld, Osmun, 1977), 132; Barry, *Dollars and Dictators*, 97-8.

100. Bradford Burns, in Jan Black, ed., *Latin America: Its Problems and Its Promise* (Westview, 1984); see also *PEHR*, I.

101. "Why Farmers Go Hungry"; figures are from the early eighties, the most recent years for which data are available. See also Frances Moore Lappé & Joseph Collins, *Food First* (Ballantine, 1978); Susan George, *How the Other Half Dies* and *Feeding the Few* (Institute for Policy Studies, n.d.).

Chapter 2

1. Krehm, *Democracies and Tyrannies*, 19.

2. Philip Russell, *El Salvador in Crisis* (Colorado River Press, 1984, 37f.); LaFeber, *Inevitable Revolutions*, 73-4. On the 1932 events, see Thomas Anderson, *Matanza* (U. of Nebraska press, 1971).

3. Quoted by Walter LaFeber, *America, Russia, and the Cold War* (Wiley, 1967), 133.

4.Lawrence Wittner, *American Intervention in Greece* (Columbia, 1982); John Lewis Gaddis, *The United States and the Origins of the Cold War* (Columbia, 1972); see *TNCW* and *Fateful Triangle* for summary in the context of the period.

5. Simon Hanson, *Five Years of the Alliance for Progress* (Inter-American Affairs Press, 1967), 1.

6. LaFeber, *Inevitable Revolutions*, 154, 161ff., 184.

7. Gordon Connell-Smith, *The Inter-American System* (Oxford, Royal Institute of International Affairs, 1966), 54.

8. James Eayrs, *In Defence of Canada; Indochina: Roots of Complicity* (U. of Toronto, 1983), 4.

9. "Crisis in the World and in the Peace Movement," in Nat Hentoff, ed., *The Essays of A. J. Muste* (Bobbs-Merrill, 1967).

10. Laurence Shoup and William Minter, *Imperial Brain Trust* (Monthly Review, 1977), 162-3.

11. Policy Planning Study (PPS) 23, Feb. 24, 1948, *FRUS 1948*, I (part 2); reprinted in part in Thomas Etzold and John Lewis Gaddis, *Containment* (Columbia, 1978), 226f.

12. Kennan was replaced by hard-liner Paul Nitze on Jan. 1, 1950, to become Counsellor to the Department of State.

13. *Report of the National Bipartisan Commission on Central America*, Henry Kissinger, chairman, Jan. 10, 1984.

14. JCS 1769/1, April 29, 1947; *FRUS*, 1947, I; reprinted in part in Etzold and Gaddis, *Containment*, 71-83. The quoted comment speaks "from the military point of view," which includes "ideological warfare."

15. See Shoup and Minter, *Imperial Brain Trust*, 136, 175-6; William A. Williams, *The Tragedy of American Diplomacy* (Delta, 1962).

16. LaFeber, *Inevitable Revolutions*, 107, 96.

17. Speech in April 1961, cited by John Lewis Gaddis, *Strategies of Containment* (Oxford, 1982), 208.

18. Walt Rostow, *The United States in the World Arena* (Harper & Row, 1960), 244; John King Fairbank, *American Historical Review*, Feb. 1969). For specific details on the intelligence and scholarly record, see my *For Reasons of State* (Pantheon, 1973), chapter I.V; *TNCW*.

19. See *For Reasons of State*, and on the postwar period, references of note 64, below.

20. Barry Blechman and Stephen Kaplan, *Force Without War* (Brookings Institution, 1978), 51.

21. Connell-Smith, *Inter-American System*, 161f.

22. Louis Wiznitzer, *CSM*, May 14, 1985; Alexander Cockburn, *Nation*, March 23, 1985.

23. "Nicaragua Bishop Says U.S. Embargo Hurts," *NYT*, May 25, 1985; "Opposition in Nicaragua Says It Is Weakened by the U.S. Embargo," *NYT*, May 10, 1985; also Stephen Kinzer, *NYT*, May 12, 1985 and *Business Week*, May 13, 1985, noting local business opposition and adverse effects on local businessmen and growers.

24. James Austin, *BG*, June 16, 1985. On US financing of *La Prensa*, see below. The embargo was "categorically condemned" by the Latin American countries; *Le Monde*, May 17, 1985.

25. Gary Clyde Hufbauer and Jeffrey Schott, *Economic Sanctions Reconsidered* (Institute for International Economics, 1985), 672, a book dedicated to Secretary of State George Shultz; *CSM*, May 16, 1985.

26. Richard Immerman, *The CIA in Guatemala* (U. of Texas, 1982), 184-5, 128.

27. For discussion, and comparison of Japanese behavior in Manchuria to the American invasion of South Vietnam, see my

American Power and the New Mandarins (Pantheon, 1969), chapter 2.

28. Timothy Garton Ash, *New York Review of Books*, Nov. 22, 1984.

29. Anderson, *Matanza*, 157; LaFeber, *Inevitable Revolutions*, 152; Allan Nairn, *The Progressive*, May 1984; see also the issue of April 4, 1985, for comment on criticism of Nairn's important study, to which we return.

30. William Y. Elliot, ed., *The Political Economy of American Foreign Policy* (Holt, 1955), 42. See my *At War with Asia* (Pantheon, 1970), for further discussion of this revealing work.

31. Gregorio Selser, *Sandino* (Monthly Review, 1981), 104.

32. V. G. Kiernan, *America: The New Imperialism* (Zed, 1978), ii.

33. Connell-Smith, *Inter-American System*, 2; Dexter Perkins, *The Monroe Doctrine*, three volumes (1927, 1933, 1937; reprinted by Peter Smith, 1965-6), I, 9-10.

34. Perkins, *Monroe Doctrine*, III, 63; Connell-Smith, *Inter-American System*, 10, 5; Perkins, II, 318, referring specifically to Mexico.

35. Gabriel Kolko, *Main Currents in American History* (Pantheon, 1984), 47; Taft, quoted by Pearce, *Under the Eagle*, 17; Connell-Smith, *Inter-American System*, 16; the reference in the latter case is to Mexico.

36. Perkins, *Monroe Doctrine*, III, 161; Millet, *Guardians of the Dynasty*, 52.

37. Perkins, *Monroe Doctrine*, III, 396.

38. Connell-Smith, *Inter-American System*, 48-9, 15.

39. Lester Langley, *The Banana Wars* (U. of Kentucky, 1983), 26; Hubert Herring, cited by Connell-Smith, 15.

40. LaFeber, *Inevitable Revolutions*, 50f.

41. LaFeber, *Inevitable Revolutions*, 54-8, 75-6.

42. Gabriel Kolko, *Politics of War* (Random House, 1968), 302f. On US oil policy in the context of general postwar global planning, see *TNCW*, chapters 2, 11.

43. Connell-Smith, *Inter-American System*, 81f.

44. LaFeber, *Inevitable Revolutions*, 78f.

45. Krehm, *Democracies and Tyrannies*, 121.

46. LaFeber, *Inevitable Revolutions*, 78f. On the same phenomenon with regard to petroleum policy, see *TNCW*, and with regard to US policy in Asia, *At War with Asia*, chapter 1. More generally, see Kolko, *Main Currents*; Stephen Krasner, *Defending the National Interest* (Princeton, 1978).

47. Kolko, *Politics of War*, 471.

48. William Roger Louis, *Imperialism at Bay* (Oxford, 1978), 481.

49. This and what follows is drawn from an illuminating study by Melvyn Leffler, "The American Conception of National Security

and the Beginnings of the Cold War, 1945-48," *AHR Forum*, *American Historical Review*, April 1984.

50. Kolko, *Politics of War*.

51. Samuel Huntington, in M.J. Crozier, S.P. Huntington and J. Watanuki, *The Crisis of Democracy* (NYU, 1975), report of the Trilateral Commission. On this commission, see Holly Sklar, ed. *Trilateralism* (South End, 1980) and *TNCW*.

52. Shoup and Minter, *Imperial Brain Trust*; see *TNCW* for a brief review. See Robert Schulzinger, *The Wise Men of Foreign Affairs* (Columbia, 1984), a much more superficial conventional history that omits the crucial material Shoup and Minter discuss while citing the "official rebuttal" by William Bundy, which condemned them for "selectivity" (*Foreign Affairs*, October, 1977). Both Bundy and Shulzinger dismiss the Shoup and Minter study without analysis as a paranoid vision comparable to that of the Far Right. Their important study was otherwise ignored. Standard histories also ignore Kennan's positions cited here, as do his memoirs. On the wartime and early postwar period, see especially Kolko, *Politics of War*, Gabriel and Joyce Kolko, *The Limits of Power* (Harper & Row, 1972), two seminal contributions to a large literature.

53. See *For Reasons of State*, chapter 1, V, for references and discussion.

54. James Chace, "How 'Moral' Can We Get," *NYT magazine*, May 22, 1977.

55. See *TNCW*, chapter 2.

56. President Lyndon B. Johnson, speeches on Nov. 1, Nov. 2, 1966; *Public Papers of the Presidents of the United States*, 1966, Book II (Washington, 1967), 563, 568; *Congressional Record*, March 15, 1948, House, 2883.

57. Dean Acheson, *Present at the Creation* (Norton, 1969), 219; see *TNCW*, 195f., for more extensive discussion.

58. Seymour Hersh, *The Price of Power* (Summit, 1983), 270, quoting Roger Morris; Morton Halperin et al., *The Lawless State* (Penguin, 1976), 17, citing Hersh, *NYT*, Sept. 11, 1974.

59. LaFeber, *Inevitable Revolutions*, 157.

60. Walter Laqueur, *WSJ*, April 9, 1981; *Economist*, Sept. 19, 1981. On the terrorist war against Cuba conducted from US bases under US government auspices, see Herman, *Real Terror Network*, *TNCW*, and sources cited. Sterling's much-admired fables may be based in part on a document fabricated by the CIA to test the veracity of a defector, then circulated through the sleazy network of peddlars of planted "intelligence leaks." See Alexander Cockburn, *Nation*, Aug. 17, 1985.

61. *For Reasons of State*, 31-37, citing documents in the *Pentagon Papers*.

62. Minutes summarizing PPS 51, April 1949, cited by Michael

Schaller, "Securing the Great Crescent: Occupied Japan and the Origins of Containment in Southeast Asia," *J. of American History*, Sept. 1982; the study also suggested that "some diversification of their economies" should be permitted. For fuller development of this topic, see Schaller; essays by John Dower and Richard Du Boff in Chomsky and Howard Zinn, eds., *Critical Essays*, vol. 5 of the *Pentagon Papers* (Beacon, 1972); *For Reasons of State*, chapter 1, V.

63. Perkins, I, 131, 167, 176f. The last phrase is Perkins's summary of "a widespread, nay, almost general, viewpoint" among European statesmen.

64. See *For Reasons of State*, 37; *PEHR*, II; *TNCW*; Joel Charny and John Spragens, *Obstacles to Recovery in Vietnam and Kampuchea: U.S. Embargo of Humanitarian Aid* (Oxfam America, 1984).

65. *At War with Asia*, 286.

66. On this matter, see *PEHR*, II, 2.2.

67. *At War with Asia*; *For Reasons of State*; *PEHR*, II; and sources cited.

68. *NYT*, May 5, 1985.

69. *WP Weekly*, April 22, 1985.

70. For the government case as presented by a respected advocate, see John Norton Moore, "Legal Issues in the Central America Conflict," *J. of Contemporary Studies* (Winter/Spring 1985); also my comments, "Law and Imperialism in the Central American Conflict," Spring/Summer 1985, and Moore's response, "Tripping through Wonderland with Noam Chomsky," in the same issue, which is quite revealing: e.g., his claim that we may discount statements of intent by the President, high government officials, the *contra* leaders, etc., as well as the pattern of actual events, because "as anyone with a twelfth-grade education understands," US policy requires congressional approval. The impossibility of executive wars and intervention should come as a great comfort to their victims in Guatemala, Laos, Cambodia, Cuba, etc. In fact, what every sane twelfth-grader understands is that civics textbooks are one thing, the real world, quite another. Another typical example is his proof that the US did not attack South Vietnam by bombing it from 1962, later invading outright; the proof is that North Vietnam invaded the South 13 years later, and according to the US government, controlled the southern insurgency. Putting the first argument aside out of charity, Moore's Communist counterparts could demonstrate by similar logic that the USSR did not invade Afghanistan, since the insurgency is controlled from Pakistan and the guerrilla groups have been attacking from Pakistan with Pakistani support since 1973 (*Far Eastern Economic Review*, Jan. 30, 1981), A few similar examples appear below, along with examples of gross misrepresentation.

Altogether, not a very impressive performance by "the staff of the Center for Law and National Security," whom he thanks for their "substantial research assistance." I am, however, indebted to Moore for pointing out that the full statement by FDN leader Calero is even more awful than the part I quoted; see chap. 1, note 19, including the omitted parts. The editors of this right-wing journal demonstrate their standards, e.g., in attributing to me the view that "U.S. actions in Grenada and Central America are no different from actions in Afghanistan"—their paraphrase of my statement: "There are, of course, numerous respects in which Soviet aggression in Afghanistan is not comparable to U.S. intervention in El Salvador [Grenada is nowhere mentioned]; a closer comparison would be to the U.S. attack against South Vietnam..." The latter comparison cannot even be heard in these circles, so offensive is it to jingoist sensibilities. This material is worth reading for its insight into the intellectual bankruptcy of these "conservative" circles and the curious incapacity to understand that chanting of government slogans does not constitute argument.

71. Roy Gutman, "America's Diplomatic Charade," *Foreign Policy*, Fall 1984.

72. General Assembly Resolutions 194 and 273; reprinted in John Norton Moore, ed., *The Arab-Israeli Conflict*, vol. III (Princeton 1974).

73. "La Prensa's editors have lobbied for continued U.S. funding of the contras, never acknowledging their human-rights violations" (Council on Hemispheric Affairs and Newspaper Guild (AFL-CIO, CLC), *Press Freedom in Latin America 1984-85*, 51, discussing the "inexcusable" government harassment of *La Prensa*); Joel Brinkley, *NYT*, March 26, 1985, reporting the grant, through a federally-financed foundation.

74. *Fateful Triangle*, 139; *Hadashot*, May 23, 1985; *Al Fajr* (Jerusalem), Aug. 9, 1985; Matti Peled, *Koteret Rashit*, Aug. 14, 1985; *Hadashot*, May 16, 1984; Dan Fisher, *LAT*, Oct. 5, 1985; *Ha'aretz*, July 10, 1985; Moshe Negbi, April 5, 1985, excerpted from a forthcoming book. On the mechanisms of self-censorship, see also Moshe Negbi, *Koteret Rashit*, June 19, 1985.

75. News conference, *NYT* June 19, 1985.

76. Stephen Kinzer, *NYT*, Sept. 9, 1985.

77. Interview, COHA's *Washington Report on the Hemisphere*, July 9, 1985. See Penny Lernoux, *Nation*, Sept. 28, 1985, for a reasoned discussion of the current situation. The US secured British recognition of the sovereignty of Nicaragua over the Miskitos, which the US regarded as "unquestionable," in 1895; Perkins, *Monroe Doctrine*, III, 40f.

78. *Human Rights in Nicaragua: Reagan, Rhetoric and Reality*, Americas Watch, July 1985; *Violations of the Laws of War by Both*

Sides in Nicaragua: 1981-1985, Americas Watch, March 1985. The former is a detailed critique of Reagan Administration lies concerning Nicaragua. On Administration lies, see also *In Contempt of Congress* and the bipartisan congressional report "U.S. Aid to El Salvador," discussing the record of the Administration in providing "insufficient, misleading and in some cases false information to Congress." Its lies to the public have become notorious.

79. Stephen Kinzer, *NYT*, Sept. 17, 1985; Shirley Christian, *NYT*, Oct. 8, 1985.

80. Fairfax Downey, *Indian Wars of the U.S. Army* (Doubleday, 1963), 32f.

81. The preferred version is that Ben-Gurion "opposed only the return of Arabs who had joined the enemy"; Marie Syrkin, *New Republic*, Oct. 21, 1985.

82. Yoela Har-Shefi, *Hadashot*, Aug. 24, 1984; Yoram Nimrod, *Al Hamishmar*, June 7, 1985; see *TNCW*, pp. 464-5, on the earlier 1979 report. An AP report on the *Hadashot* story appeared in the *Boston Globe*, without details and with an apologetic commentary (Aug. 26, 1984), but not elsewhere, to my knowledge. For more on the background, including the rejection of Arab peace overtures, see Tom Segev, *1949* (Domino, Jerusalem, 1984; Hebrew). This and other recent work based on newly available archival material will substantially revise the conventional picture.

83. Eyal Ehrlich, "Ambush on the Jordan," *Koteret Rashit*, Aug. 14, 1985. Commenting on this material, a group of dissident Israeli journalists note that contrary to what Ehrlich states, "it isn't true that no one knew about what was going on," citing protests by tiny left-wing groups and writers at the time, adding that others preferred not to disturb the victory celebrations; Report no. 19, Alternative Information Center, 14E Koresh St., Jerusalem.

84. AP, *BG*, Sept. 21, 1983.

85. Rabbi Morton Rosenthal of ADL, letter, *NYT*, Sept. 27, 1983, responding to an op-ed of Sept. 13 by Ilana DeBare; Walter Ruby, *Jerusalem Post*, Aug. 21, 1984, *Genesis 2*, Sept. 1984; Americas Watch, *Human Rights in Nicaragua*; Ignacio Klich, *Le Monde diplomatique* (Dec. 1983); Stan Steinreich, Jewish Student Press Service, *Genesis 2* (Sept./Oct. 1983). For Rabbi Rosenthal's reiteration of the ADL charges, see *Jewish Post*, Sept. 5, 1984; *Le Monde diplomatique*, June 1984.

86. *Human Rights in Nicaragua*.

87. COHA press release, Aug. 1985; Stephen Vaughn, *Holding Fast the Inner Lines* (U. of North Carolina, 1980), 194. For discussion and the broader context, see *TNCW*, chap. 1.

88. E.g., Moore, "Tripping through Wonderland," who attributes to me the claim that "progressive" forces such as Cuba, Nicaragua, and the Salvador guerrillas, have an "exemplary human rights record"—what I wrote is that their "abuses of human

rights and democratic principle, often real," are not the cause of US opposition to Cuba and Nicaragua, as is obvious from US support for far more violent regimes; the Salvador guerrillas are not mentioned; the word "progressive," which he repeatedly gives in quotes, is his invention. Moore also speaks of my "commitment to the radical regime," non-existent of course, but Moore would have no other way of interpreting heretical views with regard to the Holy State.

89. Jonathan Steele, *London Review of Books*, April 4, 1985.

90. On the technique of constraining debate within the bounds of the state propaganda system, see *TNCW* and earlier work cited; also, my "Notes on Orwell's Problem" in *Knowledge of Language* (Praeger, 1985).

91. Randolph Ryan, *BG*, Aug. 27, 1985.

92. For much further discussion, see the references of note 90.

93. 1983 Report of the House Permanent Select Committee on Intelligence, cited by Joanne Omang and Edward Cody, *WP*, March 11, 1985; Wayne Smith, *LAT*, Aug. 25, 1985.

94. Joel Brinkley, *NYT*, June 5, 1985.

95. Connell-Smith, 23f., 343.

96. LASA report, cited above; Colman McCarthy, *WP* (*MG Weekly*, March 17, 1985); Collins, *What Difference Could a Revolution Make*; Booth, *The End and the Beginning* (Westview, 1985); UCLA historian E. Bradford Burns, *In These Times*, Jan. 25, 1984.

97. Karen Remmer, in Black, *Latin America*. See also, among others, Halperin, *Lawless State*; Hersh, *Price of Power*.

98. Council on Hemispheric Affairs, April 2, 1985; also June 26, 1983; Jan Black in Black, *Latin America*; Tom Farer, "Human Rights and Human Welfare in Latin America," *Daedalus* (Fall, 1983).

99. Denis Warner, *The Last Confucian* (Macmillan, 1963), 312.

Chapter 3

1. See chapter 2, note 78.

2. *Congressional Record*, Senate, 1649, Jan. 14, 1927, cited by Philip Brenner, in Ralph Miliband, John Saville and Marcel Liebman, *Socialist Register 1984: The Uses of Anti-Communism* (Merlin, 1984); Langley, *Banana Wars*, 186.

3. Karl Meyer suggests that the source may be a John Birch society fabrication; *NYT*, Oct. 8, 1985. The incident aroused little comment, the assumption apparently being that random lies are normal and acceptable on the part of the political leadership.

Fabrication of quotes is an Administration specialty; for example, repeated attribution to the Sandinistas of the phrase "revolution without frontiers" by the President and others, with much outrage; they later conceded that this and other "quotations" have no source (*NYT*, March 30, 1985, also citing another example of such fakery, the use by Vice-President Bush of a Nicaraguan postage stamp with a picture of Karl Marx to prove that the Sandinistas are setting up a Marxist state; other stamps, he failed to mention, feature George Washington and Pope John Paul II). Though the fabrication has long been exposed as lacking any source, it continues to be used by apologists for US atrocities, e.g., by Moore, who cites it in quotes, repeatedly ("Tripping through Wonderland"); yet another example of "conservative scholarship." Note that the offending phrase, even if it existed, would be quite innocuous, just as if the leaders of the American revolution had expressed a hope that their democratic revolution would extend "without frontiers." In fact, there is a similar phrase in a speech by Sandinista leader Tomás Borge, who said in July 1981 that "this revolution transcends national boundaries," making it quite clear that he meant ideological transcendence. He proceeds to say: "this does not mean we export our revolution. It is enough—and we couldn't do otherwise—for us to export our example...we know that it is the people themselves of these countries who must make their revolutions." No one familiar with the US government disinformation system could doubt what would follow; and sure enough, in September 1985 the State Department published a document attempting to prove Nicaraguan aggressiveness, entitled "Revolution beyond our Borders," referring to this very speech, with a mistranslation of Borge's statement excised from the immediate context to make it appear that the Sandinistas themselves boast of their aggressiveness. The fraud is exposed by the Council on Hemispheric Affairs, *Washington Report on the Hemisphere*, Oct. 16, 1985. The tradition of fabrication is a hoary one. See *TNCW*, 71, and references of note 56, below, for earlier examples.

4. *NYT*, March 20, 1984, June 5, 1985; *LAT*, Nov. 14, 13, 1984.

5. Langley, *Banana Wars*, 153f., 137, 123f.; Stuart Creighton Miller, *"Benevolent Assimilation"* (Yale, 1982). 230-2.

6. Bain, *Sitting in Darkness*, 78, 66, 86f.; Miller, *Benevolent Assimilation*, 164, 65f., 95, 116, 235, 269.

7. Daniel B. Schirmer, *Republic or Empire* (Schenkman, 1972), 231, 236-9.

8. T. D. Allman, *Unmanifest Destiny* (Dial, 1984), 277, 259, 265; *Scientific American* quoted by Ronald Takaki, *Iron Cages* (Knopf, 1979), 162.

9. for specific references, see *For Reasons of State*, 114f., 127f.; *TNCW*, 198f.

10. John Goshko and Charles Babcock, *WP*, April 14, 1984. In apparent contradiction to Rubin's accurate statement, Moore ("Tripping through Wonderland") claims that "the U.S. has repeatedly raised the Cuban-Nicaraguan aggression before the Security Council." But the contradiction is only apparent; in the style of a legal advocate, Moore carefully formulates his statement so as to evade the issue while appearing to address it. What is at issue is not rhetorical allegations but rather a formal charge of armed attack, invoking the right of self-defense, and an appeal to the Security Council to act. Moore also conveniently omits the words requiring report of measures taken to the Security Council, in citing Article 51 in his "Legal issues."

11. See my "Rule of Force in International Affairs," reprinted in *For Reasons of State* from the *Yale Law Journal* (June, 1971), and "Law and Imperialism."

12. *NYT*, April 13, 1984; Julius Lobel (Professor, Pittsburgh School of Law), *Memorandum of The National Emergency Civil Liberties Committee on the United States, Nicaragua and the World Court*, April 15, 1985.

13. Anthony Lewis, *NYT*, May 28, 1984, citing an address by Moynihan at the Syracuse Law School.

14. LaFeber, *Inevitable Revolutions*, 41, 48, 53, 59; Connell-Smith, *Inter-American System*, 51-2; Selser, *Sandino*, 28.

15. Hufbauer and Schott, *Economic Sanctions Reconsidered*, 674f.

16. Millett, *Guardians of the Dynasty*, 25-6. For the full text, see Selser, *Sandino*, 28-30.

17. Booth, *End and Beginning*, 24, 50; Millett, *Guardians*, 139, 226. On National Guard atrocities, see Booth, 119f.

18. "Interview of the President by the New York Times, March 28, 1984," released by the White House, March 29.

19. News Conference; *NYT*, Feb. 22, 1985.

20. Bill Keller, *NYT*, Feb. 28, 1985.

21. Adam Pertman, *BG*, Aug. 29, 1985.

22. Joel Brinkley, *NYT*, March 30, 1985.

23. *CSM*, April 23, 1985; *NYT*, Nov. 1, 1984; *WP*, Nov. 29, 1984; *LAT*, March 3, 1985.

24. Interview with Claudia Dreifus, *Progressive*, August 1985.

25. Moore, "Legal issues"; see chapter 2, note 70, for his explanation of the logical impossibility of what the US is actually doing and has often done in the past.

26. Millett, *Guardians*, 24, 31; Langley, *Banana Wars*, 157, 160, 217.

27. Russell, *El Salvador*, 38, citing *NYT*, May 3, 1978; LaFeber, *Inevitable Revolutions*, 13.

28. Anderson, *Matanza*, 159; Kirkpatrick, cited by Bonner, *Weakness and Deceit*, 237.

29. Richard Millett, in Black, *Latin American*; Embassy Cables of May 1961 quoted by McClintock, *American Connection*, I, 149, 199; Edward Herman and Frank Brodhead, *Demonstration Elections* (South End, 1984), 98.

30. LaFeber, *Inevitable Revolutions*, 173f.; McClintock, *American Connection*, I, 64f.

31. Sam Dillon, *New Republic*, June 17, 1985; Shirley Christian, *NYT*, June 16, 1985; Chris Norton, *CSM*, July 1, 1985.

32. Julia Preston, *BG*, Feb. 7, 1984.

33. Booth, *End and Beginning*, 75-6.

34. Nairn, "Behind the Death Squads"; see chapter 2, note 29.

35. McClintock, *American Connection*, I, 23, 44, 319, 35; II, 74, 64.

36. McClintock, *American Connection*, I, 17, 33.

37. Taylor address to Inter-American Police Academy, Dec. 1965, cited in Jan Black, *United States Penetration of Brazil* (University of Pennsylvania, 1977), 143; Bernard Fall, *New Society*, April 22, 1965. Also Gabriel Kolko, *Anatomy of a War* (Pantheon, 1985), 89.

38. Nathan Twining, *Neither Liberty Nor Safety* (Holt, Rinehart & Winston, 1966), 244-5; emphasis in original.

39. Bonner, *Weakness and Deceit*, 34.

40. Brown, *With Friends Like These*, 117.

41. Letter to President Carter, Feb. 17, 1980; reprinted in Pearce, *Under the Eagle*, and *Revolution in Central America* (Boulder: Westview, 1983), edited by Stanford Central America Action Network.

42. Quoted in *Report on Human Rights in El Salvador*, 183, from State Department congressional testimony.

43. UPI, *BG*, March 24, 1983; an 80-word item, but at least it was there.

44. *Report on Human Rights*, 55-6, 102-5; Herman and Brodhead, *Demonstration Elections*, xf.

45. Robert Parry, AP, *BG*, March 22, 1985; Joel Brinkley, *NYT*, March 22, 1985; James LeMoyne, *NYT*, March 24, 1985.

46. Anne Marie O'Conner, *CSM*, Jan. 29, 1985; also James LeMoyne, *NYT*, Jan. 20, 1985. LeMoyne, *NYT*, Sept. 29, 1985.

47. McClintock, *American Connection*, I, 343.

48. Stephen Kinzer, *NYT*, March 3, 1984; Daniel Southerland, *CSM*, Oct. 12, 1984. Santivanez's testimony was impugned on the grounds that he had been given aid by critics of US government policy, an argument that would eliminate much of the testimony about atrocities of official enemies over the years. Note that Santivanez's testimony is considerably more credible than that of most defectors, since what he reports is hardly welcome news among those who hold power in the country to which he defected; in contrast, defectors who tell the story preferred by the state that

presents them to the public are naturally suspect.

49. Laurence Simon and James Stephens, *El Salvador Land Reform, 1980-81*, Impact Audit, Oxfam America (February 1981); Bonner, *Weakness and Deceit*, 199f.

50. *Report on Human Rights*, 57, 168-9.

51. *TNCW*, 387, where such exceptions as I could find are also noted.

52. COHA's *Washington Report on the Hemisphere*, Nov. 29, 1983; Chris Hedges, *CSM*, Sept. 10, 1984. The Salvadoran Army had also attacked the University in 1960, beating the rector, jailing students and employees, ransacking and destroying, and killing one person; Russell, *El Salvador*, 43. The improved performance of 1980 reflects 20 years of US training and the more direct US role, by 1980.

53. *TNCW*, 391.

54. *Report on Human Rights*, 60, 124, 126-127; Bonner, *Weakness and Deceit*, 206-7, 212.

55. Bonner, *Weakness and Deceit*, 207; *Miami Herald*, Dec. 23, 1980.

56. Russell, *El Salvador*, 135, 138.

57. Jeffrey Race, *War Comes to Long An* (U. of California, 1971); Douglas Pike, *Viet Cong* (MIT, 1966), 91-2, 101; George Kahin, *Pacific Affairs*, Winter, 1979-80. On the record of captured documents and the way they are falsified by government propagandists, called "scholars," see *TNCW*, chapter 5 (discussing Guenter Lewy) and my essay in Chomsky and Zinn, *Critical Essays*. For further discussion, see my "Rule of Force in International Affairs."

58. See *TNCW, Fateful Triangle,* for documentation of the facts and the media suppression of them.

59. McClintock, *American Connection*, I, 302; Dan Williams, *LAT*, July 21, 1985.

60. *Harper's*, March 1981.

61. Bonner, *Weakness and Deceit*, 203-4. AIFLD, associated with the AFL-CIO, is virtually an agency of the US government. On AIFLD and the US labor movement generally in Latin America see Black, *US Penetration*; Jonathan Kwitny, *Endless Enemies* (Congdon and Weed, 1984); Jonathan Feldman, "U.S. Foreign Policy Towards Latin American Labor: AIFLD, Central America & Beyond," ms. MIT, Sept. 1985, Report prepared by the Council on Hemispheric Affairs; Michael Sussman, *AIFLD: U.S. Trojan Horse* (EPICA, 1983).

62. *NYT*, Feb. 21, 1981; John Carlin, *London Times*, Sept. 28, 1984; Julia Preston, "Duarte's power thirst recalled," *BG*, May 8, 1984, report of an interview with Alberto Arene of the governing board of the Christian Democratic Party until 1980, now a spokesman for the rebel coalition in Washington.

63. McClintock, *American Connection*, 274, 277, 293; *NYT*, Feb. 22, 1981.

64. Bonner, *Weakness and Deceit*, 59, 61.

65. Chris Hedges, *Dallas Morning News*, March 30, 1985. See Americas Watch reports, cited earlier.

66. COHA's *Washington Report on the Hemisphere*, Oct. 2, 1984, citing the text of a *Playboy* interview with Duarte, parts of which were omitted from the published version; *Draining the Sea...*, Americas Watch, March 1985; also Americas Watch reports of April, August 1984. On the Reagan administration efforts to undermine human rights organizations in El Salvador and the US (and elsewhere), see Brown, *With Friends Like These*, and repeatedly in America's Watch reports.

67. Shirley Christian, *NYT*, June 3, 16, 1985.

68. Chris Norton, *CSM*, July 1, 1985.

69. "Retreat of the great reformer," *South*, March 1985; Francisco Acosta, COHA's *Washington Report on the Hemisphere*, Aug. 27, 1985; Shirley Christian, *NYT*, June 16, 1985; on AIFLD, see references of note 61.

70. John Heberle, letter, *BG*, Sept. 9, 1985.

71. *Report on Human Rights*, 169; McClintock, *American Connection*, I, 311; *Draining the Sea...*, 17; James LeMoyne, *NYT*, Sept. 13, 1984; Julia Preston, *BG*, Sept. 10, 1984.

72. Bonner, *Weakness and Deceit*, 325-6.

73. Chris Norton, *CSM*, Jan. 25, May 29, Feb. 28, 1985; *Economist*, "The president's education," July 27, 1985.

74. James LeMoyne, *NYT*, Feb. 25, 1985; John McAward, *BG*, July 9, 1984.

75. Marvin Frankel, *Newsday*, April 11, 1985; Clifford Krauss, *WSJ*, Sept. 16, 1985.

76. Steven Roberts, *NYT*, June 14, 1985.

77. Tad Szulc, *NYT Magazine*, May 25, 1980; Philip Bennett, *BG*, Sept. 25, 1980.

78. James LeMoyne, *NYT*, Feb. 10, 1985; July 10, 1985.

79. Marc Cooper, *L.A. Weekly*, July 26, 1985.

80. Editorial, *CSM*, May 16, 1985.

81. John Carlin, *London Times*, Sept. 28, 1984.

82. Sunday homily of Bishop Rivera y Damas, Jan. 3, 1982, cited by Cynthia Arnson, *El Salvador: a Revolution Confronts the United States* (Institute for Policy Studies, 1982), 84-5; Brown, *With Friends Like These*, 233, citing Kirkpatrick speech of Dec. 1, 1981; *New Republic*, Dec. 23, 1981, May 2, 1981.

83. Lord Chitnis, "Observing El Salvador: the 1984 elections," *Third World Quarterly*, October 1984; for detailed comparison of elections in Poland and El Salvador, and much relevant discussion, see Herman and Brodhead, *Demonstration Elections*.

84. Jonathan Steele, *London Review of Books*, April 4, 1985; Timothy Garton Ash, *Spectator* (London), March 31, 1984.

85. Ash, *New York Review*, Nov. 22, 1984.

86. *Washington Post* correspondent Christopher Dickey, in Robert Leiken, ed., *Central America: Anatomy of Conflict* (Pergamon, 1984).

87. *TNCW*, 39-42, 393-4; Bonner, *Weakness and Deceit*, 255f.; also I.M. Destler in Leiken, *Central America*. On the White Paper, see James Petras, *Nation,* March 28, 1981; Jonathan Kwitny, *WSJ*, June 8, 1981; Robert Kaiser, *WP*, June 9, 1981.

88. *Newsday*, April 19, 1984; *Washington Post*, Feb. 21, 1983; Bonner, *Weakness and Deceit*, 263f., 232.

89. *Background Paper: Nicaragua's Military Build-Up and Support for Central American Subversion*, Dept. of State and DOD, July 18, 1984; *NYT*, June 30, 1984.

90. *NYT*, March 17, 1985.

91. E.g., Moore, "Legal Issues," who relies on it as his primary source.

92. *NYT*, May 19, 1985.

93. Joel Brinkley, *NYT*, Aug. 10, 1985.

94. PEHR, I; Herman, *Real Terror Network*; *TNCW*, 47-55.

95. Arthur Schlesinger, *A Thousand Days* (Houghton Mifflin, 1965; Fawcett reprinting, 1967), 713-4; Joseph Smith, *Portrait of a Cold Warrior* (Putnam, 1976), 382. Thomas McCann, *An American Company* (Crown, 1976), 168-9; he withdrew the suggestion because of fears that El Salvador might retaliate against his company and when he discovered that El Salvador was getting its PR advice from a former high-ranking official of the US Defense Department, with whom he did not want to get into "a game of chess" with unforeseeable consequences.

96. Cf. William LeoGrande, *World Policy Journal*, Winter, 1984; the desperation of defenders of the government's case is revealed by Moore's reference ("Legal Issues") to the "superb job" of the vacuous document in demonstrating Cuban-Nicaraguan instigation of violence and terrorism.

97. *"Revolution Beyond Our Borders,"* US Dept. of State, Sept. 1985; Alfonso Chardy, Knight-Ridder Service, *BG*, Sept. 14, 1985; Shirley Christian, *NYT*, Sept. 14, 1985; Richard Bernstein, *NYT*, Sept. 17, 1985. On the title of the document, see note 3.

98. AP, *BG*, Oct. 21, 1985.

99. Joel Brinkley, *NYT*, March 30 1985; Brian Jenkins, *New Modes of Conflict* (Rand, June 1983), prepared for the Defense Nuclear Agency; on the military forces in the region, see Council on Hemispheric Affairs, *News and Analysis*, Feb. 28, 1985.

100. E.g., Moore, "Tripping through Wonderland."

101. Lydia Chavez, "U.S. Steps up Use of Spying Planes in Salvador War," *NYT*, March 30, 1984; Chris Hedges, *CSM*, April 6, 27, 1984; *BG*, Oct. 1, 1984; *NYT*, Sept. 30, Oct. 9, 1984. See also Russell, *El Salvador*, 137.

102. Chris Hedges, *National Catholic Reporter*, April 17, 1984; Robert McCartney, *WP*, April 12, 1984.

103. McCartney, *WP*, April 12, 1984.

104. COHA's *Washington Report on the Hemisphere*, Oct. 30, 1984.

105. Hedges, *CSM*, April 27, 1984; Herman and Brodhead, *Demonstration Elections*, xi; *New Statesman*, Dec. 7, 1984.

106. Chris Hedges, *CSM*, March 26, 1984; Americas Watch and Lawyers Committee for International Human Rights, *El Salvador's Other Victims: The War on the Displaced*, April 1984, 46f., *Free Fire*, August 1984, 39f.

107. Editorial, *CSM*, May 16, 1985.

108. *New Republic*, June 10, 1985; *NR* editor Leon Wieseltier, *NYT*, June 7, 1985.

109. Editorial, *BG,* May 22, 1985.

110. Editorial, *NYT*, April 18, 1983; editorial, *WP* (*MG Weekly*, March 10, 1985); *New Republic*, Aug. 15, 1983, March 25, 1985.

111. Ash, *New York Review*, Nov. 22, 1984; Andy Thomas, *Effects of Chemical Warfare* (SIPRI, Taylor & Francis, 1985), 33f., a review of material from British state archives.

112. Allman, *Harper's,* March 1981, *Unmanifest Destiny,* (Doubleday, 1984), 77-8.

113. "Instances of the Use of United States Armed Forces abroad, 1798-1945," submitted by the State Department to demonstrate precedent for US intervention without congressional authorization, with 200 entries (Hearings, "Situation in Cuba," Committee on Foreign Relations and Committee on Armed Services, US Senate, 87th Congress, Second Session, Sept. 17, 1962, 82-7); Langley, *Banana Wars*, 54; Stephen Kinzer, *NYT*, April 21, 1984.

114. Booth, *End and Beginning*; Millett, *Guardians of the Dynasty*; William LeoGrande, *Foreign Affairs*, Fall 1979; *PEHR*, I; *TNCW*, 16, 291.

115. Susanne Jonas, in *Revolution in Central America*; LaFeber, *Inevitable Revolutions*, 241. Excluded from the debt repayment was $5.1 million owed to Argentina and Israel for arms sales to Somoza; Goldfield, *Garrison State*, 37.

116. Juan Tamayo, Knight-Ridder Service, *BG*, Oct. 3, 1983; Philip Taubman, *NYT*, May 3, 1984; White, *Morass*, 67.

117. *Miami Herald*, Dec. 16, 1984, cited by Alexander Cockburn, *Nation*, Feb. 9, 1985 but apparently otherwise ignored.

118. *Miami Herald*, Dec. 19, 1982; *LAT*, March 3, 4 1985. For a record of CIA and *contra* attacks, see *WSJ*, March 5, 6 1985.

119. Alfred Gellhorn, *St. Louis Post-Dispatch*, June 27, 1985.

120. *Oxfam America Special Report: Central America*, Fall 1985.

121. Editorial, *NYT*, Oct. 18, 1985.

122. *NYT*, Aug. 8, 12; *WP*, Aug. 14, 1985; Edgar Chamorro, *NYT*, June 24, 1985, *New Republic*, Aug. 5, 1985; Anthony Lewis, *NYT*, Oct. 3, 1985.

123. Fred Kaplan, *BG*, June 12, 1985. After his exposures, Chamorro was threatened with expulsion from the US. The threat was withdrawn after media exposure and protest.

124. Dennis Volman, "Skepticism about Eden Pastora's 'crash' reflects his diminishing prestige," *CSM*, July 26, 1985; James LeMoyne, *NYT*, Sept. 4, 1985.

125. See David Rogers and David Ignatius, *WSJ*, March 6, 1985, for a detailed description of the CIA mining operation, based in part on a classified CIA document outlining it, in part on other governmental sources. Senior Administration officials had long conceded the facts; see, e.g., *WP*, April 10, 1984. The World Court unanimously ordered the US to "immediately cease and refrain" from such acts as "the laying of mines" (*NYT*, May 11, 1984).

126. *J. of Contemporary Studies*, Spring/Summer, 1985.

127. AP, *BG*, Aug. 23, 1985; editorial, *BG*, Sept. 21, 1985; Bob Woodward, *WP*, May 19, 1984.

128. John Gerassi, Paper presented at the annual meeting of the International Studies Association, Washington DC, March 5-9, 1985.

129. Yehuda Tsur, *Al Hamishmar*, Aug. 9, 1985.

130. McClintock, *American Connection*, I, 305.

131. McClintock, *American Connection*, II, 224; Flora Montealegre and Cynthia Arnson, in *Revolution in Central America*, 299.

132. Christopher Dickey, *WP*, April 3, 1983.

133. *NYT*, March 24, 1985; Dec. 14, 1982.

134. James LeMoyne, *NYT*, March 18, 1985; Nancy Nusser, *CSM*, April 5, 1985, quoting FDN leader Adolfo Calero.

135. *Latin America Weekly Regional Reports*, Jan. 13, 1984; Mary King, associate director of Action under the Carter Administration and a senior research fellow at COHA, *San Jose Mercury News*, Aug. 25, 1985; Duncan Campbell, *New Statesman*, Aug. 9, 1985.

136. *NYT*, June 5, 1985; *BG*, Sept. 17, 1985.

137. *BG*, Nov. 9, 1984, also citing similar comments by Connecticut Democrat Christopher Dodd.

138. *The Electoral Process in Nicaragua*, official publication of LASA, Nov. 19, 1984; see chapter 1, note 15.

139. Julia Preston, *BG*, July 29, 1985, one of the rare reports in the US press that expressed skepticism about the US government position.

140. This is a statement "smacking of supercilious quasi-racism" according to Moore ("Tripping through Wonderland"). The LASA report, he writes, "may say more about *its* sorry state of politicization of scholarship than about the reality in Nicaragua." That the election was fraudulent, contrary to the conclusions of the LASA study on the scene, is proven, for this respected legal scholar, by the fact that it was condemned by a *New York Times* editorial, a criticism by a former Venezualan Foreign Minister, a claim of harassment by Cruz (which the LASA report investigated in detail and concluded was vastly exaggerated), and a few alleged comments by Sandinista officials which do not bear on the conduct of the elections—again, a useful insight into the "conservative" mentality.

141. For confirming evidence, see *NYT*, Oct. 21, 1984.

142. *WSJ*, April 23, 1985.

143. *NYT*, Aug. 25, 1985.

144. *Nation*, April 27, 1985.

145. Lois Whitman, letter, *NYT*, Nov. 16, 1984; Jonathan Steele and Tony Jenkins, *MG Weekly*, Nov. 1984.

146. Tony Jenkins, *MG Weekly*, May 5, 1985, quoting Dr. Luis Rivas, president of the Social Democratic Party.

147. Edward Herman, *Covert Action Information Bulletin*, Spring 1984.

148. *NYT*, Aug. 18, 1985. Alexander Cockburn observes that this was apparently too much for some *Times* editor, who changed the wording in a later edition from "democratization" to "internal changes"; *Nation*, Aug. 31.

149. See *TNCW*, 70f., for references and context.

150. George Black, review of Shirley Christian, *Nicaragua* (Random House, 1985), *Nation*, Sept. 7, 1985.

151. Christian, *NYT*, Aug. 18, 1985; AP, *BG*, April 13, 1985.

152. Carla Robbins, *Business Week*, Aug. 19, 1985; Susan Kaufman Purcell, *NYT*, July 20, March 12, 1985.

153. Purcell did not respond to a request for some examples illustrating her concern, or that of the program she heads, for democracy elsewhere in Central America.

154. Robert McCartney, *WP*, Sept. 30, 1984.

155. Philip Taubman, *NYT*, Sept. 24, 1984; Alma Guillermo-prieto, *WP weekly*, Nov. 26, 1984.

156. Jim Morrell, "Contadora: the Treaty on Balance," *International Reports*, Center for International Policy, June 1985; Tom Farer, "Contadora: The Hidden Agenda," *Foreign Policy*, Summer 1985. On earlier US efforts to prevent a peaceful settlement, see Gutman, "America's Diplomatic Charade."

157. *NYT*, May 2, 1985.

158. Editorial, *London Times*, June 14, 1985.

159. Editorial, *Toronto Globe and Mail*, Nov. 12, 1984. The

editors hold that Nicaragua's relation to the US should be recognized as similar to Poland's relation to the USSR; one wonders whether they really understand exactly what they are implying. One might also note that the US has not recently been invaded through Nicaragua and virtually destroyed by a great power that is now part of a military alliance dominated by the USSR.

160. Quoted by John Saul, *Monthly Review* (March 1985). Citing the same remark, John Hanlon comments that the plan is the same for Mozambique; *New Statesman*, Oct. 19, 1984.

161. Davis, *Slavery*, 65; for the population estimate, Davis cites Sherburne Cook and Woodrow Borah, *Essays in Population History: Mexico and the Carribean*, I (U. of California Press, 1971).

162. Langley, *Banana Republics*, 119, 129, 173; Reagan cited in Barry, *Other Side of Paradise*, 339.

163. Bruce Calder, *Impact of Intervention*. The following quotes and comments on the 1916-24 intervention are from this study unless otherwise indicated; pp. 16, xiv, 100, 239-40, 39-40, 240, 123f., 161, 196, 140-1, 239, 158, 186, 249.

164. Piero Gleijeses, *The Dominican Crisis* (Johns Hopkins, 1978; expanded from the 1965 French original), 18-9, 336.

165. Gleijeses, *Dominican Crisis*, 19.

166. Langley, *Banana Wars*, 156; Abraham Lowenthal, *The Dominican Intervention* (Harvard, 1972), 24; Gleijeses, *Dominican Crisis*, 22, 27, 341.

167. Hans Morgenthau, *The Purpose of American Politics* (Vintage, 1964). Shortly after, Morgenthau, to his credit, was to abandon this conventional stance and become one of the few principled critics of the Indochina war among US scholars.

168. Pearce, *Under the Eagle*, 62.

169. For an assessment of the US involvement in the assassination attempts, see Gleijeses, *Dominican Crisis*, Appendix I.

170. Cole Blasier, *The Hovering Giant* (U. of Pittsburgh, 1976), 251f.; also Lowenthal, *Dominican Intervention*, 27f., 44f.

171. Gleijeses, *Dominican Crisis*, 88f., 97; Blasier, *Hovering Giant*, 303.

172. Gleijeses, *Dominican Crisis*, 116f.

173. Murray Marder, *WP*, Oct. 30, 1983.

174. Herman and Brodhead, *Demonstration Elections*; *PEHR*, I; Penny Lernoux, *Cry of the People* (Doubleday, 1980); Lisa Wheaton, in Sklar, *Trilateralism*.

175. Leslie Gelb, *NYT magazine*, Nov. 13, 1983; John Silber, *New Republic*, Feb. 18, 1985; Peter Kihss, *NYT*, July 5, 1982.

176. Barry, *The Other Side of Paradise*, 304; *Latinamerica press*, April 11, 1985.

177. Samuel Huntington, "American Ideals versus American Institutions," *Political Science Quarterly*, Spring 1982; correspondence, Winter 1982-3.

178. Blasier, *Hovering Giant*, 57f.

179. LaFeber, *Inevitable Revolutions*, 112f; Schoultz, in Diskin, *Trouble in Our Backyard*; Smith quoted in Blanche Wiesen Cook, *The Declassified Eisenhower* (Doubleday, 1981), 253. On the CIA coup, see Cook; Stephen Kinzer and Stephen Schlesinger, *Bitter Fruit* (Doubleday, 1981); Immerman, *CIA in Guatemala*.

180. Moore, "Tripping through Wonderland." The same intriguing conception of our "obligation" to attack Nicaragua under international law is advanced by Senator Daniel Patrick Moynihan in a speech applauding the increase of the budget for intelligence (meaning, e.g., war against Nicaragua) to the highest level "by any country at any point in history." The *Times* heading for this disgraceful performance is "Required Reading," Oct. 15, 1984.

181. Lieuwen, *Generals vs. Presidents*, 39.

182. For details, see McClintock, *American Connection*, II, 51f.

183. LaFeber, *Inevitable Revolutions*, 165; Hugh O'Shaughnessy, *New Statesman*, Dec. 1, 1967 and Marcel Niedergang, *Le Monde*, Jan. 19, 1968; AP, *NYT*, Nov. 27, 1983; Schoultz, in Diskin *Trouble*; Douglas Foster, *Mother Jones*, Nov./Dec. 1985. Like Calder and Blasier, Schoultz attributes to US planners "the best of all intentions." See also Julia Preston, *BG*, Nov. 2, 3, 1985.

184. James LeMoyne, *NYT*, Aug. 24, 1985.

185. McClintock, *American Connection*, II, 216-7, citing an unpublished manuscript by Gleijeses, Johns Hopkins University (SAIS), 1982.

186. See Juan José Arévalo, *The Shark and the Sardines* (Lyle Stuart, 1981); Juan Bosch, *Pentagonism* (Grove, 1968).

187. Lars Schoultz, *Comparative Politics*, Jan. 1981.

188. Michael Klare and Cynthia Arnson, *Supplying Repression* (Institute for Policy Studies, 1981); emphasis in original.

189. *PEHR*, I, 43f.

190. Herman, *Real Terror Network*, 84.

191. On the remarkable force of the taboo, see *TNCW*, 103f.

192. Black, *United States Penetration of Brazil*, 55, 235f.; Sylvia Ann Hewlett, *The Cruel Dilemmas of Development* (Basic Books, 1980), 170.

193. Kenneth Freed, "Desperation: Selling Your Eye, Kidney," *LAT*, Sept. 10, 1981.

194. Connell-Smith, *Inter-American System*, 164, 167; Cook, *Declassified Eisenhower*, 218.

195. Booth, *End and Beginning*, 86; James Petras and Morris Morley, in Miliband, *The Uses of Anti-Communism*; "Guatemala," 1980 Report of the London Anti-Slavery Society to the UN Working Group of Experts on Slavery; Roger Plant, *Guatemala: Unnatural Disaster* (Latin America Bureau, 1978), 86. For details and general background, see Jim Handy, *Gift of the Devil* (South End, 1984).

196. Hedrick Smith, reporting the opinion of US policy makers, *NYT*, Dec. 8, 1967; *Congressional Record*, April 13, 1967, S5054-7, memorandum introduced by George Kahin. On the elections, see

Herman and Brodhead, *Demonstration Elections*.

197. Samuel Huntington, "American ideals."

198. President Reagan, interview, *NYT*, Feb. 12, 1985; Reagan described our "good relationship" with Marcos adding that "we realize there is an opposition party that we believe is also [sic] pledged to democracy". Bush in *State Department Bulletin* 81, August 1981, 30.

199. Alexis de Tocqueville, *Democracy in America*, I, quoted by Takaki, *Iron Cages*, 80-1.

200. Miller, *"Benevolent Assimilation"*, 78, 74, citing the *New York Criterion* and *Salt Lake City Tribune*; 123, 220f., 247; Sixto Lopez, *The Outlook*, April 13, 1901.

201. Francis Jennings, *The Invasion of America* (U. of North Carolina, 1975), especially chapter 13; 46, 110, 83, 173n, 12. Editorial, *NYT*, Aug. 6, 1954; see *TNCW*, 99, for further discussion. A notable contemporary parallel is the takeover of Palestine on Scriptural authority, "dunam after dunam," with comparable disdain for the rights of the native population (if they even existed, a fact that many deny, just as myths of sparse and nomadic Indian population persisted, on ideological grounds, until recent years; Jennings, 16f.).

202. Editorials, June 20, June 29, 1954; Arthur Krock, *NYT*, June 29, 1954.

203. McCann, *American Company*, 171, 46, 59-60, 47.

204. Bernard Fall, *New Republic*, Oct. 9, 1965; James Reston, *NYT*, Feb. 26, 1965.

205. Bernard Fall, *Last Reflections on a War* (Doubleday, 1967), 33, 47; James Reston, *NYT*, Nov. 24, 1967; John King Fairbank, *American Historical Review*, Feb. 1969.

206. William V. Shannon, *NYT*, Sept. 28, 1974; *BG*, May 8, 1985.

207. Ken Anderson, *BG*, Oct. 1, 1984.

208. Editorial, *New Republic*, April 2, 1984.

209. Bonner, *Weakness and Deceit*, 160.

210. See *PEHR, II*, 3, for the curious history of this and other inventions of Western propaganda at the time.

211. Alexander Cockburn wrote in the *Wall St. Journal* that "This is language we have not heard since the Nazi era," eliciting a response from editor Hendrik Hertzberg, who claimed that the journal was "characterizing the *Administration's* view, which we were at pains to distinguish from our own." He quoted the passage above which definitively proves that his plea is an utter falsehood, as the further context makes still clearer. *WSJ*, May 17, 29, 1984.

212. Julia Preston, *BG*, Nov. 15, 1984.

213. Higginbotham, *In the Matter of Color*, 377, 383.

214. Benjamin Taylor, *BG*, Dec. 8, 1984.

215. Press Conference, Feb. 21, 1985; *NYT*, Feb. 22.

Chapter 4

1. Joel Brinkley, *NYT*, March 27, 1985.

2. David Woods, *LAT*, March 17, 1982. Lehman said he envisioned a conventional rather than a nuclear global war with the USSR—conceivable, but hardly likely.

3. See my *Fateful Triangle*, chapter 7, for a review until mid-1983; there have been other cases since and the hazards remain significant. On 1967, see Donald Neff, *Warriors for Jerusalem* (Simon & Schuster, 1984).

4. For discussion, see my articles in Michael Albert and David Dellinger, eds., *Beyond Survival* (South End, 1983; excerpted in the *Michigan Quarterly Review*, Fall 1982), and *Studies in Political Economy*, Summer 1985, from which some of these remarks are taken; also Joseph Gerson, ed., *The Deadly Connection* (AFSC, Cambridge, 1983; expanded edition, New Society, 1986); and numerous other articles, particularly by Michael Klare.

5. Graham Allison, *Essence of Decision* (Little, Brown and Co., 1971), 1, 39; cited by Ron Hirschbein in his discussion of "atomic cultism" in his *Nuclear Theologians*, ms.

6. On these matters, see *TNCW*, *Fateful Triangle*. The topics are rarely discussed in a rational way in the US—except by the Israeli lobby, which understands the matter well enough—because of Israel's holy status among American intellectuals, comparable to that of the USSR in the Communist Party, a fact regularly deplored by Israeli doves who recognize that this blind loyalty is driving their country to disaster; see the same sources for documentation and discussion; also Paul Findley, *They Dare to Speak Out* (Lawrence Hill, 1985).

7. William Arkin, *Bulletin of the Atomic Scientists (BAS)*, Oct. 1985; Fred Kaplan, *BG*, Sept. 15, 1985.

8. *The Defense Monitor*, no. 6, 1984; on the methods of calculation that inflate Soviet expenditures, see *TNCW*, 193, and sources cited, particularly the work of Franklyn Holtzman.

9. Interview, *NYT*, Feb. 12, 1985. The President's speech writers are technically correct in their deceitful claim concerning the reduction in warheads since 1967, resulting from the retirement of redundant and obsolete weapons including gravity bombs (the latter, after two serious nuclear weapons accidents involving nuclear-armed bombers) in favor of more accurate, capable and versatile weapons; for details, see Thomas Cochran, William Arkin, and Milton Hoenig, *Nuclear Weapons Databook* (Ballinger, 1984), I, chapter 1.

10. See David Johnson, director of research of the Center for Defense Information, *Inquiry*, June 1983, reviewing the Pentagon publication *Soviet Military Power*, 1983; also Andrew Cockburn, "Threat Inflation," in the same issue. On the misrepresentations and outright falsehoods in the 1984 volume, see Fred Kaplan, *BG*, April 15, 1984.

11. For an excellent discussion of this topic, see William Schwartz, et al., *The Nuclear Seduction: Why the Arms Race Doesn't Matter*, Boston Nuclear Study Group, August 1985.

12. William Bischoff, *Harvard Graduate Society Newsletter*, Winter-Spring 1985; the sample was civilian and military "security policy makers" involved in a Kennedy School program. A poll of a group of Harvard alumni attending a session on nuclear war showed that 63% regarded the likelihood of nuclear war as between "almost certain" and greater than one in a hundred—far too high to face with equanimity; 37% of the experts shared this judgment.

13. Joseph Gerson, *Nuclear Times*, February 1984.

14. See *Fateful Triangle* on the evasions of the peace movement, on Lebanese opinion, and on the scandalous failure of the media to consider it.

15. *Nuclear Arms Control*, Committee on International Security and Arms Control, National Academy of Sciences (National Academy Press, 1985), 84, 78, 87; for the text, see UN Press Release GA/6935, 13 Jan. 1984, *Resolutions and Decisions Adopted by the General Assembly*, 124-5. The Resolution, 38/76, called for a freeze "under appropriate verification" of all nuclear weapons and delivery systems, including testing and production.

16. Eric Pace, *NYT*, Dec. 10, 1982; Bernard Nossiter, *NYT*, Dec. 14, 1982; Tom Wicker, *NYT*, Oct. 7, 1985; Bethe quoted by Arthur Schlesinger, *WSJ*, Oct. 7, 1985; Barnaby, by Diana Johnstone, *In These Times*, Sept. 18, 1985.

17. William Broad, "Pershings Stir Accidental-War Fears," *NYT*, Dec. 12, 1983; Edward Dolnick, "Can computers cope with war?," *BG*, Dec. 10, 1984.

18. *Defense Monitor*, 5, 1983.

19. Walter Pincus and Don Oberdorfer, *WP Weekly*, Dec. 17, 1984.

20. Strategic weapons are defined differently by the USSR and the US. Soviet proposals refer to weapons that can strike the other superpower; US calculations omit US forward-based systems and US missiles in Europe that are aimed at Soviet targets, and the arsenals of US allies, with considerable further vagueness. We would reject the latter stance as absurd if the situation were reversed.

21. Bernard Weinraub, *NYT*, Sept. 29, 1985; "Week in Review," same day; Paul Lewis, *NYT*, Sept. 22, 1985; UPI, *BG*, Sept. 29.

22. Jeffrey Duncan, *BAS*, Oct. 1985. The facts were partially conceded in a misleading comment by Leslie Gelb, *NYT*, Oct. 4, 1985.

23. Herbert Lin, letter, *NYT*, Oct. 3, 1985.

24. *Defense Monitor*, 8, 1985. The rather significant Administration concession is briefly noted without comment by Leslie Gelb, *NYT*, Oct. 4, 1985, in the final paragraph of a 52-paragraph article on the US summit stance.

25. Edward Dolnick, "Can computers cope with war?" Dec. 10, 1984.

26. Daniel Arbess and William Epstein, *BAS*, May 1985.

27. Diana Johnstone, *In These Times*, Sept. 18, 1985.

28. John Vinocur, "Gromyko Denounces U.S. at Conference," *NYT*, Jan. 19, 1984; *NYT*, Feb. 18, 1983; Claudia Wright, *New Statesman*, Sept. 20, 1985; Diana Johnstone, *In These Times*, Sept. 18, 1985.

29. Steven Erlanger, *BG*, Oct. 1, 1985.

30. William Beecher, *BG*, Oct. 11, 1985; Anthony Lewis, *NYT*, Oct. 14, 1985.

31. *NYT*, Sept. 30, 1985; Fred Kaplan, *BG*, Oct. 28, 1984.

32. George Wilson, *BG-WP*, August 27, 1985; Jeffrey Smith, *Science*, Oct. 14, 1983; Howard Ris, letter, *WSJ*, Sept. 25, 1985.

33. Philip Boffey, *NYT*, March 8, March 7, 1985; Robert Bowman, *CSM*, Jan. 10, 1985 (his emphasis); Gerald Smith, *Business Week*, Aug. 19, 1985.

34. Hella Pick, *MG Weekly*, May 12, 1985; Charles Mohr, *NYT*, Sept. 25, 1985; Jeffrey Smith, *Science*, Oct. 4, 1985; Walter Pincus, *WP Weekly*, Oct. 14, 1985.

35. Peter Clausen, *World Policy Journal*, Spring 1985; George Ball, *New York Review*, April 11, 1985.

36. Ball, *New York Review*, April 11, 1985; Wayland Kennet, *BAS*, Sept. 1985.

37. He is in error about this; since 1970, rhetoric aside, the US has supported the Israeli occupation and blocked attempts at a peaceful political settlement, thus maintaining the tensions that are most likely to lead to nuclear war; see *Fateful Triangle*, until mid-1983, and for the period since, my paper in Chomsky, Jonathan Steele and John Gittings, *Superpowers in Collision* (Penguin, London, 1984), and my "United States and the Middle East," *ENDPapers* (Nottingham), Summer 1985.

38. Assistant Defense Secretary Richard Perle, speaking in Bonn, *BG*, July 31, 1985; *Ha'aretz*, Aug. 16, 1985.

39. The assessment is inaccurate in that it omits France, where the Paris intellectuals, in the latest phase of their recurrent frenzies, often outdo Reagan in hysterical warnings of the Soviet takeover of the world, notably those who a few years earlier were passionate Maoists and Stalinists, virtually alone on the world scene.

40. *Foreign Affairs, America and the World 1983* (Winter 1983).

41. George Lardner, *WP Weekly*, Sept. 9, 1985.

42. Randall Forsberg, President and Executive Director, Institute for Defense & Disarmament Studies, 2001 Beacon St, Brookline MA 02146, March 1985.

43. Henry Kissinger, *American Foreign Policy* (Norton, 1969), 28; for more on this topic, see *TNCW*, chapters 1, 2, 6.

44. See George Ball, *New York Review*, Nov. 8, 1984, April 11,

1984, for a number of such quotes; Ze'ev Blitzer, *Al Hamishmar* (Israel), Oct. 27, 1983, reporting Reagan's comments to Tom Dine, head of the Israeli lobbying group AIPAC, while thanking him for "the behind-the scenes efforts of the pro-Israeli lobby to mobilize support in Congress for the continued American presence in Lebanon."

45. "From Cold War to Cold Peace?," *Business Week*, Feb. 12, 1949; *Economist*, April 13, 1985.

46. LaFeber, *America, Russia, and the Cold War*; for an important contemporary discussion, see James Warburg, *Germany—Key to Peace* (Harvard, 1953). The incident has largely disappeared from history.

47. Leffler, "The American Conception of National Security"; see also the discussion of his paper in the same issue by John Lewis Gaddis and Bruce Kuniholm, raising no serious question concerning his thesis, and Leffler's response. See also Kolko and Kolko, *Limits of Power*, for extensive background.

48. Michael Evangelista, "Stalin's Postwar Army Reappraised," *International Security*, Winter 1982/3.

49. Stephen Cohen, *New Statesman*, Feb. 8, 1985; Amos Perlmutter, op-ed, *NYT*, April 30, 1985.

50. Gaddis, *Strategies of Containment*, 356-7; his emphasis.

51. Henry Kissinger, *The White House Years* (Little, Brown, 1979), 57, 65; for discussion of this much praised and utterly fatuous document, see *TNCW*, chapter 6.

52. Gaddis, *Strategies*, viiin, his emphasis.

53. Basil Davidson, *Scenes from the Anti-Nazi War* (Monthly Review press, 1980), 93, 152; Smuts cited on p. 17; Davidson was a participant-observer in British intelligence in southern Europe.

54. Stephen Ambrose, *Rise to Globalism* (Penguin, 1971), 58.

55. Davidson, 233f. See Kolko, *Politics of War*, for discussion of Italy and the general pattern in Europe and Asia. For a brief review of CIA activities in Europe, see Halperin, *Lawless State*, 36f.

56. Wittner, *American Intervention in Greece*; Johnson cited on p. 303. Christopher Hitchens, *Cyprus* (Quartet, 1984).

57. D. F. Fleming, *The Cold War and its Origins* (Doubleday, 1961), I, 501-3; citing *NYT*, Nov. 19, 1949.

58. Linklater, et al., *Fourth Reich*, 135. See this study as well as John Loftus, *The Belarus Secret* (Knopf, 1982), and a six-part series by Kai Hermann, "A Killer's Career," *Stern*, from May 10, 1984, based on interviews in Bolivia and US government documents. See also Alan Ryan, *Quiet Neighbors* (Harcourt, Brace, Jovanovich, 1984); documentation from US intelligence provided in the *Stern* series indicates that a good deal is covered up in the account by Ryan, who directed the US Justice Department investigation of Nazi war criminals. For more on the entire matter, see Peter Dale Scott, *Covert Action Information Bulletin* (Fall, 1985).

59. Loftus, *Belarus Secret*, 68ff., 77f.; Thomas Powers, *The Man Who Kept the Secrets* (Knopf, 1979); NSC 68; reprinted in Etzold and Gaddis, *Containment*.

60. See Hermann, "Killer's Career," for interviews with intelligence operatives and Bolivian officials on these matters.

61. Eugene Kolb, letter, *NYT*, July 26, 1983.

62. Linklater, *Fourth Reich*, 168f., 173-4.

63. *NYT*, May 7, 10, 1985. On the attitudes of Roosevelt, Churchill and others at the time, see my *American Power and the New Mandarins*, chapter 1.

64. Linklater, *Fourth Reich*, 198, 17f., 270, 279f., 288f. On the remarkable career of delle Chiaie, see Stuart Christie, *Stefano delle Chiaie: Portrait of a Black Terrorist* (Refract publications, London, 1984).

65. Jenkins, *New Modes of Conflict*, 6, 2.

66. Blasier, *Hovering Giant*, 63.

67. Cited by Morton Halperin, *Militarism and Freedom* (Riverside Church Disarmament Program, July 26, 1981), 3.

68. Bruce Cumings, *The Origins of the Korean War* (Princeton, 1981), xxi, 349; estimates for Cheju Island by John Merrill, in Cumings, ed., *Child of Conflict* (U. of Washington, 1983). See also Gavan McCormack, *Cold War Hot War* (Hale & Iremonger, Sydney, 1983); Jon Halliday, in Miliband, *Uses of Anti-Communism*.

69. Schulzinger, *Wise Men of Foreign Affairs*, 106.

70. See *American Power and the New Mandarins*, 337-8, for references and discussion; Jennings, *Invasion of America*, 19, 153.

71. Fred Kaplan, *Wizards of Armageddon* (Simon & Schuster, 1983), 289, 155f. (his emphasis); Bundy cited by Gaddis, *Strategies of Containment*, 206.

72. David Ottaway and Walter Pincus, *WP* (*MG Weekly*, March 17, 1985); Pincus, *WP* (*MG Weekly*, Jan. 23, 1983); Pincus and Don Oberdorfer, *WP Weekly*, Dec. 31, 1984.

73. Ottaway and Pincus, *WP* (*MG Weekly*, March 17, 1985); Fred Kaplan, *BG*, March 7, 1985.

74. Leslie Gelb, *NYT*, June 8, 1983.

75. Cochran et al., *Nuclear Weapons Databook*, I, 13; Robert Komer, "What 'Decade of Neglect'?," *International Security*, Fall 1985. On the Carter programs and the crisis exploitation, see *TNCW*, 189f.

76. Economists Walter Heller and James Tobin, cited by Richard Du Boff and Edward Herman, "The New Economics: Handmaiden of Inspired Truth," *Review of Radical Political Economics*, Aug. 1972.

77. Cited by Gaddis, *Strategies of Containment*, 204.

78. See the analysis of Soviet power by the Center for Defense Information (*Defense Monitor*, January 1980), concluding that it peaked in the late 1950s, declining since in capacity to coerce and

influence. The absolute power to destroy, of course, constantly increases, for both superpowers and others as well.

79. See Fred Bergsten, *Foreign Affairs* (July 1971), on Kennedy's concern for developing new markets for Japan.

80. Harold Brown, Report to Congress on the budget and defense programs, Jan. 29, 1980; NSC 141, cited by Kaplan, *Wizards of Armageddon*, 137-8.

81. Walter Pincus, *WP Weekly*, Oct. 7, 1985.

82. Alfred Chandler, Joseph Monsen, *Daedalus*, Winter, 1969; Wilson quoted in Richard Barnet, *The Economy of Death* (Atheneum, 1969), 116.

83. Gaddis, *Strategies of Containment*, 93-4, 204.

84. Felix Rohatyn, Interview, *World Policy Journal* (Fall 1984).

85. "From Cold War to Cold Peace?"

86. On the concerns over economic stagnation at that time, and the reasons for the recourse to military Keynesianism as a way out, see Kolko, *Main Currents*, 317-8.

87. Robert Reich, "High Tech, a Subsidiary of Pentagon Inc.," *NYT*, May 29, 1985.

88. *Business Week*, April 8, 1985.

89. "Pentagon Spending is the Economy's Biggest Gun," *Business Week*, Oct. 21, 1985.

90. *Economist*, Sept. 7, 1985; *Le Monde*, April 9, 1985 (*MG Weekly*, April 28, 1985).

91. Samuel Downer, quoted by Bernard Nossiter, *WP*, Dec. 8, 1968.

92. Stephen Daly, *NYT*, Sept. 9, 1983; on the differential response to such atrocities depending on who is the perpetrator, see my "Notes on Orwell's problem," in *Knowledge of Language* (Praeger, 1985).

93. Even this lunacy was solemnly reported by the media, which have yet to update the story with the information that the secret official US list of 14 "Libyan terrorists" was in fact a list of prominent members of the Lebanese Shiite party Amal, including its leader Nabih Berri and the religious leader of the Lebanese Shiite community, most of the rest being aging Lebanese politicians; to compound the absurdity, Amal is strongly anti-Libyan. The document was obtained by the *New Statesman* in London; Duncan Campbell and Patrick Forbes, *NS*, Aug. 16, 1985. They note that on Dec. 7, 1981, at the height of the furor, Reagan told the world press: "We have the evidence and he [Qaddafi] knows it." Libyan denials were "laughed off, and were of no avail in killing the story."

94. As noted, the shift, both in programs and rhetoric, began in the late Carter Administration.

95. Norman Podhoretz, *NYT*, Oct. 30, 1985.

96. LaFeber, *Inevitable Revolutions*, 108, 110.

97. Lars Schoultz, *Human Rights and United States Policy Towards Latin America* (Princeton, 1981), 219; the Senate had opposed an earlier proposal to this effect in 1958. Charles Maechling, "The Murderous Mind of the Latin Military," *LAT*, March 18, 1982.

98. Ruth Sivard, *World Military and Social Expenditures 1981* (World Priorities, 1981, 8); Paul Quinn-Judge, *Far Eastern Economic Review*, Oct. 11, 1984. One consequence, he notes, as a "major political gap for the new regime," since "the south was stripped of the trained, disciplined and presumably committed young cadres who would have formed the backbone of the present administration"—a propaganda victory much exploited in the West, since this contributed to a North Vietnamese takeover.

99. See p. 52-53, above.

100. Hans Morgenthau, *In Defense of the National Interest* (Knopf, 1951), 80-1.

101. It is an achievement not quite matched in the USSR, with regard to its invasion of Afghanistan; see my "Notes on Orwell's problem."

102. Alain Besançon, *New Republic*, Feb. 18, 1985; Besançon, until recently a hard-line Stalinist, has now undergone the stylish Paris conversion to fantasies about the "impotence" of the West before the Communist onslaught. "US official says N-war foes suffer 'Protestant angst'," *BG-LAT*, Nov. 26, 1981. The official was Pentagon fanatic Richard Perle. This was before the Catholic Bishops had spoken out strongly on the issue, after a bout of "Catholic angst."

Chapter 5

1. Thomas Ferguson, "Party Realignment and American Industrial Structure," *Research in Political Economy,* 6.1-82, 1983.

2. Crozier et al., *Crisis of Democracy*; chapter 2, note 51, above.

3. Kolko, *Main Currents*, 25f. See this important study for background throughout.

4. Ferguson, "Party Realignment"; his emphasis.

5. Kolko, *Main Currents*, 30; Palmer in David Brion Davis, ed., *The Fear of Conspiracy* (Cornell, 1971).

6. Murray Levin, *Political Hysteria in America* (Basic Books, 1972).

7. On some of the means employed within the ideological system, see the essays, mostly written through the 70s, in *TNCW*;

also *PEHR* and Herman, *Real Terror Network*. Material sampled in earlier chapters provides additional illustrations.

8. Thomas Edsall, *The New Politics of Inequality* (Norton, 1984), 13, 55, 107f., 117f. Edsall is a political reporter for the *Washington Post*.

9. Heritage Foundation, *Mandate for Leadership*, 1980, cited by John Saloma, *Ominous Politics* (Hill & Wang, 1984), 16. Saloma was the first president of the liberal Republican Ripon society. Some indication of the intellectual level of latter-day "conservatism" is given by the material cited earlier from the *Journal of Contemporary Studies*, which considers itself "scholarly," published by the right-wing Institute for Contemporary Studies, founded by Edwin Meese and others in 1972; Saloma, 12.

10. Bertram Gross, *Friendly Fascism* (South End, 1983).

11. Edsall, 142, 177, 152; chapter 4, generally.

12. Thomas Ferguson and Joel Rogers, "Labor Day, 1985," *Nation*, Sept. 7, 1985; Reagan quoted by Joshua Cohen and Joel Rogers, *On Democracy* (Penguin, 1983), 26. For further discussion, see Frank Ackerman, *Hazardous to our Wealth* (South End, 1984).

13. The journal of the Newspaper Guild observes that the policies of the Reagan Administration are causing "the most significant...restrictions" on access to government information "since the end of voluntary censorship in World War II," citing numerous Administration actions "restricting access to information and editorial freedom" and proposed legislation which shows that "more threats are coming." *Guild Reporter*, March 22, 1985; see *Human Rights Internet Reporter*, May-August 1985, 563-4, for summary.

14. Ira Glasser, Executive Director, ACLU, open letter, Feb. 24, 1984; see *In Contempt of Congress and the Courts: The Reagan Civil Rights Record* (ACLU, Feb. 27, 1984), for a review of the government's contempt for the law on the domestic scene.

15. Subsequently, an all-white jury in a largely black county convicted a black voting rights activist from the Southern Christian Leadership Conference of abusing the absentee voting process, the Justice Department's first conviction. Five other defendants were found not guilty; in four of these cases juries were racially mixed. *NYT*, Oct. 17, 1985.

16. Andrea Bernstein, "Battle in the Black Belt," *Progressive*, October 1985; William Schmidt, *NYT*, Sept. 29, 1985.

17. Ferguson, "Party Realignment."

18. On this matter, to which we return, see Cohen and Rogers, *On Democracy*.

19. Quoted by Saloma, *Ominous Politics*, 22.

20. Steve Curwood, *BG*, Oct. 3, 1985.

21. John Patrick Diggins, *NYT Book Review*, Oct. 20, 1985.

22. I intend to take up this matter elsewhere, and therefore will not go into details here. See Peter Biskind, "Vietnam: a TV history," on the PBS series, and my article on the companion volume by Stanley Karnow, in *Race & Class* (London), Spring 1984. For general discussion, see references of note 7.

23. On the character of such efforts as exist to come to terms with the "radical critique," see *For Reasons of State*, 42, 56f.; Christopher Lasch's introduction to Gar Alperovitz, *Cold War Essays* (Doubleday Anchor, 1970).

24. Ferguson, "Party Realignment." See Walter Dean Burnham, "The 1980 Earthquake," in Thomas Ferguson and Joel Rogers, eds., *The Hidden Election* (Pantheon, 1981), for discussion of the general topic, and Saloma, *Ominous Politics*, chapter 5.

25. Daniel Yankelovich, *Issues in Science and Technology* (Fall, 1984); Richard Severo, "Poll Finds Americans Split on Creation Idea," *NYT*, Aug. 29, 1982, reporting a Gallup poll; 38% accepted divine guidance of evolution. On Reagan's views, see p. 189, above.

26. AP, *BG*, Oct. 21, 1985.

27. Saloma, *Ominous Politics*, xvii, xi.

28. Ferguson, "Party Realignment," his emphasis.

29. *Ibid.* See also his "From Normalcy to New Deal," *International Organization* (Winter 1984).

30. Cohen and Rogers, *On Democracy*.

31. For some recent general discussion of this and related matters, see William Domhoff, *Who Rules America Now?* (Prentice-Hall, 1983). Ferguson observes that until 1856, members of Congress received no regular salaries, "a subtle touch unappreciated by later analysts" ("Party Realignment").

32. Kolko, *Main Currents*, 284.

33. Quoted by McCann, *An American Company*, 45.

34. *TNCW*, 64; also *For Reasons of State*, chapter 7.

35. See *TNCW*, chapter 1.

36. Cf. LASA, "Electoral Process in Nicaragua," 30-1.

37. Stephen Kinzer, *NYT*, Oct. 23, 1984.

38. Robert Eisner, *NYT*, July 8, 1984; Samuel Bowles, *NYT*, July 4, 1984; Emma Rothschild, *NYT*, Oct. 28, 1984; Lawrence Klein, *LAT*, May 8, 1984; *Business Week*, Oct. 22, 1984, citing a study of the Urban Institute, *The Reagan Record*.

39. Lucia Mouat, *CSM*, March 14, 1985; Thomas Oliphant, *BG*, Aug. 28, 1985; Ferguson and Rogers, "Labor Day, 1985"; Andrew Malcolm, *NYT*, Oct. 20, 1985, particularly the accompanying charts.

40. Cohen and Rogers, *On Democracy*, 33; William Leuchtenberg, "The 1984 Election in Historical Perspective," *Newsletter*, National Humanities Center, Spring 1985; on the analysis of the 1980 elections, see *TNCW*, 56, and sources cited.

41. Peter Grier, *CSM*, Nov. 9, 1984; Adam Clymer, *NYT*, Nov. 11, 1984; *BG*, Nov. 2, 1984.

42. Vicente Navarro, 'The 1984 Election and the New Deal; an Alternative Interpretation," *Social Policy*, Spring 1985; data in the following paragraph are from this article.

43. Navarro, "1984 Elections"; Edsall, *New Politics of Inequality*, 17. Moynihan voted along with the rest.

44. Grier, *CSM*, Nov. 9, 1984; Cohen and Rogers, *On Democracy*, 33; Leuchtenburg, "1984 election"; Edsall, *New Politics*, 181f., 197, 201.

45. Burnham, "The 1980 Earthquake."

46. Adam Clymer, *NYT*, Nov. 19, 1985.

47. *Business Week*, April 26, 1982.

48. John Rielly, *Foreign Policy*, Spring 1983; Charles Kadushin, *The American Intellectual Elite* (Little Brown and Co., 1974). In Kadushin's sample of "elite intellectuals," only a handful opposed the war on principled grounds—what he called "ideological grounds"; that is, the grounds on which all opposed the Soviet invasion of Czechoslovakia.

49. Albert Speer, *Inside the Third Reich* (Avon, 1970), 287.

50. For a recent discussion of these matters, see Michael Albert and Robin Hahnel, *Marxism and Socialist Theory* and *Socialism Today and Tomorrow* (South End, 1981).

51. For some remarks on this matter, see my "Soviet Union versus Socialism," MS., 1985, and for further discussion, see Albert and Hahnel, *Socialism*.

52. See *For Reasons of State*, 25.

53. For many examples of relevant strategies and tactics and discussion of their logic see Albert and Dellinger, *Beyond Survival*, Albert and Hahnel, *Socialism Today and Tomorrow*, and Cohen and Rogers, *On Democracy*.

Index

Abrams, Elliot, 29, 32f, 112, 141
Acheson, Dean, 51, 69, 191
Accuracy in Academia, 229
Accuracy in Media (AIM), 229
Acosta, Francisco, 111f
Adams, John, 45
Adams, John Quincy, 58
Afghanistan, 56, 79f, 126, 217ff, 266
Africa, 41
AIFLD, (see American Institute for Free Labor Development)
Aldridge, Edward, 179
Alexander, William, 72
Alexander I, Czar of Russia, 67
Allende, Salvador, 69, 82f
Alliance for Progress, 37, 39f, 45f, 58, 96ff
American Civil Liberties Union (ACLU), 20, 227, 238
American colonies, 256
American Institute for Free Labor Development (AIFLD), 109, 111f
Anti-Defamation League of B'nai Brith, 77ff, 133
Arbenz, Jacobo, 154, 164
Arévalo, Juan José, 50, 154f, 201
Argentina, 21, 33ff, 122, 157, 199, 201
Arnson, Cynthia, 158
Ash, Timothy Garton, 56f, 118, 125f
Atlacatl Battalion, 6, 25, 33, 113, 122f
Atlantic Charter, 43, 45, 47, 195
Augsburg, Emil, 197

Ball, George, 186
Barbie, Klaus, 35, 198ff
Barnaby, Frank, 177, 182
Batista, Fulgencio, 62
Bell, James, 88
Bell, John, 100
Ben-Gurion, David, 77
Bennett, Tapley, 152
Berle, Adolf, 55
Bernays, Edward, 165, 235
Besançon, Alain, 219
Bethe, Hans, 177
Bishop, Maurice, 71
Block, John, 41
Boland, Edward, 133
Bolívar, Simón, 58f
Bolivia, 36, 198, 200f
Bonner, Ray, 79, 109

Borge, Tomás, 270
Bosch, Juan, 150f
Bosworth, Stephen, 31
Botswana, 74
Bowman, Robert, 184
Bracken, Paul, 178, 181
Brazil, 40, 53, 159, 161
Brezhnev Doctrine, 59
British Parliamentary Human Rights Group, 117, 139
Brown Brothers Bank, 4, 94
Brown, Harold, 207f, 215, 217
Bryan, William Jennings, 87
Bryan-Chamorro Treaty, 91
Buckley, Tom, 7
Bundy, McGeorge, 204
Bundy, William, 187
Bush, George, 53, 161, 270
Business Week, 190, 209
Butler, Smedley, 94
Byrnes, James, 64

Cabanas, 25
Calero, Adolfo, 11, 13, 74f, 277
Cambodia, 17, 21, 52, 69ff, 106, 118, 168, 248, 266
Canada, 41
Caritas, 22, 24
Carter, Jimmy, 8, 14ff, 34, 102ff, 127f, 156ff, 202, 205, 214, 222f, 226, 236, 239, 242, 245, 248
Casey, William, 129
Castillo, Fabio, 96
Castro, Fidel, 66, 69
Central American Court of Justice, 91
Chace, James, 68
Chalatenango, 24
Chamorro, Edgar, 13f, 93, 131, 133
Chandler, Alfred, 208
Chaing Kai-shek, 55
Chile, 68f, 161, 167, 199, 201, 218
China, 55, 66, 203
Christian, Shirley, 141, 142f
Churchill, Winston, 43, 45, 63, 87, 126, 195, 248
Clements, Charles, 5f, 9, 25f, 108
Clausen, Peter, 186
Clifford, Clark, 45
Cockburn, Alexander, 22
Cohen, Joshua, 233f
Colombia, 61, 196
Columbus, Christopher, 146
Commager, Henry Steele, 232
Committee on Public Information, 78

CONDECA (Central American Defense Council), 98
Congo, 218
Constable, John, 123
Contadora, 81, 143f
Coolidge, Calvin, 86
COSEP (Higher Council for Private Enterprise), 132
Costa Rica, 37f, 39, 61
Council on Foreign Relations, 55, 143; War and Peace Studies groups, 203
Cruz, Arturo, 12, 13, 14, 17, 137, 138
Csorba, Laslo, 229
Cuba, 5, 54, 55, 56, 62, 66, 82, 83, 84, 98, 119, 172, 175, 266
Cyprus, 196
Czechoslovakia, 196, 218

Darlan, Jean, 195
Dartiguenave, Philippe, 87
d'Aubuisson, Roberto, 23, 103, 104, 132, 201
Davidson, Basil, 194, 195
Davis, Benny, 204, 205
Dayan, Moshe, 77
DeLauer, Richard, 186
delle Chiaie, Stefano, 200, 201
D'Escoto, Miguel, 169
de Tocqueville, Alexis, 162
Diggins, John Patrick, 229
Dodd, Christopher, 277
Dominican Republic, 5, 46, 61, 62, 71, 86, 98, 146, 147ff, 161, 218
Doueimah massacre, 76
Duarte, José Napoleón, 16, 19, 21, 22, 24, 25, 26, 27, 33, 101, 102, 106, 107, 109ff, 138, 168
Dulles, Allen, 198
Dulles, John Foster, 53, 160, 198
Durenberger, Dave, 171, 172, 180
Duvalier dynasty, 146

East Berlin, 218
East Timor, (see Timor)
Edsall, Thomas, 225, 226
Edwards, Don, 227
Egypt, 173
Eisenhower, Dwight D., 68, 101, 203, 206
Eisenhower, Milton, 160
Elliot, William Yandell, 58
El Playón, 112, 113
El Salvador, 5ff, 30, 32, 33, 35ff, 39, 45, 54, 62, 66, 75, 90, 95ff, 98, 99, 122ff, 129, 130, 134, 135, 141, 156, 161, 167, 169, 200ff, 214, 218, 222, 245
Enders, Thomas, 132
Etzold, Thomas Herman, 48
Evangelista, Michael, 192

Fairbank, John King, 52, 166
Fall, Bernard, 100, 165, 166
Ferguson, Thomas, 222, 231ff
Ferraro, Geraldine, 243
Fiallos, Ricardo, 104
Fletcher, James, 181
Fontaine, Roger, 89
Ford, Gerald R., 158, 248
Forsberg, Randall, 188
Fortas, Abe, 63
Four Freedoms, 45, 47
Fox, Edward, 32
France, 54, 62, 64, 65, 128, 173, 196, 198, 216, 284
Funston, Frederick, 87

Gaddis, John Lewis, 48, 193, 194
Garcia Villas, Marianella, 123f
GATT, (see General Agreement on Tariffs and Trade)
Gehlen, Reinhard, 197, 198
Gelb, Leslie, 152
General Agreement on Tariffs and Trade (GATT), 53, 91
Gerassi, John, 133
Germany, 190, 192, 193, 198
Gerson, Joseph, 176
Giddings, Franklin Henry, 162
Gomez, Leonel, 108
Good Neighbor policy, 44, 62, 63
Gordon, Lincoln, 159
Gorman, Paul, 92
Graham, Daniel, 186
Gualsinga river, 33
Grant, Ulysses S., 88
Great Britain, 59, 61, 62, 64, 65, 126, 136, 173, 195, 196
Greece, 45, 64, 69, 89, 195, 196, 218
Grenada, 34, 71, 72, 173, 214
Gromyko, Andrei, 179, 182
Gross, Bertram, 226
Guatemala, 5, 8, 28ff, 35, 37, 39, 40, 52, 53, 54, 55, 61, 66, 75, 82, 98, 99, 104, 108, 119, 120, 129, 154ff, 160, 161, 164, 199, 201, 218, 235, 266
Guazapa region, 5, 25, 26f, 108

Haiti, 8, 46, 71, 86, 146, 149

Hamilton, Lee, 138
Harkin, Tom, 101
Hart, Gary, 205, 242
Healy, Peggy, 130
Heller, Walter, 206
Henriquez, Francisco, 149
Herman, Edward, 158, 201, 229
Hernández Martínez, Maximiliano, 43f, 62, 95
Herzog, Chaim, 77
Hispaniola, 146ff
Hitchens, Christopher, 32
Hitler, Adolf, 35, 55, 79, 86, 154, 189, 194, 198, 199, 201, 248
Ho Chi Minh, 46, 51, 68
Honduras, 4, 11, 12, 15, 35, 37, 39, 40, 83, 104, 120, 129
Hoover, J. Edgar, 224
Howard, Michael, 57
Humphrey, John, 3
Hungary, 27, 217, 218
Hunter, Miguel Bolanos, 119
Huntington, Samuel, 153f, 157, 161, 223

Iklé, Fred, 54
Immerman, Richard, 55
Indian Wars, 22, 76, 87, 162, 163, 203
Indochina, 216, 218, 246
Indonesia, 17, 70
International Court of Justice, 11, 14, 89, 90, 91
International Red Cross, 19, 22, 23, 24, 124, 159, 248
Iran, 69, 72, 218
Israel, 29, 30, 34ff, 38, 73ff, 108, 123, 128, 133, 157, 173, 176, 187, 199, 282
Italy, 69, 195

Jackson, Andrew, 228
Japan, 41, 55, 66, 67, 175, 193, 197, 207, 212
Jay, John, 3
Jefferson, Thomas, 58, 169
Jenkins, Brian, 122, 201
Johnson, Lyndon B., 68, 98, 120, 152, 196
Johnson, Samuel, 169
Journal of Contemporary Studies, 289

Kellogg, Frank, 85
Kennan, George, 48, 49, 50, 57, 65, 68, 157, 158, 198
Kennedy, Edward M., 101
Kennedy, John F., 6, 37, 40, 45, 46, 50, 57, 96, 97, 99, 119, 151, 172, 173, 189, 203, 206, 207, 208, 209, 213, 214, 216, 244, 245, 255
Kennet, Wayland, 186, 187
Keyserling, Leon, 209
Khmer Rouge. 17, 168
Khrushchev, Nikita, 172
Kirkpatrick, Jeane, 8, 15, 20, 33, 75, 91, 95, 117
Kissinger Commission, 48
Kissinger, Henry, 55, 68, 69, 70, 83, 188, 194
Klare, Michael, 158
Kleiner, Michael, 35
Knox, Philander, 92
Kolb, Eugene, 199f
Kolko, Gabriel, 224, 234
Komer, Robert, 205
Korea, 66, 196, 197, 202, 203
Krehm, William, 5, 43, 63
Krock, Arthur, 164

Lansing, Robert, 59, 87
Laos, 45, 52, 70, 71, 72, 82, 161, 266
Laqueur, Walter, 66
Las Hojas massacre, 113
Lasswell, Harold, 235
Latin American Studies Association (LASA), 137, 138, 256
Lau, Ricardo, 104
Lebanon, 74, 108, 176
Lehman, John, 171
Lenin, Vladimir, 86
Levin, Carl, 179
Levitsky, Melvin, 31
Lewis, Anthony, 91
Lewy, Guenter, 259, 273
Libya, 214
Lieuwen, Edwin, 261
Lin, Herbert, 180
Lippmann, Walter, 235
Loftus, John, 21
London Times, 144
Lopez, Sixto, 163
Los Llanitos massacre, 25, 32f
Lucas Garcia, Romeo, 31, 157

MacMichael, David, 110
Madriz, José, 92
Maechling, Charles, 216
Magaña, Álvaro, 16
Mahnke, Horst, 197

Majano, Adolfo, 109, 110
Marcos, Ferdinand, 161
Martin, John Bartlow, 151
Matamoros, Bosco, 122
Matanza, 44, 62, 95
Mayer, Ferdinand, 149
McCann, Thomas, 165
McCarthy, Joseph, 225
McCloy, John J., 198
McFarlane, Robert, 180, 183
McKinley, William, 87
McNamara, Robert, 178
Medici, Emilio, 159
Medrano, José Alberto, 98, 103
Mejia Victores, Oscar, 32
Melman, Seymour, 215
Mencken, H. L., 213
Mesopotamia, 126
Metternich, Prince Clemens von, Chancellor of Austria, 67
Mexico, 46, 88, 119
Miskitos, 11, 74, 75
Mondale, Walter, 171, 183, 188, 242, 243
Monroe Doctrine, 58, 59, 64, 67; "Roosevelt Corollary," 60, 61; "Wilson Corollary," 61, 64
Monsen, Joseph, 208
Moon cult, 199
Moore, John Norton, 94, 166, 168, 270, 271, 275, 278, 280
Morgenthau, Hans, 149, 218
Morison, Samuel Eliot, 163
Morocco, 66
Mothers of the Disappeared, Committee of, 22f, 110
Motley, Langhorne, 93
Moynihan, Daniel Patrick, 90, 170, 242
Mussolini, Benito, 199
Muste, A. J., 46

Namibia, 74
Narkis, Uzi, 77
National Security Council (NSC), 144, 191, 205; NSC memorandum 48/1—65, 68; NSC memorandum 68—198, 203, 215, 224
Neier, Aryeh, 16, 26
Netherlands, 41
New Republic, 117, 125, 167f, 170, 203
New York Times, 164, 165, 166, 176, 180, 235

New York Times on elections in El Salvador and Nicaragua, 140
Nicaragua, 4, 8, 9ff, 35, 37, 38, 39, 53, 54, 60, 62, 71, 72ff, 82, 85, 86, 89ff, 97, 98, 106, 111, 120, 121, 126, 127ff, 135, 141, 167, 169, 171, 173, 187, 202, 235, 236, 245
Nitze, Paul, 204, 207, 208
Nixon, Richard M., 55, 68, 69, 83, 120, 158
North, Oliver, 131
NSC, (see National Security Council)

Obando y Bravo, Miguel, 78
Ochoa, Sigifredo, 24, 26, 30
Olds, Robert, 60
Olney, Richard, 59
Orfila, Alejandro, 73
Organization of American States, 73
Ortega, Daniel, 14, 53, 56, 143
O'Sullivan, Kenneth, 136
Otis, Elwell S., 87
Oxfam America, 9, 39, 129, 130

Pakistan, 80, 266
Palmer, A. Mitchell, 224
Panama, 197
Panama Canal, 61
Pastora Gomez, Eden, 128, 131, 132, 133, 134
Patterson, Robert, 64, 100
Paxson, Frederic, 141
Perle, Richard, 219
Peterson, Howard, 191
Pettit, Jethro, 9, 10
Philippines, 8, 70, 86, 87, 88, 161, 162, 163, 196, 218
Piedra, Alberto, 156
Pike, Douglas, 107
Pinochet, Augusto, 199, 201
Podhoretz, Norman, 216
Poland, 218, 228
Polisario, 66
Pol Pot, 21, 106, 118, 248
Ponchaud, François, 168
Pratt, William V., 44
Puerto Rico, 8
Purcell, Susan Kaufman, 143

Quiché Province, 30

Rabin, Yitzhak, 77
Race, Jeffrey, 107

Ramirez, Atilio, 103
Rauff, Walter, 199
Reagan, Ronald W., 8, 12, 18ff, 24, 29, 31ff, 33, 37, 53, 54, 73, 74, 75, 77, 79, 80, 81, 85, 86, 91, 92, 117, 118, 128, 137, 144, 161, 169, 174, 177, 183, 184, 185, 187, 200, 202, 204, 206, 207, 208, 209, 214, 222, 225, 226, 231, 236, 239, 240, 242, 243, 244, 245
Red Cross, (see International Red Cross)
Reich, Robert, 211
Reston, James, 166
Ríos Montt, Efrain, 29, 31, 32, 134, 199
Rio Sumpul, 15, 105, 112
Ris, Howard, 184
Rivas, Luis, 278
Rivera, Brooklyn, 75
Rivera y Damas, Arturo, 106
Robelo, Alfonso, 138
Rockefeller, Nelson, 198
Rogers, Bernard, 182
Rogers, Joel, 233, 234
Rohatyn, Felix, 209
Rojas, Marroquin, 155
Romero, Oscar Arnulfo, 16, 18, 22, 50, 102, 103, 118, 222
"Roosevelt Corollary," (see Monroe Doctrine)
Roosevelt, Franklin D., 37, 43, 45, 47, 154, 195, 201, 233, 240, 248
Roosevelt, Theodore, 61, 63, 87, 88
Rostow, Walt, 51
Rowe, David, 203
Rubin, Alfred, 90
Rudel, Hans Ulrich, 199
Ryan, Randolph, 80

Saloma, John, 232
Samuelson, Paul, 209
San Juan del Norte, 127
San Martín, Ramón Grau, 62
Sandino, Augusto, 127
Santivanez, Roberto, 104
Sassen, Alfons, 199
Sassen, Wim, 199
Schlesinger, Arthur, 119
Schoultz, Lars, 157
Schwend, Friedrich, 199
Scowcroft Commission, 205
Selser, Gregorio, 58
Shannon, William, 21, 166ff
Shultz, George, 53, 86, 93, 136, 138, 169

Shur, Michael, 36
Silber, John, 152
Sin, Jaime, 103
Singlaub, John, 133
Sino-Soviet bloc, 55
Sivard, Ruth, 216
Six, Franz, 197
Skorzeny, Otto, 199
Smith, Gerald, 185
Smith, Jacob, 87, 88, 163
Smith, Walter Bedell, 154
Smuts, Jan Christiaan, 194
Somoza dynasty, 5, 8, 13, 37, 62, 71, 92, 97, 98, 102, 104, 127, 128, 148
South Africa, 74, 169
Spain, 200
Speer, Albert, 248
Stalin, Joseph, 190, 194
Stankievich, Stanislaw, 197
Steele, David, 139
Sterling, Claire, 66
Stevenson, Adlai, 89
Stimson, Henry, 63, 64
Sulzberger, Arthur Hays, 165
Syria, 176
Szulc, Tad, 115

Taft, William Howard, 59
Taylor, Maxwell, 100
Teller, Edward, 186
Thailand, 196
Thorndike, Edward, 235
Thorpe, George, 86, 149
Timor, 21, 45, 248
Toriello, Guillermo, 52, 218
Toronto Globe and Mail, 145, 172
Trevor-Roper, Hugh, 164
Trilateral Commission, 223, 230, 265
Trujillo, Rafael, 148, 150
Truman Doctrine, 45, 69, 195
Truman, Harry, 209, 210
Tsongas, Paul, 137
Tueni, Ghassan, 176
Turner, Stansfield, 94
Turkey, 64, 69, 172, 173, 191, 196
Twain, Mark, 3, 26
Twining, Nathan, 101

UNCTAD, (see United Nations Conference on Trade and Development
United Nations Conference on Trade and Development (UNCTAD), 91
Ungo, Guillermo, 101

United Fruit company, 4, 119, 154, 164, 165, 235
United Nations Charter, 89, 90
Uruguay, 8, 53
US petroleum policy, 61, 62
USSR, 4, 20, 27, 34, 44, 52, 53, 54, 56, 57, 64, 65, 69, 79, 80, 81, 119, 126, 136, 173, 174, 177, 178, 179, 180, 182, 183, 184, 185, 190, 191, 192, 194, 198, 202, 217, 219, 231, 251

Vanderbilt, Cornelius, 127
Venezuela, 53, 119, 197
Vides Casanova, Carlos, 168
Vietnam, 6, 22, 30, 51, 52, 66, 67, 68, 70, 80, 82, 84, 99, 100, 107, 120, 124, 126, 127, 161, 165, 166, 196, 219, 222, 244, 247, 252, 256, 266

Walker, William, 127
Waller, Littleton W. T., 86, 88, 163
War and Peace Studies Project of the Council on Foreign Relations, 47, 49, 65
Washington, George, 76
Watt, David, 187
Webster, Daniel, 89
Weinberger, Caspar, 184
Weizmann, Chaim, 77
Western Sahara, 66
Wiesel, Elie, 36
White, Robert, 108
Wiggins, Armstrong, 74
Will, George, 20
Williams, Murat, 6
Willkie, Wendell, 240
Wilson, Charles E., 208
"Wilson Corollary," (see Monroe Doctrine)
Wilson, Woodrow, 5, 46, 59, 61, 63, 81, 86, 146, 147, 149, 224
Wisner, Frank, 198
Wofford, Lawrence, 227
World Court, (see International Court of Justice)
Wriston, Walter, 229

Yarborough, William, 99

Zamora, Mario, 109